Secular Bodies, Affects and Emotions

Also available from Bloomsbury

Confronting Secularism in Europe and India,
ed. by Brian Black, Gavin Hyman and Graham M. Smith
Spirituality, Corporate Culture, and American Business, James Dennis LoRusso
Alternative Salvations, ed. by Hannah Bacon, Wendy Dossett and Steve Knowles
French Populism and the Discourse on Secularism, Per-Erik Nilsson

Secular Bodies, Affects and Emotions

European Configurations

Edited By
Monique Scheer, Nadia Fadil and
Birgitte Schepelern Johansen

BLOOMSBURY ACADEMIC
LONDON • NEW YORK • OXFORD • NEW DELHI • SYDNEY

BLOOMSBURY ACADEMIC
Bloomsbury Publishing Plc
50 Bedford Square, London, WC1B 3DP, UK

BLOOMSBURY, BLOOMSBURY ACADEMIC and the
Diana logo are trademarks of Bloomsbury Publishing Plc

First published in Great Britain 2019

A catalogue record for this book is available from the British Library.

A catalog record for this book is available from the Library of Congress.

ISBN: HB: 978-1-3500-6522-2
          ePDF: 978-1-3500-6523-9
          eBook : 978-1-3500-6524-6

Cover image © MadisonKnox/Shutterstock

Typeset by Integra Software Services Pvt. Ltd.
Printed and bound in Great Britain

To find out more about our authors and books visit www.bloomsbury.com and sign up for
our newsletters.

Contents

List of Figures

Notes on Contributors

Katie Aston is a Research Associate at Newman University, Birmingham. She was recently awarded funding by the Understanding Unbelief project to research secular and non-religious beliefs about dying and the end of life. Her research interests span material culture, art, cartoons, secularism, atheism, humanism and ritual practices, within the disciplines of sociology, cultural studies and anthropology.

Marian Burchardt is Professor of Sociology at the University of Leipzig. He is currently studying how nation states and urban actors regulate cultural differences and public space and how these regulations affect the practices, socialities and subjectivities of ordinary citizens. He is completing a monograph on the impact of nationalism on religious diversity.

Judith Dehail is Associate Professor in Aesthetics and Cultural Mediation in the Department of Arts at Aix-Marseille University and is affiliated with the Laboratoire d'Etude en Sciences des Arts. Her research interests include the mediation of knowledge and art in museums and the practices of museum visitors and library users.

Matthew Engelke is Professor in the Department of Religion and Director of the Institute for Religion, Culture, and Public Life, at Columbia University. An anthropologist of religion, he is the author of three books and is currently working on a monograph concerning humanist funerals in London.

Nadia Fadil is Associate Professor of Anthropology at the IMMRC (Interculturalism, Migration and Minorities Research Centre), the University of Leuven. She works on Islam in Europe, both as a living tradition and as an object of governmental regulation and societal debate. More broadly, her theoretical interests pertain to questions of subjectivity and power, ethical selfhood, embodiment and affect, post-colonialism, race and secularism.

Mar Griera is Associate Professor at the Department of Sociology, Universitat Autònoma de Barcelona, and Director of the research group on sociology of religion (ISOR). She has published extensively on issues of religious minorities, public policies and national identity.

Stacey Gutkowski is Senior Lecturer in Conflict Studies in the Department of War Studies, King's College London. She is Co-Deputy Director of the Centre for the Study of Divided Societies there and Co-Director of the Nonreligion and Secularity Research Network. Her work interrogates the relationships between war, peace, religion and the secular in Jordan, Iraq, Egypt, Afghanistan, the United States and the United Kingdom. She is the author of *Secular War: Myths of Religion, Politics and Violence* (I.B. Tauris, 2013).

Pamela E. Klassen is Professor in the Department for the Study of Religion, cross-appointed to Anthropology, at the University of Toronto, where she is also Vice-Dean, Undergraduate and International in the Faculty of Arts and Science. Her most recent publications are *The Story of Radio Mind: A Missionary's Journey on Indigenous Land* (University of Chicago Press, 2018) and *Ekklesia: Three Inquiries in Church and State* (University of Chicago Press, 2018), co-authored with Paul Christopher Johnson and Winnifred Fallers Sullivan.

Carolin Kosuch is a historian and religious studies scholar currently working as a postdoc researcher at the German Historical Institute in Rome. She is the author of a book on German-Jewish anarchists, *Missratene Söhne. Anarchismus und Sprachkritik im Fin de Siècle* (Vandenhoeck & Ruprecht, 2015), and her current project is a comparative cultural history of cremation.

Lois Lee is Research Fellow at University of Kent. Her research interests centre on the nature of the existential in modernity, with an empirical focus on non-religious populations. She is the author of *Recognizing the Non-Religious: Reimagining the Secular* (Oxford University Press, 2015).

Claudia Liebelt is Assistant Professor in Social Anthropology at Bayreuth University. Her current research and teaching pertain to gendered notions of beauty and aesthetic body modification in Turkey, extending to questions of normativity, intimacy, class, embodiment, secularism and Islam. Among her recent publications is an edited collection *Beauty and the Norm: Debating Standardization in Bodily Appearance* (Palgrave Macmillan, 2018).

Karsten Lichau is a research scholar at the Center for the History of Emotions, Max Planck Institute for Human Development in Berlin. His research interests include the historical anthropology of the body and the senses, with a special focus on sound history and the history of emotions. He has published on the social and cultural history of the face, and, more recently, on the role of sound, emotion and religion in staging politics.

Géraldine Mossière is an anthropologist and Professor at the Institut d'études religieuses at the University of Montreal. Her research interests include religious diversity, religious mobility, spirituality and healing, new believing subjectivities as well as the researcher's subjectivity in the field. The author of *Converties à l'Islam, Parcours de femmes en France et au Québec* (University of Montreal Press, 2013), she is currently heading ethnographic projects on various dimensions of conversion.

Monique Scheer is Professor of Historical and Cultural Anthropology at the University of Tübingen, where she also serves as Vice-President for International Affairs. She has co-authored *Emotional Lexicons: Continuity and Change in the Vocabulary of Feeling*

(Oxford University Press, 2014) and is currently completing a monograph on the cultural history of enthusiasm.

Birgitte Schepelern Johansen is Associate Professor at the Institute for Cross Cultural and Regional Studies, Migration Studies and Minority Studies, University of Copenhagen. Her most recent publication is *Hate, Politics, Law* (Oxford University Press, 2018), co-edited with Thomas Brudholm.

Jennifer A. Selby is Associate Professor of Religious Studies and affiliate member of Gender Studies at Memorial University of Newfoundland, Canada. Her research considers Islam in contemporary France and Canada, focusing on secularization theory, Muslim studies and gender. She has recently published *Beyond Accommodation: Everyday Narratives of Muslim Canadians* (with A. Barras and Lori G. Beaman, University of British Columbia Press, 2018).

Riem Spielhaus is Professor of Islamic Studies with a focus on education and cultures of knowledge at the Georg-August-Universität Göttingen and a department head at the Georg Eckert Institute for International Textbook Research. Her most recent publications focus on knowledge production on Muslims in Europe and Islamic practice in Germany.

Acknowledgements

This edited volume was prepared by an author's workshop held in February 2016 at the University of Tübingen, Germany. We are grateful for the generous support of the Fritz Thyssen Foundation and the University of Tübingen for the organization of this workshop. We would also like to thank the keynote speakers Pamela Klassen, Matthew Engelke, Rebbeka Habermas and Charles Hirschkind as well as all the participants at the workshop for contributing to the highly stimulating discussions which took place there. All the volume's contributions profited from this initial conversation, as well as from the very incisive comments from anonymous reviewers, whom we thank for the time they took for their careful readings. We would also like to express our thanks to Lalle Pursglove and her team at Bloomsbury for shepherding this project to publication.

From its inception at a café in Berlin in 2014, this volume was inspired through readings of the pathbreaking work of scholars like Talal Asad, Charles Hirschkind and, not least, the late Saba Mahmood. The conversations she opened and her invitation to critically inquire into the affective and bodily textures of 'the secular' profoundly shaped our approach and the conception of this volume. Though she was not able to attend the workshop, her thinking has been part of the project from the beginning. We would therefore like to dedicate this book to her memory and to the influence she has had, and will continue to have, on a generation of scholars of religion and the secular.

Secular Embodiments: Mapping an Emergent Field

Monique Scheer, Birgitte Schepelern Johansen, Nadia Fadil

With few exceptions, studies of secularity have not paid much attention to its embodied, affective components or lived practices. Approached either as a particular kind of social and political arrangement, as an ideological project or as a result of the changing, perhaps diminishing, role of religion, secularity has most often been examined at the macro-level of whole societies, of policy issues and of philosophical stances. And while the study of religion took a material and sensory-affective 'turn' some time ago, looking more assiduously at practices, embodied experiences and emotional attachments, the same cannot be said for the study of the secular. This book is about how we can think about the secular as something that is practised, felt and experienced. Rather than focusing on how it is expressed in formalized legal-political arrangements or in abstract ideas about the proper place and role of religion in society, we focus on secularity as a social and cultural reality, richly textured by embodied performances as well as commitments, attachments, hopes, obligations, fears and joys. It proposes that if we want to better understand the processes through which certain forms of religiosity can become objects of concerns and anxieties, if we want to understand the stakes that people have in upholding and performing ways of life designated and understood as secular and if we want to understand the ongoing transformations of shared narratives about ultimate meaning and of the rituals which uphold them, we need to anchor the study of the secular in actual bodies in actual places.

This turn towards 'lived experience' took place in religious studies quite some time ago. Not only has the debate over the priority of 'myth or ritual' been around since the beginning of religious studies but a more recent move particularly by scholars of American religion has been influential. As early as the 1980s, they sought to move beyond the focus on institutional, dogmatic or narrative histories and to take an ethnographic approach to their research (e.g. McCarthy Brown 1991; Orsi 1985). Postulating that practice was prior to belief and materiality was inseparable from and indispensable to spirituality, they soon joined forces with scholars interested in the visual and material culture of religious practitioners, the art, architecture and objects of belief (e.g. MacDannell 1995; Meyer 2009; Morgan 2010). By the early 2000s, there was a thriving community of scholars studying the way people carry out their belief, how religion 'happens' in spaces, bodily movements and postures, sensual perceptions and emotions. The same cannot be said of secularity, whose study has remained more firmly oriented towards its dogmatic formulations and institutional manifestations, particularly among political scientists and sociologists, but even among anthropologists, who look at the different forms these arrangements take in different societies.[1]

Perhaps the most obvious reason why the embodied aspects of the secular have not hitherto received much attention is the way in which the object of study itself is commonly construed. In its political articulations, the secular is nearly always represented in ways that empty it of any such affective and emotional textures, for example by emphasizing neutrality, impartiality, factuality, rationality and reason as its constitutive features (Connolly 1999). Those very areas which self-describe as secular (not only science, law and medicine but scholarship generally, for example) are typically predicated upon an exclusion of the emotional, affective and sensorial from their operations, often relegating these aspects to domains deemed 'private' or 'subjective'.[2] This construal is further associated with a particular kind of secular self, which Charles Taylor has described as 'buffered' (2007), implying a disconnect between the body and the world (cf. Asad 2011), which must be created and upheld in all sorts of everyday performances. Thus, emotional containment is expected from judges in courtrooms, civil servants and bureaucrats, all illustrations of how the very idea of a 'secular public' is performed by individuals in their continuous display and expectation of a certain comportment. Though this self-presentation and self-cultivation is coded as 'rational' or 'neutral' in opposition to the 'irrational' and 'emotional', we suggest that it could also be viewed as a certain mode or style of affectivity invited by an ordering of the social known as 'secularism'. This ordering is upheld – as anthropologist Webb Keane has suggested – by a 'moral narrative of modernity', that is, a normative history of self-mastery and emancipation, processes releasing 'the true character of human agency' (Keane 2013: 160). He urges us, as well, to look more closely at the 'practices which make secular modernity an inhabitable project' (163), pointing out that secularism not only is an immaterial idea but also takes on a material reality. Thus, we should 'sharpen our focus on the concrete environment for thoughts, values, beliefs: the context that supports and instigates them, such as bodily habits, clothing, kinds of media and the visual imagery they support, the layout of buildings and cities, ways of talking, all that makes them plausible and inhabitable' (164–65). To this list we would add that the secular is not per se 'un-emotional' even when it is presented as adhering to the ideals of objectivity and rationality. Rather, these ideals are underpinned by a specific mode of emotionality (which might be referred to as subdued or contained), as well as by emotions *about* secularity. One need only engage briefly the ways in which such claims about the merits of objectivity, rationality and neutrality can be made and defended, or look at the practices that characterize the social institutions typically designated as secular (e.g. bureaucracies, politics or science) to recognize that the secular can also be a very emotional affair indeed (Bear and Mathur 2015). The repeated controversies over religious symbols in public places, the moral panic that surrounds current conversations on religious extremism, the affect-laden reactions to perceived offences against the deep-seated sense that religious blasphemy has a place in public discourse (such as the Danish cartoon controversy) – all of these can also be viewed as 'secular affect' in the sense Saba Mahmood has suggested (2006).

By taking into consideration secular bodies, affects and emotions, this volume seeks to contribute to an ongoing conversation about the ways that the concept of the 'secular' and 'secularization' has been increasingly destabilized, from within and without academic discourse. The standard argument that the secular emerges out of the religious (by separating itself from it) has led to an examination of the ways that the two categories are actually co-constitutive, never really completely separate from one another and that the differentiation between them continually threatens to collapse. Each of the chapters in this volume demonstrates from different perspectives the impossibility of the secular as a substantially independent entity. There is no situation in which the secular can be seen to exist in the pure form that some conceptualizations of it postulate; it is always intertwined with and dependent upon the religious. The very same can be said of another conceptual pair: rationality and emotionality, and the mental abstraction and embodied materiality typically ascribed to each side. There is a growing body of research in cognitive science that emphasizes the embodied character of thought,[3] and the turn to emotions and affect in the humanities has been fuelled in no small measure by the realization that emotions are never really completely separate from cognition (Rosenwein 2002). The connection of the concepts body, affect and emotion in the title may, at first glance, seem to reproduce this binary, assuming in some unproblematic way that emotions are essentially physiological processes. However, the practice-oriented approach to all three concepts we subscribe to implies that they are understood in a manner that goes beyond the mind/body binary. The body is always a 'mindful body' (Scheper-Hughes/Lock 1987) and affects and emotions are, in our view, 'embodied thoughts' (Rosaldo 1984: 143). This position responds to work in the history and anthropology of emotions that has so emphasized the cognitive side of emotion that it has often neglected its embodied dimension, overlooking a rich literature on the anthropology of the body in which sensation, sensibility, affect, emotions and feelings play a key role.[4] The title of this introduction takes its cue from the 'embodiment approach' in this literature (Csordas 1990), in which the body is twofold: subject and object (I 'am' my body, but I also 'have' this body). Thus, in this collection, the body figures as a canvas for self-presentation as well as a medium for experience, often as feelings or moods, individual and shared. Emotions give the body 'speech' as much as the body provides the self with an instrument for expression. Subjectivity is itself to be found at the nexus of body and mind: 'I' arise as a specifically positioned, gendered, classed, racialized, religionized subject through embodied actions of thought and feeling. These can be experienced as active and passive (I 'think' my thoughts, but they also 'think' me); the subject emerges through processes of self-fashioning which are conscious and unconscious, controlled and uncontrolled. Thus, the secularity of a subject will not only be found in her propositional knowledge but also in the embodied actions of perception, emotion and comportment.

In this same vein, we would suggest that the study of the secular should not so much lie in an attempt to capture what it *is*, but rather to reveal what it *does* and how it *works*. Our central argument is that the secular is not so much a 'thing' than a formation which operates through the selective marking of practices, habits and life-forms as neutral, universal and 'real' (see also Asad 2003). This volume seeks to understand how this occurs by looking at how the body and emotions are implicated in this process. We are thus interested in documenting the ways in which artefacts, subjectivities or imaginaries become understood, addressed and represented as universal and neutral through a series of bodily and emotional operations. This will help us to understand more fully how the secular works in everyday life and why, in spite of its 'impossibility', it can mobilize emotionalized commitments. In the following, we will discuss the conceptual background motivating the studies gathered in this volume, our understanding of the secular, of the secular body and of secular affect and emotions.

From the study of secularization to the study of the secular

In assessing the recent scholarly turn towards the secular, it is important to recall how these developments are related to a series of older debates that have been at the heart of the sociological and anthropological study of religion. To be sure, the process of secularization has been a persistent theoretical framework for thinking about religion in connection with modernization (a scholarly trajectory ranging back at least to de Saint-Simon, Comte, Durkheim and Weber). The main spirit of this early sociological engagement was to understand the changing and diminishing role of religious institutions (most notably the church) and to anchor this change in broader societal developments such as urbanization, structural and functional differentiation, increasing pluralization and individualization – all processes that contributed to an increasing disenchantment of the world. These early works provided a fertile breeding ground especially for sociological research during the latter half of the twentieth century, characterized by a shared interest in describing and understanding secularization as a process (Dobbelaere 2002). What characterized most of this work was an occupation with religion – its size, shape, place and role in society – as the yardstick for assessing forms and degrees of secularization, typically based on a pre-given notion of religion.

The diagnosis of a decrease of religion in public space (or even more generally) has come under considerable critique, to the point that some consider it obsolete. This development, described by some as a 'post-secular' turn (Habermas 2008), reflects a changed assessment of the role of religion within public life and the growing awareness that religious commitments, often manifesting in politicized movements, continue to play a vital role all over the world, even in Western Europe. This change has generally been marked as 'new', but it is important to note that this awareness was already present in the early 1960s, the heyday of the secularization thesis (Tschannen 1992). One must only recall the early discussions (Lauwers 1974; Martin 1969, 1978) or the later more vociferous debates (Berger 1999; Dobbelaere 1999; Stark 1999) among sociologists of religion to realize that the empirical validity as well as epistemological building blocks of this paradigm have always been hotly contested. In particular, the Parsonian notion that religion figures as a self-referential system has been the object of several critiques, especially from a constructivist theoretical angle (Beckford and Hampshire 1983; Lauwers 1974; Luckmann and Berger 1991 [1966]; Martin 1969). While these debates have resulted in certain revisions of the paradigm, in particular its early claims about religious privatization (Beyer 1994; Casanova 1994), the presupposed functionalist and Parsonian theoretical framework remains an important point of contention.

Critiques of secularization, as well as its implicit concept of religion, hold a strong tradition in the fields of sociology, anthropology and religious studies (Cantwell Smith 1978). At the heart of these critiques is the understanding that the study of religion and the secular co-implicate each other. The question then becomes one of just how to conceptualize this intertwinement. It has become rather commonplace and hardly controversial to note that traces of religion (particularly when it is loosely defined as 'the sacred') can be found in secular activities, that secular institutions participate in religion when they enlist ritual performances and/or seek to generate a kind of 'collective effervescence' that was one of Durkheim's fundamental features of religion. These assumptions can be derived from a sociological secularization paradigm, which would argue that secularity never fully rids itself of its religious roots. Having stated that the notion of a linear process of secularization is difficult to uphold, however, we prefer to derive this observation from the anthropological approach that focuses on the genealogy of the secular and religious as co-constitutive and therefore dependent on one another to make sense. The work of Talal Asad, especially his argument that religion figures as a product of modern discursive processes, has been pivotal in this respect. His seminal essay 'The Construction of Religion as an Anthropological Category' (1993) is well known for its trenchant critique of essentialist, liberal Protestant views on religion (as represented in the work of Clifford Geertz). But his essay is also important because it proposes we study authorizing processes that create 'religion' as a classificatory device rather than assuming there is already such a thing as 'religion'. This perspective is inspired by a radically constructivist position combined on the one hand with a pragmatic philosophical perspective which seeks to understand how social phenomena are turned into meaningful realities through material and linguistic interventions, and on the other with a critical theoretical perspective that looks at the role of power and ideology (see also Asad 1979; Scott and Hirschkind 2006).

This perspective has had a profound influence on current studies of secularization. Secularization is no longer viewed as a gradual disenchantment of society, a quasi-natural evolution in which religious beliefs and practices lose their validity and relevance. Instead it is seen as expressive of an underlying 'grammar', a set of forceful distinctions, connections and logics, which precedes and organizes this often conflictual process (Asad 2003; Mahmood 2016). The secular grammar, Asad suggests, not only creates and enforces a defining distinction between religion and the secular but re-organizes and re-evaluates a broader set of categories such as knowledge, belief, rationality, irrationality, factuality, history and transcendence. If a central characteristic of secular societies resides in the consistent and continuous problematization of 'religion' (Agrama 2012), then neither religion nor the secular are a priori categories, but the result of incessant discursive deliberation (Sullivan 2009). It is precisely through not only this deliberation but also enactment of what counts as 'religious' and 'secular' that they each come to light. This also implies that the secular is not merely an absence of religion but a complex set of operations with describable features, produced through its co-constitutive relationship with a certain understanding of religion. Several recent studies have therefore sought to account for the discursive and material iterations of these distinctions in everyday settings, such as in the context of the law and citizenship (Agrama 2012; Fernando 2012; Sullivan 2009), educational contexts (Johansen 2011) or in international politics (Hurd 2008). Most of them have, however, refrained from examining the affective and embodied dimensions entailed in these processes. Yet such distinctions are experienced in and become real for living, breathing, feeling bodies. In the lived, felt and enacted reproductions of the divide between the religious and the secular, each acquire a presence, a materiality, which makes them real to us. This has, perhaps, been sufficiently demonstrated for religion. But by analogy: if the secular is not merely the absence of religion, it is also not 'simply there'; it must be made present by discursive and embodied practices. And since it is inherently unstable, they must be iterated, stored as bodily knowledge and made to feel 'natural'.

When Charles Hirschkind (2011) asked the question of whether there is a secular body, his answer was quite ambivalent. If the secular is an impossibility, how can there be a secular body? But if we conceptualize the secular as an operation of drawing boundaries, then perhaps the secular body is one that does the work of discernment, of sensing and reacting in ways that make the divisions between the secular and the religious seem somehow grounded in nature. When emotions and affects are viewed as visceral reactions more or less detached from rational thought – as is the commonsense view – they are considered incapable of dissimulation, investing them with a truth value that 'mere opinions' cannot have. Furthermore, reactions of taste and sensibility are also considered to be outside the purview of reasoned debate (*de gustibus non est disputandum*). Thus, a 'secular affect' as an embodied, affective response to an offence to the secular sensibility argues for the truth of the secular and shuts down any deliberation over it. What we seek to explore in this volume is how this sensorium comes into being; how it is maintained, defended and transmitted; and what specific shapes and contours it can acquire. What are the dogmatic formulations in discourse, and where are the sites of pedagogy, the training grounds for secular sentiments and affects?

Bodies can be secular

The body, whether understood as a metaphoric or material reality, has long figured as an important site of anthropological and sociological investigation, a privileged entrypoint to account for the material sedimentation of social structures and cultural norms (Bourdieu 2006 [1977]; Douglas 1980 [1969]; Turner 1984). Once the secular is conceived of as a particular social order based on a specific logic, it becomes clear that it will also become embodied and produce certain understandings of 'proper' – in this case unmarked, universal – bodies. Joan Scott (2009), for example, has shown how, historically, secularism has intersected with the matrix of gender and sex – coining the term 'sexularism' – and how this has been constitutive for determining what kind of bodies can in fact be considered neutral and abstract. The same applies for the category of race. Western Europe, in particular, has recently been at the front stage of public controversies around the sartorial practices, bodily habits and linguistic expressions of Muslim minorities whose behaviour has been either marked as incongruous with the values of neutrality, perceived as a potential threat for the cohesion of the national and social body (Fadil 2014; Moors 2009), or as potentially reinstating moral gender codes that a generation ago were at the centre of counter-cultural struggles for a free society (Verkaaik/Spronk 2011). These controversies are often viewed as indications of a multicultural society in crisis, but we can equally consider them to be evidence of a continuous *racial* demarcation and exclusion of religious minority groups as other. Gil Anidjar (2003) and Mayanthi Fernando (2014) have already noted that in the continental European tradition, a distinction between race and religion can hardly be made for the way others (such as Jews and Muslims) have been demarcated during the largest part of the nineteenth century. Current controversies are thus reminiscent of the continuous entanglement between secular and racial formations through the marking of certain bodies as other.

The invitation to approach the secular through the lens of embodiment has also been present in scholarly work on secular*ism* for quite some time. In *Why I Am Not a Secularist* (1999) William Connolly points towards the ways in which secularist politics (not least of the Kantian pedigree) have sought to ignore or even exclude the visceral register from the domain of public reason. This exclusion was (and is) intrinsic to the creation of a public sphere that can lay claim to universality, because it is freed from the density and particularity of actual lived life. This is what Asad calls a myth of secular democracy: a political regime that claims to be based on universal reason, in which the political elites seek to contain religion as well as passions (Asad 2003: 61). Yet at the same time, secularist politics still work to create and deepen passionate attachments to certain forms of life, just as they draw on particular ethical sensibilities in order to make sense (Connolly 1999: 164). According to Connolly, public political conversation is an intersubjective endeavour, and as such, it takes place within the framework of historically contingent experiences of trauma, joy, love, grief and anger, which have all left their imprints on those partaking in the conversation. So even though 'secular presentations of reason and moral discourse remain tone-deaf to this second register of intersubjectivity, they nonetheless depend upon it in order to stabilize those practices' (Connolly 1999: 26). As materializations of bonds as well as divisions between people, and thus an intrinsic part of the political, emotions draw the body into the secularized public sphere.

While the sensibilities and corporeal formations through which secularism is realized (i.e. the political articulations and social implementations of the idea of a separation of religion and public life) centrally occupies us here, in this collection we also seek to examine the historical backgrounds and broader cultural phenomena related to the body, its limits and its relations with its surroundings, which undergird secularist politics. So while there might not be *a* secular body, as Hirschkind suggests (2011), there certainly seem to be important understandings and enactments of the body associated with the secular.

One such important understanding is, as briefly mentioned above, that of a body organized according to a clearly demarcated inside and outside, for example the idea that the body is sealed off from its surroundings by the surface of its skin. This spatially delimited unit functions as a container for, among other things, emotional experience. This scheme has been widely discussed and criticized from various angles (not all which share our interest in the secular), and scholars have, among other things, argued how this 'sealing off' of the body has contributed to the idea of an authentic space inside that is simultaneously outside the scope of political governance (see for example Merleau-Ponty 1962; Lutz and Abu-Lughod 1990; Taylor 1992, also Brown 2006). In *Formations of the Secular*, Asad continues these critiques and discussions of the interiorization and hence privatization of affect and passion by relating them to the private/public distinction so fundamental to the secular grammar (2003: 75). Thinking specifically about pain, Asad argues that the secular as cultural formation creates a body whose own affective experience of pain becomes the highpoint of subjective authenticity, while the pain of others becomes inflected with doubt, because it can never be finally known and hence confirmed as a public reality (2003: 80). Secular interpretations of pain thus tend to render it private and passive, because it – qua interiorization – is considered inscrutable.[5] In a different scholarly tradition (and with a different normative aim), Charles Taylor (2007) has also pursued the issue of the inside/outside scheme, arguing that the sealing off of the body goes hand in hand with disenchantment. Disenchantment, Taylor argues, relegates intentional agency only to mindful subjects, and the only mindful subjects are those residing within the human body (2007: 30). Thus, the emptying of the world of spirits and powerful agents is perpetuated by a new understanding of the self, not as porous to spirits and capable of being distributed, but a buffered self that stands in a kind of discontinued relationship with the world (2007: 539ff). Such a world only allows for representation, not incarnation, and so these mind/body, self/ world divides involve a particular cultivation of the senses: that we learn to interpret what we experience according to this (re)location of agentic forces, understand how to distinguish the symbolic from real presence and enact the associated scheme of interiority/exteriority.[6]

For both authors, the body in the secular imaginary (Asad) and the immanent frame (Taylor) is also embedded in a narrative of emancipation and self-mastery. For Asad it implies, among other things, the emergence of a particular economy of pleasure and pain, where '"history-making" and "self-empowerment" can progressively replace pain by pleasure – or at any rate, by the search for what pleases one' (2003: 68). While pleasure is considered to be a natural, healthy state, pain becomes a passive state to be overcome through individual agency (whether by being dissolved or relocated) – an understanding of pain and agency that makes it difficult to comprehend pain as something that actively takes part in constituting relationships (2003: 84). For Taylor, too, the secular is, among its many aspects, also a narrative of human emancipation and maturation, a narrative that posits the secular body as a body that has become adult, liberated from repressive traditions and capable of enduring the realities of life without recourse to supernatural explanations and powers (Taylor 2007: 575, also Keane 2013). In her above-mentioned work on the 'sexular' body, Joan Scott (2009) continues these reflections, showing how – in the actual historical situations through which gender equality and liberation became formulated as abstract ideals – the distinction between private and public and the privatization of passion was (and is) feminized, making some bodies particularly eligible for secular/sexular emancipatory projects. the colonized woman the veiled woman (8). And in a more recent contribution, Stacey Gutkowski examines how a secular *habitus* (in the Bourdieuan sense) informs current warfare by attending to the ways in which secular sensibilities and perspectives on (religious) difference predispose British security logics within a 9/11 context (Gutkowski 2012).

These brief outlines obviously do not do justice to the complexity of arguments at stake, and neither do they cover all that has been said about secular bodies, affects and emotions (see for example Jakobsen and Pellegrini 2008; Mahmood 2009; Pellegrini 2009). Yet, they do bring forth some of the analytical predicaments that may arise when we attempt to approach the embodied aspects of the secular. Not only do they show that hard lines between inner and outer, between the body as surface and the body as self, between feelings, thoughts, emotions and sensations are hard to draw; they also make evident how the secular, despite attempts to operationalize it through clarifying definitions and distinctions, is indeed a slippery thing. The secular, as Wendy Brown has rightly stated, 'can suggest a condition of being unreligious or antireligious, but also religiously tolerant, humanist, Christian, modern or simply Western. And any effort at settling the term immediately meets its doom in conflicts among these associations' (2013: 4). If the secular is conceptualized as 'the water we swim in' (Hirschkind), our present age (Taylor) or the underlying grammar of a society or world-order that understands itself as modern (Asad), then a serious attempt at analysis cannot solely be interested in the practices through which the boundaries between 'religion' and 'the secular' are explicitly (re)produced and consolidated (Greil and Bromley 2003; Johansen 2011). Rather we are invited to consider all aspects of life, where such boundaries are working implicitly or as a remote or even forgotten point of reference. By implication, often our object of analysis may just as well be described through other, equally broad and vague notions such as modern, liberal, Christian, Protestant or Western. The project of understanding secular embodiments entails the question of how to disentangle and distinguish between the more or less unconscious habits and styles of cosmopolitan, urban secularism, the more self-conscious commitment to secular humanism as *Weltanschauung* and a rather mainline, middle-class liberal Protestantism (see Engelke 2014). When are we looking at a specifically secular body, and when might it be considered a modern or scientific one? Or are they deeply nested within each other? Does it make sense at all to create an overarching category of the secular body for comparison, or should we restrict ourselves to identifying various locally and historically specific understandings of the secular? These questions may not all be completely resolved in this volume, but thoughtful engagement with these complexities characterizes all its chapters. Taking up the uncertainty and ambivalence with which Charles Hirschkind answers the question 'Is there a secular body?' (2011), we seek to maintain a productive tension between these various intersecting categories. The essentially contested nature of the concept itself is part of what has invigorated the conversation in this area, and hence the case studies presented in this book do not conform to and advocate a single definition of the secular. Rather they are intended to display the broad range of analysis that becomes possible when putting the proverbial flesh on the bones of what, almost fifteen years ago, Asad called 'the secular imaginary' (2003: 6).

Are there secular emotions?

As we stated at the outset, considering the conventional understanding of the secular as rational, objective and neutral, one might think that the notion of secular emotions is an oxymoron. Indeed, the secular grammar itself organizes the spaces for religion and non-religion according to concepts of inner and outer, private and public, such that religion is something private and interior, whereas the public space and public discourse should be religion-free. This reduction of religion to subjective experience has been intensely critiqued in religious studies, where it has also been noted that it is characteristic in particular of Protestant understandings of religion (Asad 1982) and conflates religious belief with emotion (Proudfoot 1985). Because emotion is viewed per se as interior and subjective, it appears to be the medium proper to religious belief, encoded in an Enlightenment logic as something opposed to rationality. That is to say, emotion and religion provide two dimensions of 'irrationality' which stand opposite to reasoned thought and public discourse and should be strictly divided from it. Emotion, like religion, threatens individual agency and freedom; we can be in thrall to our passions (or even just feelings and intuitions) the way we are to a deity, 'enchanted' by their power. Banishing emotion from interactions thereafter deemed objective and neutral can thus also be seen as a kind of disenchantment, like the one which divides the supernatural from the natural and banishes spirits and gods from the earthly plane. In this sense, secularity may not, by definition, include emotionality. Even to claim there is such an entity as 'secular emotions' is therefore already a destabilization and critique of this secular logic, a re-enchantment of the secular from two sides, the religious and the emotional.

Just as the shift from the secularization paradigm to a more nuanced view of the secular has generated new research questions and perspectives, so has the recent 'turn to affect' or 'emotional turn' (Gregg/Seigworth 2010; Plamper 2015; Wetherell 2012) been highly productive. It has invited us to consistently address the ways in which the social is mediated by complex visceral experiences that orient and attach bodies to particular ideas, places, objects and to other bodies. Our linking of bodies, affects and emotions in the title of this volume points to a particular conceptualization of emotion that should be made clear at the outset: The initial impetus for the emotional turn was fuelled by claims that emotions were not irrational but rather to be taken as seriously by historians and social scientists as thoughts and spoken words (Rosenwein 2002). Thus, there was a preoccupation with the relation – or indeed, conflation – of emotion and cognition as well as the importance of language and emotional terminology for emotional experience (Lutz 1988; Lutz/Abu-Lughod 1990). More recent theoretical developments have sought to realign emotions with the body, and our exploration of the secular body is inspired by this scholarship which places feeling, emotion and affect on a continuum with bodily sensations and comportment without neglecting its cognitive content.

One such 'rematerializing' approach to emotion, referred to most generally as 'affect theory', emphasizes emotion's physical intensity, sometimes viewed as pre-cognitive and pre-linguistic (Massumi 1995, 2015).[7] The interest here is in the potential for affective force to guide human action and judgements (Navaro-Yashin 2012), for its role in social affairs – for better or worse (Berlant 2011; Connolly 2002) – which goes deeper ui is prior to discourse. Though it has been harshly criticized for reinstating a mind/ body dualism it claims to undermine and for assigning political power to physiological processes (Leys 2011), it does two things important to the project of understanding secular bodies: First, in its focus on the collective, shared, atmospheric qualities of affect, it questions the interiority of emotion and thus the private/public, personal/ political divide on which secularism is based. Second, it seeks to draw attention to the performative and embodied dimension of discourse, to break with the focus on the meaning of language and other signifying practices and look instead at their effects.

Thus, the interest in affect comes rather close to earlier sociological discussions which sought to de-privatize and exteriorize emotion, such as Norbert Elias's critique of the *homo clausus* (Elias 1998), which some sociologists of emotion have built on, arguing that emotions happen not inside a person but between people (Burkitt 1997; Wetherell 2012). Emotions mediate relations between subjects through facial expressions, bodily postures, tone of voice and gestures as much as with words, with verbal statements, about which much more has been written. Reddy's concept of emotives (2001) focuses on the speech act, the first-person statement ('I am angry' or 'I love you'), but also invokes the performative power of speech. Though he is careful to distinguish the speech act emotive from that of performative (the emotive can backfire, which a performative – if the conditions are right – theoretically cannot), his concept helps shift the focus from the content of emotional expression to their effects on the subject as well as on those he or she is addressing, activating their bodies as well as provoking their cognitive processing.

Another approach to emotion that seeks to locate it within a person, closely tied to bodily movements and activations, and yet recognize its dependence on socialization and relationships between people, is inspired by practice theory and particularly Pierre Bourdieu's notion of *habitus*. Instead of viewing emotions and their intensities as bodily *states*, this approach suggests we view them as bodily *practices*. According to this view, emotions are not something we have; they are something we do (Scheer 2012), thus allowing us to analyse them as we do any other cultural practice. Whereas affect theory is more interested in disruption, this approach emphasizes the habituation of emotional responses and intensities in specific social constellations, training the body to perform a certain way as part of interaction with spaces and objects (Reckwitz 2012), as well as with other bodies and perhaps invisible agents. Many of the contributions to this volume, in their exploration of the ways that secular bodies are cultivated, experienced and presented, implement approaches to the emotions from within this family of theoretical offerings emphasizing the performative, embodied and relational aspects of feeling.

Moral geographies and arenas of secular embodiment

As we have shown thus far, the question of lived and embodied secularity has been initiated in theoretical arguments. This volume seeks to implement these insights in empirical studies of concrete situations and practices, historical and current. We approach this question from two angles: In one, the secular body is posited, enacted and cultivated in a conscious effort to live a secular life clearly demarcated from a hegemonic religious way of life. This religious hegemony can be largely imagined, as in the case of secular humanists in Britain today, or quite real, as in nineteenth-century Italy, twentieth-century Quebec or twenty-first-century Istanbul. Though these studies also show how the secular/religious divide continually collapses or is at least the source of much unease and ambivalence, it seems to have its clearest articulation of bodily style in these settings. But it is also clearly formulated in reaction and opposition to a perceived threat by non-secular bodily habits, such as wearing Jewish orthodox headgear or the burka in public spaces. When these latter practices are viewed as minoritarian, the secular body is postulated as hegemonic: 'this is how we live here'. In the process, certain forms of dress or comportment (such as presenting the face) are discovered to be secular. The other angle from which to look at the secular body is in practices not self-consciously secular but felt to be normal in public spaces. The task then is to delve into the ambivalence of what bodies are being asked to perform in spaces rather newly (and unstably) understood to be secular. When people take up – or are asked to take up – a secular habitus in their capacity as citizens, regardless of what their personal convictions regarding religion may be, the boundary-making of the secular operation runs directly through them. The performance of a secular habitus for a state bureaucrat or questionnaire form inculcates and enforces feelings that conform to the secular norm. But there is space for resistance, as when the supposedly secular stance of using birth control is construed as a spiritual practice.

As different as the secularism of the public sphere and secularism as a personal belief system may seem, when presented side by side, it becomes apparent that in all cases the porosity and instability of the boundary between the secular and the religious is evident, as well as the work that is necessary to uphold it. Though very different in origin and motivation, in both situations, bodies and feelings are cultivated, which illustrates Asad's claim that '[t]he secular … is neither continuous with the religious that supposedly preceded it' – as a nationalist ritual or reverent pose in a museum might be assumed to be – 'nor a simple break from it' (2003: 25) – as a cremation procedure or humanist wedding would be thought to represent. These case studies take us into not only the complex interpolations of the religious, non-religious and political dimensions of everyday life but more specifically into the practices through which secular realities are experienced, sustained and challenged.

The secular imaginary (in all its different forms and shapes) is, of course, a global one. Although we have chosen to focus on regions which can be characterized as distinctively European in this volume, we are not suggesting that secularity as an ideal and practice is restricted to them. Rather, we seek to interrogate the notion of Europe that practices of secularism seem to contain. In so doing, we suggest that Europe should be considered not merely as a geographical zone but also a cultural project guided by a series of ideals and promises and realized through a vast and varied number of practices and institutions. Secularization, modernization, constitutionalism, democracy, human rights and national sovereignty are territorialized as European (or Western) even as they are sought after, institutionalized and defended elsewhere as well. To describe this volume's focus as European therefore refers less to the fact that most chapters take a site within a European state as their geographical locality (which they do), but more to the point that they all trace and explore the embodiment of concepts, institutions or practices that have largely emanated from Europe (in the narrow geographical sense), and which are still part of Europe as a broader cultural project. Thus, this book also examines how cultural underpinnings of the secular are bound to certain geographical imaginaries and how both are crafted and embodied through the distinct mobilization of affect and the senses.[8] In a similar vein, the religions that form the backdrop of the secularities discussed in this volume are by and large all of the so-called Abrahamic genealogy. This is not to suggest that secularity is not pertinent to majority Hindu or Buddhist societies – on the contrary, it is a topic of rising interest (see for example Quack 2012; Bubandt/van Beek 2012; Binder 2017; Streicher 2016). Rather, our focus has been on current debates within Europe which are centred on Christianity and Islam. We should also add that we have focused on *Western* European settings which do not take the situation of post-socialist societies into account. The specific ways in which secularism played out under Soviet, socialist and/or communist governments – for example as a top-down institutionalization of atheism and public display of anticlericalism which led to a differently motivated revival of religious engagement in the public sphere after 1989 than in the West – has had repercussions on post-socialist forms of lived secularism that could – and hopefully will – fill a volume of their own.[9]

In the following studies on the secular body, affect and emotions, we are looking at three areas, each with slightly different understandings of the body. The first part of this volume, *Bodies and Other Secular Things*, approaches the body as something people 'have' and must handle in some way, in life as well as in death. There is a secularity of this body strongly inflected by scientific discourse, which determines how one handles it and governs feelings about it, just as one would handle other scientific objects. Setting the stage for the ongoing exploration of the semantic field around the secular and the religious that the volume provides, Pamela Klassen traces how contraception has been conceived by churches as well as by social science as a key indicator and motor of secularity. The 'contraceptive body' is construed by them as a secular body, though the women using these emancipatory technologies embed them in a far more complex practice that traverses secular/spiritual boundaries. Jumping back about a century, Caroline Kosuch's chapter finds the same kinds of ambivalence in the way cremation emerged as a flagship cause of the freethinker's movement throughout the second half of the nineteenth century in Germany and Italy, working to create a secular (dead) body through an education of feeling towards it. Lois Lee's chapter highlights the importance of recognizing varieties of secularism. She exemplifies how this plays out in the ways that 'atheist worshipper' can be conceptualized and the multiple layers of embodiment these mobilize. The closing chapter in this part by Judith Dehail investigates how museums of music history in France and Germany cultivate a particular secular spectator by arranging their displays and providing a certain pedagogy for the body interacting with those objects.

The second part, *Being Secular*, presents cases in which a secular way of life is consciously sought and cultivated. The first is located in Great Britain's growing community of secular humanists and looks at how they conduct rituals in explicitly non-religious ways. Taking weddings as specific examples, Katie Aston shows how they not only express particular attitudes towards personhood, characterized by sincerity and personal agency, but also seek to instantiate them through affective gestural repertoires. In Claudia Liebelt's chapter, aesthetic body modifications are the primary vehicle for Kemalist Turkish women to perform their self-understanding as secular. Geraldine Mossière spoke with Quebecois born before the Quiet Revolution of the 1960s, now non-believers and passionate about *laïcité* but at the same time emotionally attached to the Catholic Church's style and its historically hegemonic role in the province. Stacey Gutkowski examines another case in which religion and culture are difficult to differentiate, identifying 'reasonableness' as a distinctive performance of the self as secular *hiloni* in Israel. By indirectly and often unintentionally facilitating and rendering opaque practices of Israeli governance over many aspects of Palestinian life, this way of being secular becomes implicated in state sovereignty.

Gutkowski's chapter provides a bridge to the third part, *Making Secular Citizens*, in which a secular sensibility is discovered or enforced through encounters between individual actors and a state apparatus or institution addressing them as citizens adhering to a specific arrangement of state-church relations, religion and public space. Karsten Lichau's examination of the invention of the 'moment of silence' in the early twentieth century as a secular performance of commemorating the dead reveals it to be a highly complex performance of ecumenism and nationalism that does not come easily. In the twenty-first century, the state becomes preoccupied with assuring its religious minorities adhere to the secular social order and in so doing, present its citizens with dilemmas in which they must choose whether to enact themselves as secular or not. Jennifer Selby examines what happens when the French state, seeking to discern which marriages are genuine, confronts prospective partners with challenging questions about their feelings and their secularity. Birgitte Schepelern Johansen and Riem Spielhaus look at how the production of quantitative knowledge about Muslims in Europe, through polls and surveys, serves as a site for producing as well as appeasing anxieties about Muslims' capacity for being appropriately secular. Marian Burchardt and Mar Griera investigate the feelings articulated in Spain over the wearing of burkas in public places, a classic example of secular affect. Finally, Matthew Engelke offers some reflections on the case studies in this volume and draws out further implications for an anthropology of the secular body.

With this introduction, and indeed with the volume as a whole, it is our aim to bring more clearly into view how the secular structures not only institutions but subjectivities, how it is made not only plausible but indeed appear to be the natural state of affairs in modern societies, something that can only happen through materialization. Nothing would appear to us more natural than those parts of ourselves we do not fully govern – our bodies, our feelings – and yet our relationships to them are deeply shaped by patterns, which have come to form the 'common sense' of society. Investigating the way that we inhabit the secular, and secularity inhabits us, we hope, will contribute to a broader project of critical scholarship on cultures of liberal democracies and 'modernity' that, while not seeking to undermine their intentions, remains vigilant in identifying their limits, weaknesses and pitfalls.

Part One

Bodies and Other Secular Things

Contraception and the Coming of Secularism: Reconsidering Reproductive Freedom as Religious Freedom

Pamela E. Klassen

When a woman slips a diaphragm snugly against her cervix or swallows a pill at the same time every morning so that she can engage in sexual intercourse with a man without becoming pregnant, what is the nature of her act, and who decides? More than half a century ago, the Supreme Court of the United States legalized contraception for married (implicitly) heterosexual couples across the nation. In a 1965 ruling on *Griswold v. Connecticut*, in which Estelle Griswold was fighting to keep open her Planned Parenthood birth control clinic in the face of state attempts to shut it, the court ruled that the constitutional right to privacy entailed that married couples had the freedom to use contraceptive tools to prevent pregnancy. By 1972, the Supreme Court had extended the right to access contraception to all people, married or unmarried (Gordon 2002). Since that time, academics and church leaders alike have often pinpointed the legalization of contraception as a key juncture in the rise of what they called a secular society, in which women and men made decisions about what to do with their bodies without guidance from religious, mostly Christian, teachings.[1]

Five decades later, a 2014 Supreme Court ruling heightened the presumed secularity of contraception, but this time by limiting women's access to contraceptives. In a case that turned not on the right to privacy but the right to religious freedom, appellants challenged what was called the 'contraceptive mandate' in President Obama's Affordable Care Act (ACA), by which employers were required to provide insurance plans that covered contraceptive costs. In an interesting twist for legal scholars, the evangelical Christian owners of Hobby Lobby, a craft supplies company with a workforce made up largely of women, deployed an innovative use of religious freedom. Hobby Lobby's lawyers successfully argued that the government was infringing not only the owners' right but also the corporation's right to religious freedom by mandating the company to provide insurance that gave their employees access to contraception such as IUDs and emergency contraceptives (Gedicks 2015; Griffin 2015; Sepinwall 2015). In the wake of the 2016 election and the subsequent attacks on the ACA, the Republican government further weakened the contraceptive mandate, continuing to frame it as an infringement of religious freedom.

In this chapter, I ask how this shift came about: How did a woman's access to contraception move from being understood as part of her constitutional right to privacy to becoming legally recognized as an inherent threat to the religious freedom of others, both people and corporations, far removed from the realm of her intimate relations? Has a tacit agreement that contraception is secular helped religious freedom to trump reproductive freedom? Whose arguments and experiences have been narrated in this shift? Which genres of testimony – theology, medical evidence, poetry – are given authority, and by whom? My answer, in part, rests on analysing changing definitions of the 'religious' and the 'secular' and the pressing weight these words can levy on the bodies of women.

Women's reproductive bodies have long been fertile sites of political wrangling, on which both nations and churches have built their authority through symbolic and coercive means, often with the concepts of religion, spirituality and the secular at close hand (see Ginsburg and Rapp 1995; Cady and Fessenden 2013; Griffith 2017). Contraception has been a particularly slippery battleground on which such wrangling takes place (Griffin 2015; Weiner 2017). Sometimes fought for as a tool of women's self-determination and sometimes fought against as threat to the religious liberty of others, contraception is a fascinating site for exploring the power of the word 'secular', as a designation that can enable the privileging of profoundly patriarchal – in the sense of rule by men – visions of what counts as a religious or secular body.

In recent years, numerous scholars have pointed to the ways that the power of the secular is formed out of oppositions that are in fact 'entanglements' (Bender 2010). Historian Joan Scott has offered a provocative reversal of the usual story that secularization led to women's emancipation, coining the term 'sexularism' to argue that projects of secularism in the Christian West were *founded on* and helped to *produce* inequality and political exclusion of women. According to Scott, even within modern European secular visions 'sex [was] restricted to a reproductive mandate, issued not in the name of God but of national salvation' (Scott 2017: 88). Depending on its population needs, the state might desire that certain women use more or less contraception, making reproductive mandates not solely the preserve of churches.

The concepts of religion, the spiritual and the secular are always contested, because they are powerful categories for organizing human social and political life, including modes of gendered embodiment (Lofton 2017). Contraception, neither inherently secular nor inherently religious, is a tool with profound consequences for particular women and for the collectives of which they are a part. As Kathryn Robinson argued, fertility and contraception are not only questions of the individual subject: 'Women do not live as social isolates; they belong to families, kin groups, status groups, classes, villages, nations, all of which encompass power relations that may impact on fertility' (Robinson 2001: 48). Particular contraceptive tools may provoke specific ritual and religious challenges: 'For example, the problems of the "menstrual chaos" associated with the injectable contraceptive Depo Provera is especially troubling in cultures where there are intimate, even sacral, associations of femininity and menstruation … The use of modern contraception inscribes bodies in a different way, locating them within different sets of power relations which may intersect with the old' (Robinson 2001: 50). Contraception has a spiritual politics.

To think of women's use of contraception as embodying a spiritual politics runs counter not only to some Christian theological traditions but also to prominent scholarly narratives of contraception as a driver of secularization in the twentieth century. Scholars including Charles Taylor and Callum Brown have suggested that for a woman to gain control over her cycles of fertility was for her to emerge as a secular actor, not bound by religious codes of sexual conduct. At the same time, those perspectives on contraception most often deemed religious by scholars and the law are held by people who oppose access to contraception, such as the Catholic hierarchy and some Evangelical Christians, including those in the 'Quiverfull' movement, in which women are to place the fate of their fertility and sexual health entirely in the hands of God (DeRogatis 2014; van Geuns 2016).

Despite sharing similar histories as imperial exports with complicated pasts, reproductive freedom and religious freedom are seldom thought together (Wenger 2017). But what if, in keeping with millennia in which women have marked their menstrual cycles and clocked their fertility with rituals, prayers and technologies meant to achieve *and* to forestall pregnancy, contraception can itself be considered a religious practice that qualifies for freedom? My aim here is not to argue with legal rigour that access to contraception is a religious freedom right. Instead I frame the regulation of fertility as part of a broader spiritual politics that some women understand to be at the heart of their selves and relations. A woman's right to choose may well be situated within a history of secular bodies as those that insist on personal autonomy unbeholden to Christian doctrine. However, women choosing to be sexually active but not procreative have also framed fertility with spiritual narratives. Adjudicating their contraceptive practices as post-biomedical bodies, these women become what Rayna Rapp called 'moral pioneers', making ethical and pragmatic choices about their fertility and sexual health shaped by discourses and tools at once medical, legal and spiritual (Rapp 1999; see also Klassen 2001).

Unpacking how contraceptive-using women were cast as secular bodies is critical for understanding how access to contraception shifted from an issue of reproductive freedom to one of religious freedom. In what follows, I first discuss how the idea of the secular came to be attached to women's use of contraception by both scholars and religious leaders. I then give a brief history of the changing availability and techniques of contraception in North America. I focus particularly on debates among Protestant and Catholic women and men about legalizing contraception sparked by the advent of the Pill in 1960. Far from being a settled secular tool, some advocates even came to argue that to use contraception was redemptive or a 'sacred choice' (Cahill 1966; Maguire 2001). Finally, I argue that to analyse the spiritual politics of contraception, it is essential to listen to the voices of women in a different register than the doctrinal or the legal, which so often reduce complex issues to dichotomies of right and wrong, winner and loser. Women have contemplated their reproductive horizons, by which I mean their ability to foresee and to plan for their childbearing, in a range of genres, including the scholarly essay, fiction, art and music. Considering these genres together allows us to see how women's reproductive horizons are never simply secular or religious.

Making contraception secular

Despite the active efforts of Jewish and Christian groups to secure access to contraception as a religious value and a legal right and despite decades of Catholic women making use of IUDs and the pill, both bishops and historians came to frame women's use of contraception as a secular act. In the 1940s, the National Catholic Welfare Conference (NCWC), a clerical organization committed to combatting anti-Catholicism and bringing Catholic perspectives into public discourse, defined secularism as 'the practical exclusion of God from human thinking and living' (cited in Holscher 2016: 155). The NCWC would later become the United States Conference of Catholic Bishops, the organization leading the charge against the contraceptive mandate and providing 'ethical directives' for health-care policies directly informed by Catholic doctrine, in which they directed Catholic hospitals to ban contraception (United States Conference of Catholic Bishops 2009).

Catholic legal scholar John T. Noonan Jr. similarly used the word 'secular' in contradistinction to a God-infused inner life in his 1965 survey of Catholic doctrines regarding contraception. He argued that 'secular law' – or state law – was a force of coercion that operated differently from the church's moral teaching: 'Unlike a history of secular law, however, where the meaning of a rule may be measured by its effective sanctions, the history of a moral doctrine must be, chiefly, an account of what was taught. The application of a moral rule is effected primarily not by agencies of compulsion but by an individual's accepting it in his heart' (Noonan Jr. 1986: 2). Noonan, who served on the papal commission on birth control, knew that many Catholic women in the 1960s chose to follow secular law regarding contraception even while considering themselves committed Catholics in their hearts.

More recently, several scholars have worked with an assumption of the secularity of contraception. In her careful 2004 history of US Catholicism and contraception, Leslie Woodcock Tentler repeatedly used the phrase 'the secular politics of birth control' to denote the actions of contraception advocates, including politicians and Catholic laypeople. Similarly, she described priests in the 1920s who delivered pre-marital instruction as increasingly frustrated by 'wholly secular views on marriage and sex' held by young couples, noting that one priest blamed mothers for challenging priests' authority when teaching their daughters about contraception (Tentler 2004: 7 and 40). If Catholic mothers were instructing their daughters about birth control, however, were their teachings necessarily secular?

In more direct causal arguments, both philosopher Charles Taylor and sociologist Callum Brown have correlated women's access to reliable contraception to the coming of secularism (see also Dobbelaere 2002: 168). For both men, contraception was part of a broader questioning of sexual ethics that became part of a secular age. According to Taylor, the modern social imaginary of the secular reimagined political power, social organization, human nature and even sexuality itself in such a way that an earlier respect for supernatural spirits, transcendent forces and social hierarchy has been displaced by a focus on the natural goodness of ordinary life and immanence, in a world of distinct individuals for whom religion could be a 'choice' and not an obligation. Writing from an agonistic Catholic perspective, Taylor contended that secular sexualities, and contraception and homosexuality in particular, pose a strong challenge to traditional views of Christianity: 'This terribly fraught area in Western Christendom, where the sexual meets the spiritual, urgently awaits the discovery of new paths to God' (Taylor 2007: 767).[2]

Historical sociologist Callum Brown also pointed to the 1960s as a particularly charged time when the sexual met the spiritual. Brown focused on the importance of contraception and changing gendered patterns of women's roles in family and work as demographic keys to the 'secular revolution' in Anglo-American contexts (Brown 2012: 12). Noting contraception in particular, Brown argued, 'By the early 1990s in USA, 80 to 85 per cent of Catholic women were reported as approving the use of the pill, whilst in UK in the 1990s the issue was recognised by Catholic scholars as the single greatest impediment to young women's faith' (Brown 2012: 171). That Catholic scholars saw contraception as the greatest impediment to young women's faith, however, does not reveal how women themselves understood the spiritual stakes of contraception. As Jennifer Selby and Diana Gustafson have shown, there is a continued 'resilience of Christianity for how women understood their reproductive bodies' (Gustafson and Selby 2016: 24) even in supposedly 'de-Christianized' places.

Faced with more pregnancies and births, the ethical choice for some mothers was to choose not to procreate. As Peter Schneider and Jane Schneider argued in their study of the increasing use of *coitus interruptus* over the twentieth century in a largely Catholic Sicilian town, 'for the mass of those who engaged in withdrawal – especially the women – no purely secular consciousness was necessary' (Schneider and Schneider 1995: 192). Despite transgressing Catholic teaching which barred *coitus interruptus*, their attempts to control their reproductive horizons suggest that for these women consciousness was, in the words of Rosalind Petchesky, a 'series of "negotiations" back and forth between ideology, social reality, and desire' (Petchesky 1990: 367).

If contraceptive practices are not necessarily secular, does that make them religious? Despite the boundary that some Christians draw between themselves and the secular as a 'God-excluded' realm, scholars have shown that in North America secularism is often better described as Christian secularism, or even Protestant secularism (Fessenden 2007; Jakobsen and Pellegrini 2008; Klassen 2011; Sullivan 2007). As a result, when supposedly secular law adjudicates Christian claims to religious freedom, these claims are more recognizable than those of non-Christians. As Winnifred Sullivan argues, the rise of religious freedom claims has awakened a new interest even from non-Christian groups to secure 'the muscular hierarchical demands of the rights of churches' (Sullivan 2015: 237). Religious groups seeking such rights are often highly gendered, with a strong preference for heterosexual marriage as the proper sphere for sexual relations (Pellegrini 2015; Shachar 2001).

As the example of contraception in the Catholic Church shows, however, courts often fail to consider the complexity of in-group contests over gender and sexuality. Discussing the Obama administration's attempts to negotiate with Catholic bishops over the contraceptive mandate, Leslie Griffin wrote as follows: 'Although the government frequently referred to the reproductive rights of women, it never took into account the religious liberty of Catholic women to make their own decisions of conscience about contraception without the bishops' intrusion' (Griffin 2015: 1420).

When a male celibate bishop defines the contraceptive mandate as an infringement on religious freedom for all Catholics, his version of freedom overwrites that of the majority of Catholic women, who use contraception.

The risk, then, is that understanding a woman's choice to use contraception as a secular practice renders unimaginable, or at least unspoken, the very possibility that regulating her fertility might be a moral, spiritual or religious act. Considering contraception and religious freedom in the context of workplace accommodations, Isaac Weiner argues that scholars need to better account 'for the ways that religious claims are produced and animated through public controversies and within the marked-as-secular spaces of labour and law' (Weiner 2017: 56). When women's bodies are themselves marked as secular, it becomes particularly important to attend to the voices of women who have imagined fertility and its regulation otherwise.

Changing contraceptive mentalities

Prior to the legalization of contraception, women in North America lived with serious constraints on their abilities to chart their own reproductive horizons. Though communities of women, especially midwives, had long cultivated knowledge of contraceptive techniques for the spacing of children, these means were not always reliable. The constraints on women differed depending on their social status. Upper-class white women had greater access to doctors who would fit them for diaphragms or perform tubal ligations for medical reasons. Poor women, especially if they were African American, Mexican American or Indigenous, were less likely to have access to freely chosen medical means of contraception. Instead, they were more often subject to medically prescribed coercive sterilization as a systemic form of racist population control and reproductive injustice (Lira and Stern 2014; Stern 2015).

Whether women's means of contraception were chosen or coerced, the pressures on them to remain quiet about their fertility practices were great. The scholarly study of women's fertility control is what Jessica Marcotte called an 'agnotology' – the study of the history of ignorance about women's practices of contraception (Marcotte 2016). While some scholarly ignorance was a result of women actively keeping such knowledge to themselves, it also came from scholars' acceptance of racist tropes. As Algea Othello Hale explained, social scientists long ignored the reality of 'family planning by black women', preferring instead the explanation that declining birth rates among African Americans in the late nineteenth century were caused by venereal disease (Hale 2007: 298).

During the early days of the struggle for legal access to contraception, women and men fought for people's right merely to learn about contraceptive methods (Bagge 2013; D'Emilio and Freedman 1988: 222). The Comstock laws, first instituted in the 1870s, outlawed sending supposedly 'obscene' information about contraception, let alone shipping contraceptive devices, via the US post (Beisel 1998). The American Medical Association supported laws restricting access to contraception until the 1930s, and even later, medical school curricula included little information about contraceptive methods (D'Emilio and Freedman 1988: 244). Across Protestant and Catholic churches, leaders shared a 'broadly Christian stance' of opposition to what they called a 'contraceptive mentality' as sinful, selfish and socially dangerous (Tentler 2004: 6). In the approving eyes of a Catholic archbishop, this alliance 'tied the state's law to God's law' (Cushing quoted in Griffin 2015: 1414).

Feminist historians have pieced together the politics of birth control in America, demonstrating remarkable diversity in attitudes, including perspectives that understood contraception as a kind of religious practice (Gordon 2002; Griffith 2017). The extant archive of women's knowledge and use of contraception, however, is vastly overshadowed by the books, papers and theological pronouncements written by men that condemn contraception. The most voluminous of these textual traditions is found within Catholicism, as Aline Kalbian has discussed, and is based largely on the theological ruminations of celibate men who considered contraception a question of moral evil, in which a woman could sin against the sacrament of procreative marriage and the potential of conceiving a life (Kalbian 2014). If a mentality – or *mentalité* – can be gauged in part by the volume of print culture that testifies to it, it would seem that men have a more prolific contraceptive mentality than do women.

Even when contraception was illegal in North America, women found ways to regulate their fertility, often in cooperation with men: the most popular methods pre-legalization were condoms, the rhythm method and *coitus interruptus* (Tone 2012: 320).[3] Also popular were 'feminine hygiene' products, a euphemism for products with multiple uses, one of which was the prevention of pregnancy. Most notoriously, a woman could purchase Lysol to use both as a germicide to clean her counters and a spermicide to douche the walls of her vagina (Eveleth 2013). Despite the fact that it was known to poison women to the point of death in some cases, women still turned to Lysol even in the 1970s, as one of the cheapest, if also unreliable, means for preventing pregnancy (Westoff and Ryder 1977).

Already by the 1930s, in the face of rising pressure from the birth control movement, several Protestant and Jewish organizations approved qualified use of contraception for married couples (Griffith 2017; Tentler 2004: 73). With the release of the pill in 1960, and partial legalization of contraception in 1965, doctors could now prescribe contraceptives to married women solely for the purpose of avoiding pregnancy, without being cloaked as treatments for other health-related diagnoses. The pill also revolutionized when and how women used birth control, as Andrea Tone noted: 'unlike condoms and diaphragms, oral contraceptives separated sex and procreation completely – a woman swallowed her pill in privacy, irrespective of the day's sexual agenda' (Tone 2006: 261). A medication developed in part by John Rock, a Catholic doctor, the pill was a product of state regulation which attracted critics from diverse political perspectives: Catholic bishops opposed it for what they considered to be its moral effects, black nationalists condemned it as a tool of racist genocide and feminists protested the paternalism and the sloppiness of the drug's approval testing process, raising concerns about its safety (Critchlow 1999; Marks 2010). Swallowing her pill in privacy did not mean that a woman's contraceptive act was without public consequences.

Redemptive contraception

The debate over contraception in the 1960s did not adhere to divisions of secular and religious. Many advocates spoke openly as Jews, Protestants and Catholics, and churches and synagogues worked with Planned Parenthood (Christie 2002; Davis 2005; McLaren and McLaren 1997). Eager to address contraception as a religious question in the 1960s, liberal Protestants and Jews critiqued sexual double standards that came at the expense of women and 'committed significant time and energy to writing and speaking about the need for new and creative religious thinking about sexual ethics' (Griffith 2012: 477). For these North Americans, access to contraception was a requirement for living a faithful life.

John Rock became one of the pill's most vigorous public defenders, writing and speaking on television as a self-described Catholic. An obstetrician, gynaecologist and father of five, Rock formed his view of contraception while working in a rhythm method birth control clinic, where he saw the toll that multiple unplanned pregnancies took on the bodies and lives of his patients. Since the notoriously unreliable rhythm method had received the Pope's blessing in 1951, Rock hoped to convince the Pope that the pill was also a method based on the rhythms of a woman's cycle (Critchlow 1999: 115).

The 1960s were an era of growing medicalization: just as the pill turned contraception into a medically prescribed concern, so too did medical doctors and researchers become increasingly emboldened to comment from their medical expertise on the moral issues of the day (Gordon 2002: 115). Interviewed in 1964 by journalist Katie Johnson for a popular Canadian news show, Rock argued that 'coitus' was 'the binding act in marriage', and that contraception which allowed a mother and father to care for their family by spacing their children did not lessen the sacredness of this bond (Johnson and Rock 1964). For Rock, the use of contraceptives was not a secular failure of moral living but an act in keeping with the procreative principle of Catholic theology.

When Johnson inquired why the Catholic Church was opposed to contraception if it was theologically sound, Rock replied that the church needed to listen to laypeople who had come to accept contraception through theological deliberation: 'In Catholic teaching, the individual's conscience is what he must follow, providing his conscience has been properly formed.' When Johnson pressed further to ask if contraception could also be used for pre-marital or extra-marital sex, Rock demurred, at least for Catholics: 'Any manifestation of sex which leads to, strengthens, fortifies monogamy is good. And any use of sex or sex organs that does not do this is bad.' Bridging theological arguments with those of population control, Rock also cited the need to 'separate copulation from population'.

Some Catholic leaders also cautiously defended the pill. Canadian Archbishop Philip Pocock, replying to a letter from a woman parishioner who condemned the pill as ungodly, drew on tropes of the drunken husband and 'deficient' children:

> Not infrequently situations arise which cause a good Catholic wife and mother to ask herself if God does not wish her to exercise discretion in bringing more children into the world. Suppose she is the mother of four or five small children,

some of whom are mentally deficient, and she is married to an unemployed, alcoholic husband who appears regularly to insist on his rights? (Pocock quoted in Meenan 2011: 218)

Pocock suggested that for such a woman to limit her husband's 'approaches' to the infertile times in her cycle might not be sinful. While not openly critiquing the idea that a husband had the right to force his wife to have sex, Pocock insisted that challenges faced by 'very devout Catholic mothers' in negotiating their sexual lives was a question that 'moralists must answer' (Pocock quoted in Meehan 2011: 218). According to some, his cautious support of contraception later cost him the chance to become a cardinal in the Roman Catholic Church (Meehan 2011).

In the 1960s, Catholics supporting access to contraception were emboldened by legal scholar John Noonan's cautious appeal to the papal commission on birth control that doctrine should be considered living, and thus changeable (Noonan Jr. 1986 [1965]). While Noonan's research helped lead the papal commission to encourage the Pope to loosen the church's restrictions on contraception, likely the best known of US Catholic theologians to address the issue was Noonan's mentor, John Courtney Murray, a Jesuit theologian who argued for respecting 'the religious freedom of non-Catholics to use contraception' (Griffin 2015: 1415; McGreevy 2004: 245; see also Allitt 1995; Haberski 2012). Arguing that contraception was an issue of 'private morality' and noting that some US religious groups had deemed it acceptable, Murray advised that the Catholic Church should not oppose its legalization: 'because Americans of different religions disagree in good faith about the morality of contraception, "laws in restraint of the practice are in restraint of religious freedom"' (Murray quoted in Griffin 2015: 1415). For Murray, contraception was not an inherently secular threat.

In 1968, the year after Murray died, Pope Paul VI chose to ignore the majority report of his papal commission and condemned the use of contraception in *Humanae Vitae* (Paul VI 1968). Many Catholics protested, including clergy, laypeople and most dramatically, a growing cohort of Catholic feminist theologians. Just two months after Pope Paul VI promulgated *Humanae Vitae*, the Canadian Catholic Bishops released a statement in response, colloquially known as the Winnipeg Statement. They went beyond thinking of contraception as a question of religious freedom for non-Catholics to argue that even a Catholic priest or counsellor, following the tenets of moral theology, might find that the right course of action was to recommend contraception to a woman (Appleby 1999; Sheridan 1991).

Scholars among the first formally trained generation of Catholic women theologians argued even more strongly in favour of artificial contraception. With a pragmatic bent, Jane Furlong Cahill compared the punishments meted out to Adam and to Eve for their 'original sin':

Since we have never hesitated to remedy Adam's specific punishment 'working by the sweat of his brow' by labour saving devices, why should we hesitate to put reasonable control back into woman's role as a human wife and mother by scientifically slowing down her obviously hyperactive fertility? This is all the more reasonable since we hold that women as well as men have been redeemed by Christ from the effects of Original Sin and marriage raised to the dignity of a sacrament for the obvious purpose of sanctifying the recipients. (Cahill 1966: 469)

Cahill then articulated a redemptive theology of contraception: 'May not contraception then be considered a kind of restoration of Eve and her daughters – a real form of redemption?' (Cahill 1966: 469). Touching on the spirituality of desire, Cahill also decried the rhythm method as a 'moral evil' for perverting the cadences of marital sexuality, since for many women, sexual desire peaks with ovulation (Cahill 1966: 473; Toates 2014: 152).

Writing her own agnotology of contraceptive spirituality, Cahill concluded:

> The current teaching as I see it stems from a serious, though understandable, ignorance of the Fathers of the nature of woman and human sexuality which has unfortunately been transmitted to the present day. But just as a man's role in life cannot be completely summed up in his role as a father, so neither can woman's role in life be designated solely by her role as a mother. (Cahill 1966: 474)

Cahill's theology of redemptive contraception challenged maternal essentialism while remaining dedicated to sacramental, heterosexual marriage (cf Delgado 2014).

The 1960s discourse of the morality of contraception arose in the era of Vatican II, when Catholics and Protestants experimented with ecumenical dialogue (Hoyt 1967; see also Hannah 1965). As Protestant churches came to call for 'freer laws on abortions', however, and abortion was legalized in the 1970s, this dialogue became strained. Once women in the United States and Canada gained legal access to contraception and abortion, those Christians who considered themselves part of a contraception-averse church were no longer in alignment with what many inside and outside of churches were now calling secular law and society. As Leslie C. Griffin has shown, Catholic bishops were among the most perplexed by this change: 'At the beginning of the twentieth century, the American Catholic bishops inhabited a church-friendly regime of anti-contraceptive laws due to no effort of their own' (Griffin 2015: 1412). By the 1970s, however, debates over abortion 'thrust the bishops back into politics, and, eventually, provided them with the opportunity to put contraception back into the political and legal spotlight' (Griffin 2015: 1415). Such politics included excoriating Catholic feminist theologians who supported women's access to contraception (Day 2012; Farley 2006).

The bishops' twenty-first-century targeting of contraception is not a mere smokescreen for their opposition to abortion. Long before the controversy over the Affordable Care Act, Catholic organizations doggedly fought against 'contraceptive equity' legislation that sought to make contraception broadly accessible to low-income women (Griffin 2003; Kalbian 2014). In a 1990s era of hospital mergers, access to contraception was often limited regardless of which hospital did the merging: when Catholic hospitals were taken over by non-religiously affiliated institutions, they often insisted on a clause that required the new entity not to provide contraception or abortion services, and when Catholic hospitals did the taking over, they removed any contraceptive services (Flood 2006; Fogel and Rivera 2004; Rodgers 2002). Limiting the availability of contraception more generally has real consequences, especially for women living in rural and remote areas where access to contraception may be difficult enough already (Fogel and Rivera 2004). Anti-contraception mentalities have also affected other areas of women's health, such as treatment for ectopic pregnancies (Anderson et al. 2011; Foster et al. 2011; Manian 2014).

In their new fight against the contraceptive mandate, the Catholic bishops have insisted that contraception is a moral, not a medical, issue, borrowing, ironically, from the feminist critique that pregnancy and childbirth are not diseases automatically requiring medical intervention. Arguing that contraception does not treat a 'medical' condition and is thus not insurable, the bishops, ironically, also supported men's 'medical need for Viagra' (Griffin 2015: 1418). Pope Francis' exhortation, *Amoris Laetitia* (2016) or the 'Joy of Love', underscored the anti-contraception message of *Humanae Vitae*, further supporting the American bishops. No longer able to count on a wider culture that shared the view that contraception was immoral and should be illegal, contraception-averse Christians developed a new argument rooted in the idea of religious freedom.

Reimagining the spiritual politics of fertility

Scholars of religion and the secular should note that the resurgence of contraception as a contested political issue in North America can be witnessed not only in court battles focused on religious freedom but also in feminist art, fiction, television and music. For example, inspired by Margaret Atwood's *The Handmaid's Tale*, a dystopian portrait of Christian patriarchal fundamentalism, women dressed as Handmaids came to protest for legal access to contraception and abortion in the streets and state legislatures of the United States. This performative protest suggests that the spiritual politics of fertility are expressed in multiple registers which reimagine fertility's perils and pleasures against varying histories of sexism, colonialism and racism.

At a bodily level, women have long used amulets, herbs, prayers and rituals to influence their fertility, either to bring about pregnancy or to avoid it. At a cosmological level, 'fertility rites' was long the term of art that scholars used to describe collective rituals to cultivate divine and earthly power (Frazer 2012; Harrison 1922). Feminist scholars have brought these bodily and cosmological aspects together to discern a spiritual politics of fertility. Carol Delaney argued that 'procreation theories', or the ways that people understand and narrate the significance of the fertility of both women and land, profoundly shape religious or cosmological systems and the lives of women (Delaney 1991: 9). In a comparative argument focused on sacrifice, Nancy Jay went further to argue that the power of women's fertility was so awesome and threatening to men that they invented new rituals of 'rebirth', including baptism, to counter the creative power of childbirth: 'sacrifice is remedy for having been born of woman' (Jay 1992). As Jay showed, many religious systems built community through gendered hierarchy and exclusion in which 'the blood of menstruation and childbirth is the quintessence of impurity' (Jay 1992: 77).

Ritualized practices of childbirth and menstruation (at once a sign of fertility and of not-being-pregnant) do not stem solely from hierarchical exclusion, however. In her study of 'religions dominated by women', Susan Sered found that patrilineal and male-dominated religions were most concerned to control women's reproductive horizons. By contrast, 'in women's religions what we often find is that women's control of her own fertility is somehow sacralized or institutionalized. Apparently, religions that sacralize or institutionalize women's control of their own fertility are anathema to patrilineal societies' (Sered 1996: 62). When patrilineal religions have sought to dominate matrilineal societies, as in the case of Catholic missionaries to Indigenous nations, the sacredness imputed to fertility has often led to the disempowerment and denigration of women-centred spiritual practices of fertility.

Kim Anderson, writing of Anishinaabe practices of family planning, argued that twentieth-century Catholic anthropologists who claimed that Cree and Anishinaabe women did not use contraception were likely misreading the situation due in part to their theological views. Their ethnographic findings were also compromised, as Anderson shows, by women's sense that they should keep their fertility practices secret from anthropological inquirers. In her own oral history research, she found many accounts of contraception: 'These stories demonstrate how older women managed *madjimadzuin*, "the human Milky Way," through their family planning practices.' With a recurring theme of limiting the number of births in order to ensure that mothers survive to care for their children and to 'live to see their grandchildren', these contraceptive stories led Anderson to conclude that '[f]amily planning was undertaken to ensure the survival of the people' (Anderson 2011: 42). The spiritual politics of fertility are polyvalent, shaped by histories of racism and resistance, generational memory and the vulnerability and resilience of bodies in relation (see also Duncan 2005; Fraser 1998).

In addition to scholars, feminist artists have also reflected on the moral and bodily significance of rituals of fertility. Vanessa Dion Fletcher, a Potowatomi/Lenape performance and visual artist, has critically juxtaposed Indigenous traditions of menstrual rituals with medical and consumer approaches to menstruation and fertility to revisualize the 'reproductive body'. Her textile exhibit *Mark Blot Spot Stain*, inspired by Indigenous women's beading traditions, stitched red beads on fabric to represent the stains of her own menstrual blood, while her installation *Own Your Cervix* alluded to the 1970s women's health movement, inviting guests to come to the gallery to 'visualize your cervix' with a speculum. Complete with a waiting room and examination room, the exhibit aestheticized and spiritualized the cervical self-exam (Dion Fletcher 2016, 2018). Dion Fletcher's restaging of this key symbol of the 1970s women's health movement echoed this earlier challenge to the medicalization of women's reproductive bodies through invocations of spiritually informed self-knowledge (Gaskin 1990; Our Bodies Ourselves n.d.). Questioning settler colonialism, land and memory through new rituals and representations of menstruation and medicalization, Dion Fletcher's art evokes a feminist and Indigenous spiritual politics of fertility.

In a differently spectacular intervention, Beyoncé's visual album *Lemonade* also restages colonial histories, through songs and images of African American women's practices of asceticism and pleasure. Reciting the poetry of Somali-British poet Warsan

Shire and combining Christian and Yoruba-inspired imagery, *Lemonade* is a testament to the sacredness of sexuality far beyond the horizon of the reproductive. With a cast of powerful black women, *Lemonade* calls out cheating husbands, racist police violence and male violence against women at the same time that it frames female sexuality as possessing kaleidoscopic spiritual depths. An artistic feat in which the spiritual meets the sexual, *Lemonade* has provoked new efforts to build a textual tradition of black women's sexual ethics, as Candice Benbow's *Lemonade Syllabus* demonstrates (Benbow 2016a, b). Black women's interpretive reception of *Lemonade* frames it as a new archive for reclamation, according to scholar Regina Bradley, in which Beyoncé 'sift[s] through the forced silence regarding the physical, social and spiritual violence of slave women to locate the quiet of black women's endurance ….[T]he antebellum south serves as an entry point for Beyoncé to recognize the historical and cultural horrors of black womanhood while reclaiming the survival techniques passed down over time' (Bradley and Hampton 2016). One of these survival techniques was contraception (Hale 2007).

Hinting at contraceptive douching in her recitation of Shire's poem 'Denial', Beyoncé intones, 'I bathed in bleach and plugged my menses with pages from the Holy Book.' With the pages of the Bible soaking up the blood that signals the absence of pregnancy, Beyoncé brings the word of God directly into a woman's body in a manner at once sacrilegious and sacred, and not mediated by men (Beyoncé 2016). As her remarkable performance when pregnant with twins at the 2017 Grammy Awards demonstrated, Beyoncé very consciously makes use of what art historian Cecile Fromont called a 'golden dreamscape of maternity figures and mythical women', including Oshun, Mami Wata and the Virgin Mary (Cecile Fromont in Raiss 2017). Telling a redemptive story with her powerful, singing, fertile body, she crossed freely among the maternal, the desiring and the divine (Hobson 2016).[4]

Beyoncé's allusive performance was not that of a secular body. If the secular in North America is so deeply inflected by Christianity, however, it is worth remembering that the Christian story is based not only on the crucifixion but also on the incarnation. Christianity is a complex social imaginary whose power depends on the combined control and celebration of the maternal body (Klassen 2015). Neither of these social imaginaries – the secular or the Christian – can fully encapsulate the complexity of a woman's decision to use contraception to control her fertility.

Menstruation, pregnancy and childbirth are experiences with profound effects on women's engagement in their political worlds, shaped by the criss-crossing forces of class, race, gender and sexuality. As Justice Ruth Ginsburg quoted her predecessor, Justice Sandra Day O'Connor, in her dissent to the Hobby Lobby decision, 'The ability of women to participate equally in the economic and social life of the Nation has been facilitated by their ability to control their reproductive lives' (Ginsburg quoting O'Connor in Gostin 2014: 785). This control is never absolute but it is also not necessarily secular, in the sense of excluding gods or goddesses from one's thinking or living.

Women cannot afford to ignore legal arguments when it comes to their reproductive bodies. But arguments cast purely in a legal genre might well result in competing religious freedoms going head to head in a courtroom, with women's bodies hanging in the balance. Next to the power – and impotence – of papal decrees or legal judgements which restrict women's access to contraception are stories, poems, art and music that name women's sexuality as a powerful source of ethics and relationality when it is procreative and when it is not. Artists, writers and musicians show the importance of cultivating fluency in other genres of address in order to challenge the binary of secular and religious that has long channelled the spiritual politics of fertility through a perspective largely oriented by the visions of men.

A Secular Corpse? Tracing Cremation in Nineteenth-Century Italy and Germany

Carolin Kosuch

In March 1884, the British newspaper *The Referee* promoted a new way to deal with human remains:

> Folks of every rank and station,/We beg your kindest approbation/For Cremation./ Let individuals and the nation/Support the latest innovation/In Cremation./And in your wills leave intimation/You will not be a cold collation,/For hungry worms a further ration,/But have the final consolation/Of clean and swift annihilation/By Cremation. (Parsons 2005: 114)

During the last quarter of the nineteenth century, similar calls echoed throughout Switzerland, Sweden, France, Denmark and the United States.[1] Cremation became the subject of many leaflets, brochures and newspapers. Extensively propagated by newly founded cremation societies, the topic was seized by scientific congresses and parliaments.[2] The Kingdom of Italy, created in 1861, and the German Empire, established only a decade later, spearheaded this discourse.[3] Both countries' movements for cremation benefitted from liberal and radical-liberal attitudes that politicized the values of reason, progress and advancement.[4] The practice of cremation gained fervent support among natural scientists, physicians active in politics and a small but growing interested public of merchants, lawyers, artisans and members of the free professions (Conti et al. 1998: 91–105). Many of the natural scientists and physicians among the cremationists were motivated by their enlightened and often materialistic belief that they could answer the questions of health, life and morality more profoundly than Christian clerics, as well as by the desire to mould self-determined, civilized citizens (Mantegazza 2010: 85).[5] While campaigning for cremation, they committed themselves to advancing a 'civilizing mission' (Pini 1885: 7).

All the European cremation movements reflected the anti-Catholic, anticlerical political positions common at the time (Weir 2014: 271f.),[6] but in Italy this stance was additionally encouraged by the unresolved 'Roman Question', the growing anti-modernist attitude of the papacy and its reluctance to support the young nation state. Italian cremationists provoked massive ideological arguments with the Catholic

Church, not least due to their ostentatious sympathy for laical Freemasonry.[7] Aligning themselves with the politicized notion of progress, they strived to overcome the generally negative *Risorgimento* image of the 'backward Italian south'.[8] In a nutshell, cremation triggered a debate between fiercely opposing parties, both struggling for the prerogative to interpret the Italian present and future.

In order to enforce their medico-political-ideological aim and to justify its urgency, cremationists also relied on the increasingly widespread notion of hygiene.[9] The hygienic paradigm, nourished by a general fear of epidemics like cholera or typhus, which periodically raged throughout the continent in the nineteenth century, was fed by a prospering sector of professional and semi-professional public medical lectures and publications that spread the latest theories on miasma, germs and possible routes of transmission through air, water and soil.[10] At the same time, cremation advocates often sought to link the practice to pre-modern traditions – not, of course, by promoting the cremation of corpses on open pyres in Europe's urban centres, but rather by claiming they were adapting an ancient tradition to modern science and engineering (Lueger 1908: 120–27). British anthropologist Mary Douglas's remarks on the human tendency to 'force one another into good citizenship' according to 'certain moral values' defined by 'beliefs in dangerous contagion' thus seems to have found their confirmation in cremation and its technology (Douglas 1966: 2f.).

With their highly critical stance towards religion and religious institutions and their tendency towards rationalization and worldliness, cremationists can be considered prototypes of secular subjects.[11] Nevertheless, their writings also contain a solemn, at times even poetical, language, appealing remarkably frequently to certain emotions vis-à-vis the corpse, seemingly at odds with their science-centred paradigm. I suggest that what at first appears to be a contradiction actually points to an overlapping of the religious and the secular as well as the reliance of a secular stance towards the corpse on emotions ranging from reverence to disgust and horror. In this chapter, I would like to examine the interrelation of the secular and the religious, which – following Talal Asad – comes from the fact that '[t]he secular … is neither continuous with the religious that supposedly preceded it … nor a simple break from it' (2003: 25), by analysing certain practices and wording found in both German and Italian cremationist publications. In so doing, I will attempt to show 'how contingencies relate to changes in the grammar of concepts – that is, how the changes in concepts articulate changes in practices' (2003: 25).

Equality in purity: The immortal ashes of the nation

Anatomist, geologist, autodidact, hobby inventor and one of the most influential and creative proponents of cremation in nineteenth-century Italy, Paolo Gorini (1813–81)[12] not only shared the patriotic belief of his liberal combatants but exceeded their enthusiasm in many ways. Much a child of his times, Gorini was deeply influenced by both the national and social revolutionary movements Mazzini and Garibaldi had launched (Beales and Biagini 2002) and moulded by the romantic colouring of the Risorgimento (Ginsborg 2011), which 'expresses not only imagination and feeling, but also a distinctive form of patriotic fervour, at once noble and melancholy' (Cranston

1994; 99), His work combined scientific curiosity, devotional commitment and liberal beliefs. Initially, he worked as a teacher trying to educate his students to be open-minded and free from prejudices, but later he invented explosives and offered his help to the city of Milan during the uprising of the Cinque Giornate (1848), the response to the Habsburgian siege.[13] Gorini's unorthodox methods and topics of research ranged from anatomical preparation to the exploration of volcanoes. His book *Sull'origine dei vulcani. Studio sperimentale* [On the Origins of Volcanoes. An Experimental Study] (1871) reflects his anti-Catholic, materialistic, positivistic concept of life and matter and offers a solution to the mind-body problem[14]: According to his theory, life and matter pass through an endlessly flowing cycle that starts with minerals and ends with human beings. As stated by Gorini, every material stage of the cycle forms a distinct and essential part of a well-defined realm; the plutonic power he discovered during his observations of volcanic lava, however, seemed to him to unite each and every material form in the universe. Observing this, he concluded that matter is never lost from nor added to the cycle. In Gorini's vision, everything is thus part of a steady and unavoidable process of transformation. Indeed, Gorini denied the existence of human free will, understanding the soul as an ephemeral by-product of the self-organization of matter, and the body as a purely mechanical unit (Gorini 1871: 512–18).

Resting on pluralized, heterogeneous political and cultural conditions,[15] Gorini's scientific and liberal convictions, together with his criticism of Catholicism as a form of institutionalized exploitation that caused inequality, constituted the secular core of his beliefs (Gorini 1871: 533f.). These seemingly secular convictions, however, were also based on the myth of liberalism (Asad 2003: 57) and reflected Masonic positions that substituted and imitated Christian ones.[16] Consequently, Gorini, in his secularity, by no means renounced transcendent beliefs: His interpretation of the plutonic stream, characterized as the creative principle of the universe, the artist, the demiurge, turned out to be a monistic[17] one that also contained elements of pantheism. Thus, in Gorini's theories, science, liberalism and anti-Catholicism converge in a religious pattern that plainly shows the entanglement of the religious and the secular.

It was against the backdrop of his theory of life and matter that the anatomical preparator Gorini[18] was first faced with the question of cremation: In 1872, Mazzini, Pater Patriae, died. Mazzini was an outstanding representative of the Italian nation and its previous struggle for freedom. At the time of his death, the liberal movement was in desperate need of a symbol to convey its strength and power; thus, after a controversial debate, some of Mazzini's combatants decided that his corpse should be embalmed and preserved for public exhibition. This 'artificial sanctification' (Luzzatto 2001: 13) through the use of modern chemistry – regardless of its secular setting – recalls the Catholic belief that a body showing no signs of decomposition is proof of sainthood (Angenendt 1994: 149–52). Here again, by making Mazzini's corpse a national relic intended to be worshiped by his fellow Italians, secular grammar relied on religious precedent.

Gorini was in charge of the project's practical realization and reflected on his work and his emotions in *La conservazione della salma di Giuseppe Mazzini* (The Preservation of Mazzini's Corpse) (1873). Facing the body of the deceased hero aroused feelings of shock and wonder in Gorini (1873: 6, 46). While Mazzini's spirit would live on in the Italian nation, his body would soon succumb to the work of worms if treated in the traditional way. Here, the liberal scientist Gorini argued for the modification of nature according to human values and requirements. Whereas the British, though living in the most industrialized country in the world, did not dare to consider this step, the Italians would not hesitate to include even the corpse in the project of civilizing their nation, Gorini explicated (1873: 34f.).

It was no accident that he placed his fellow Italians at the vanguard of a modern, forward-looking, enlightened and rational paradigm (Dalmas 2012).[19] The Italian national movement was composed mainly of liberals and democrats who were influenced by the culture and traditions of Western Europe and permeated with anti-Catholic notions (Isabella 2009). The internal division of Italy into a north regarded as modern, rational and progressive and a south looked upon as a superstitious and backward 'inner Italian Africa'[20] led some of the proud patriots fighting for the dawn of their nation to feel that Europe's established nations wrongly perceived them as inferior. As liberals, Gorini and the Italian cremationists tried to combat this feeling with their progressive stance towards the corpse: for them, cremation emerged as the Kingdom of Italy's ticket not only to modernity – a strongly ideologized concept – but also to a top position in Europe's hierarchy (Monsagrati 2004: 130).

As Gorini emphasized, only those who, like Mazzini, had served their country devotedly were meant to be embalmed and preserved for the memory and moral instruction of future generations in perpetuity, or at least for a certain period of time (Gorini 1876: 225f.).[21] His moralizing opinion aligned with the convictions of another advocate of cremation, Ferdinando Coletti, a professor of pharmacology. In his campaign for cremation, Coletti highlighted that a cremation urn kept in the family home would strengthen relations between the generations and spark 'a moral regeneration' (Coletti 1866: 229–32, 237–40). Without cremation, an 'enormous sea of the deceased' would fill Italy's cemeteries, leaving no space for the living, Gorini (1876: 16) added. From his point of view, the Christian tradition of burying the dead was an unhygienic and almost barbaric habit: He confessed that he had always suffered with the deceased, carelessly left behind in cold soil. Untamed, wild nature, who took back from the buried corpse the substances she once used to build the body, was to be overcome by creating 'an insurmountable obstacle'. The corpses of the deceased were to be treated 'less cruelly' and saved from the 'injustice of time' (1876: 13). For Gorini, cremating the corpses of average citizens was to grant them equality: just as embalmment preserved Mazzini's corpse, their remains would be preserved in the form of indestructible ashes. Gorini's casting of cremation as a way of saving and preserving the dead (as opposed to destroying them) found its echo in the charter of the first Italian cremation society promoting cremation: 'submitting to the living innocuous relics for preservation, produced in a simple and economic way' (Municipal Archive of Gotha 1884: 3).

Cremation, as outlined by its Italian proponents, would prevent the corpse from being reabsorbed by nature. Yet, in Gorini's concept, it should not entirely inhibit this process of reclamation: lightweight components could escape during the combustion process and through the chimney find their way back into the plutonic cycle of life (Gorini 1879: 17). In this way, according to Gorini, modern man, by means of his technology, would accelerate natural processes and perfect, not thwart, them (Gorini 1876: 11). The ashes, an element of culture created by man and collected in the urn, however, would – at least in theory – be divested from nature forever as a symbol of human superiority and self-determination: 'The artist [the creative principle of the universe] was well advised to keep hidden, because once detected he would have to subordinate himself strictly to human rules and follow human commands' (Gorini 1871: 496).

Gorini's work did not stop at theory and anatomical preparation: After a series of attempts, he constructed a working crematory furnace that fulfilled the needs of Italy's cremation movement better than the already existing furnaces engineered by Polli, Brunetti and Clericetti (Pini 1885: 128–32). His simple mechanism worked discretely, producing odourless, pure white ashes free from any contamination. It thus lived up to the central demands of the medical-cultural concept of hygiene and aligned with the modern notion of deference as connected to cleanliness and individuality. It was implemented in various Italian cities as well as in Woking, a city near London.

Here I pause to draw a first conclusion: For nineteenth-century Italian cremationists, the buried corpse and its decay were unbearable. It was the purified, clean corpse in the form of ashes saved from nature's implacability that they idealized.[22] They seem to have implicitly connected the dead body buried in the ground, conceptualized as an element of nature, with pre-modern times and with the Catholic idea of man, an idea that according to the cremationists was oriented towards the afterlife, dirt and disease. They rejected this idea: A pure, precious, innocuous and honourable 'modern corpse' was one that had been sanitized by fire and refined by science and technology; it no longer required the sanctification of clerics. The emphasis cremationists laid on the preservation of the body was a result of their disbelief in the Catholic concept of the soul and its afterlife. Notwithstanding these divisions, the religion-infused secularity of the Italian cremationists tended to rely on a specific Catholic model, re-reading and re-modelling the meaning of the saint's body or of fire as a secular element of purification for the sinner's soul. The grammar of the secular thus follows not just from modernity modelled on Protestantism but the religious specificities of a society: the 'religious-secular divide [seems to] acquire specific cultural meanings' (Asad 2003; Burchardt and Wohlrab-Sahr 2013: 606).

Together with the clean corpse, cremationists addressed refined emotions they believed would bind the precious deceased (Gorini 1879: 28), physically purified by fire, to the community of the living:

> Oh mothers! Think of your poor children who lie in the ground. The flowers and the cold marble covering their graves cannot save them from decay; it is as if they lie in a garbage heap. It is horrible, but true. In the name of sentiment, I therefore call on the mothers to promote cremation. And in the name of sentiment I ask for the support of the mothers and wives; and in the name of this religion of the heart I invite everyone to stand up for cremation, not just as the most hygienic and rational system, but as the only one that corresponds to the needs of the heart, securing devotion. (Margarita 1876: 38)[23]

No other than in the Italian case, German-language promotion of cremation in the press adopted an anti-Catholic polemic, too, constantly reporting on the horrible burial fosses in Naples and Palermo and railing against the grotesque burial vaults of Capuchin monasteries, where corpses hung down from the ceiling in their clothes, evoking disgust and revulsion.[24] It advertised cremation as a process that ensured feelings of true, pure love, memory and noble commemoration, and beautiful, poetic devotion. Even though he was critical of cremation, the following observations from Paolo Mantegazza point to feelings common on both sides of the Alps and provide a bridge to the next section of this chapter:

> Our funeral rites will undergo two major changes, one hygienic and one moral. From the moral point of view, we expect a more serious morality and less hypocrisy. In former times, we buried the deceased because we were Christians; now we have to become cremationists because we are human. Free from hypocrisy, purified by fire, and guided by science, our funeral rites will be both improved and more subtle. Leaving behind those mystical and superstitious beliefs, they will reflect pure human affects, serious, but filled with the holiest poetry. (Mantegazza 1989: 679f.)

Feeling secular? The politics of disgust

Without a doubt, the anti-Catholic, civilizing, hygiene-promoting mission adopted by nineteenth-century cremation movements was a unifying force that brought together individual national cremation societies in a transnational network with regular meetings during various congresses.[25] Periodicals like *Die Flamme* and *Phoenix* reported the history of cremation, the movement's worldwide advancement and the juridical or clerical challenges hindering its progress.[26] The strong mutual influence between Italian, German and other cremationists was reflected in their publications and articles, in which they even cited each other and translated each other's writings. Any distinctions made between their emotional approaches, therefore, must be tentative. The intensity of the invocation of specific emotional terms and the degree of affection expressed in emotional language in the writings of natural scientists on cremation, however, reflect the specific background of each national cremation movement and can thus be differentiated.

Italian and German cremationists shared a feeling of disgust towards 'putrefaction', a politicized term they used to advance their case. In the age of positivism, in which hopes were raised for mankind's final victory over nature, disgust signalled a distance that defined the 'unclean corpse' as the radical 'other' for the modern individual (Kristeva 1982). The Italians' disgust seems to have stemmed from both hygienic and moral considerations: decomposing corpses were thought to contaminate the water, soil and air,[27] but they were also seen as 'poor dead' who had been left behind due to cruel and inhuman Catholic convictions that lacked any 'true' deference. In Germany, on the other hand, where cremation was promoted against the backdrop of a secularity shaped by Protestantism, particularly its refusal of the worship of (bodily) relics and the invocation of saints,[28] the emphasis was placed on putrefaction and the decaying corpse itself, which was considered 'disgusting'.[29]

Despite these nuances in the emotional setting of disgust – a setting that reflects the significance of the body in secularities based on either Catholic or Protestant culture – the tendency to alienate the corpse in both cremation movements was objectified and amplified by a campaign for a broad and general installation of mortuaries that would separate the corpse from the family, the home and domestic scenery (Baginsky 1874: 29; Laqueur 2015: 211–362). For many cremationists, the still quite common contemporary custom of sharing the house with the laid-out deceased was unacceptable. According to them, the custom was related to connotations of poverty and hardship and thwarted their attempts to identify their nations with progress and civilization.[30] After the physicians assigned to the post-mortem examination issued their final judgement, the corpse, the cremationists thought, no longer fully belonged to the world of the living; it was thus supposed to be stored intermediately in a public building erected exclusively for this purpose. Subsequently, the dead body, perceived as potentially dangerous to the bereaved, was placed into the public sphere anew only after the purifying process of cremation.

As the endeavour to create distance between the corpse and the world of the living merged with a sense of revulsion, Italian and German cremationists additionally began to focus on crime and moral offence, which likewise conflicted with their image of the enlightened, physically clean and morally good modern man. German cremationist publications, to emphasize these issues, reiterated stories about corpses buried without combustion that became the objects of some of the most flagitious crimes. Articles, brochures and books reported the theft of clothes covering already buried bodies, the rape of deceased beautiful young women, the exploitation of decomposing corpses for commercial purposes and the systematic feeding of animals with body parts (Küchenmeister 1875: 47–50).[31] Thus combustion, in their view, would have a twofold civilizing effect, cleansing and purging both the body and society.

Strikingly, the corpse became 'the other' only when contrasted with the living[32]; when allowed to remain in the realm of the dead, the corpse and the ashes produced from it maintained their humanness. Consequently, both corpse and ashes had to be separated from other inanimate substances: 'Technology has to secure the discreteness of combustion in furnaces that exclusively cremate human bodies' (Küchenmeister 1875: 58).[33] These claims aligned with Gorini's efforts to produce pure human ashes free from any contamination and to keep them in an urn dedicated to the remains of a single individual, not in collective ash containers. Just as in cases where the body was buried in the earth, it was the funeral service[34] that drew the allegorical line of demarcation between the living and the dead in cremation. A very short, but nonetheless disturbing, moment of uncertainty seems to have existed in the symbolic transition that took place during the process of cremation, one in which the 'no longer human' was 'not yet metamorphosed': The corpse to be cremated was placed into a coffin that, once closed, was meant to remain untouched by human hands. It was a machine and not a human that placed the corpse in the furnace. Thus, human engineering bridged the gap between the two orders of human definition:

It will be difficult for many if they think that the coffin is touched by human hands after the funeral and shoved by them into the combustion chamber. A simple mechanism would allow us to avoid this scenario. Upon being lowered, the coffin would be guided on to an adjustable platform and from there directly into the furnace by simple tracks. No human hands would touch it; they would have only to open and close the door of the combustion chamber. (Küchenmeister 1875: 180)[35]

The German cremationists' feelings of disgust towards the dead and their desire to separate them from the living were embedded in a complex emotional setting marked by the sensation of horror. Their disgust was accompanied by an intense fear of being buried alive[36] and fuelled by massive discomfort at the idea of decomposition taking place in the grave without some form of civilizing control. An unpleasant feeling of shame over the disintegrating, stinking corpse evoked the embarrassment that completed this emotional setting.[37] While German and Italian cremationists shared a feeling of deference towards the departed, the German cremationists, unlike the Italians, took feelings of respect to be unquestionable obligations, not elements of a romanticized love or a moral bond between the generations (Trusen 1855: 12). Gorini expressed a sense of 'compassion' and 'loving memory' towards the dead; the German physician and leading cremationist Reclam spoke of 'awe' and 'serious contemplation', reflecting a certain distance evoked by a fearful reverence for the deceased. Nevertheless, the German cremationists' vocabulary also included affective and emotional figures as they at times turned to the concepts of love, care, memory and poetry. Their motivation, though, was political: the use of these concepts was a response to actual or anticipated critiques, intended to diminish the gap between the columbarium and the cemetery (Reclam 1874: 608–10).[38] Having said that, 'sentiment' often appeared as a devalued, pre-rational category: 'People assume that the memory of our beloved ones expires much sooner in the columbarium than in an earth burial. It is incredible how thoughtlessly these catchwords from the sentimental sphere are repeated' (Küchenmeister 1874: 145).[39]

What united the emotional spectrums of the Italian and German cremationists was their common focus on the aesthetic aspects of cremation; this emphasis was in line with the stress they put on the world of the living as opposed to the world of the beyond.[40] Like Gorini, the German physician Küchenmeister attacked religious customs; to him, they were a form of mental obtuseness which had to be 'cut open with the scalpel of reason' in order to fight 'inner aversions' (Küchenmeister 1874: 144).[41] The more educated the people are, the more refined their aesthetics become, he thought, thus making them less tolerant of offences against the senses of sight and smell (Küchenmeister 1874: 143). Thus, he argued, his contact with skeletons in his professional life made his flesh creep, whereas the presence of urns did not arouse the same feelings (Küchenmeister 1874: 145): 'Urns neither offend anyone with their stench prior to excavation nor with their appearance during excavation' (Küchenmeister 1874: 145). The cremationists, it seems, related the purified, inodorous, non-hazardous and bodily unspecific ashes to the beautiful, good and aesthetically appealing.

One of the first to promulgate cremation in the nineteenth century as a forgotten but once highly appreciated custom in Germany was Jacob Grimm. In a memorandum written as early as 1849, he concluded that cremation had been an Indo-Germanic custom practised by all of the tribes and peoples who belonged to this language area

(Grimm 1850: 78). The Saxons and Frisians had feared the closed grave, Grimm stressed (Grimm 1830: 81), but he also connected their preference for the pure, brightly shining, lively flame over the lazy, mouldy earth with productivity and forward progress (Grimm 1850: 79f.). This observation reflected Grimm's national pride and sense of liberty and superiority: He labelled the distant, pre-modern relatives of the industrialized British as modern due to their practice of cremation. He presented this Germanic custom[42] as evidence of a morally advanced national culture that had initially been unspoiled by Christianity. Just as the Italian cremationists justified modern cremation by relating it to Greco-Roman antiquity (Cucaro 1883: 14–23), Grimm, within the context of a modern appreciation for and sacralization of history as the source of truth, portrayed non-Christian, pagan history as the foundation of the grammar of nineteenth-century secularity (Metzger 2011: 165–70).

As in Gorini's writings, a monistic world outlook (Gregory 2012) underpinned Grimm's reasoning; like Gorini he relied on a cyclical model of matter in motion, stressing cremation would not dampen any amazement at the seed generating new life (Grimm 1850: 83f.). Many of the subsequent articles, publications and presentations on cremation followed this pattern. German and Italian cremationists differed, however, in the aspects of cremation that they emphasized. Gorini, Pini and their fellow Italian cremationists focused on the association of cremation, especially when contrasted with earth burial, with scientific and hygienic progress, liberty, freedom of choice and individuality – which was to be expressed post-mortem in a 'civilized' and 'equalizing' funeral that, they thought, engendered feelings of loving memory better than the Catholic customs they fiercely rejected. German cremationists, on the other hand, paid more attention to the idea of utilization.

The basic concept of utilization was laid out by Dutch physician Jacob Moleschott,[43] who, after holding academic positions in Germany and Switzerland, became a senator in the Kingdom of Italy. His work *Der Kreislauf des Lebens* (The Circle of Life) (1852), with its materialistic and atheistic reasoning, argued for the implementation of positive, not metaphysical, knowledge. Moleschott postulated the immortality of matter; he saw it as eternally circulating and renewing itself, determining the animate world and all the human beings within it. In Moleschott's vision, both mental activities and the soul were pure aspects of matter, inseparably bound to it. While Gorini shared these ideas, Moleschott, as a professional physiologist, took them further. In his chemical studies on the ashes of various animate substances, he itemized the occurrence of several minerals and chemical compounds. He found that these components play a decisive role in the process of growing healthy tissues (Moleschott 1855: 157). Phosphorus in particular, named after Lucifer, the light-bearer (Emsley 2000) – an interesting coincidence, when we think of Moleschott's highly ideologized scientific, 'secular' mission – seemed essential to build the brain and secure its functioning (Moleschott 1855: 158f.). Moleschott made these observations in the context of his beliefs about earth burial: the dead, he thought, were consigned to decay in their graves only because of the outdated idea that the mouldering bones would one day be resurrected. It would be much more useful, he thought, to keep the matter of corpses in motion, enabling instantaneous material regeneration. He denounced the waste of the phosphorus stored in the graveyards (Moleschott 1855: 460) and campaigned for its reutilization: 'If we could cremate our dead, we would enrich the air with carbon dioxide and ammoniac and the ashes would fertilize our heaths, bringing life to new cereal plants, animals, and humans' ('Eine Stätte der Todten' 1895: 1740f.; Moleschott 1855: 462).

Together with Moleschott's book, this argument for utilization spread among German materialists like Ludwig Büchner and finally found its way into the monistic theory of Ernst Haeckel, who further popularized the idea of the material foundations of the scientific system of belief in his 'Monistenbund' (Küchenmeister 1875: 58; Trusen 1855: 3).[44]

Büchner's *Kraft und Stoff* (Force and Matter) (1855) supported and expanded Moleschott's thoughts. He denied the idea of individual resurrection (Büchner 1864: 199), blaming modern man's weak will and reluctance to return to the world the elements he received from it. Relating Christian crypts, which he rejected, to greed, he noted that those buried in a crypt keep for themselves not only all the precious components of their bodies but also their jewellery (Büchner 1864: 31). It was through cremation that these negative habits and emotions could be substituted by a generous, altruistic, 'higher' moral principle for the benefit of all (Büchner 1864: 109, 242f.).[45] Here we find traces of Büchner's belief in the superiority of a secularism based on Protestantism over the stereotyped Catholic Christian: reason, simplicity, virtue and modesty are contrasted with quasi-baroque dissipation and abundance. German cremationists took Büchner's ideas about the inferiority of earth burials and fleshed them out in their works, looking for evidence that earth burials were responsible for the leaching of nutrients from the soil. One such author, the physician Bernstein, listed crop failure and population decline, both important factors in the ruin of many once flourishing cultures, as potential results of this leaching of the soil. He warned that without cremation the achievements of modern culture could be in danger (Bernstein 1874: 36, 47).

With the concept of utilization, materialistic cremationists attempted to assuage feelings of disgust towards and a desire for distance from the corpse with the idea of a quick and complete re-integration of its elements into the cycle of matter through cremation and the distribution of the ashes in fields. The procedure of combustion, according to this theory, not only counter-balanced feelings of disgust but also neutralized them along with unwelcome moral qualities like greed and selfishness: the corpse, which had once been alienated from the community, could be absorbed in the community of the living anew, thus securing their advancement. Simultaneously, the once foreign, distant and disgusting corpse would become something positive, something that no longer stood in opposition to the sphere of the living (Kristeva 1982).

Emotions and the secular: A conclusion

Nineteenth-century modernity[46] was led by paradigms such as hygiene and technology as well as civil progress, challenging the Christian worldview and framing itself as secular. In the case of cremation, this entailed the cultivation of emotions surrounding death and the corpse – both of which had become worldly and material – that differed from the Christian model. In Italy, a sense of equality that reflected the democratic and the liberal notion of the nation state aroused a feeling of compassion towards the corpse. The preserved ashes of the cremated objectified both a feeling of superiority over nature and, at the same time, monistic hopes of re-integrating the elements of a former human into nature's cycle of matter during the process of combustion. German cremationists, on the other hand, expressed a higher degree of disgust towards the corpse in their writings. They toned down feelings of revulsion towards the corpse by proposing the quick re-integration of its chemical compounds into the world of the living.

The arguments given in favour of cremation and the related concepts also point to an overlapping of the religious and the secular that took place over the course of the dissolution of earlier traditions surrounding death into a rich plurality of practices, beliefs and emotions. Neither was the theory of cremation free from transcendent contents nor did those who opted for cremation refuse Christian rituals or even beliefs per se. In Italy, prominent members of the Italian cremation societies (Società per la cremazione dei cadaveri di Milano 1880)[47] spoke words of mourning for the cremated – not Catholic priests, who were not officially allowed to attend cremations until 1963 (Davis and Mates 2005: 107–16). German Protestants, though uncertain how to deal with the new custom of cremation, were more conciliatory,[48] adapting Protestant ritual to cremation.[49] In line with this re-arrangement, the meaning of the Christian emotional vocabulary moved along the instable border between the religious and the secular. Deference, for example, was invoked both as a sentiment and a duty, as if the deceased needed to be properly buried and bemoaned;, otherwise, they were not able to enter the realm of the dead and threatened the living with their ongoing presence. Secular forms of ritual purification enacted this deference as much as Christian forms did.

In the nineteenth century, particularly among cremationists, the meaning of purity seems to have shifted. Deference was an obligation ensuring that hygienic requirements were met; the corpse was purified in a microbiological sense so that the living were protected from physical harm. Simultaneously, the ashes (hypothetically) guaranteed that the deceased would be eternally remembered. They symbolized the continued existence of the once human, whom the bereaved could thus approach with a caring, yet respectful, emotional distance (as in Germany) or loving affection (as in Italy). All things considered, Christian and modern deference are comparable because they share concerns: in both cases, the care of the dead involves the essential task of protecting the world of the living; both notions of deference require that memory and continuity be secured. Emotions and the corpse go hand in hand: the meaning and treatment of both were remodelled, not re-invented, by cremationists. Combustion simply accelerated a process that took years in the soil.

Despite the adaptability of the new custom of cremation, and despite the fevered cremation movements with their largely urban character and the passionate propaganda launched by their members, annual cremation statistics before 1900 hardly reached a four-digit level. In modern societies, cremation never managed to replace Christian earth burial entirely; it remained, and still remains to this day, one option among many

(Davis and Mates 2005: 433–37).[50] In the nineteenth century, committed cremationists speculated as to why cremation was failing to become a widespread practice. As shown above, they found their answer in the emotions of their contemporaries. They observed a general fear of the inability to feel in the face of ashes kept in a columbarium what was felt at a grave in a cemetery towards the deceased:

> Many are discouraged by their inherited or at the least acquired sense of deference, yet not by the fast destruction of the beloved outer form through combustion, but by their incapacity to feel the same way in the face of the ashes kept in the columbarium as in the face of the deceased buried in our ancestor's cemetery, which even atheists appreciate as a solemn place. ('Urnenhaine' 1899: 2875f.)

German and Italian cremationists, it seems, suffered under the apparent unwillingness of mourners to be convinced by political arguments or medical-hygienic education. They interpreted their inability to produce appropriate emotions as a fear of being cut off from something vital over which religion held a monopoly: the enchanted, the solemn and the sacred. In their attempt to compensate for the perceived lack of these vital elements in their proposed treatment of the dead, cremationists were confronted with a choice: either rely on religious foundations or invent a new tradition. The first option implied denying the differences between cremation and Christian ways of dealing with corpses, though partially negating the views that originally had led them to promote cremation. The second required cremationists to draw on the enchanted, the solemn and the sacred themselves in order to create a successful new tradition. Thus, it was not without reason that nineteenth-century cremationists made use of arts and architecture to offer refined edification and utmost elevation in a secular setting. It was in this way that they attempted to create a new tradition whose emotional draw prevailed over that of religious tradition within the context of a modernity founded on a deep entanglement of the religious and the secular.

Observing the Atheist at Worship: Ways of Seeing the Secular Body

Lois Lee

In 2010 architects Tom Greenall and Jordan Hodgson were commissioned to design what became the 'Temple of Perspective' (de Botton 2013), rechristened 'the Atheist Temple' in media treatments.[1] The client was British public philosopher Alain de Botton and, though the building was never built, an impression of the Atheist Temple appears in de Botton's 2013 volume, *Religion for Atheists*.[2] The temple was in fact one of the several buildings designed for this volume; the project also resulted in designs for a 'Temple to Love', a 'Shrine to the Mayfly', and a 'Shrine to Care', among others. But it was the Atheist Temple that featured most prominently in the volume and wider media discussions, including coverage in the British *Guardian* and *Telegraph* newspapers and *Timeout* magazine. In 2012, a model of the building was also presented at the British Royal Academy's flagship Summer Exhibition.

In this chapter, I explore how we can make sense of the imagined visitor to this imagined space to help understand the 'cultivation of the distinct sensibilities, affects, and embodied dispositions that undergird secular forms of appraisal and practice' (Hirschkind 2011: 633). In so doing, the chapter responds to the provocation from anthropologist Charles Hirschkind that scholars address the question, 'what is a secular body?' and explore what our 'answers – or refusals to answer – tell us about the practical and conceptual contours of the secular and secularism' (Hirschkind 2011: 633). The provocation is a welcome one, since the meaning of the 'secular' has remained remarkably elusive (Lee 2015; Taylor 2007), even though the term itself has become familiar and widespread – possibly because many discussions are theoretical, speculative and/or engage with the secular in very general terms. The problem we arrive at is summed up very concisely by Hirschkind (2011: 641) when he says, 'while the statement, "He [or she] lives a very religious life" gives us some sense of the shape of a life, "He [or she] lives a very secular life" tells us almost nothing (except, negatively, that the person does not engage in practices of worship)'.

In this chapter, I argue that Hirschkind's frustration arises, at least in part, from the limitations of the critical approach that Hirchskind uses to think about the secular. I propose an alternative, one that builds on productive tensions between critical secular studies and another approach, non-religious studies, which have largely developed in parallel. Where critical scholars tend to work with secularity *qua* regime, framework or context, non-religious studies scholars work with secularity *qua* the experience and outlooks of non-religious individuals and populations. Bringing these approaches into conversations presents a helpful third approach, one which accepts the view that phenomenal secularity (that which is designated secular by actors, including academics) has distinctive qualities to it, but that these are more numerous and more complicated than the encompassing notion of secularism that critical scholars use allows (Lee 2015; cf. Burchardt et al. 2015; Wohlrab-Sahr 2011; Wohlrab-Sahr and Burchardt 2012).

In this approach, we can pull at that richly detailed tapestry that critical scholars call secularism to reveal the warp threads upon which it all relies, and thereby open our analyses to the many different tapestries that might be woven about them. To this end, the chapter explores the value of recognizing some of these foundational threads – what I refer to as the *immanent-secular, secularism, non-religion* and *non-traditional existentiality* – as analytically autonomous from one another, so that we can imagine not only 'an immanent life' but also 'a secularist life', 'a non-religious life' and 'an existential life' in ways that give meaningful impressions of those lives. As Monika Wohlrab-Sahr (2011) argues, critical studies of secularism have been enormously productive yet they hit a wall if they insist on working genealogically to the exclusion of all else. I hope to show that developing analytical concepts from that genealogical work will help us find new pathways forward, while also addressing major issues within the two dominant approaches to secularity: the tendencies in critical secular studies to generalize and in non-religious studies to naturalize what it means to be secular. I begin by setting out these two approaches.

Two approaches to the secular

Over the past two decades, new approaches to and sometimes pushing beyond the secular have started to build momentum and take form. The most significant of these are critical secular studies and non-religion studies. The heterogeneous body of work known as critical secular studies addresses Western modernist forms of secularism as a broad ideological, political or cultural framework and is associated with philosophical and anthropological scholars such as Talal Asad (2003), Webb Keane (2007), Saba Mahmood (2005), Charles Taylor (2007) and others. The burgeoning, equally diverse, non-religious studies engages much more with identity, experience and subjectivity of people identified (by themselves or by others) as irreligious or non-religious, as well as with the cultures that manifest in activist organizations, new congregations like the Sunday Assembly and in everyday experiences and performances of difference from religious 'others'.[3] This work is most commonly undertaken by sociologists and psychologists, but also by anthropologists, who often work with non-religious actors who participate in organized forms of non-religion (see for example Luehrmann 2011, Aston, this volume, and Engelke, this volume).

Though these two scholarships have often developed in parallel and have not engaged with each other as deeply as they might have (cf. Beckford 2012),[4] they both shift attention from the secular as a measure of religion's absence towards an idea of the secular as describing a set of experiences and cultural formations, which are concrete and necessarily instantiated in material forms, including the human body. In identifying secularity as socio-cultural experience, these scholarships both make and instantiate 'cultural turns' in the study of secularity (cf. Wohlrab-Sahr and Burchardt 2015). But, though they are animated by overlapping theoretical concerns and empirical foci, they also have significant differences that have allowed them to develop in relative isolation from one another: critical work focuses especially on how distinctions between religious and secular that in some way prioritize the secular are made – on secular*ism*, that is – and on the power and influence that secularists and -isms exert (Lee 2012, 2015; Wohlrab-Sahr and Burchardt 2012); non-religious studies focus much more on non-religious populations, especially on individuals' experiences and subjectivities, as well as charting the characteristics of those populations.

Underlying these differences are other distinctions. Critical secular studies' cultural turn is driven by a critique of the secularity and secularisms of Western governments and other authorities, and tends to the view, often implicit, that religious actors are more vulnerable to these powers than non-religious ones are. Underlying much of this work is an emancipatory goal for religious people and traditions, by educating the secularist out of the naïve notion of religion that they are perceived to hold innocently or wield strategically over the religious. This scholarship has led to a much richer understanding of how a particular and powerful secularist attitude has shaped and continues to shape the social world. On the other hand, though, it has tended to make generalized remarks about what secular actors say, think or do, while its empirical work has focused on *religious* actors in relation to broader secular frameworks or contexts (Lee 2015: 60; see also Hirschkind 2011: 635). Consequently, its cultural turn is incomplete in the sense that it has not yet fulfilled the potential of its own logic since it does not pay equal and sustained attention to the non-religious actor as existing, impactful and embodied, nor to the nature, heterogeneity and contingencies of non-religiosity and the invested interests that structure it.

In the second strand of work, scholars have started to recognize non-religiosity (often referred to as 'secularism' in north America, or as 'atheism' in a number of Protestant and post-Protestant contexts)[5] as concrete and meaningful in the formation of subjectivities and societies. This second cultural turn (of sorts) is much less concerned with distinctions between religious and non-religious – frequently, in fact, pointing to similarities between them, such as a common capacity for moral thought and ethical practice. Rather, it seeks to recognize and understand a set of positions and experiences that are identified in contradistinction to religious ones, that is, as non-religious (Lee 2012, 2015; Quack 2014), and which have not been widely studied until recently (Lee and Bullivant 2012). Because this work responds to a disparity between the large number of non-religious people and cultures on the one hand and the small number of detailed empirical treatments on the other, it is empirically focused.[6] If Talal Asad has produced the canonical works of the critical secular tradition, and social anthropology and political philosophy provide its disciplinary home, Colin Campbell's 1971 volume (reprinted in 2013), *Towards a Sociology of Irreligion*, is the touchstone for those working in this second area, and scholars from sociology and psychology are its main contributors.

By different means, this scholarship has produced its own picture of the secular individual – describing them in terms of their demographic profile, their participation in social movements and their health and well-being. However, this work has not always been sufficiently critical of the secularization paradigm, so that the secular individual is still often understood negatively, in terms of the religion they are without and the outcomes of this without-ness, rather than in terms of the new beliefs and cultural formations that these individuals hold or participate in. The cultural turn here is methodological rather than conceptual, recognizing the secular individual as a subject, yet not necessarily identifying secularity as a mode of subjectivity per se. A second issue is that, in addressing hostile accounts of the non-religious person, this work is sometimes defensive, and therefore desensitized to ambivalences. Its real limitation, though, has been the relative lack of qualitative accounts of so-called secular populations, illustrating that, as with the critical secular studies project, the logic of this second cultural turn is in some sense unfulfilled.

When Webb Keane describes secularism as 'a project, not a return to some natural condition from which humans deviated' (2013: 161), he provides a neat summary of the two visions of the secular that I have outlined above: one that is primarily critical of the secular as an ideological project, and another that takes non-religious populations and outlooks seriously in its methodology but does so in order to better prove a naturalized, universalist account of the secular. In this chapter, I draw attention to the value of a third option – something between the naturalized idea of secularity as the condition of being unencumbered by religion as – of just being normal – and the ideological notion of secularity as a project. It arises from looking in more detail at micro-level secularity (as non-religious studies do) but attending much more closely to the cultural contexts that shape bodily experience, habits and sensibilities (as critical secular studies scholars do). I argue that searching for secularity as cultural formation but doing so through close attention to the non-religious subject leads to the need for a much broader armoury of concepts to describe the different layers to this secularity and, ultimately, a move away from the idea that those layers configure in a single, coherent, stable and predictable cultural formation that we can call the secular.

Many-layered secularity

Despite the wide-ranging work undertaken within the two broad and heterogeneous approaches identified above, there is potential to expand current understandings of the secular. There is by now enough work around 'non-religious subjectivities' (e.g. Baker and Smith 2015; Lee 2015; Mumford 2015) to show that the purely negative account of secularity as being without religion is insufficient. On the other hand, though, the complex of attributes that critical secular studies identifies as secular is so very – perhaps unwieldingly – thick that it can be challenging to apply it to micro-level experience and practice. What I propose is that we identify and disentangle the threads that form the warp of the tapestry critical scholars present us with – that richly described, thickly historical, ideological secularism that elides with Western modernity, and its nation-state politics, rationalism and scientific epistemology. In so doing we can isolate finer-grained concepts that help us to describe and understand what it means to live 'a secular life' in more nuanced terms and, significantly, explore the multiplicity of ways in which it is possible to be secular. I want to set out four main ways of thinking about secularity and understanding secular bodies, all of which arise from past fieldwork with English people who identify as not religious or non-religious (Lee 2015).

First is secularity as immanence in the Kantian sense – a way of describing the realities that manifest in the 'immanent frame' (Taylor 2007). This secularity involves an immersion in 'this-worldly' space and time that is contrasted with a capacity to transcend them both – to view this world from an 'other-worldly' plane or to understand secular time in relation to eternity. This notion of secularity is close to the traditional, Christian one (Knott 2005; Taylor 2007), and in my work, I use the term 'secularity' solely to describe this particular warp thread. I find it sufficiently specific and concrete to imagine what a 'very secular life' might entail: a life lived with a limited or dampened temporal awareness and imaginary capacity. Presuming that this kind of radical here-and-now-ness is quite rare as a general condition, in practice this secularity might be most evident in *periods* of life that are more secular than others, or in particularly secular domains, moments or situations. Alternatively, we might think about secularity as a framework, as Taylor (2007) does, one that does not eradicate experience of transcendence but nevertheless curtails it in important ways. In opposition to Hirschkind's argument that the concept of the secular offers nothing that other concepts (rationalism, liberalism, modernism) do not already describe, I hope to demonstrate that this idea of secularity as immanence helps us describe something distinctive.

Though scholars have repeatedly tried to trouble the idea, secularity is most commonly located in a binary with religion. Secularity in the narrower, Christian sense is, however, more accurately contrasted with *eternity*, or conceptions of eternity brought about through transcendence. The eternal actually has a place *within* critical notions of secularity, as in the idea that secularity connotes a type of worldview – a philosophy of life, existence and reality that is, commonly identified as materialist or humanist (e.g. Keane 2013: 159). I use the concept of 'existentiality' (or sometimes meta-existentiality) to describe the relationship that humans have with the eternal, since this relationship is also one with the nature and perimeters of our own existence. Historically, religious traditions have been central to the cultivation of existential experience, but the notion of existentiality I develop in my work (e.g. Lee 2015) is one of several recent attempts to also engage with 'philosophies of life' outside of traditional religious contexts (see Taves 2016). This emerging scholarship shows that secular individuals have the capacity to imagine beyond their physical, secular existence and thereby conceptualize (in a very broad sense) that existence in ideas, symbols and practices (Baker and Smith 2015; Lee 2015; Mellor and Shilling 2010; Taves 2016).[7] This idea of non-traditional modes of existentiality is the second thread I want to unweave from that tapestry of secularism, and then recast claims about it as hypotheses. The extent to which 'modern' modes of existentiality are materialist (Keane 2013), humanist (Taylor 2007) or post-modern and agnostic can be approached then as empirical questions, and open ones, since a sociology or anthropology of existentiality or worldview is just beginning.

Though the terms 'secular' and 'secularism' are often used interchangeably, I follow Asad (2003) and some others in insisting on the need to distinguish between them. The third key analytic concept that can be unwoven from critical notions of the secular is, then, secularism, understood narrowly as a theory, ideology or other system of constructing the secular, that is, of *demarcating* social and psychic domains in which immanent concerns have primacy and *specifying* the nature of that primacy (Lee 2015, 2016). Experience, ideas and cultures concerning the eternal and the existential may play a role in these domains, but secularity implies that this role is at least secondary to governing logics derived from immanent concerns (Lee 2015, 2016). In general terms, to live a secularist life would be to proceed through the world constantly engaging with – advocating, questioning – ideas about the relevance and legitimacy of the transcendent in particular domains: to be responsive to discussing transcendent existential topics with friends, for example, but resistant to, even shocked by, these themes being raised in a job interview setting; to visit a designated place of worship to kneel in prayer, but resist the idea of kneeling in prayer on a city street.

The benefits of thinking about secularism as a warp thread rather than a whole tapestry include the opportunity to explore diverse secularisms, including religious ones as well as non-religious ones. This means that, instead of seeing secularism and non-religion as intrinsically bound together, we need to disentangle them. This brings us to a fourth key concept of non-religion, understood in relational terms to describe the phenomena that are primarily identified in contradistinction to the religious (Lee 2012, 2015; Quack 2014). Embodied non-religiosity might be irreligious, for example: in past fieldwork with non-religious Britons I met people who were consciously training themselves to 'un-learn' or de-habituate what they saw as superstitious habits, such as throwing salt over the shoulder for good luck. Others talked about less conscious experiences of 'un-disciplining', such as feeling physically repelled by certain religious beliefs and practices – muscular resistance to bowing the head in prayer in the context of Christian worship, for example, or passionate, visceral anger experienced by the bereaved confronted by religious ways of memorializing the dead. As well as irreligious modes of non-religion, though, others describe another kind of embodied non-religion, in which they experience sensations of excitement and wonder in relation to religion that is charged by their sense of otherness from it – by their sense of religion as exotic, for example (e.g. Lee 2015: 34). Significantly, non-religiosity sometimes has to do with the immanent world (having to do with mundane matters of clerical corruption, for example), but not always: the anger felt by the person mourning in a non-Christian way is non-secular when it is driven by an alternative idea about the nature of eternity; the sense of religion as exotic can arise from a sense of having differing beliefs about the nature of existence. Again, this is the kind of nuance that conflating non-religion, secularism and secularity can obscure.

All of these concepts – the immanent-secular, existentiality, secularism and non-religion – offer, then, distinctive approaches to thinking about ways of living and about the body that are not encompassed by concepts like modernism, rationalism or liberalism. To imagine the possibilities of this approach, I now turn to another work of imagination: a vision of an 'Atheist Temple' and of the 'atheist worshipper' who might occupy it.

The atheist at worship

Courtney Bender has recently proposed that sociologists and anthropologists interested in the everyday realities of religiosity engage more closely with the way in which public, governmental and elite actors 'not only imagine, but experience' what she describes as 'post-religious' modes of religion, spirituality and secularity (2016b: 102, 104, 107). In this work Bender explores another unrealized architectural project: Frank Lloyd Wright's plans for Broadacre city in the United States. Bender's analysis is primarily spatial, and I have likewise taken a spatial approach in consideration of the Atheist Temple elsewhere (Lee 2017). But space and the body are inseparable (Knott 2005; Vasquez and Knott 2014, in Lee 2017), and here I turn attention to how the spatial shapes and is shaped by 'body pedagogics' (Mellor and Shilling 2010), in processes which might cultivate distinctive modes of 'sensibilities, affects, and embodied dispositions' (Hirschkind 2011).

The imagined Atheist Temple is a skyscraper, with an internal space comprised of a single, dramatically elongated atrium. In a beautiful image of the building (Figure 4.1) produced by the architects and circulated in the media, the building is imagined in the heart of the City of London, surrounded by the distinctive skyscrapers of London's financial district. Another image shows a cross-section of the building (Figure 4.2), in which we see a single figure: a man, standing alone, dwarfed by the cavernous space that rises towards an open view of the sky and from which a dramatic shaft of light

Figure 4.1 Temple to Perspective, London, courtesy of Thomas Greenall.

Figure 4.2 Temple to Perspective, cross-section, courtesy of Thomas Greenall.

descends. In exploring multi-layered ways of thinking about the secular body, the following section considers the ways in which existentiality, the secular-immanent, secularism and non-religion are manifest in the building itself and the imagined bodies that occupy it.

The atheist worshipper and the existential body

The mode of existentiality that the Atheist Temple is designed to cultivate as bodily sensation closely conforms with the existential humanism that critical secular scholars often anticipate as part of a secular cultural complex.[8] The building's architects reference humanistic tenets explicitly in describing the building's form. In the architect's words, 'the entire history of life on Earth' is depicted on the walls of the 46-meter high space, with '[e]ach centimeter of its height equate[d] to one million years of life'; and, at its base, a single band of gold – 'one meter from the ground and no more than a millimeter thick' – represents the existence of humankind. The outside of the temple is also inscribed with 'an interpretation of the human genome sequence', which the architect says is 'a celebration of one of humankind's greatest achievements, while simultaneously a reminder of our fragility'. It is by these means they intend that a visitor to the temple should leave 'with a renewed sense of perspective'.[9] These ideas and representations reference a materialist conception of existence, but it is also explicitly human-centred – in its valorization of human capacities and achievements in human knowledge (the genome sequence), in its foregrounding of humanity over other animals (the gold band) and in its adoption of a human gaze which the temple's titular sense of perspective is relative too. Humanity's existence is the temporal standard against which existence of material reality is measured and conceptualized; the latter is not represented as relative to the history of life in general on earth, nor to the history of primates or any other life form, nor to the history of earth itself; nor is it relative to the human lifespan, nor the lifespan of a particularly feted individual. Rather – and archetypically for existential humanism – perspective is scaled to the history of humanity as a species.

The architects clearly intend that visitors to the Atheist Temple engage intellectually with these representations and frame their life in humanist perspective. But this humanism is also cultivated as a bodily experience, since the form of the space and the body's relation to it encourage the occupant of that space to experience it through particular bodily sensations also associated with humanist traditions. The space encourages the imagined visitor to take on the role of worshipper by experiencing their body as small – 'fragile', as the architects put it – and by responding to the story of existence told on its walls through bodily practices of quietude, reverence, awe and wonder, since the long, narrow atrium space would not only dwarf the visitor but encourage his or her eye upward, following the visual lines of the tapering walls to the apex and drawn to light that only enters the space there. The intention is that the building will exert its force on the body of visitors, so that they experience themselves as smaller, less significant and more alone than they did in the streets outside; perspective is in this way something that is wrought upon the body.

The building is also designed to isolate the individual body, so that the visitor's experience is focused entirely on his or her intellectual and physical relation to a set of existential ideas. In her discussion of Evangelical-Christian body pedagogics, Anna Strhan (2015: 68–69) develops Michel Foucault's ideas about moral reflexivity as an embodiment of Christian subjectivity and Jeremy Carrette's focus on silence as an aspect of this subjectivity. She shows how the British Evangelicals she works with 'seek to disciple(in)e themselves and each other through different kinds of silence' (2015: 69). A similar bodily repertoire is referenced in the Atheist Temple, in which worshippers are encouraged to respond through awe, reverie, interiority and quietude – though it is also striking that the Atheist Temple perhaps invites visitors to experience the space and the existential in solitude, rather than as part of a communal silence.

These embodiments of humanist existentiality can be understood in relation to wider existential experience in the UK. For one, the architects necessarily draw on the existential cultural conventions in the context in which they live and work, since they intend that people will be able to make sense of the space when they visit it, the more so because the Atheist Temple project had a 'missionizing' objective to convince people that existential practice and the spaces that facilitate them are needed in contemporary societies (De Botton 2013). The design therefore reflects modes of existential thought and practice that are more widely cultivated though bodily as well as intellectual disciplining. Consider, for example, a practice that Rachael Shillitoe (2017) observes in fieldwork exploring religion and non-religion in British primary schools: Shillitoe describes how one school she worked with responded to the legal requirement to practice daily collective worship by reading a poem that encourages the children to reflect on things they were grateful for. These assemblies cultivated an embodied practice of gratitude, imparted by an authority figure to a group, consumed collectively and in silence, and construing gratitude as something that is manifested through self-reflection (rather than through expressive action, say). William Connolly writes about 'little *moments*' of 'gratitude in existence' (2011: 651, my emphasis), and my research documents how individuals can experience such moments as sparked by an immediate object (a reason to be grateful), or as if out of nowhere (e.g. Lee 2015: 179). Yet Shillitoe's work demonstrates how registering gratitude and experiencing it in certain ways is cultivated through practice. Through such practices, people learn to recognize some phenomena (and not others) as existentially significant, and to notice them as existential under particular conditions – in quiet spaces, for example.

The Atheist Temple also references specifically humanist traditions of cultivated bodily sensation. There is, for example, a tradition of exploring humanist existentiality through sensations of awe. This might be cultivated through viewing what media historian Alexander Hall (2017) calls 'humanist blockbusters' – the expensive BBC science and nature programming of the twentieth and twenty-first century that uses emotive language, sweeping scores and richly cinematic cinematography to inculcate an intensely emotional experience of wonder in response to humanist narratives of existence.

This form of existential humanist sensibility is particular and can be differentiated from other forms of humanist sensibility. An instruction comparison can be made here to another work of architectural imagination: Frank Lloyd Wright's vision for Broadacre city, which Bender explores in her work (Bender 2016a, b). Of particular interest is Lloyd Wright's design for an 'automobile objective', which involved a planetarium, restaurant and scenic, high-up viewing point over the suburban vista. Like the Temple to Perspective, proposals for the automobile objective were unrealized; and, like the Temple to Perspective, the architectural vision was explicitly concerned with creating existential experience – which Bender describes somewhat ambiguously as 'post-religious religion' (Bender 2016b), and which is popularly termed 'spirituality' in the United States and sometimes also in the UK context. The mode of existentiality that Bender identifies is recognizably humanist: she shows how it celebrates human achievement, especially technology, and is founded on a sense of human progress, and that there is an explicit attempt to cultivate these ideas in how people physically use and experience the building.

Beyond those significant similarities, though, there are also striking differences between the two humanisms. Greenall and Hodgson's temple is imagined in the heart of the city of London; Lloyd Wright's automobile objective is imagined within a mid-century American suburban context. While the Atheist Temple encourages the visitor into a position of stillness, the visitor to Broadacre's automobile objective is mobile, moving up and around the edifice of the building by motorcar; in this building the individual does not look up to the apex; he or she comes to occupy it, and looks down upon and across the vista before him or her. In Bender's subtle analyses, she uses the concept of the 'technological sublime' to explore how Lloyd Wright's vision recalls romantic nineteenth-century images of the white man – as it was, and is also in Lloyd Wright and Greenall and Hodgson's imaginations – gazing down upon the world, awestruck partly by its mystery, partly by his feeling of confident mastery over it. The human visitors are invited to be impressed by the world out there, as they are in the Atheist Temple; but in Broadacre they are not encouraged to feel this through a sense of their vulnerability or fragility, but their strength and authority.

There is not space here to unpack the differences between these existential humanist imaginaries in detail, but this sketch indicates the heterogeneity of humanist existentialities, shaped by their locations in geo-cultural contexts and capable of leading to distinctive modes of bodily experience – through the relationship of the body to its environment (below-ness versus above-ness; stillness versus movement), through emotional repertoires (awe, reverie, humility; awe, facility, authority) and through practices of sociality (idealization of isolation and solitariness; idealization of participation and movement in small, probably domestic units). Instead of generalizing about secular worldviews, then, these kinds of analyses can show how secular existential projects have 'shaped, articulated, broadcast, and provided space for [people] to experience their "spiritual" selves' (2016b: 106) in distinctive ways.

The atheist worshipper and the non-religious body

For Hirschkind, the one thing that the concept of secularity might tell us about a person is the negative information 'that the person does not engage in practices of worship'. For Hirschkind this is meagre knowledge, yet recent years have seen the development of relational studies of different kinds of negative positioning as a major strand in non-religion studies, associated with my own conceptual work around non-religion (e.g. Lee 2012, 2015) and typified by Johannes Quack's anthropological field theoretical approach (Quack 2014).[10]

In the Atheist Temple, non-religious relationality is manifest in at least two different ways. First, non-religiosity is visible in the identity that the building manifests – taken on by the visitor incidentally, by participating in a space itself identified through non-religious categories.[11] Non-religious identities are commonplace in places like the UK, especially since they are sometimes carriers of existential meaning, particularly in 'detraditionalized' contexts like the UK, where new existential orientations are rarely consolidated and codified in centralized institutions; that is, in the absence of positive ways of identifying their existential beliefs and worldviews, individuals turn to the non-religious concepts that are available to them (Baker and Smith 2015; Lee 2015; Mumford 2015). Non-religious identities are not always carriers of existential meaning, though, and may have other kinds of significance. As significant identities, they are also the main point at which we can see the secular as a manifestation of socio-cultural positionality – as *habitus*, in Bourdieuisian terms (see also Gutkowski 2012).

In past work, I have discussed a passage taken from a piece in the *London Review of Books* (LRB), a well-known British literary magazine, in which the author describes '[m]iddle-class white atheists like me [who] sail around on our bikes to buy our coffee beans in Broadway Market or Victoria Park Village', the latter being fashionable, increasingly middle-class areas in the East End of London (Meek 2011: n.p.). One thing the passage illustrates is how non-religiosity intersects with other aspects of identity such as socio-economic status, ethnicity and gender (as we learn from the gendered identification of religious others elsewhere in the piece), as well as the way in which all of these identifications are embodied. In the LRB example, the author's non-religious identity is manifest in the occupation of a certain body (white, male) and certain spaces (Broadway Market), in physical practices (cycling in particular, mobility in general) and in cosmopolitan patterns of consumption (expensive coffee, travel). The imagined visitor to the Atheist Temple (Figure 4.2) echoes Meek's portrait: the image shows a white man, apparently middle class since he wears the accoutrements of professional employment. A second picture (Figure 4.3) produced by the architects also depicts a white man, this time in more casual attire but occupying a similar socio-cultural space. Both men are pictured in a building that itself is the creation of men in middle-class occupations and echo the profile of public atheists in the UK as elite, white and male, from de Botton to Richard Dawkins (Bullivant 2010; Sheard 2014). The building itself is located within the City of London, one of the most affluent regions of the city and the world (Lee 2017).

We would be wrong to take this representation of the atheist body at face value: although atheists are likely to be white in the UK, they are commonly female and as likely to have lower socio-economic status as not. It is significant, though, that the *idealized* non-religious body takes this form. Imagined bodies shape real bodies, through psycho-social processes of socialization as well as the reproduction of power relations that influence imagined bodies and real bodies alike. Bullivant (2010) contrasts the white male figureheads of British public Atheism with the 'wild' female figurehead of US atheism in the person of Madalyn Murray O'Hair, whose certainly strange story (involving kidnapping and murder) has recently been adapted into a Netflix film. These different bodies are significant, not only because they influence the way in which non-religious actors are positioned in social contexts, as Bullivant shows, but because they are produced by those contexts – are manifestations of them. The Atheist Temple draws attention to the way in which the bodies of the non-religious laity and representations of those bodies work alongside leaders' bodies and their representations to shape how non-religious bodies are imagined and produced.

The body imagined in the Atheist Temple is also meaningfully non-religious in a quite different sense, through the relationship of otherness established in its vision of the atheist at worship. As we have seen, the body is encouraged to experience its existentiality through a particular emotional repertoire and practices of comporting the body. These draw extensively from Christian, especially Protestant, modes of understanding and being existential, which are historically significant in the UK and bound up with dominant discourses about religion and Britishness. Indeed, British non-religion often references these traditions, for example in describing non-religiosity through God- and belief-focused concepts (e.g. atheism, non-believer,

Figure 4.3 Temple to Perspective, interior, courtesy of Thomas Greenall.

unbelief) that also derive from these traditions. These religious traditions are also visible in the imagined Atheist Temple – in cultivating the sense of existentiality as best experienced in private and quietness, and encouraging internal reflection and experiences of humility and awe in relation to the transcendent (Strhan 2015: 68–69; cf. Schmidt 2000). Though the transcendent is represented by human knowledge rather than God, these other Christian modes are largely intact. Moreover, the space itself references the familiar conical spires of Anglican and other church buildings in the UK, so that the relation of the imagined body to that space also replicates Christian modes of embodiment.

Many scholars have traced these kinds of cultural ties between Christianity and secular modernity. However, the objective is often to challenge the idea that modernity involves a complete break from religious pasts, and this work tends to emphasize cultural continuities – the way in which secularity is, in important ways, really religious. By contrast, relational approaches to non-religion suggest that the way in which new cultural formations are differentiated from traditional forms is significant, and that the production and reproduction of non-religiosity is a process of cultural transformation. Scholars working more closely with irreligion and other forms of non-religion have come to recognize that non-religion always manifests something of the religion it is othered from (Campbell 2013 [1971]; Davie 2013), yet it would be wrong to say that non-religion simply reproduces religion. Rather, processes of othering bring something new into being.

In the Atheist Temple, a humanist existentiality draws on religious, especially Protestant traditions, and demonstrates an unbroken 'chain of memory' (Hervieu-Leger 2000). But it also a non-religious space, which echoes Protestant traditions in order to challenge and overthrow them. One of Alain de Botton's broad objectives is to reshape the public sphere according to his own vision of the public good – something seen elsewhere in his work, such as his Living Architecture initiative, which aims to expand the role of contemporary architecture in popular culture. His Atheist Temple is one attempt to shape contested public space that the Church of England has dominated. At the same time, de Botton's project is situated in opposition to more radically anti-religious forces, which would like to see spaces (and other resources) dominated by religions eradicated rather than shared with non-traditional existential cultures.

Visitors to the Atheist Temple would be implicated in these forms of non-religious distinction-making. Some non-religious actors would refuse to participate: many people who experience their non-religiosity as a physical recoil from practices that reproduce the bodily pedagogics of the religion(s) they reject might feel uncomfortable in the temple. Those who try to 'un-discipline' or 're-discipline' their bodies as part of a process of 'nonreligionisation' (Lee 2014) or 'atheisation' (Sheard 2014) might actively reject the project, as the prominent anti-theist public figure, Richard Dawkins, has done, seeing the notion of an Atheist Temple as 'a contradiction in terms' (Booth 2012: n.p.).[12] These kinds of reactions also demonstrate how the Temple to Perspective allows visitors to be non-religious in certain ways but not others: it explores and creates post-Protestant experience but does not offer the same kind of opportunity for those who experience themselves as other to other religious traditions. In these different ways, the Atheist Temple might affirm experiences of (certain forms of) non-religious otherness, while also allowing people to experience religious practice in new ways and inscribe it with new kinds of meaning in relation to non-traditional existential cultures.

The atheist worshipper and the secularist body

We can also understand the visitor to the Atheist Temple in terms of secularism: practices of differentiation-making between the immanent or this-worldly and the transcendent existential or other-worldly, and the prioritization of the former in certain domains or in general.

Most significantly, the Atheist Temple creates a space for the body to experience the existential and eternal as set apart from the non-existential and secular. Rather than engaging with this-worldly life, the building creates a forum in which the visitor solely engages with existential conceptualisations. The purity of this existential function contrasts with the role of the existential and the secular in comparable religious spaces. In fact, a practical turn in the study of religion has called attention to the integration and significance of secular practice in religious life. Be it cooking in mosque kitchens (Kuppinger 2017) or the cleaning of Church buildings (Day 2017), the status of such activities as secular or existential is often blurred. Yet in the Atheist Temple there is no kitchen, no offices, no cleaning cupboards (Lee 2017: 139). Its sole purpose is for existential reflection, so that it not only cultivates reflection as a mode of existentiality but also cultivates an embodied understanding of a distinction between spaces in which existentiality is in general more (or less) relevant, more (or less) legitimate.

By helpful contrast, Lloyd Wright's automobile objective has several secular functions intermingled with its existential ones. Not only do the automobile objective and the Atheist Temple express alternative humanist existentialities but also different forms of secularism.

Is there a secular worshipper?

If we acknowledge that atheists can engage with alternative philosophies of life, which are experienced through practice as well as through thought, the idea of an Atheist Temple and an atheist worshipper is not contradictory in the way that, for example, Richard Dawkins imagines. By contrast, if we resist the critical secular scholar's tendency to collapse several meanings into the concept of secularity and instead salvage the traditional, Christian sense of the term – as one in which transcendent existential concerns become in some way secondary to this-worldly, immanent concerns – the idea of the secular worshipper becomes problematic. Strictly speaking, the secular cannot be worshipped and still be secular, since to worship the secular is to reflect upon it and thereby transcend it. But thinking in terms of a secular sensibility more generally, the Atheist Temple if anything attempts to *exclude* secular life and sensibility, as we have seen, rather than cultivate it. In this temple, the imagined worshipper is called away from and out of secular time and the concerns of immanent life; he or she is fully immersed in transcendent existentiality, not only metaphorically but viscerally, since the visitor's body is at once absorbed into the cocooning form of the atrium and raised above it, carried up and into the unseen world beyond the window at the apex.

The non-secular nature of the Atheist Temple relies on distinctions between immanent and transcendent, secular and existential, and this may make the secular relevant to bodily experience within the temple. If the atheist worshipper focuses on the existential within the temple, this focus is partly achieved by distinction from the secular bodies moving about outside of it. The physical stillness that the temple seems to encourage likewise contrasts with the mobile and mundane bodies in the city streets beyond. Georg Simmel sees entranceways as intrinsic to processes of human sense-making, 'through a capacity to connect and separate things' (discussed in Strhan 2015: 29–31).[13] In this way, the Atheist Temple attempts to divest visitors of their secular sensibilities at the door, yet would derive some its affective power from the visitor's transition – though partial and imperfect – from secular to existential as the visitor enters (or leaves) the space. Though the Atheist Temple would perhaps not cultivate a secular body, it might then cultivate a *de*-secularizing of the body as part of its attitude towards what it means to engage in existential thought and practice. If Greenall and Hodgson's temple would not cultivate secular sensibilities within its confines, therefore, it might inform secular sensibilities outside of it, while also cultivating a form of existential secularism that strictly separates and delimits the existential within the world.

Conclusion

Charles Hirschkind's scepticism about the concept of the secular demonstrates, quite rightly, that our enquiries need to be brought down to earth if we are to know whether and how the concept has any real analytic force. In this chapter I have argued that new methods of disentangling the concept of the secular into a series of narrower, more specific and more concrete analytic categories is one useful outcome emerging from the empirical study of the non-religious person in non-religious studies, and that these concepts stand to help us to get a better handle on the phenomena that critical scholars are also interested to account for. In exploring the Atheist Temple, these concepts – immanent secularity, ideological secularism, relational non-religiosity and non-theistic but still transcendent existentiality – all help us to imagine and think about different modes of embodiment that might emerge therein.

Distinguishing these separate threads also helps to address issues within both critical secular studies and non-religion studies. Building on both bodies of work, the multi-dimensional and multi-faceted approach I advocate tries to cut across their tendencies to focus on secular contexts and on secular individuals (but *not* secular subjectivity) respectively. This is an affirmation of Hirschkind's method of investigating the cultural waters that we swim in by exploring the movements, contortions and sensations of the swimmer. If I also end up agreeing with Hirschkind that we should indeed be sceptical of existing notions of the secular, this is not, however, because I also find it difficult to imagine distinctively secular lives and bodies (as he does), but rather because I find it difficult to imagine a single coherent way in which this might be so.

In theory, my approach argues that what we have meant by the secular in fact captures several discrete characteristics, all of which are not captured by other concepts. But in practice, too, these categories help us respond to an emerging emphasis in scholarship on the historical multiplicity of secularities (Burchardt et al. 2015; Wohlrab-Sahr and Burchardt 2012), which in turn calls into question that idea of one dominating secular or secularist formation through which we can understand vast socio-cultural domains over extensive periods of time. In fact, one lesson of critical scholarship might be precisely that we would be wise to question the conceptual framework bestowed on us by ideologies invoking the secular – that recognizing them as ideologies (as critical secular studies allow us to) should invite us to reconsider whether those ideologies should set the terms of the discussion.

This chapter presents only a tentative exploration of how conceptually disentangling layers of secularity might impact understandings of the body, and its limitations include a focus on the imagined body, rather than an ethnographic account of real bodies in action. Even in conceiving of the secular body in new ways is, however, a leap of imagination that may open up new opportunities for identifying and understanding the nature of secularity as embodied in future empirical projects. The separate ways of describing the secularity of the body set out here allow us to consider, for example, the way in which these layers of secularity can be tangled together, as well as the possibility that they are not always so. It is this last possibility that indicates that the single category of the secular, which has, over recent years, carried us on a long and enriching journey, may at some point prove a roadblock to our attempts to deepen our enquiries and understanding.

Secular Objects and Bodily Affects in the Museum

Judith Dehail

Originally founded in France in order to support the newborn Republic, the public museum takes part in the implementation of a specific set of understandings, which can be identified as secular. Notably, it strives to create a realm governed by a scientific programme, which is to be intellectually understood in the same way by all its visitors. And, as I will argue in this chapter, the museum setting also conveys a specific pedagogy of the senses (as suggested by Hirschkind 2011) which enforces a specific relationship to the exhibited objects. That is to say, the museum participates in cultivating a secular body. But this body does not merely reproduce the ideal of distanced, unemotional, scientific objectivity. Like the secular-religious entanglement (Asad 2003), the practices employed cannot escape their interrelationship with affects and motivations that run counter to the self-understanding of the museum as a non-religious space. The shaping of secular bodies is therefore constantly subject to destabilizing moments.

This argument will be built on case studies conducted in two musical instrument museums: the *Musée de la Musique* in Paris and the *Grassi Museum für Musikinstrumente* at the University of Leipzig. Drawing on a discussion of some of the literature in museum studies, which argues for continuity between church and museum in Western societies, I will focus on another way that museums are religious-secular spaces, namely through the transformation of the objects on display. Specifically, I will consider how the function of the musical instrument is transformed inside the museum, becoming, in a sense, 'secularized'. Interviews conducted with conservator-restorers will show the role played by the practices and affects of these professionals in this change of the object's status. Finally, interviews conducted with visitors in the two museums will offer a view into their reactions to the way the instruments are exhibited and the pedagogy of the senses to which they are being asked to submit as well as the experience they describe, which demonstrates the constant destabilization of the secular 'grammar' (Asad 2003).

Shaping a secular body: The museum exhibition as a disembodied ritual

In order to contest the generally accepted opposition between religious and secular regimes, a number of authors have pointed to resemblances they identified between museum buildings and spaces dedicated to Western Christianity. According to Brian O'Doherthy, the modern gallery can be characterized as a space 'constructed along laws as rigorous as those for building a medieval church', in which works of art, just like religious truths, must seem 'untouched by time and its vicissitudes' (1986: 14–15). For Peter Van Mensch (1990), a continuity between church and museum emerges in the case of the assignment of a new function to an old religious building: transforming this type of monument into a museum is often perceived as the least problematic solution. Hans Belting sees church and museum as being sometimes interchangeable. For example, the exhibition *Seeing Salvation*, held at the National Gallery of Art in London (2000), attracted a high number of visitors who 'came because they couldn't find any more inside the churches the images of what they believed in' (2007: 60).

By showing continuity between church and museum buildings, these authors question the generally accepted understanding of the museum visit as a neutral frame facilitating the acquisition of objective knowledge, pointing to its ceremonial character. Furthermore, Carol Duncan conceptualizes the entire exhibition site of the museum as a ritual, which the visitors enact. Using the example of the Art Museum,[1] she intends to analyse 'the hidden ... ritual content of secular ceremonies'.[2] Just like visitors to holy places, she argues, museumgoers 'bring with them the willingness and ability to shift into a certain state of receptivity'. She uses the term 'liminality' to describe this 'particular kind of contemplation and learning experience and demanding a special quality of attention' (Duncan 1991: 91), thanks to which the visitors are passively guided through a programmed narrative and perform a rite that brings them to enlightenment (Duncan 1995).

The performance of the museum ritual by visitors has indeed had a political dimension since the beginning of the public museum, as shown by Eilean Hooper-Greenhill. She analyses how, right after the French Revolution, the museum was used as a means of establishing the newly born Republic. According to her, the museum can be viewed as another 'disciplinary technology' (Foucault) – such as the school or the prison – that creates 'docile bodies' (1992: 168). Tony Bennett's concept of the 'exhibitionary complex' allows him to analyse the role of social regulator that the museum plays. He sees this institution as a place of exhibition of bodies and objects (1995: 59) in which the crowd constituted of museum visitors learns to regulate itself through its own observation. Besides the will to control the crowd, the museum is also concerned with the idea of 'civilizing' the visitors (especially the working classes). A number of mechanisms are therefore used in order to regulate their behaviour, like a set of rules which had to be respected inside the museum.

Historical studies on how 'the habits of art spectatorship' (Rees Leahy 2012: 4) were inculcated towards the end of the nineteenth century highlight a particular training: visitors were learning a particular way of viewing inside the museum, which was soon to become considered 'common sense': in a museum, visitors are to walk at a slow pace while keeping their distance from the works of art, granting them a prolonged and concentrated gaze. Julia Noordegraaf indeed argues that, by the end of the nineteenth century, visitors no longer needed rails or any such restrictions preventing them from touching the paintings – which therefore disappeared or became less visible – because they had 'internalized the proper reading of the museum script' (2004: 162). The acknowledgement of this process led Barbara Kirshenblatt-Gimblett to observe that the museum is a school for the senses' and that its sensory curriculum has a history (2000: 7).

Indeed, this process reveals the dominance of the sense of vision in the exhibition space and, along with it, a disregard for the other senses. As noted by Constance Classen, objects in a museum are 'for the most part, only to be seen, not felt, smelt, sounded and certainly not tasted' (2007: 895). Fiona Candlin interestingly shows that this used to be otherwise and analyses the shift from what she calls 'tactuality' to visuality within the museum (2010: 58–90), the introduction of the museum imperative: do not touch. She demonstrates the importance of class in this evolution, since it is precisely when the museum was becoming more accessible to the lower classes that touch was forbidden for the visitors.

As this literature demonstrates, the museum is not only a prime example of the instability of the secular/religious distinction but also a space in which bodies are schooled in a certain comportment and feelings – in this case, towards historical objects, which also transgress the secular-religious boundary. The pedagogy of the senses at play in the museum also relies on the implementation of a new relationship with the material objects on exhibit, one that is specific to this secular institution.

Theorists of the museum have long been fascinated with the transformation of the status of the objects that come through its doors.[3] What defines this transformation is the idea that the objects entering this secular space lose their original function and acquire a symbolic one in its place. Taken away from their actual place of belonging, the museum objects are 'elected to stand as witness to beauty, identity and civilization' (Jeanneret 2011: 121). According to Krzysztof Pomian (1987), all collection objects have one thing in common: that their usefulness has been definitively done away with. He employs the term 'semiophore' to define these objects that have no use value but which, in this state, fully reveal their significance. And according to the expression of museologist Georges-Henri Rivière (1989), the museum object as 'symbol-object' summarizes a complete epoch or an entire culture. This means, for example, that musical instruments that become part of a museum collection are freed from their past as objects and embody a new symbolical significance within the exhibition. They shall no longer be played and will instead stand for a musical historical period, a music style, a famous musician, a technique of fabrication and so on. The exhibition of the object indeed represents the culmination of this transformation as it makes it possible, through installations such as showcases, to fully establish the necessary condition of the distance between subject and object.

The transformation of the museum object has also been described by art historians as a process of secularization. Hans Belting (1994) shows that what we call a work of art today has not always been considered as such. He indeed describes how the image slowly transformed over time into an art object, losing its original cultural function and its inherent power to acquire a social status through the discourse on art, the artist and the artist's style (see also Morgan 1998 and Elkins 1998). For Olivier Christin there are 'converging effects of the Byzantine iconoclasm and the emergence of collecting' (2002: 176). He explains how, at the turn of the sixteenth century, the iconoclasm 'throws on the market' (2002: 178) a large number of works of art (such as images and altarpieces) that used to be linked to a specific place of worship and to a particular function. These objects then shift status and function as they are integrated in private collections, where they are valued not for what they represent or for the functions they used to fulfil but because of their formal qualities and of the notoriety of the artist who created them. The newly developed collecting practices therefore lend the image an unprecedented value and an equally noble end. Finally, as a 'separated' space, specifically intended for the love of art and for aesthetic pleasure, the museum confers a 'sacred reload' on the image (Christin 1991).

Museologist Crispin Paine studies the redefinition of religious objects – previously used in liturgies – once they enter the museum, noting that, while losing their previous function, they acquire new significance and values, as well as 'a new personality'.[4] This secularization process is, I would argue, primarily characterized and supported by the fact that the practices that used to involve the object and which gave it a practical function in the church service have been replaced by a secular bodily relationship to the object, which removes it from its usefulness.[5]

Museums, science and the technique of secularizing the musical object

In the musical instrument museum, most of the objects exhibited are not actually used in religious ceremonies before they enter the collections. However, one could argue that the process they undergo can still be characterized as a secularization if we consider the radical change in the way they are handled outside and inside the museum. The museum creates a secular space in which the objects should be perceived and referred to differently from they would be outside. The process of their transformation into defunctionalized objects is observable diachronically as well as synchronically, through the conservation practices of museum conservators and restorers. Therefore, I will first look briefly into the way these practices evolved throughout the twentieth century, focusing more particularly on the shift that occurred after the 1960s in order to shed light on how the idea of professionalism and of scientificity were, at that time, reframing the way musical instruments had to be handled inside the museum space. I will then use interviews with conservator-restorers to analyse the role these professionals play as individuals in the secularization of the instrument, focusing on the way the museum shapes a new bodily relationship between them and the musical instrument.

Although the way musical instruments are preserved in the museum has, as we will see, evolved quite dramatically during the last century, it seems to have been consistently true to one principle: the quest for authenticity. Towards the end of the nineteenth century, the movement later called 'early music revival' and characterized by the will to rediscover forgotten musical repertoires was growing roots in Europe (see notably Fontana 2008; Gétreau 1995). At the end of the 1880s, musical instrument collectors were forming early music ensembles using the instruments of their collections in order to revive repertoires that had fallen into disuse. Their purpose was to reanimate this music in a way that would be as close to the original – as authentic – as possible. They were therefore performing these repertoires on the instruments for which they had originally been composed, and this justified, for them, putting those instruments back in playing order, regardless of the nature or importance of the restorations and modifications this might imply. The instruments were indeed merely considered as a way to access music. As this trend was mushrooming within the amateur milieu, it began to settle in the museum as well, and public collections in turn became tools for the rediscovery of the music of the past.

Restoration of musical instruments was not the exclusive consequence of the influence of the early music revival movement. A common practice of museum curators was to entrust instrument makers and repairers with instruments of their collections even though there was no intention for these instruments to be played.[6] These craftsmen acted out of habit, namely, using the same techniques they usually would use for 'active' instruments belonging to musicians. However, one consequence of the early music revival movement was that this phenomenon of restoring collection instruments to playing order became much more frequent. This is why it can be seen as a main trigger for the major shift that occurred in musical instrument museums' conservation policy.

It is indeed in the context of the growing success of the early music revival movement that the International Committee for Museums and Collections of Musical Instruments (CIMCIM) was created in 1960 as part of the International Council of Museums (ICOM). The founding of this committee corresponds to the beginning of important changes in the way the instruments of museum collections were to be conceptualized and thus handled. It filled the increasing need among museum workers in contact with musical instruments for a space in which they could exchange opinions about conservation matters[7] and eventually feel part of a professional body. During the first meeting of CIMCIM, a plan of action was adopted by the members stating the necessity to create 'a guide-treatise on restoration and conservation, and to formulate provisional recommendations for the conservation of musical instruments' (CIMCIM 1960: 18) as one of its highest priorities. The third motion, entitled 'Conservation and restoration of musical instruments', noted that 'concerning restoration, two specific and contradictory problems arise'. The motion points to the paradox between the necessity to carry out 'integral technical restoration of instruments which may be incomplete or in a bad state of preservation' in order to restore the instruments to a playing condition and 'the danger involved in this type of restoration of permanently impairing their value as historical documents by too much guesswork or too many repairs' (1960: 19).

A few years later, CIMCIM published a document giving directives for the conservation and restoration of musical instruments of public collections (CIMCIM 1967). It discouraged the practice of modernizing historical instruments and emphasized the importance of documenting all actions performed on the instruments. The stated aim was to avoid 'non-scientific restorations' and the establishment of 'a method both rational and meticulous to restore the instruments' that would be based on 'the outcome of the most recent research'. Following this publication, conservation and restoration practices began to evolve progressively in the museums in charge of musical instrument collections. A notable change is the idea, rapidly gaining ground around that time, that museums should not have recourse to external professionals (instrument makers and repairers) anymore but should make room for a new type of profession for the restoration of musical instruments, tailored especially to their particular requirements. These new professionals would be trained to understand the specificity of the status of the musical instrument as a museum object and would work along the lines of a clearly defined deontology.

CIMCIM, however, later published two additional documents concerning the conservation and restoration of musical instruments, in 1985 and in 1993. The modifications proposed in these documents show the further shift of attention that occurred in those years from the idea of finding the authentic music of the past using historical instruments to the perceived necessity of preserving the original substance of their materiality. That the musical instrument is, above all, a document is an idea that emerged at that time, along with which the conception that any physical contact with (and obviously any restoration on) the instruments should be avoided as it could result in an irremediable loss of information. The recommendations published in 1985 therefore advised how to 'regulate the access to musical instruments of public collections' (CIMCIM 1985: 1). They encouraged drastically limiting situations where the instruments would be touched by anybody other than qualified museum professionals in exceptional cases where it would serve an attested scientific purpose. It logically forbade, for example, that the instruments of a public collection be played 'for motives of idle curiosity or individual pleasure' (CIMCIM 1985: 6). The document published in 1993 was directly referring to the first version of the recommendations, stating that '[s]ince 1967, the science and goals of conservation have ... progressed.' The term 'restoration' had disappeared from the title of this document, erased by the now singular acceptable practice of conservation (i.e. to prevent the instrument from deteriorating, with a minimal-intervention approach). The latter practice was defined by 'the application of scientific principles to the treatment of museum objects, with an emphasis on documentation and research' (CIMCIM 1993). This mutation of the terminology mirrors the transformation of the musical instrument's status in the museum. From intermediary or tool, it has become an end in itself, which materially crystallizes, and therefore documents, the authenticity of the past. This transformation also implies that a distance is set with the instrument: as museum object, and according to the ideals of museum conservation, it should no longer be touched.

At this point, I would like to look into the actual role that the conservator-restorers (later referred to only as conservators) play in the secularization of the instrument in the museum. My goal is not to produce a comprehensive survey of their working methods, but rather to concentrate on the subjective component of their adherence to the deontology of their museum profession and on the adjustments that this might imply for them. I hope to show that the secularization of the object relies in large part on the conversion of their embodied practices to fit the requirements of the museum and on their conviction in accomplishing a valuable mission for society.

What first characterizes the work of conservators is the specificity of the way they look at (and metaphorically listen to) the musical instrument. This look imposes a certain restraint on the part of these professionals because it is the object itself that 'justifies our gesture', as one Parisian conservator explains.[8] 'The main point is to have an exchange with the object', states another conservator in Leipzig.[9] 'It is very important for me to put the instrument down, to sit in front of it and to see what the instrument tells me, or rather what it wants to tell me .... It is essential to listen to the instrument.' Only then can the temptation to act on impulse out of habit or personal inclination and to 'correct the object' be avoided (Sachs 2003). This specific way of looking at the instrument is clearly differentiated from other types of approaches outside the museum, and therefore has to be actively interiorized. The conservator quoted above explained having to 'completely relearn' a new relationship with the instrument when he decided to become a museum conservator after having worked as a violinmaker.

> There [in the lutherie workshop where I used to work], I was building new instruments. They had to be smooth, they had to have a nice surface, and look really new. When I started working in the museum, I learnt that here, it was considered as a danger to try and beautify everything. It took me a while to realize 'OK, you have to base your approach on the object itself, you have to see what the instrument tells you'. ... It was a phase of relearning, of a new way of thinking. It happened quite fast, in the first four years after I started working at the museum.[10]

The relearning phase that this conservator refers to recalls the idea of a rite of passage, during which he converted to the specific approach to the museum's musical instruments. At least inside the secular space of the museum, he abandoned his past way of handling the instrument and instead adopted practices that value, above all, the authenticity of the substance of the object.

A former museum conservator,[11] now working as an instrument maker, building copies of historical instruments, explained how her past museum career exerts fundamental influence on the way she works today. Contrary to most early instrument makers, who build non-rigorous copies (i.e. often without having seen the historical instrument), her main concern is to stay true to the original object. 'I don't see myself as an artist creating new instruments', she explains. 'Because I come from the museum, I grew up in a museum, I base my work on research, I try, with my instruments, to be as close as possible to the original.' Although she is very much aware of the 'margin of interpretation' that she might not be able to avoid in the copies she will produce, she still constantly strives to 'abstract [her] personality' from the process of building an instrument. She is indeed motivated by the main criterion, learnt in the museum, of the quest for authenticity, which she perceives as objective. It is because she strongly adheres to the idea of respecting this criterion, and because she is driven by the will to serve the original material object that she refuses, for example, to adapt her copies to the desires and special requests of the musicians who order them. She explains that if one of them asked her to create a copy, that is to modify or adapt a specific component that would not exist in the original instrument, she would say, 'I don't think I would do it. I would try and persuade them to change their mind or I wouldn't build the instrument.' The difficulties that she faces (financially, in particular) show that this absolute loyalty to the original, which is at the heart of her work as an instrument builder, actually stems from a real conviction.

It is one thing being in a museum, having a fixed job and building a copy when you don't need to earn money [from it], but if you are on the market and you need to earn money from your instruments, it is much more difficult.[12]

However, in order not to have to make any compromises with her instruments, she tries 'to earn money with other means', and, for example, founded a music label. The fact that she prefers not to produce the copies rather than to compromise her deontology illustrates the power of the conviction that, even though it originated in the museum, still drives her work today: a belief therefore so strong that it can live on outside the secular space of the museum.

The conservators' conviction in the absolute value of the original material object is linked to the powerful idea of being part of a higher mission that has a direct positive impact on society. 'Personally, I always have the feeling that we are mediators between the maker of the original instrument and the future generations for whom we prepare [those instruments]', confides another conservator.[13] This conviction therefore plays an important role in the continuity of the specific status of the instrument in the museum. Through their daily practices, the conservators uninterruptedly act as depository of this status. This is notably observable in the way they voluntarily limit their perception of the object and do not allow themselves to think of its dimension of sound. For instance, the instrument maker mentioned above[14] explained how, for a long time after leaving her museum job and starting to build copies that would ultimately be played, she did not reflect on the dimension of sound in her instruments. It is only when she was forced to notice the considerable improvement in the sound of the first fortepiano copy she had built many years ago that she began to acknowledge this aspect of the instrument. 'At the beginning, because I had worked so long in a museum I did not think about [the evolution of the sound], but now that I mostly work as an instrument – maker ..., I have to say, when the instruments are new, they have to be played! It is almost as if they had to wake up.' In the same way, this conservator tells about his experience during the rare event of the production of a CD using the historical instruments of the museum. In the frame of this project, he exceptionally had to be attentive to the sound dimension of the instruments selected for the recording. He talks here about a specific fortepiano:

Usually, I always strive to protect everything and to make everything look nice and well arranged for the visitors and suddenly, it was about ensuring that it would sound well; it's a completely different approach. And I enjoyed it also. I didn't have to do much, I had to tune it, make sure it stayed tuned and harmonize the sounds, but this experience, to see that it was then producing good music, it was fantastic!
[I ask: do you miss this otherwise, not being able to do this more often?]
[Long silent pause] It would have to be truly part of my mission ... In this case I could ... It's also a nice job to ... make the instruments sound, to bring out the full richness of the sound and all these kinds of things. But it is not my mission here.[15]

Through this brief overview of conservators' practices, it is possible to witness a new relationship to the object being implemented inside the secular space of the museum. Musical instruments that were used to produce music are put at a distance. They lose their use value and acquire a symbolic one instead. Now valued for the authenticity of their original substance, they should no longer be played or touched. By incorporating specific practices while working with musical instruments inside the museum, museum conservators not only shape their bodies and skills in order to fit the requirements of the museum but also become key actors in the creation of secular objects. In being faithful to the deontology of their profession, they indeed uninterruptedly activate a specific regime of truth regarding musical instruments that characterizes the museum. An interesting fact, however, is that they do not seem to do so because they feel obliged to or because they have simply been told it is the right thing to do, but because they act out of conviction. In some cases, they have converted to this secular way of looking at the instrument and later stay true to this point of view, even if they do not work under the authority of the museum anymore. This suggests that they personally engage in this way of thinking and therefore brings one to wonder if the nature of the underlying feeling of their conviction is actually so different from that which stirs the religious believer. The specific way with which they relate to the objects is, however, thoroughly defined as secular and rational, illustrating, as one could argue, the praxis of the secular 'grammar' (Asad 2003).

The secular body shaped by the museum exhibition is therefore one that builds on a visual relationship to the objects around it. It has learned that these defunctionalized objects are meant exclusively for thorough, calm and silent contemplation, leading to the acquisition of scientific knowledge. As we will see in the next part, this assumption might, however, be challenged by a more detailed look into the visitors' experience.

Questioning the secular ritual, inhabiting the museum institution

Visitor, speaking about the reason why she brought her grandson to the museum: 'It's to get him accustomed to places … Actually, he was speaking in a low voice; he knew that it was a place where you can't raise your voice … In principle [the museum] is a rather specific place, not religious, but almost … It's for him to get used to it.'[16]

The state of 'liminality' that describes, according to Duncan (1991, 1995), the increased receptivity, or the act of making oneself available for contemplation and learning, of the visitors inside the museum is illustrated by the way some visitors relate to certain instruments they encounter in the exhibition rooms of the museums in which I conducted field research. Some visitors indeed describe a feeling similar to what Stephen Greenblatt calls 'wonder' and defines as the 'power of the object displayed to stop the viewer in his tracks, to convey an arresting sense of uniqueness, to evoke an exalted attention' (1990: 20). For instance, a visitor to the Parisian museum for musical instruments, a professional violinist, describes how he found himself in a state of enchantment as he encountered the instrument he specifically came to see. Seeing it in real life provoked immediate wonder, with no past or future: 'I felt really lucky to see the 1724 Sarasate, the Stradivarius which is my most favourite instrument since I'm [sic] like fifteen. I was really happy to see it … It's beautiful.'[17] This visitor came to the museum with a readiness to experience 'one of those momentary cultural epiphanies' (Bazin, cited in Duncan 1995: 477). He had prepared to be aesthetically touched and transported out of the present moment, and the sight of the admired object helped him achieve this particular emotional state. It could be pointed out that the exhibition setting in which the famous Stradivarius violin is presented helped him achieve this specific state. Standing in the middle of the room inside an isolated showcase,[18] lit in a dramatic manner, the violin is indeed sublimated and given an epiphanic character.

One could therefore argue that this specific feeling – aesthetic (visual) transcendental pleasure – relates to what Charles Hirschkind describes as 'sensibilities that fit into the game of secularism'. Just like the 'honed sensibilities of the Romantic poet' evoked by Hirschkind, it has been 'encompassed by and appropriated within the narrative of the secular emancipation from religion' (2011: 643). This feeling therefore relates to the 'religious shadow' (2011: 643, and also underlined, in the specific case of the museum, by the above-mentioned authors) of the enterprise, led by the museum, of promoting secular ideals. This could explain why, more than being tolerated in the exhibition spaces, this aesthetic emotion is encouraged. The museum exhibition therefore seems to illustrate quite well the 'gap' highlighted by Hussein Agrama (cited in Hirschkind 2011: 644) 'between the ideals secularism promotes and the realities that it establishes'.

The interviews I have done with museum visitors, however, also reveal other kinds of emotions, which do not seem to be dictated by the ritualized 'script' implemented by the museum, but rather seem to go against it. One of the most common reactions that I observed is indeed the frustration felt by the visitors at being forbidden to touch the exhibited instruments. The transformation of the instrument into a defunctionalized symbolic object inside the museum, along with the consequent enforcement of a distance from it, is perceived as a groundless fetishization. According to the visitors who express this frustration, the instrument should indeed, on the contrary, only be defined through its use value (i.e. as a tool for producing music).

At the same time, those visitors demonstrate – in varying degrees, as we shall see – an understanding for the position in which the museum is. They are aware of the constraints of conservation that the museum faces and that, in this context, getting closer to the instruments would most likely endanger their material substance, as in the following example:

> Visitor: You always wish to have the haptics [to be able to touch the objects], but I understand that on the other side, it doesn't work to have 500-year-old instruments and to allow anyone who wants to play on the instruments to do it; this is naturally understandable. … I like to look behind the façade; this why I would have sometimes hoped, for example with the neo–Bechstein grand piano, that the cover would be open, that you would be able to see the electronic sound pickup system. I had already seen one in Berlin, but I think that it would make it optically easier to understand for people if it was open. But then you would need to put these Plexiglas panes of course, which is financially not really … I can imagine why you don't do this with all of them.[19]

This understanding also extends to the museum's supposed struggle of the project of making instruments available to play inside the exhibition galleries. Even though they 'would like to play' some of the instruments exhibited, visitors imagine that it is logistically 'complicated to organize something like this and make it happen' and therefore give up their wishes.

This compassion for the museum and understanding for the constraints imposed by its mission of conservation, its architecture or its limited financial means testify to the visitors' willingness to shift to a specific state of mind when they enter the museum, recalling – once again – liminality. Even though they have desires that are linked to their relationship to music outside the museum, once inside they are disposed to 'look at themselves and their world with different thoughts' (Duncan 1998: 477). Often, in their discourse, they oppose the opinion, which they express and then qualify as personal – that instruments should be played – against a general idea of a common good for which these desires are worth suppressing. Communication theorist Joëlle Le Marec has shown that the specificity of the relationship between museum and visitors relies on the fact that visitors benevolently trust the museum institution and on the fact that its sole intention is to accomplish its social missions in the best possible way.[20] This is already palpable, she has argued, in the readiness and availability with which visitors generally engage in a conversation with interviewers who conduct research inside museums (Le Marec 2007, 2013). One could argue that this trust and deference towards the institution relates to the ritualized character of the museum identified, among others, by Duncan (1991, 1995).

In what could be characterized as a second 'nuance' of visitors' reactions, the balance between the two 'emotionalities' described above (active trust and acceptance of the authority of the museum versus personal desire to touch the instruments) changes. The visitors realize that playing the instruments of the exhibition is not allowed, but they find it difficult to resign themselves to not touching them, not getting close to them in order to see them better and not trying them out. The rationally conceivable constraints of conservation of the instruments in the museum do not outbalance the desire to experience the object in a different way other than exclusively by looking at it. 'It really annoys me when I see that really good instruments are behind glass cases and cannot be used', explains one visitor.[21]

> I always have the need, when I see a good instrument, to take it in my hands and to try it. And it is not possible there [in the exhibition of historical instruments].[22] I still pressed a couple of keys of a piano [his wife who is also taking part in the interview laughs and nods, clearly embarrassed] but I was scolded right away. ... It is not possible to do it differently, I can see that of course ... but it's ... There were multiple times where I would have liked to try [and thought] 'how does this sound?'[23]

This tendency among visitors of both musical instrument museums (Paris and Leipzig) to touch the musical instruments on display is a largely observed fact, first by museum guards as well as by conservators. Typically, visitors will hit an unprotected drum with their fingers or press on a couple of keys of a clavichord, sometimes consciously crossing barriers and walking over podia – among other obstacles – in order to reach the instrument. Some visitors also mention their resistance to their own desire to touch, defining it as a noticeable good deed: 'I was surprised that [some of the instruments] are exhibited without any protection, because there must be lots of people who want to touch them. So I was quite surprised … But I resisted!' Another visitor proudly notes, after visiting the museum with her family: 'We were well-behaved. We didn't touch too much.'

A third type of reaction features extreme positions of visitors based on strong claims about musical instruments. In these cases, the idea of apprehending musical instruments only visually is truly difficult to accept, and visitors find ways to bypass museum rules and actually play the exhibited instruments. This adaptation of museum policy is nonetheless rare, as the visitors who form this last category are intensely involved either in a museum practice or in a musical practice.

The three categories of reactions presented here form a gradation illustrating the negotiated character of the interactions between the two 'emotionalities' felt by the visitors and the way the outcome of the interaction conditions their experience of the museum. This rather conflicting negotiation can also be inferred from the way visitors very often refer to the child as a catalyst in order to justify their request for a change in the way the musical instruments are presented.

> Visitor, after saying that he finds it frustrating not to be able to touch any instrument in the exhibition: As an adult let's say that it is OK but as a child it must be rather disappointing … Maybe it is my childishness that tells me it is good to manipulate things … To see instruments is nice, but musical instruments, you want to touch them. Make them sound, make them resonate, hit them, scratch them, all of these things![24]

In some cases, no frustration is actually voiced for oneself. The only reason genuinely identified as valuable for a disruption of museum rules is thus the only people who haven't yet submitted to them: children. 'I didn't miss [being able to touch the instruments] so much', explains a visitor. 'I know the principle of museums. But for younger people it would be good to have instruments that could be manipulated.' One possible interpretation of these reactions is the following: visitors' desire or the drive to touch the instruments is repressed by the internalized museum rules and by the attachment and respect felt for this institution. The repressed desire comes back, however, metamorphosed into the shape of the child's innocence.

The Freudian paradigm only emphasizes the idea that the way visitors experience the secular space of the museum is conditioned by a constant internal negotiation between feelings of apparent conflicting nature.[25] On the one hand, they feel respect and trust – relating to the 'religious shadow' identified by Hirschkind (2011) – for this institution, for its social missions and the knowledge it exhibits. They have incorporated the rules and norms of behaviour that the museum promotes, and they wish to honour them. On the other hand, they experience a powerful desire if not to disobey, at least to question these rules and their appropriateness. They are driven by other strongly embodied practices that are linked to the relationship to music that they continuously build outside the museum. The visitors thus do not simply passively enact a prescriptive ritual; they wish to inhabit the institution and therefore to adapt its policies. The ritualized character of the museum exhibition identified by Duncan as a surreptitious frame manipulating museumgoers' behaviour is, in this case, unveiled by the visitors themselves, who directly address it and see it as grounds for negotiations.

Conclusion

I have attempted to show how the museum institution is one of the places where we learn to have secular bodies. Taking into account the similarities pointed out by some authors between church and museum, I have considered the museum visit as a secular ritual. I have tried to provide an analysis of the rules and norms that shape this ritual and of the bodies of the visitors who enact them. Visitors are taught to respect a specific hierarchy of the senses inside the museum, and therefore the exhibited objects should only be looked at and not touched, felt or smelled. They also learn to place themselves in a state of heightened receptivity in order to attain intellectual enlightenment. In doing so, they attune themselves to being receptive to secular emotions. I have also looked at the secularization of the object inside the museum as a set of specific practices in which the museum object is entangled. I have analysed the discourse and working habits of conservator-restorers in order to highlight the importance of their affects, personal engagement and conviction in the transformation of the musical instrument into a defunctionalized object with scientific relevance. One could therefore argue that, by embodying these practices, museum visitors and professionals carve the border between religious and secular. However, the conflicting 'emotionalities' observed in the last part of the chapter, provoked by the frustration felt by visitors of not being able to touch the exhibited musical instruments, also exemplify the constant destabilization of this inscription. As part of the process that shapes secular bodies within the museum, this conflict contributes to shedding light on the complexity and diversity of practices, discourses and knowledge that continuously redefine the boundary between secular and religious.

Part Two

Being Secular

Formations of a Secular Wedding

Katie Aston

This chapter will explore the humanist weddings as sites in which we may come to grasp one outline of the secular body, its accompanying emotional, ethical registers and speech acts. In particular, I will explore secular self-fashioning (Hirschkind 2011: 639) and the negotiations made by humanist celebrants who perform these rites. What will become apparent through the discussion below is the way in which the person is framed as an individual being – rational and sovereign. This kind of conscious self-fashioning demonstrates how secular humanists cultivate what Asad calls 'the rhetoric of sincerity' (2003: 52 cited in Hirschkind 2011), arguing that being 'true to oneself' is both a moral duty but also presupposes a certain kind of sovereign self, displayed through acts of sincerity.

This particular discussion of secular moral and ethical concerns draws from the work of Webb Keane, specifically his work on sincerity (1997, 2002, 2006) and his work on secularism as a moral compulsion (2013). In addition, I will demonstrate how the body is the means through which secular and ethical concerns can be attained. This view of the body draws on the work of Saba Mahmood's and her study of Islamic prayer in which she defines the body as 'not so much as a signifying medium to which different ideological meanings are ascribed, but more as a tool or developable means through which certain kinds of ethical and moral capacities are attained' (Mahmood 2001: 837).

It is important, however, to make a distinction between the overt and the more subtle forms the secular body takes (Lee 2015: 88). In a previous work (Aston 2015) I have examined overt expressions of non-religious worldview clothing, for example (see also Lee 2015). In this chapter, however, I will explore the more subtle negotiations of interior and exterior lives, as they emerge/reveal themselves through the wedding ceremony.

My examination of the secular humanist body and its emotion registers draws from data collected between 2011 and 2013 during fieldwork with British secular humanists. The research I undertook was a multi-sited ethnography, exploring the material and visual manifestations of what I called 'nonreligious' expressions (see Aston 2015; Lee 2012). As part of the research I worked with celebrants who had been trained by Humanist UK (formally *British Humanist Association* or BHA) to perform non-religious weddings and funerals, and members of the public accessing this service. The data includes interviews with approximately 10 celebrants who performed ceremonies on behalf of Humanist UK. I also examined wedding scripts and interviewed 15 couples who were either planning a humanist wedding or had already had one. These weddings will form the main focus of this chapter.

Humanist UK

Founded as the BHA in 1965, Humanist UK has a longer history as part of the *Union of Ethical Societies*, which were instituted in the latter part of the nineteenth century with the aim of 'disentangl[ing] moral ideals from religious doctrines, metaphysical systems and ethical theories' (Campbell 1971: 74). Humanist UK has continued to cultivate these principles today. The organization today promotes itself as '*the* national charity working on behalf of non-religious people who seek to live ethical and fulfilling lives on the basis of reason and humanity' (humanism.org.uk, emphasis added). Humanist UK is an organization of activists, and at present runs a number of secularist campaign on issues which include challenging the automatic appointment of Bishops to the House of Lords and arguing for representation of non-religious (including humanist) perspectives on the religious education curriculum in the UK.

In his exploratory essay, Charles Hirschkind suggests that 'a secular person is someone whose affective-gestural repertoires express a negative relation to forms of embodiment historically associated (but not limited to) theistic religion' (2011: 368). But, as I will argue below, there is no clear negative relation to religion in the secular humanist milieu. Although humanist ceremonies are an alternative to religious ceremonies, they are also an alternative to prescriptive, secularized civil ceremonies. But it is worth mentioning a further concern of secular humanists regarding religion: the perception of religious control on the body. This concern has manifested historically in the 'free-thought' movement, from which Humanist UK emerges (see Royle 1980 or Schwartz 2010, 2013 for a feminist perspective). These movements began to promote rights to abortions and challenged divorce laws and free speech regulations. As noted above the campaigns of the Humanist UK continue to centre on these ethical issues, plus more contemporary concerns such as female genital mutilation, gay rights (including marriage rights), assisted dying and faith schools.

Figure 6.1 'Please don't label me.' Image courtesy of Humanist.co.uk.

Participants I interviewed were particularly passionate about the Humanist UK campaigns against faith schools (Figure 6.1) and for assisted dying. The narratives of these campaigns included a concern for the segregation of children on the grounds of faith and the moral right to control your own life and death. This kind of campaigning drives a secular humanist narrative about the sovereign self and the cultivation of the social body and underpins some of the discussion below.[1] This kind of work assumes a number of things about personhood, particularly of universal human rights and freedom of individuals versus cultural freedoms and tradition. Finally, the body is framed as a site of anxieties and conflict, typically between secular humanist groups and their 'others'. But it is worth emphasizing again that this does not mean only the 'religious' other.

As well as campaigning, the organization also provides pastoral services, and at the time of my research, had a network of just over 300 celebrants accredited by them to perform non-religious ceremonies (see also Engelke 2014, 2015a, 2015b). Typically, they offered provision for members of the public who wanted non-religious alternatives to life-cycle ceremonies celebrating birth, marriage and death. Humanist UK began performing these ceremonies as early as the 1960s. Only in recent years, however, have these become formalized, introducing a programme of accreditation and training for celebrants and increasingly sophisticated marketing material.

The third strand of the Humanist UK work was the facilitation of local humanist groups. These Humanist UK-affiliated meet-ups are usually places for debate and discussion, and indeed this is part of their appeal for many (Engelke 2015a). Many humanist celebrants also attend local humanist groups (there are approximately sixty groups nationwide). During my research I interviewed Lavender and Karl, two celebrants from south London, who explained that they had set up one such local group, which gave people 'a space to talk to people about their thoughts [and] just make friends with like-minded people' but caveated that 'the group did not always just talk about [humanist] issues'.

What is important to recognize about the work of Lavender, Karl and other celebrants included in this chapter is that their humanism was an active and lived worldview. Lavender explained to me that

> I'm like humanism in action. [Matthew Engelke's] findings are that
> people who become celebrants are not wanting to engage on such an
> intellectual level as much as a doing humanism. … I'm like that, I'm not
> so keen on these intellectual discussions.

Celebrants' work differed from these local groups, and during their work with the public, they were not always likely to encounter committed humanists. It's important to recognize they were not anti-intellectualist, but almost all celebrants expressed to me an awareness of the practical limitations of a purely intellectual approach to humanism, and of rationalism. Indeed, not all celebrants supported the local humanist groups for this very reason.

In June 2012 I met Melissa at her home in Devon, where she invited me to stay for the weekend to observe two ceremonies she would be performing. She explained to me on a walk around the local Devon countryside that she had attended a couple of her local humanist meetings but had found them deeply frustrating. Her particular group had been anti-Christian and focused on a rationalist, scientist critique of theology and religions more generally. While these arguments may have rung true for her on a theoretical level, they did not seem relevant to her own work with grieving families, or during weddings. Funerals especially, but also weddings and naming ceremonies, seemed like inappropriate times to most celebrants to discuss such theoretical matters. But more than this, humanism for many was much wider than simple questions about why people should not be religious: it served as a pragmatic alternative for those who could not find space in institutionalized religion.

This is one of the central arguments of this chapter, that secular humanist rituals are performances which can challenge the view of the 'secular' as a merely 'cold' or 'rational' ontological position, insistent on emptying the world of religion. Contra to some early presentations of the secular worldview, as highly intellectualized and rationalist, for example 'new atheism', my ethnographic material will expand this definition. I will show that secular humanists desire more than the emptying out of religious ritual and that the wedding ritual act can act as an introduction to possible avenues in which the secular might be expressed emotionally, ethically and bodily.

What is secular humanism

My participants tended to self-describe as humanist. Being secular was an implicit part of this identity; however, when made explicit my participants typically meant they were 'without religion'. When using the terms 'secularism' or 'secularist' participants tended to refer to the removal of religion from state apparatus. Humanism on the other hand was typically understood as a positive identity, defining people by what they believed rather than what they didn't. Nevertheless, a secular add-on was considered an unnecessary qualifier, as my participants felt the absence of religion was an essential part of being humanist. In this chapter I choose to make the secular explicit and will refer to my participants as *secular* humanists. Moreover, the worldview of the self-described humanists I introduce below shares characteristics with a number of anthropological analytical descriptions of the 'secular'. I want to make clear in this chapter that I draw a parallel between these emic and etic models. In doing this I don't want to ignore the humanist aspect of this phenomena, in favour of the analytical category secular.

To expand on my definition of the secular, or more precisely secular humanism, I draw on the work of Webb Keane (2006, 2013). Webb Keane states that secularism is more than simply returning the world to a former 'natural condition' or a freedom from religious impediment. He suggests. instead, that secularism includes an impetus for change, what he calls the 'moral narrative of modernity' (2013). Undergirding this narrative is a sense that people 'ought' to recognize their own agency and that the consequence of failing to recognize this is in fact a moral error. The moral impetus, therefore, comes from an insistence on 'restoring agency to its proper subjects' (2013: 159) or replacing gods with humans. Keane suggests this is a narrative of liberation from illegitimate rulers, but also from traditions given in 'scriptures, unreal fetishes such as their religious rituals and relics' (160) and this agency is embodied by free and critical thinking. Modern subjects are characterized by knowing themselves 'to be the true agent of [their] actions, in contrast to those non-moderns who displace their own agency onto gods, demons, spirits, and so forth' (160). This self-knowledge therefore places 'moral weight on distinguishing interior state from exterior worlds' (Keane 2006: 12).

This is a useful framework particularly because my participants made a number of claims about the right to autonomy, freedom and self-mastery – affording them their proper recognition (Keane 2013: 163). In addition, I consider the moral weight of this term and the associated term 'secularism'. Webb Keane's definition of the 'moral narrative of modernity' is of particular use:

> Arguments about agency, rationality, or freedom for instance, are tacitly informed by assumptions that self-transformation is not only a central aspect of historical progress, but also a good that exceeds local systems of value. (Ibid.)

So secular modern subjects who adhere to this narrative differentiate themselves from subjects who impute agency to entities that the outsider does not recognize, such as an interventionist God (ibid.). As the chapter unfolds, it will become clear that secular humanist weddings are oriented within a typically secular cosmology, which rejects the transcendental and any celestial bodies. Even where religion is embraced, it is dealt with in a manner that does impact on the secular humanists' capacity to adhere to their own sincerely held beliefs. Furthermore, the ideal of the unique and personalized wedding makes primary the individual and his or her freedom of choice, apparently typical of the liberal secular modern. Finally, Mahmood's definition of the body is therefore crucial, as it demonstrates the means through which secular humanist moral capacities are attained. This chapter centres on the way in which the above moral presumptions are enacted and attained through a ritual, and certain liberal and secular assumptions become 'embodied'.

Marrying in the UK

If you want a legally recognized marriage in England or Wales, couples can choose a 'religious' ceremony which has to be held in a building which has been officially recognized as religious by the state. Or they can choose an essentially secular civil ceremony. These ceremonies are performed typically by state-employed registrars, and there are rules dictating the content of these ceremonies. For example, although you can include poems and songs of your choice within the ceremony, there can be no religious references at all within the ceremony. According to the Marriage Act of 1994, premises for civil marriages must be secular, and '[m]ust have no recent or continuing connection with any religion, religious practice or religious persuasion which would be incompatible with the use of the premises for the solemnisation of marriages' (Marriage Act 1994).

It should be noted that in the UK it has been possible to have a secular civil ceremony since the Marriage Act of 1836. According to the *Office of National Statistics*, in 1872, forty years after this act, only 10 per cent of marriages were civil ceremonies. However, over a century later, by 2011, 70 per cent (174,600) of the 247,890 weddings performed in England and Wales were civil ceremonies. It is worth noting that 2015 has seen the lowest number of weddings in England and Wales on record, and there is indication of a gradual decline in weddings overall. Data comparison between 2014 and 2015 suggests, however, there has been only a slight decline in civil ceremonies among opposite-sex couples (1.6 per cent) compared with a greater decrease in religious ceremonies (8.0 per cent) (Humanist UK 2018; ONS 2018). In fact, over the last century, there has been a significant decline in religious ceremonies, particularly those conducted by the Church of England.

Humanist ceremonies are a comparatively new phenomenon, although they are not currently legally recognized despite campaigns by Humanist UK. Nevertheless, the humanist celebrant network of England and Wales is now growing, linking together approximately 310 trained celebrants. There has also been a rise in humanist weddings over the last decade; in 2004 there were 287 opposite-sex humanist weddings conducted, and according to the ONS' most recent data, in 2015 this rose to 975 (Humanist UK 2018).[2]

Celebrants conduct on average nearly seven times more funerals than weddings. As such, the majority of celebrants become accredited to conduct funerals (approximately 270), doing only a few additional naming and weddings on an ad hoc basis. The remaining celebrants train only in weddings and/or baby-namings. There does not seem to be a financial incentive to perform more funerals. For comparison, the celebrant fee is around £300–£800 for a wedding, £120 for a naming and around £120 for a funeral. Instead reason for this disparity is partly preference: some celebrants feel like they are doing more positive, ethical work in conducting funerals. There is also greater demand for funerals as there is currently no secular state alternative to religious rites. Nevertheless, in spite of having a civil non-religious alternative, nearly 1,000 opposite-sex couples are opting for humanist weddings. The following section considers why this might be and starts to examine how secular humanists define what they are, as much as what they are not.

The religious alternative

On 26 May 2012, I attended the wedding of Fiona and Bobbie. Not long after the wedding we met to discuss their choices and their experience of the humanist ceremony. Despite any initial reservations about what humanism was, the key motivation for Fiona and Bobbie having a humanist ceremony was not wanting a religious or civil ceremony. Neither Bobbie nor Fiona described themselves as religious, although since the wedding both were happy to identify as humanist. Fiona also described herself as 'spiritual', although she did not elaborate on what this meant for her. Neither visited church, even for Christmas or Easter celebrations, and seemed disinterested in organized religion. They had considered a blessing after the wedding to appease Bobbie's Catholic mother, but eventually decided against it. In fact, it emerged that they were annoyed at the idea of non-religious friends having church weddings. Bobbie stressed that he thought it was nonsense:

> I don't hold it against people if they want to get married in church, but the bullshit they went through, having to make out they believe in God even though I know for

sure they don't … although maybe now they would say they do … but it's, all these bloody meetings, none of them have seen the vicar since.

It was common for my participants to express annoyance at people having religious ceremonies when it was not consistent with their worldview. Some went as far as to call this out as hypocrisy. Others spoke of feeling alienated by the doctrinal aspects of a church wedding. As Luna, a young female celebrant, said of her own, if not slightly exaggerated experience:

> [In a church] you find yourself sitting back and thinking about what you're going to eat for dinner because you don't believe in that bit, or you watch the bride and groom and know that they don't either. It's all a bit of a farce.

What is clear from these descriptions is that the secular humanist felt alienated in the church context. Furthermore, having a ceremony that is not compatible with the beliefs of the couple (in this instance, non-religious couples having church ceremonies) is considered 'bullshit' or farcical. Such actions are ridiculed and often prompted passionate responses from my secular humanist participants, some even suggesting this was hypocrisy.

The civil alternative: The legals

Fiona and Bobbie were equally dismissive of religious and civil ceremonies. They felt the latter was too cold and rigid. Nevertheless, since humanist weddings are not legally binding, Fiona and Bobbie still had to perform a civil ceremony and chose to do this the day before their humanist wedding. Their experience of the civil registry process only increased their negative view of the civil ceremony. Both Fiona and Bobbie had small families, so they invited only their mothers and one guest to the 'legals'.[3] Their fathers were estranged from them, and neither had been invited to the wedding. Despite this, the couple were disappointed to find out that only their fathers were eligible to sign their wedding certificate. This coloured their ceremony and experience of that day, as it did not reflect their family setup and cemented their view that this ceremony was not compatible with their view that the wedding should reflect them as a couple.

This kind of experience was common, and the civil ceremony was often described as bureaucratic and formulaic. I interviewed Rebecca over the phone in the summer of 2012. We talked for nearly an hour, with her enthusiastically reminiscing about her wedding, despite it being six years ago. She explained that her humanist wedding was, for her, the 'real wedding', although she confessed to having little mention of humanism in the ceremony and couldn't really tell me what it was. Nevertheless, she was dismissive of the civil ceremony the couple had to undertake, stating that she and her husband had 'treated it as a joke'. The registrar had been 'the worst example'. She mimicked her 'dull' voice saying: 'You have all your friends and family gathered here today'. Rebecca thought this must have been part of a set script and explained that the registrar had read it monotonously, by rote, without amending it to the actual circumstances. As it turned out a number of their family were not present and Rebecca complained: 'It just wasn't the case. We had just the bare minimum of two witnesses.' The civil ceremony was perceived as 'rote', and thus did not honestly reflect anything about the couple.

The humanist wedding

For the reasons outlined above, the civil and religious weddings alienated many secular humanists, often making them feel excluded or detached. These ceremonies are often emptied; they are too disenchanted, and as such, secular humanists set themselves apart from these ceremonies as much as from religious ceremonies. Instead, they claim to offer something specific and concrete to couples: something meaningful. The organization argues that their ceremonies are

> all founded on the shared values and beliefs of Humanism. A Humanist ceremony is therefore *more than, and different to, a merely secular occasion*. (British Humanist Association 2013: 2, emphasis mine)

This means that their ceremonies are more than simply absent of religion, but they encompass and incorporate humanist beliefs and values.

So what sets humanist weddings apart from these other alternatives? The descriptions above demonstrate the incompatibility of religious weddings and civil ceremonies with the secular humanist worldview, particularly because they were perceived as fixed, rote and impersonal. In addition to the gradual decline in the number of Brits declaring themselves as Christian, or engaging regularly with the church (ONS 2012), there has been an increased demand for personalized ceremonies, particularly bespoke funerals (Funeralcare 2011). However, recent research on weddings, including my own, suggests that there is also a growing market for bespoke weddings. In their review of British weddings, Julia Carter and Simon Duncan have found couples are beginning to opt for 'distinctiveness' over 'lavish consumption' (2017: 5).

The ceremonies marketed by Humanist UK attend to these trends, and the organization specifically market their ceremonies as non-religious, personalized alternatives to religious rituals and the strap line for their weddings is 'your wedding, your way'. In addition, their training not only covers conducting the ceremonies but constructs a bespoke event. Usually when interviewing couples, I would ask what defined their wedding as humanist. Most responded that 'it was personal' or 'it reflected us'. As further evidence of this, after attending one humanist wedding with a celebrant named Melissa, we found ourselves behind a huddle of guests who were talking over the ceremony. One remarked: 'It felt like Ben [the groom] was speaking. I could hear his words; the words were really nice.' As such, personalization appears to be a significant reason people choose humanist ceremonies, as they are perceived and often experienced as unique and moving personal event. Not only this, personalization becomes a defining feature of their 'humanist' content, as I will explore further below.

So how is this personalization achieved? It is typical for a humanist ceremony to be written from scratch. After an initial conversation by telephone, the celebrant will make a family visit. A visit can last a couple of hours and is essentially a semi-structured interview in which the celebrant elicits information about the couple and boils it down into a first draft of the script. A few months after their first meeting, and three of four drafts of their script later, Fiona and Bobbie were reunited with their celebrant on 26 May 2102.

Their ceremony took place in a woodland ceremony circle, named Hornbeam Cathedral, owing to the large circle of hornbeam trees. Alongside complex decisions around religious or civil ceremonies, their decision to marry outdoors was a central part of Fiona and Bobbie's reasons for having a humanist wedding. To complement this setting, Fiona had chosen a colour scheme for the wedding: rose pink, pistachio green and antique cream. These aesthetic decisions tied the colours and setting into the theme of a forest wedding. But more importantly through childhood Fiona had enjoyed this aesthetic, sharing photos of herself in loose, long dresses in woodland settings. This childhood image had then later been transposed onto the framework of a wedding. The humanist wedding was the only way to ensure this childhood dream was met, as there is no way at present to have a legally recognized ceremony in this woodland area.

The couple's sartorial choices were central to their decision-making and again demonstrated a focus on personalizing their day (Figure 6.2). Fiona's was white, with a flowing loose fit, and she had on her head a garland of pink roses with green and pink ribbons. Bobbie had decided to wear a kilt in his family tartan of green, indicating his Highland heritage. The mother of the bride had found a corduroy dress in green with pink roses. The visual fit of this dress was clear, but it had another more poignant presence. The dress was the same that Fiona's mother had worn on the day that Fiona was taken home from the hospital after being born. It was apt then that Fiona's mother was to 'give her away', taking her daughter over another threshold, and of course this was more fitting to Fiona's family arrangements. But what is obvious too from the image of the couple is how the celebrant consciously shied away from ostentatious clothing, a point I will elaborate in my discussion below.

Fiona and Bobbie's wedding ceremony lasted around half an hour. The couple were situated in front of the celebrant, facing the guests, and occasionally each other (Figure 6.2). The guests were told by the celebrant that this ceremony had been chosen by the couple because they wanted it to be 'personal to them and to the promises that they are making to each other', and a brief definition of humanism was given: '[The] belief in the one life that we know we have. The time to be happy is now; the place to be happy is here. And humanists know that the way to be happy is to lead good lives, respectful of others and taking responsibility for our lives and our actions.'

This was a fairly standard definition of humanism, typical of all of the weddings I attended, and scripts I was able to see. It was fairly normal too that it should come early in the ceremony. Celebrants explained to me that some couples who were having a humanist ceremony for purely pragmatic reasons would often suggest leaving it out completely. Celebrants were reluctant to do this, and a description of the type above was usually a minimum requirement. Humanism was usually not mentioned explicitly during the rest of the ceremony, but as I will elaborate below, it was implicit in other aspects of the wedding ritual and script.

Figure 6.2 Sartorial choices: The couple and the celebrant. Photo courtesy of the author.

Following the introductions, the celebrant then tells 'the story of us'. The celebrant constructs this directly from the interview with the couple, usually telling the story of how the couple met. Fiona and Bobbie had included a story about their meeting five years earlier; the celebrant Linda told us, 'Fiona was wearing hot pants and wellies, a memorable combination.' There is usually some humour involved if this is suited to the couple, and on this occasion the story of Fiona and Bobbie elicited quite a lot of laughter from their friends and family. This kind of personalization helped create an intimacy with the guests, who required existing knowledge of the couple to fully appreciate the nuances of the story or 'in jokes'.

Couples could also include bespoke vows in the ceremony. I met Ed and Aileen in their north London home, and they had been married less than a year when I interviewed them. They joked about how their vows promised: 'When the zombie invasion comes' Ed would 'forsake all others to protect [Aileen]' and to 'turn off the bedroom light four nights out of seven'. This focus on the quotidian offers practical and tangible examples of how people may incorporate values such as compromise and time spent together into the marriage itself. Therefore, the bespoke nature of these wedding extends beyond aesthetics and fashions; it offers couples the means to make concrete promises to each other, in place of making abstract promises to 'love, honour and obey'.

It was not only crucial for the ceremonies to be personal, but couples also talked about humanist ceremonies allowing them to do something more than legal or religious ceremonies might. Jess and Tim were a young, well-spoken, confident, but reserved couple whom I met in Gloucester at their local wine bar. Their wedding had not taken place and they were in the planning stages. They explained that they were interested in a formal wedding, unlike Ed and Aileen's, or Fiona and Bobbie's. While humanist ceremonies do offer complete freedom for the couple, this had not been the motivating factor. Tim stated:

> We're otherwise not trying to be different for any particular reason – want to keep other bits, they work – it's just the legal and the religious bits that don't. We come from a background where there is more than just the legal part to a wedding.

But even this is an expression of their personal preference – it was the capacity to negotiate what goes in, and out, that was key. For them, the point of a humanist ceremony was to conduct the wedding publicly, recognizing that it was people in their lives that endorsed the union – not a God or supernatural being. It was important to Tim and Jess to take out anything that was remotely archaic or religious, so rather than saying, 'being gathered here in the presence of God', they wanted to refer to 'friends and family'. In fact, the personalization of a humanist wedding is contingent on a network of family.

The secular humanist worldview holds that this is the only life we, as individuals, have. Humanism, in this organized context, is described as a view of the world (a philosophy). Their website states, 'Humanism is understood as an ethical and fulfilling non-religious approach to life involving a naturalistic view of the universe' (humanism. org.uk). Their tagline, 'For the one life we have', refers to the central tenet of secular humanist ontology, that there is no life after death. Secular humanist ceremonies are therefore scripted and choreographed to emphasize the temporal/spatial framework of the here and now, and a personal, biographical time line. The celebrant introduces humanism in the ceremony as 'a belief in the one life that we know we have'. This is consistent with the naturalistic worldview of secular humanists and what Taylor calls the 'immanent frame' (2007). In addition to this, secular humanists explicitly recognize the ethical imperative that people take responsibility for their own actions; that we are relational beings, one human to another; and that we are responsible for the maintenance of these relationships. As such, the wedding becomes a key site to enact secular humanist ontology and ethical requirements, not only because this is a life-cycle ritual but also because it consciously roots itself in the present moment, and the finite lives of the marrying couple.

It is no accident that humanist ceremonies maintain a clear structure and 'arch'. In interviews all celebrants commented in one way or another on the way in which the efficacy of the ceremony rested in the balance of low and high points. Celebrants therefore consciously design the ceremony with the ring exchange as the peak moment. The vows preceding Fiona and Bobbie's exchange of rings formed promises that would be the 'basis of their commitment and their marriage'. The guests remained silent at this stage. The best man came forward with the couple's rings. These were simple and inexpensive, awaiting a time when they would be able to afford to fashion new rings from heirlooms.

> The ring is an ancient symbolic way of expressing lifelong love and commitment, as the circle, having no beginning and no end, is complete and infinite, a symbol of wholeness, eternity and peace. They represent an embrace which binds without imprisoning, a support that reassures without restricting. Wedding rings are worn permanently and with pride. (Script for Fiona and Bobbie, May 2012)

The ring exchange is an expected, recognizable moment. More often than not, there is an emphasis on love as enduring but changeable. Humanist weddings therefore reflect this monogamous norm: that we can have one partner with the hope and expectation of longevity. This is not, however, considered realistic for *all* people, and some will make this clear in the vows they choose, using terms 'as long as possible' rather than the unfashionable phrase 'till death do us part' (Bauman 2013: 5). In fact, many of those eschewing the more definitive vows were children of divorce. As one couple put it, they wanted to come into marriage with their eyes open, and to speak of 'forever' would create an 'elephant in the room', as their divorced parents would be sitting watching.

Yet, as is often the case in humanist weddings, on Fiona and Bobbie's request, the celebrant had lifted these words from the Book of Common Prayer, which contains this line 'till death do us part'. In other ceremonies couples had asked for other, equally formal vows, such as 'Will you love her, comfort her, honour and protect her, and, forsaking all others, be faithful to her as long as you both shall live?' Simon Charsley, in his description of weddings in Scotland, describes these 'call and response' vows as passive (1991). Yet, their inclusion in the humanist ceremony was often precisely because some couples wanted to avoid the anxiety of having to remember personalized promises. Others wanted to maintain the authority and weight conveyed by this kind of language.

So humanist weddings can often look like religious weddings or, more importantly, like a Church of England ceremony. This ensures solemnity. After the wedding I spoke with Linda, who had conducted Fiona and Bobbie's ceremony, asking about the inclusion of the phrase 'till death do us part', a line that Fiona previously described as 'morbid'. Linda explained that humanist ceremonies, because they are created for the couple, need to be rooted in some sense of tradition or formality at certain points in order for the outsiders to recognize it as a ceremony proper, to sense that there has been an occasion and that the couple are not just 'being silly'.

Ritual seriousness and sincerity

Finally, celebrants were keen to emphasize the humanist ceremonies were creative and honest; they did not lack something in the absence of religion. Moreover, they emphasized that these were celebratory events – even funerals – that promises only this life, so humanists felt it should be enjoyed and remembered. This is echoed in an article written by self-declared atheist Susanne Moore in *New Humanist* magazine. This was a personal piece, in which she deliberates over the style of ceremony she should have to mark the birth of her third child. Moore insists that she 'loves ritual' and asserts that one of the problems she has with 'new atheism' is that it fixates on ethics, 'ignoring aesthetics at its peril' (2013). In order to succeed in 'celebrating humanity', she argues that a recognition of secular humanist alternative rituals was necessary, as was attention to the sensual and the celebratory. Secular humanism should be more than simple intellectualism and needed to address the functional and universally human nature of ritual. Moreover, she feels she should not have to give up poetry and the excitement of ritual just because she gives up God. Narratives are, after all, 'fundamentally human'. She has reservations about excessive rationalism, in which the sensual world is rejected. Ceding all the flowers, incense, flames and offerings to 'religion' makes secular humanists 'look like a bunch of Calvinists'. She states that 'ultra-orthodox atheism' may have come to 'resemble a rigid and patriarchal faith itself' and wants to challenge both these conceptions of 'austere' atheism (Moore 2013).

But being presented with a blank slate, couples and celebrants were left with dilemmas. They often became entangled in what had gone before. Celebrants and couples often had to draw on existing ritual scripts, even if these are religious; something colloquially referred to as 'pick-n-mixing'. What is crucial in these assemblages is cultivating what Asad describes as the 'rhetoric of sincerity' (2003: 52). The primary selling point of the humanist wedding is not that it is not religious but that it allows the self/selves to be authentically and sincerely reflected to others. In order to express 'themselves', a couple (or families) may draw on religious or spiritual material within their ceremonies. The religious language which appears in these nonreligious ceremonies does so with the aim of being authentic or sincere, a point I will expand on below.

One example of 'pick-n-mixing' can be found in Fiona and Bobbie's wedding. It was decided that the couple would plant a tree in their ceremony circle, to root their marriage in that space. When we arrived in the ceremony circle, I noticed four objects in the space which looked like small shrines (Figure 6.3). These objects were referenced in the ceremony as part of the tree-planting section:

> We have conducted our ceremony between the earth altar and the air altar. *For those of you who follow astrological predictions, this has added significance as Bobbie is an earth sign and Fiona is a water sign.* So in planting this tree, we will combine those elements still further, as our [groomsmen] will refill the earth around the tree, providing stability and nutrients. (Script for Fiona and Bobbie, May 2012, emphasis added)

Figure 6.3 The ceremony circle: Altars to wind and water. Photo courtesy of the author.

What is notable here is the way in which the celebrant distances herself and others from the tradition of astrology by stating 'for those that believe'. Such rhetorical distancing can tell us much about the desire to express one's authentic self, while not inhibiting others from doing the same. In his case Linda does not want to diminish any meaning these signs might have for the couple, who are central to the ceremony.

In my fieldwork, however, it became clear that there were factions of humanist celebrants, some who were adamant not to include religious sentiment or content in their ceremonies and others who were less able to be so certain on the issue. Melissa and Luna fell clearly into the latter category. Luna remarked:

> Essentially the couple are at the forefront and then we work out what they are comfortable with. So I wouldn't want to read something religious, but if they have someone who wanted or needed to, who felt comfortable with that, I'm lenient, I'd consider a Rabbi or something, or a person reading a passage that means loads to them. I'm not sure I have a right to tell them they can't do that, *as long as I'm not representing it or giving it any authority, who am I to say yes or no?*

It is this leniency, she felt, and this ability to work with the couple and what they want that draws people to a humanist rather than civil ceremony. Luna is realistic that at least a third of her couples are not 'card-carrying Humanists', and this should be OK.

As another example of this, over the weekend spent with Melissa, we discussed the shifts that had occurred throughout her life: from a non-religious upbringing, to becoming a Quaker, to a psychology course that influenced her move from 'faith' to her current humanist ideals and practices. Melissa explained that when she was a practising Quaker, she 'enjoyed the hour of silence but found some of the things that were said more difficult', in particular the reference to spirits. She recalled that in business meetings people would say, 'I felt moved [by the spirit] to say this' and she would think, 'No you weren't!'. Her concern here was that those people were falsely imputing agency on the spirits for actions they should be taking personal responsibility for. Eventually, for Melissa she could not reconcile this set of values or her naturalistic perspective with being a Quaker and left. I also asked Melissa about including spiritual or religious language in her ceremonies. I had been told by one bride whom Melissa had married that they had had a pagan ceremony, and that Melissa had been asked to welcome an approaching white witch or spirit. Melissa seemed surprised when I mentioned this: 'No — I would feel very uncomfortable saying things [like that]. I think I was once asked to say that I could see [an entity emerging in the distance] — but I couldn't say that as that wouldn't be what I was seeing.'

Both of Melissa's descriptions point to the fact that she could not give agency to anything improper. Something she, Linda and Luna recognized is a requirement to remain true to their own beliefs, while accommodating those of others. While some celebrants had no concern saying religious words or drawing on religious frameworks precisely because they did not believe words could be magic, these three were keen to stress the reality of their beliefs and the world as they saw it.

Conclusion

The secular humanist rituals described above dramatize social and moral imperatives and they offer insight into ontological and epistemological frameworks, precisely because they are markers of 'this-worldly' activities, with a focus on the here and now. In creating new ways of articulating secular humanist values, particularly finding space for authentic and sincere self-expression, they also seek to generate certain feelings and emotions: laughter at some points, a sense of awe and solemnity at others. In concluding this chapter, I want to show how Keane's definitions are helpful for thinking through the ethnography presented, but that we may go further than Keane in showing how sincerity and authenticity are intertwined. In fact, the moral compulsion to be authentic is undergirded by a requirement to be sincere. As Hirschkind argues, being 'true to oneself' is both a moral duty but also presupposes a certain kind of sovereign self, displayed through acts of sincerity, which are embodied and have emotional effects (2011: 639).

As I have shown above, the ceremonies focus the gaze on the person and the body through laughter, on sensorial displays or personal artefacts. Moreover, celebrants attempt to physically reorient the ceremonies towards the couple and away from themselves, by dressing in a muted and unremarkable way (see also Engelke 2015a: 29). As such, participants in the wedding are drawn into the experience of that couple in a visceral way – through their involvement and guided focus on the couple. Interestingly,

I was alerted to this kind of physical inclusion, when observing the weddings of couples whom I did not know; I noted that I did feel quite alienated at points in the ceremony, as I lacked the necessary familiarity with the couple to laugh along sincerely. However, this embodied engagement in the ceremony is precisely the kind of experience celebrants want to induce. The point is to personalize the ceremonies – to be true to oneself. But also, these are attempts to create experiences which are entirely different from the secular civil ceremony and the religious (usually Christian) ceremonies.

My research highlights secular humanist assumptions through the visceral reactions positively experienced by my participants as above. But their negative experiences at both religious and civil ceremonies are also telling. In particular, Luna's description of attending a church ceremony is rich with descriptions of distance: being physically at the back of the church and mentally off somewhere planning her dinner. She was not, as secular humanists expect of their own weddings, in the here and now. This demonstrates a level of discomfort with religion, particularly publicly expressed religion.

Luna's experiences and the protestation of Bobbie that non-religious friends having religious ceremonies was hypocritical are also demonstrations of moral positions. For my participants, they chose humanist ceremonies, in part because of a moral imperative *not* to have a church ceremony because it *ought to* hold some level of meaning (Keane 2013). Akin to Latour's 'belief in belief' (2010), the church, like religion, is marked out as a space with particular meaning for those that 'believe'. This can also be expanded to other kinds of beliefs about gods, spirits or 'fetishes', as Melissa and Linda's experiences show. The key point, however, is that if you do not adhere to certain beliefs, performing as if you do is not 'sincere'. More than this, what my participants demonstrate is a tolerance of religion, but an intolerance of insincere adherence to any belief or religious practice.

I have demonstrated how religious content can be included where there is appropriate reason to do so (e.g. cultural or personal resonance with that material). However, while some celebrants will tolerate religious or spiritual content, it is often important to distance themselves from it. For Keane, the 'moral narrative of modernity' is one of liberation from illegitimate rulers, but also from traditions given in 'scriptures, unreal fetishes such as their religious rituals and relics' (2013: 160). The actions of the celebrants Linda and Melissa do more than this; they demonstrate not only the requirement to liberate oneself from 'unreal fetishes' but the desire to demonstrate personal responsibility and sincerity. They contrast themselves with those who do believe, but also positively reinforce their own sincerely held secular humanist beliefs, particularly their self-mastery.

Finally, as I note above, secular humanism is about more than the emptying out of religion from religious rituals. These rituals tell us about the emotional registers of secular humanism, about the focus on love and kinship and the orientation of the secular humanist within a naturalistic framework. The ceremonies are presented as celebrations of humans and humanity, and as displays of positive humanist beliefs, not only as the negation of religion. As such, they shift us from a secular which is purely about intellect, rationality or the mind. Instead, secular humanism is demonstrated here to be a deeply felt, emotional and affective worldview.

Complex Feelings: Catholicism, Gender and the Postsecular Subject in Quebec

Géraldine Mossière

In the province of Quebec (Canada) like in many other secular settings, the visibility of the religious practices of newcomers as well as their claims for public recognition triggered lively debates that dramatically shifted the issue of secularity in the realm of public controversy, social tensions and possible fragmentations. First, in 2007 to 2008, a controversy followed the implementation of a Canadian federal legal measure known as 'reasonable accommodation' that aimed at facilitating accommodation of the religious practices of minorities in public spaces, namely in the workplace and in schools. In the aftermath of lively public debates on the social desirability and acceptability of such accommodations, the Quebecois government commissioned two experts (Charles Taylor, a philosopher, and Gérard Bouchard, a sociologist) to launch a large public reflection over the role and conditions of the integration of religious minorities into the local cultural and social landscape. Among others, the commissioners recommended state intervention with a ban on the wearing of obvious religious signs for civil servants or representatives of the state, including kindergarten educators. The Liberal government never legislated in this regard, either for lack of interest in societal issues or for lack of time before it lost power, or for both, thereby neglecting collective concerns over the definition of Quebecois identity and the possible role Catholicism may occupy in this setting. Some commentators proposed that the commission aimed more at cooling down the public turmoil caused by the push for reasonable accommodations than it did at setting up a legal framework to delineate minorities' claims. Indeed, the commission gave the public the opportunity to express their feelings over the presence of minority groups but did no more than witness the expressions of fears, resentments and hostilities emerging from local individuals as well as from civil actors with respect to religiously and culturally diverse populations henceforth present in the province.

In 2012, four years after the Bouchard-Taylor commission, the *Parti Québécois*, whose agenda draws primarily on provincial sovereignty, won the provincial election partly by resurrecting collective mobilization over issues of national identity. This programme reached its climax when the government proposed the adoption of a Charter of Values (*Charte des valeurs*) that was explicitly designed and presented as a counter-balance for minorities' religious claims. It was not long before the plunge was taken towards portraying the latter as threats to what was described as the Quebecois national identity. The so-called national values mainly advocated gender equity, along with Francophonie and a nebulous view of secularism (*laïcité*), and they purposely depicted religious tenets as male-sexist and patriarchal (Klassen 2015). In a population that thus far had established social categories based on people's migrant status, language and religion, the debate tore apart the province between promoters of 'laïcité' on one side, and advocates of accommodations on the other side, and blurred the lines between groups self-identified as Catholic, religious minorities as well as among the unaffiliated people that self-declare either as atheist, agnostic, spiritual or secular.

Interestingly, both controversies eventually shifted the collective conversation around the issue of gender equity that was portrayed as the benchmark to assess the degree of civilization of otherness, and therefore their potential for recognition. Drawing on the presumption that religions have an oppressive effect on individuals and notably on women, the proponents of this ethnonationalist discourse claim that the state should guarantee gender equity by means of a political regime they call 'laïcité' (from now on 'laicity'). The paramount role of these two controversies in the construction of a 'laic' and nationalistic rhetoric that celebrates the 'Quebecois' identity has been abundantly documented (Bilge 2012, 2013; Bilge et al. 2010; Benhadjoudja 2017). Scholars' reading of the construction of identity nationalism in Quebec addresses laicity as a narration that shows how social actors interpret and instrumentalize this political regime (Ferrari 2009) on the basis of their social and everyday experience of otherness, and specifically their relationship to Islam and Muslims, all the while confusing laicity and secularization (Benhadjoudja 2017). Such literature comes into conversation with critical studies like Joan Scott's (2017) views on the relationship commonly held between secularity, sexual emancipation and gender equity, and Sara Farris's (2017) innovative concept of 'femonationalism' that qualifies right-wing nationalists instrumentalizing women's rights upon political and economic agendas.

While these critical views focus on the sexular ideology of the majority to stigmatize and subjugate minorities, they say little about how and why such rhetoric take roots in specific settings. In the province of Quebec, it can only be enmeshed with a secularization process that occurred as late as it did unexpectedly and rapidly, after long decades of collusive agreement between the political power and the Catholic Church that had become involved in social institutions and symbolic domains. This period that came to an abrupt end in the aftermath of the Quiet Revolution that started in the late 1960s was followed by a reform of national immigration policies in 1967 that facilitated new and larger waves of migrants originating from non-Western countries, resulting in the diversification of the cultural and religious landscape.

By illustrating how the discourse on gender equity has found fertile ground in the context of the province, this contribution proposes to historicize this rhetoric and to situate it in the local imagination.[1] Following Anderson's (1991) views on the role of emotions in national myth-making, I will show how this narrative revolves around an ethnonational myth that stems from an emotionally transformed relationship to Catholicism. Borrowing on Fortier's (2016) look on the policy of affects in embodying political ideals and shaping social and public life, I hope to complement Scott and Farris's discussion on sexualism and femonationalism by introducing the issues of affect and attachment in these processes. Unlike Scott, who situates it within a larger historical discourse on gender that may find modulations and transformations across time, I will consider these representations as part of Quebecois secular cosmology, without arguing whether it resonates with the history of the province. As myths rely on symbolic systems, they also bring about high emotionality around the objects, gestures, words and narratives that convey implicit and shared meanings. Myths hinge therefore on the emotional dimension of human beings that underlie their deeds and practices. In this contribution, I argue that Quebecois myth draws on a particular reading and emotional experience of Catholic history. As this myth is tested by contact with otherness, it also enmeshes Catholic heritage with secularity in subtle and complex ways. As it depicts the subjugation of women seized by the Catholic clergy as a pre-secular moment, it also works as a political ethos to frame collective and individual emotions and build the secular Quebecois body as opposed to the religious one. The notion of political ethos is defined as a 'culturally standardized organization of feeling and sentiment pertaining to the social domains of power and interest' (Jenkins 1991: 140). Although a political ethos is also constructed by states as politicized affect, I focus more on the subjective and phenomenological experience of such collective sentiment by examining individuals' narratives, given that life narratives construe personal and social experiences as meaningful components of an individual and collective myth that unfolds in shared memory.

By reporting the narratives of an ethnographic project that I conducted among Franco-Quebecois (Francophone Quebecois of French national origin) who were born before the Quiet Revolution and raised as Catholics, I account for the ways in which some components of this population hold an affective and embodied paradoxical attachment both to Christianity and secularism, and depict the latter as the continuation of the former. Emotional discourses here reveal a visceral denial of the impact and role of the Catholic Church but also moments of embodied attachment and recognition of its paramount role and of the cultural Catholicism in shaping modern Quebec society. Statistics confirm this apparent contradiction (Wilkins-Laflamme forthcoming): according to the 2011 census, 75 per cent of Quebecois identify as Catholics, although this number does not say anything about the level of practice that has dramatically decreased in the province in the last decade (in 2013, only 18 per cent of the population attended masses one a month, and 11 per cent at least one a week). The same data show that the number of unaffiliated reaches 12.1 per cent of the total population, a number on the rise, covering laics, a-religious or anti-religious people and atheists, agnostics and humanists.

In this chapter, I focus on these categories of so-called unaffiliated respondents and consider them as revealing of the underlying dynamics regarding the emotional construction of secularity in the aftermath of Catholic hegemony. While the narratives I have collected echo the common debate that Saba Mahmood (2009) frames as opposing the secular to the religious threat – more usually framed as religious extremism – they also shed light on the normative conceptions of subject, religion and secularization that, in Quebec, bring the issue of memory and gender into the discussion. I first briefly present the ethnographic research and how anthropological literature on emotions may provide an insightful framework to understand my respondents' narratives.

Life narratives among Quebecois babyboomers: An ethnographic project

The ethnographic research I have been conducting since 2014[2] focuses on the generation of Franco-Quebecois babyboomers defined as Francophone people who were settled in Quebec for at least two generations. They are people who were born Catholic in the 1950s, a time when children were socialized in school institutions by means of lessons called 'petit catéchisme'. The project aims at documenting the religious trajectory or 'meaning paths' these individuals have experienced as their biographical path was shaped first by ultramontane Catholicism that was deeply enmeshed in all domains of the society, and then by the dramatic changes the Second Vatican Council introduced,[3] which were linked with broader cultural shifts. While the church's withdrawal left an ethical and symbolic void in the province, the religious landscape was soon filled by the new religious and spiritual resources stemming from the diversification of the province, however, not without launching a collective discussion on the conditions and possibilities for this new social fabric to frame a *vivre ensemble*. With a methodology based on life narratives, I situate the babyboomers' life cycle as it resonates with the religious, spiritual and cultural new design of the province, coupled with the social, political and global changes and uncertainties that are continuously shaping collective identity. Following Ricoeur (1988), I see narratives as constructions that are designed so as to give meaning to biographical experiences and to the social and political conditions of their production. In Quebec, these experiences are seen through the challenges related to the secularization process and to the encounter with alterity. Each informant is met twice, with a six-month delay, in order to better grasp the changes and transformations as well as the reconstruction of these narratives with their discrepancies, hesitations, doubts and contradictions. The informants were first interviewed in 2014, when the Charter of Values was under debate, while the last informants are currently holding their second interview.[4]

Respondents were asked to recall and report their biographical path in relation to their religious experience and the social and political events that the province was going through. This includes questions dealing with education, family life, marriage, parenthood, health, divorces and break-ups, bereavements and so on, and these alongside Quebec's social and political events. Drawing on these data, I try to sketch the respondents' context of living and universe of meaning. The 38 respondents that I have met may be described as follows: nearly half of them are men (21) while two-thirds are born after 1952 (23), the eldest being 88 years old. More than two-thirds of the respondents live in Greater Montreal (29) and belong to a middle-class socio-economic category[5] (33). Single respondents (16 with 4 after a divorce), married (13 with 1 second marriage) or living in cohabitation (8 with 2 after a divorce) are distributed quite equally, with only one widow.

Religious identifications, however, are variegated: five respondents claim they are atheist, with two mentioning their humanist values; two say they are agnostic, with one showing curiosity for energies and martial arts; and one embraced Islam. Six respondents claim to be unaffiliated ('nones'), though three of them demonstrate a Buddhist-inspired form of spirituality or a religious quest. The twenty-four respondents who identify as Catholics have diverse religious beliefs and practices: five claim they are non-believers and non-practitioners, although one of them is committed in his parish's social activities; two have reconverted to Catholicism; two depict themselves as believers and practitioners, though one circumscribes her practices within the private sphere; interestingly, seven define their practices with diverse and creative labels: three as 'part-time' for important occasions ('Catholique à gros grain', or 'sort of Catholic'); three as 'minimal' and strictly private; one as 'personal practice'. A single respondent states he is distanced from practice and belief. What is more, two respondents identify with Catholicism but they nuance this self-ascribed identity with features like 'by default' or 'with reserve'. Five respondents claim they distance themselves from Catholic identity and beliefs, all the while demonstrating a deep attraction for the church's material culture and the aesthetics of rituals, which qualify them to belong to an unexpected category of 'non-believing practitioners'.

All these respondents received religious socialization during childhood through social institutions (schools, churches), whereas the influence of parents is more diverse, with some being described as distanced from religion and others as themselves 'victims of a religious discipline embodied without subjectivity'. Unsurprisingly, respondents report they questioned their religious heritage at the time of adolescence, quite often in the aftermath of a personal move, quest, travel, curiosity that led them to shift their standpoint on Catholicism. This was sometimes a result of the knowledge they developed about other religions, by reading, surfing on the net, meeting other people of various faiths and by travelling.

The respondents were invited to frame religious beliefs, belonging and path within their personal biography, and to revisit their relationship to religion by mobilizing the language of reflexivity, intimacy as well as subjectivity. As such, the exercise of putting the self into narration draws on language, including non-verbal language, as a form of 'emotion talk' (Lutz/Abu-Lughod 1990); it performs a personal commitment to one's own and to collective memory.

Narratives, emotions and the construction of the self

In a context where secularism is usually associated with modernity and rationality, it may appear to be an oxymoron to look at the emotional dimension of subjectivation in order to understand the construction of the secular self. To clarify this process, we need to problematize the relationship between emotions, embodiment and the subject.

The anthropologist Michelle Rosaldo first delineated the concept of emotions by relating the realm of interiority and subjectivity with embodied experiences that are culturally and socially informed. According to her, the self and affects are modelled by cultural tropes as well as by social relationships. Fortier (2016) goes further and distinguishes emotions and affects by defining the latter as 'a generic category of emotions and feelings, including embodied and sensory feelings through which we experience the world, and through which worlds, subjects and objects are enacted and brought forth'; it follows that affects are '*at once* deeply felt and embodied *and* social and public' (p. 139). For Rosaldo, the expression of emotions includes a social action as well as a particular language on the self, which leads her to consider emotions as 'embodied thoughts':

> Emotions are thoughts somehow 'felt' in flushes, pulses, 'movements' of our livers, minds, hearts, stomachs, skin. They are embodied thoughts, thoughts seeped with the apprehension that 'I am involved.' Thought affect thus bespeaks the difference between a mere hearing of a child's cry and a hearing felt – as when one realizes that danger is involved or that the child is one's own. (Rosaldo 1984: 143)

As she argues that emotions also express a sense of personal commitment of the subject to the social world,[6] Rosaldo considers emotions and emotional expressions not only as discourses on the self and society but also as actions to take so as to impinge on them. Interestingly, Reddy (1997) emphasizes the auto-transformative capacity of the emotional discourses and deeds, arguing that expressing affects transforms what is felt in reality. Emotional acts and expressions would therefore have the ability to make true what they refer to or what they represent as they intersect the experiences of feeling, will and power, or of feeling, thinking and creating. This 'emotional' linguistic category where the referent emerges through its wording would therefore bear its own effectiveness.

While this literature suggests that embodied emotions are situated upstream of the discursive process, I contend that the exercise of narrating the self and of construing collective memory actually acts as a channel for embodied emotions, that is to say that tropes or 'embodied thoughts' that take form within these narratives are part of a technology of self-fashioning where narration ritualizes the self and the group. In other words, as affects follow feeling rules that are embodied in the flesh, they also frame the narrative performances through which the subject produces herself. For my respondents, conveying emotions within a narrative form conditions a specific process of subjectivation (Foucault 2001) that governs the formation of the secular subject. In this perspective, 'emotional language' is the means through which secular subjectivity becomes performed.

In Quebec, the decline of the Catholic Church in Quebec also meant the loss of the Christian trope and grid to read and feel the world. This void left an open space for emotional life and embodied experiences to become criteria for the comprehension (*Verstehen*) of the self and the environment, and to celebrate the quest for sense of authenticity of the secular subject like the philosopher Charles Taylor (2002) has argued. In the next sections, I show that the production of the secular subject hinges on the visceral assertion of the unencumbered self, freed from the influence of any institutional authority and eager to give centrality to the emotional dimension of his reading of the collective experience. The ambivalent emotional experience that this narrative conveys actually vacillates between detachment and resentment with respect to the religious historical institution, on the one hand, and at the same time affective attachment and recognition of its cultural contribution to local identity and memory, on the other hand. In interviews, the affects that display this ambivalence were materialized through the semantics as well as the non-verbal expressions (laughs, silence, repetition, hesitation etc.) that gave rhythm to the narratives.

Ambivalent feelings: Attachment, rejection and the shaping of Catholic post-secularism

While gender equity as well as the emancipation of women work as a collective Quebecois political ethos, it frames a complex structure of feelings regarding the collective legacy of Catholicism. As a matter of fact, whether my respondents identify as atheist, agnostic or humanist, their critiques of religion are neither total nor absolute. Rather, they balance from detachment or resentment – in particular when it comes to articulating their contemporary secular and liberal personae around gender issue – and attachment or affection – when it comes to contrasting themselves form 'illiberal' others. As contacts with religious alterity challenge the common collective narrative, ambivalences and contradictions also reveal emotional dynamics of attachment and rejection to Christianity, its materiality, symbolic realm, ethical message as well as social and political role. When faced with ethical and religious otherness, these local affects seem driven by a deeply anchored cultural anxiety that takes its roots in the regime of collective survival that dominated consciousness for long and that is still vivid among certain segments of the population (Burchardt 2017). This affective tie is best expressed through the nostalgia that narratives somehow convey and that conflates these ambiguous feelings with a complex assemblage of individual and collective memory of Catholicism (Hervieu-Léger 2008). In her study of nostalgic Kemalism in contemporary Turkey, the anthropologist Özyürek presents 'memory as a presentist act that reconfigures contemporary, rather than past, relations and structures of power' (2006: 154) through affective-based representations that qualify founding myths and ideologies. Likewise, Svletana Boym (2001) considers nostalgia in a prospective way in that 'the fantasies of the past determined by the needs of the present have a direct impact on the realities of the future'; nostalgia would then intersect individual biography and the biography of groups or nations. The narratives I have collected show indeed how personal affect is infused with collective memory. As they put into play fragments of collective memory, these complex feelings are part of what Boym labels 'reflective nostalgia' that 'dwells on the ambivalences of human longing and belonging and does not shy away from the contradictions of modernity'. While this ethics of the doubt draws on the tension between longing and critical thinking, the study of Quebecois narratives reveals the various dimensions of their attachment to Catholicism and the complex structure of feelings they unfold. For the Francoquebecois I have met, reflective nostalgia is torn apart between the irrepressible attraction of feeling home, and the lingering anxiety of reviving past trauma.

Most respondents rationalize the role of religion and present it as a positive asset in times of social, economic and cultural anomy, mentioning the coping role it may hold in context of social and personal turmoil. For example, Marc comments: 'It [religion] must exist for some people. They need it, they live in countries that are very different from ours. Often you hang on to what you can. It is not always thought and established with rules but it is according to where you are that makes that it could be something else.' This rationale of religions presented as a comfort, a resource or a need that helps answer existential questions related to death and quest for meaning displays its own ambivalence when respondents relate it to their biographical experiences when, as children, they were exposed to the 'petit catéchisme' and its disciplinary measures that aimed at embodying a moral ethos. The emotional ambiguity unfolds in narratives between the fear of God's ire, the struggle for salvation and the sanction of hell on the one hand, and feeling of openness, tolerance, liberation, solidarity, charity and affection on the other hand. Interestingly, two respondents situate the shift from the latter to the former in their life cycle when, as teenagers, they started to question religious norms and challenge notions of sin. As references to individual sexual awakening and to the liberation of gender relationships embody this definition of religion, they also conflate it with collective memory. For example, Pierre comments the presence of Catholicism and its social impact: 'At one point, there were a lot of nuns in schools, hospitals, it was a big thing! It was for the better but it was conducted by a bunch of chauvinist men who were trying to make everybody believe that it would turn bad if we did not go to the church.'

Ambiguously enough, Catholicism is also seen by many as playing a formative role in the Quebecois national identity. Most of my respondents report a large attachment to the contribution Catholicism had as much regarding their personal experience as for the development of social institutions in Quebec, and to its modernization to some extent. Narratives refer to Catholicism as a shelter and a protection for the anxiety and feeling of threat of English assimilation Quebecois experienced, subtly suggesting thereby that Catholicism could play a similar role in coping with the supposed threat posed by the issue of integration of religious minorities in the province. For instance, Pierre acknowledges: 'I believe that we live a Judeo-Christian civilization and that our social and political structures, all our history has been heavily influenced by religion. In our societies, some very nice things, we owe them to religion. The Quiet Revolution, well ... but it remains that religion and religious institutions have had considerable contributions in our history', a contribution that some respondents propose to extend in the present, by recycling churches' spaces for social events, for example, 'not in a religious spirit, but simply, in a spirit of society' (Bruno). This nostalgia of Catholic heritage enmeshes with present, future as well as individual's and society's progress as some respondents also consider Catholicism as a springboard for learning and adapting to be in the world. For some respondents, their religious education positively conveyed rules to follow and, more specifically, the sense of the sacred, as well as it prepared them to open themselves to otherness. For example, Jeanne says, 'Catholicism led me to know better other religions, Buddhism, Hinduism, to be curious about what others believe, how others live, it brought me this, I am sure of it.' A few respondents also expressed feelings of gratitude when they mentioned the opportunities and tools that Catholicism taught and granted them in order to develop their own critical view on religion, which ironically opened the way to visceral feelings of indignation with respect to religions' treatment of their followers. For Marc,

Catholicism has had a positive impact because it opened my eyes … I have been able to compare what they said and what they were doing and to see that it was not compatible, it was nonsense. I went to St Peter's (Basilica) in Rome. I saw all the wealth, so much wealth! And if you go to China too, in some temples, the Buddha is in gold. And poor kids have nothing to eat, is it relevant?

While the decline of the Catholic Church that follows this critical stance on religion is now experienced as a collective-shared trope that encapsulates individuals and emotions regarding Catholicism's historical role, these narratives also reveal the emotional ambiguity and the complex interplay of rejection and attachment to the church that dominates my respondents' relationship to Catholicism and, more largely, to religions in the public and private spheres.

The intriguing category of respondents who claim no beliefs while reporting a peculiar type of practice sheds light on some of the determinants of the emotional dialectics that governs the formation of the secular in Quebec. A few respondents with agnostic profiles actually turn their religious institutional heritage into an aesthetic lively experience. Their attachment to Catholic materiality and liturgy supports the *poiesis* of their life where religious and spiritual symbolic systems trigger feelings of contemplation and fascination as well as a sense of embodied sacredness. Here, historically informed sensitivity to Catholicism shifts into the realm of sensorial and bodily experience, which value emotional and religious aesthetics. For instance, Bruno regrets that when the Quebecois rejected the Catholic Church, they denied at the same time the historical and architectural beauty of the churches as well as the impressive solemnity of their rituals. Jean (75, Montreal, non-believer practitioner) compares his artistic leisure to prayers:

Praying, this is like a way to elevate yourself … It is this capacity that belongs to man to get out of himself … For me, it is an artistic process. When I was retired, I started to follow painting lessons and I found it amazing because for one hour, I was doing something and I was only doing that. It was my pleasure and I was like going into a trance. And I think that there is a lot of beauty in religious manifestations, a lot of beauty, in the monuments, in the prayers, in the rituals, there is beauty.

As respondents cherish this sensorial and bodily experience they relate to feelings of sacredness, they shy away as soon as this set of symbols is ascribed institutionalized meaning, which they associate with men's intervention. Lyne's trajectory exemplifies this process: 'I realized I really like some rituals in Catholicism, I like to going on my knees, I like hearing the songs, but I get annoyed by the lyrics, they seem empty of meaning for me.' Lyne compares Catholic liturgy to Buddhist rituals whose focus on experience is highly attractive to her:

I went to some Tibetan teachings and I couldn't believe in what they were saying' regarding reincarnation, if you die you can come back as an earthworm, that doesn't stick with me. But I very much like their rituals, getting on your knees and totally lying down, they would do it five times. I like hearing them singing,

I especially like the Tibetan sounds, I can feel they fill my body. But I do not like hearing their translation in French, it loses its magic!

While Quebecois secular subjectivity conflates in complex ways in both resentment and attachment to the Catholic Church, and to a larger extent to institutionalized religion, it also shifts religious sensitivity in the realm of sensorial experiences that unfold on the body as an unencumbered site. It follows that the emancipation of the body from any ideological constraint makes it a site of individual and collective emotional historically informed expression. As resentment with respect to Catholicism draws on the status and representations of the body, the sensations and experiential possibilities that the body may also provide turn the tensions between sacred experience and singular institution into a common celebration of spirituality. In Boym's view, nostalgia and modernity do not come into contradiction since the former would 'not merely be an expression of local longing, but the result of a new understanding of time and space that made the division into "local" and "universal" possible'. Indeed, resentment towards the church is conveyed through a narrative that substitutes a vision of a universal and flexible spirituality for overall religious dogma depicted as fixed and symbolically limited. For example, Lyne considers that quitting the Catholic Church opened up her mind because 'when I talk about my values, like mutual aid, you find it in Catholic religion. But for me, this is universal, you can find it anywhere. I can also give it a much more social meaning. This is survival.' In this narrative, Catholic heritage is described as part of a universal cosmology that revolves around nature as a means for true reconnection of man to himself. This reconnection triggers a sense of personal harmony that is embodied in feelings of wellness and emotional balance. As for Pierre, he wonders whether religion is a need and he explains: 'Maybe … You always need to have a spirituality in some ways. Me, I find it in readings, I like …. I feel … I come from the seaside and it always touches me when I go back there, the sound of the waves, the stars, the evenings.'

This feeling of unity that overcomes the ambivalent reflective nostalgia is rationalized within a humanist frame, like Annette's narrative reveals:

The purpose of humanity is to bring human beings toward more perfection. They are not at war, they help each other, they share positive values. They develop themselves, how should I say … at their best. The purpose of humanity is to be a human being who is open to others. It is to be a human being who tries to do his best all the while respecting others and his environment.

This shift from Catholic values to the humanist repertoire is common to all our respondents, including those who self-identify as atheist. Bruno reports:

[Our philosophies] should be based on a certain idea of the common good and living, and which rules we should give to each other. My freedom finishes where yours starts. And then we should find the best way, but I do not need something above me who is gonna tell me … and who got it from an external force to do that.

Visceral and vivid rejection of Catholic authority is therefore balanced by a pragmatic concern for ethical and aesthetic issues, especially when the project of identity transmission to offspring is at play. Bruno's narrative exemplifies how education project is negotiated between a rationale thinking based on agency and liberal choice, on the one hand, and the yearning for being part of a family heritage informed by collectively shared catholic legacy on the other hand:

> I raised my son with the same principles of education that my father gave me. Not with the same methods but I would say with the same principles. I mean: 'this is it, you have to do that.' Still, I hope that what I ask my son to do makes more sense than what my father used to ask me to do. In other terms, I used to tell my son to do things because I thought it was the right thing to do while my father used to tell me to do this because the priest had advised him to.

As narratives show the lingering presence of Catholic memory and experience, they also unfold individual and collective reflective nostalgia in the politics of doubt that conflates the Quebecois Catholic material and social heritage and the complex structure of affects it shaped, with a yearning for sensorial experience and a longing for a renewed global ethics.

The construction of a collective myth and its ritualization

The critical discourse on religions that I have collected hinges on gender issue as well as on the local cause of the feminist battle to justify itself. While this embodied narrative on the freedom of women and emancipation of female bodies leverages local myths that describe the *Grande Noirceur* as a period of oppression for women and family life, it also contributes to the delineation of the collective memory within local secularized tropes. After the British Conquest of 1760, the population of Quebec (Canada) plunged into a regime of cultural, economic and political survival to which the Catholic Church largely contributed by governing large segments of many social institutions and shaping local consciousness in an ideology of resistance to British political and cultural hegemony. This period that is now remembered as the *Grande Noirceur* (the Great Darkness) came to an abrupt end during the 1960s and 1970s while the long-standing regime of survival fixed a feeling of cultural anxiety in local affects (Burchardt 2017). Driven by the process of liberalization and modernization of the province and in the aftermath of long and internal debates, the Catholic Church gradually withdrew from the social institutions it had regulated thus far (schools, hospitals) and lost much of its social and political control over local population as well as individual and collective conscience. This radical moment, known as the Quiet Revolution, mainly focused on the condition of women, who are usually depicted as the primary victims of the long Catholic domination. During this time, women were seen as being subjugated within their marriages as well as by priests as they were prohibited from using contraception and urged 'not to impede family', that is to have many children. While this politics of family is now depicted as a strategy of resistance to the British invaders and was supposedly delineated by local elites to oppose French Canadians' demographic force to the British economic and political domination, it was followed by a liberalization process that mainly revolved around the emancipation of women. The latter drastically modified and, in one sense, 'deinstitutionalized' gender relationships for more equity and individual autonomy with a decline of normativity, notably regarding matrimonial practices, parenthood and cohabitation. With such transformation of social behaviours came along new practices regarding religion, as well as what is more often called 'spirituality' when the country opened its doors to new cultural and religious diversity. As a result, coupled with the revitalization of Indigenous spiritualties, the province became a fertile ground for the hippy transnational movement and the sexual liberation it promoted.

The narratives I have collected insightfully exemplify the paramount role that the issue of the condition of women plays in the construction of the founding myth of modern Quebec. As the discursive rejection of Catholic heritage subtly conflates with the celebration of women's autonomy, it is subsumed in an overall critical discourse on institutional religions and the status they grant to women. Like Scott (2017) observed in France, this yearning to distance from religion builds the secular body and its sensibilities by defining the secular subject negatively around unauthorized gestures, postures and emotions associated to religion. Notions of embodiment and virtue are thereby recast within a feminist frame in such a way that the sexularist discourse emerges as one of the pivotal elements around which secularism comes to be articulated. The respondents I met share deep emotional resentment towards all religions they depict as oppressive institutions, all of which are immediately related to the Catholic Church's style and to its historical hegemonic role in the province. The Catholic Church is criticized for the abusive authority its officials (priests) exerted over the population, mentioning paedophilia, domination of the body and sexuality of women and normative construction of gender relationships. Bruno (64, Montreal, self-identified as atheist) says, 'it is more the churches than the religions. I think that the churches, let's say the priests or even the imams, it is all the same stuff. Those are people who want to control the society. For me, this is very very clear when I look at history. This is what happened, they allied with political power to control the population.' In this context, historical poverty deprivation of the Quebecois population is seen as a condition that facilitated social oppression, like Marc (72, Montreal, self-identified as atheist) explains: 'some people went to the boarding schools because the families were too large and there was nearly nothing to eat. So they were sent to the boarding schools so that maybe they become clergymen. But we came to learn that they did not all become priests. They were abused [sexually] more than anything else.'

Discursive sensibilities centre around the historical fight for women's social recognition and legal rights that seems to be embodied in a particular gendered habitus where women are attributed autonomy and agency as normative and naturalized qualities:

> The Quiet Revolution changed the world, I mean it brought freedom, sexual freedom, freedom of thought, freedom for women. In 1961, women were not allowed to borrow money at the bank, their husbands had to sign. And they were not allowed to vote, they were only allowed in 1947. And this happened because we

rejected religion. Because if we stayed like the Irish people, who refused divorce, referendum, well … Here it happened, differently. Possibly there are pros and cons. I must say the clergy is really important in Quebec too, French language has been protected thanks to them. (Pierre)

The negotiation of the secular in Quebec therefore heavily hinges on a historically informed visceral sensitivity to women's sexuality and freedom. Jeanne (68, Montreal, agnostic) compares the veiled Catholic nuns who cloister in convents to Muslim female believers who demonstrate their faith in public spaces: 'In Islam, all women have to veil, this builds a power relationship between veiled women and ordinary women, it is a relationship of superiority. It makes the Muslim woman looks like the pure woman, the woman who does not commit any sin. She reflects a sense of purity in some way, you see, *they* are pure, while *we* are impure!'

While the women's narratives embody disruptive feelings regarding virtue, men report critical thoughts regarding patriarchal control and gendered inequity. Pierre (70, Montreal, agnostic) comments, for instance, that 'when you look at women in religions, you realize that all religions are male. God is a man, Allah, Buddha. Try to find one woman in there, except one servant like Mary, except Mary Magdalene. It seems to have been invented by men so as to get control over women. For me, this is what religions are made for.' The positive contribution of men to the construction of this myth on women's subjugation by religion is validated by the only woman in our sample who self-identifies as atheist:

I have had an *avant-gardiste* father in that my father was committed in our education. He had two daughters and he used to take care of us like today's fathers are required to take care of kids. He changed diapers, he took us out, he drove us to our activities. I had the father that all other kids were dreaming about: He used to drive us to our activities and the other kids' fathers were not there. Me, my father used to come, I was proud, I was happy! At home too, actually, I believe it is my father who used to help more for homework. He was more patient than my mother.

As the recognition and promotion of emancipation of women and gender equity are part of modern Quebecois discourse, these tenets get a performative value when they come to encounter other religions in a context where the presence of practising religious minorities in the local landscape puts the founding myth of the modern Quebecois society to the test. When our interlocutors respond to non-Christian traditions, they celebrate the freedom of Quebecois women and ritualize criticism of the subordinated role and status of women in other religions, driven by the presumption (derived from their memory of Catholicism) that religions oppress women.

Nearly all respondents report they share great interest in understanding religions and the majority of them say they have studied, explored or travelled so that they could be in touch with all kinds of religious traditions. The sense of others' religion they supposedly developed allows them to extend their criticism of Catholicism to all religions with the exception of one respondent who considers Buddhism as more respectful of the human being than any other tradition, mainly because of its non-theistic approach. For example, Marc gauges each religion through the lenses of the status it attributes to women:

> Religions, this is a male society: Buddhism, I cannot embrace this one because, since I am someone who always pushes women to accomplish themselves, I cannot buy this concept. This is totally opposed to what I have always supported all my life. Islam, women are nothing in Islam and I cannot support that. Equity is equity! You are born with a particular colour, this is not your choice. What about the *kirpan*? This is even worth more? Because women, they do not even exist!

During an interview, Jeanne openly agrees as far as the presence of religious minorities is concerned, except when it comes to the status of women:

> When I attend Muslim activities, sometimes in the park next door, and I see women sitting alone and men sitting alone by their side; men are dressed with shorts, very light and very stylish and when I see women dressed with their potato sack, and they are not really smiling and they are stuck in little packages all together, and then I tell myself there is a lack of communication between men and women. And we would not like to return back … we would not like to go back to this in Quebec, to this control of religion over men and women. Because in the 1960s, in Quebec, if I remember well, there were a lot, really a lot of black dresses [nuns].

The hesitations and perplexity that frame the respondents' narratives embody fears and apprehensions regarding the resonance of new religions with shared memory that is experienced as a collective trauma. This critical view of religions revolves around a Manichaean distinction between categories of religion that are acceptable because they are respectful of individuals and their social milieu, and others that are considered sectarian and deemed as dangerous. This ideological distinction between religions relates to a Western orientation that Masuzawa (2005) has brought to light by showing how, following a linguistic comparative approach, Buddhism has been related to Indo-European religions and portrayed as world religions capable of intellectual subtleties, as opposed to Islam that is ascribed to the Semitic category, whose significance would be more limited.

At the same time, respondents report awareness that religious offences and crimes stem less from the institutions themselves than from the men that compose them. They mention the violent nature of men and their ontological inclination for power. For example, Pierre said: 'Look, all that occurs on the planet, not to mention what we do not know. Because religions they are not transparent, we do not even know what happens. Wherever men are, there is brutality.' As the presence and visibility of religious minorities is depicted as a threat to this local identity, the discursive rejection of religious practices is lived as affective moments that trigger collective celebration of secular values, among which gender equity is represented as the core of Quebecois identity. Examining the role of the non-secular in the construction of secularism in Quebec therefore emphasizes the zones of tensions, doubts and affects, and indeterminacy where it is negotiated.

Conclusion: Religious sensitivity and the 'post-secular subject'

Revisiting biographical narratives in the light of the (omni)presence of the Catholic Church in Franco-Quebecois everyday life and Quebec social structure shows the affective ambivalent relationship that the Quebecois maintain with Catholicism as their historical collective experience and, as a consequence, the recognition of the role of Catholicism in the construction of secularity in Quebec. These narratives construct the Quebecois secular subject around a 'secular affect' (Mahmood 2009) that is embodied on women's sexuality and social freedom that is seen as the privileged site of critique of Catholic memory, and the Church's subjugation of family life. However, Catholicism, notably in its post-council version, is also felt as a renewed, favourable and tolerant paradigm that facilitates the experience of modernity, secularism and a relationship to diversity; in this regard, it plays a special role in framing post-secular consciousness and subjectivities.

As the secularization of the province occurred within a short and drastic period of local transformation, it is likely to epitomize the process at work in the transformation towards secularization. The role of women's emancipation in secular discourse is indeed nothing new; it is part of a master standardized rhetorical narrative that has been circulating in the secular world and has lately found fertile ground as an authoritative voice in the province of Quebec. In Quebec however, while critiques against the abuses of the Catholic Church and, to a great extent, traditional religions are framed upon common tropes of rejection of religious institutions that are part of Quebecois modern mythology, narratives and their embodied thoughts actually display an affective relationship to Catholicism that is seen as facilitating the secular common identity. This contribution shows how secularization coalesces the emotional rejection of Catholic common history, the attachment to current Catholic heritage and their visceral projection on relationship to Otherness. This complex structure of feelings allows the construction and the perpetuation of local myths, whose sustainability paradoxically depends on their emotional potential to mobilize individual and collective remembrance; the production of the post-secular sensitivity that follows suggests that secularism could be a historically contingent process.

In his discussion on post-secular societies, Habermas (2008) alludes to the affluent societies, to which he includes Canada, 'where people's religious ties have steadily or rather quite dramatically lapsed', while religion is still assigned a public influence and relevance, following the example of the vicarious religion the sociologist Grace Davie (2000) identified in Great Britain. In Europe, the influence of religion would derive from the growing presence and visibility of immigrants' religiosity, the role religious institutions play in public debates and influence of religion on globalization processes. As all these elements contribute to produce a post-secular consciousness, the sociologist Michelle Dillon (2012) puts forth the idea of a post-secular Catholicism in Catholic settings. The narratives of my respondents suggest indeed that in Quebec, Catholicism plays a significant role in shaping of local consciousness. However, this post-secular imagination would not draw on the public involvement of the Church in public sphere since the Quiet revolution has deprived the institution of any legitimacy with respect to social and political affairs. Rather, it relies on the constant work of memory over which individuals and society give themselves to, as a collective ritual, thereby turning the lingering presence of Catholicism into a vivid nostalgia that shapes local affects and builds a post-secular sensitivity. As the singular historicity of Quebec made Catholicism and the Church the drivers of the secularization process in the province, it also granted them prominent part in the interplay between local affects and a political ethos, and the hectic path of the post-secular subject.

Secular Self-fashioning against 'Islamization': Beauty Practices and the Crafting of Secular Subjectivities among Middle-Class Women in Istanbul

Claudia Liebelt

In his essay on the secular body, Hirschkind wonders why it is that the statement '"He lives a very religious life" gives us some sense of the shape of a life, [while] "He lives a very secular life" tells us almost nothing (except, negatively, that the person does not engage in practices of worship)' (2011: 641).[1] For the residents of contemporary Istanbul, the latter statement may not sound as non-sensical as it possibly does elsewhere and for others. What is more, in an atmosphere of political tension and the common rhetoric of an increasing secular-Islamic divide of society after the consolidation of power and increasingly authoritarian rule of the conservative, pro-Islamic Justice and Development Party (Adalet ve Kalkınma Partisi, AKP), 'the secular body', for many of my research participants in Istanbul, assumed a concrete shape and role. In this chapter, I focus on a particular group of middle-aged to elderly women, those commonly termed '(self-)conscious menopausal women' (*bilinç sahibi menopozlu kadınlar*) in the public discourse (Erol 2011), who were confronted with the first signs of ageing during the early boom of the urban beauty sector in the 1990s, a period in which the menopause became public knowledge in Turkey. The following will show how self-identified secular women of this generation readily understood their secular self-fashioning through bodily practices and public performance as an act of immediate concern.

While the 'secular-Islamic divide' may have little explanatory value as an analytical term in regards to Turkey at large, it has a strong mobilizing potential in everyday life and, as Deniz Kandiyoti put it, in its recent past assumed the quality of a 'national obsession' (2012: 514). Far from being merely an abstract notion or argument, on the background of the political, cultural and economic marginalization of the secular elite in recent decades, the defence of 'secular' lifestyles, spaces and aesthetics has become a deeply embodied, classed, gendered and affect-laden disposition. While they might share little else, for many middle-class women I met as part of an anthropological research project on the role of beauty for the making of middle-class femininities in various beauty salons and clinics, fitness clubs and tattoo studios in various parts of central Istanbul between 2013 and 2015, 'secularism' was an ethical self-fashioning they carried on and with themselves into the public space.

In analysing the fashioning of their secular subjectivities, I shall take care not to repeat the hackneyed argument of Turkey as a country torn between its Western (purportedly secular) and Muslim identity. While Istanbulite women may self-identify as secular, they continue to live in what Sertaç Sehlikoğlu (2016: 144), following Babayan and Najmabadi (2008), calls an 'Islamicate context' that is characterized by shared sensibilities over public sexualities and a particular culture of *mahremiyet* (intimacy). Nevertheless, similar to the playing of 'romantic poets' cassettes in Cairo's public space described by Hirschkind, there is a secular form of urban middle-class self-fashioning that at least from the perspective of those who perform it 'contribute[s] to the project of the secular' by being 'part of the movement of negation and overcoming by which the secular emerges from the religious' (2011: 643). The aesthetic sensibilities in question 'are not [in themselves] secular (nor religious, for that matter), but ... have been encompassed by and appropriated within the narrative of the secular emancipation from religion' (2011: 643).

Coined by Greenblatt in an analysis of sixteenth-century artists, 'self-fashioning' implies 'a characteristic mode of address to the world', which has the power 'to impose a shape upon oneself [as] an aspect of the more general power to control identity – that of others at least as often as one's own' (1980: 1). Similar to what Greenblatt describes, in Turkey's current political climate, embodied self-fashioning for secular middle-class women involves 'some experience of threat, some effacement or undermining, some loss of self' (1980: 9). For the secular and often, but not exclusively, Kemalist middle-class women this chapter will go on to portray, this threat is typically described as one of Islamization and includes a sense of loss of cultural and economic hegemony as well as what Berna Turam (2013, 2015), in her recent work on spatial politics in the Istanbul neighbourhood of Teşvikiye, has analysed as an encroachment of a sense of 'freedom'. Nevertheless, it would be a mistake to describe my interlocutors' self-fashioning as merely defensive or reactive: in their everyday workings, secular dispositions, the following will show, may be exclusive, combative and forceful in their ontological claims to knowledge and truth.

In this chapter, my aim is to analyse the relation between a particular gendered and embodied form of everyday self-fashioning and the 'secular' in Turkey's recent past. In what ways can we speak of secular bodies, secular spaces and secular aesthetics within the urban space of Istanbul? And finally, given the fact that this chapter focuses on middle-aged to elderly female residents in rather wealthy inner-city neighbourhoods, what kind of self-evident 'truths' and everyday bodily practices are tied to the fashioning of proper secular selves in these particular spatial settings? Drawing on Setha Low's concept of 'embodied spaces', I understand the beauty salon as just such a space for its customers, namely a 'location where human experience and consciousness take on material and spatial form' (2003: 19). As argued by Sehlikoğlu (2016) in her work on women's physical exercising in Istanbul, in a context where concerns about women's public sexuality are shared widely, the construction of femininity always also has a 'space-making' aspect to it. Sexualized practices such as beautification or exercising, the following will show, are linked to boundary-making dynamics in social, moral and spatial terms.

This chapter proceeds with an outline of the study of secularism and, in a section on my methodological framework, the study of the gendered (secular) body in Turkey. Based on ethnographic data, the chapter is divided into two sections: (i) secularism as an embodied disposition in a particular historical line of tradition, namely that of Republicanism, with the normative, gendered ideal of a beautiful Republican woman informing current debates on intimate matters such as the application of lipstick, and (ii) the territorial claim of secular' urban spaces by interlocutors, who feel threatened by a creeping Islamization of society and the emergence of a new, pious bourgoisie; here, I offer vignettes from a beauty club and a nail bar in two urban neighbourhoods commonly described as secular.

To sum up, my aim is to show that secularism in present-day Istanbul is not only spatialized but deeply embodied and affective. Not least, it is an ethical claim to knowledge on the universal nature of woman (and man), with beauty figuring as a strong signifier of values that my secular interlocutors in Turkey commonly associated with secularism, namely freedom, discipline, joy and Europeanness.

Investigating Turkish secularism in its changing meanings

Created in a unique historical trajectory, due to ongoing transformations in the constellations of power, the meanings of secularism in Turkey are changing. While some scholars argue that claims of Turkish national belonging were never truly divorced from being Muslim and Sunni (cf. Kandiyoti 2012: 516), for many decades, secularism was clearly a state project and an identificatory reference for its hegemonic elite. It was first introduced with the 1928 amendment to the newly founded republic's constitution of 1924, by way of removing the declaration that the 'religion of the State is Islam'. In its 1937 constitution, the Turkish republic was officially declared secular, *laik*, to be exact, deriving from the French principle of *laïcité*. In fact, *laiklik* became one of the six principles of the state ideology of Kemalism, prescribing the state's position as one of active neutrality rather than of a strict separation between state and religion. Religious symbols and institutions such as religious orders, schools, Islamic clothes or the *fez* (male headdress during Ottoman period) were discarded or banned. The Roman calendar was adopted alongside the Roman alphabet and the day of rest moved from the Muslim Friday to Sunday.

In contrast to José Casanova's conceptualization of modern secularism as a 'transcultural' phenomenon, Jenny White (2013: 4) has emphasized that in Turkey, practices of both religion and secularity 'are highly culturally specific'. In Turkey, she sees a particular culture of secularism at play that exemplifies 'struggles over blasphemy of the sacred' (2013: 4). The early cadres attempted to replace Islam with a civil religion that centred, Esra Özyürek (2006) and Yael Navaro-Yashin (2002) argued in their insightful ethnographies on the topic, on the figure of the founding father of the republic, Mustafa Kemal Atatürk. Navaro-Yashin especially analysed the way the Turkish state in the 1980s and 1990s employed a rhetoric of nationalist secularism that cast religion as counter-progressive, while at the same time engaging in the self-declared secular cult of Kemalism. The discourse of secular Kemalism, according to Navaro-Yashin, was tied to a particular form of statism that in the Turkish nineties was 'coeval with violence [against Kurds and Cypriots, for example]' (2002: 202), and certainly helped the Islamic movement to achieve electoral victories on almost all levels of the state, ultimately transforming the relationship between secularism, Kemalism and the state.

In the early 2000s, when the Islamic movement had managed to form the government, but not yet taken the state apparatus, Esra Özyürek (2004, 2006) observed that the state ideology of Kemalism, and with it, secularism, began to move from the public into the private spheres; subsequently, secular symbols, such as Atatürk posters or buttons came to be displayed as part of a personal emotional attachment to the principles of the early republic. Amid the rise of an 'Islamist' elite, a more popular 'secularism of the street' (Kandiyoti 2012: 522) or 'secular populism' (Tambar 2009) emerged in this period that was concerned about the encroachment of secular rights and spaces. In 2007, hundreds of thousands participated in the so-called Republican Marches to protest the ruling party candidate for presidency and the lifting of the headscarf ban in public buildings under the slogan of 'Turkey is secular and will remain secular' ('*Türkiye laiktir laik kalacak*').

In the aftermath of the secularist Republican Marches and as the old secularist elite was replaced by a new, more openly Islamic one, Berna Turam describes how in Turkey's largest city of Istanbul, a 'new territoriality emerged ..., which was largely symptomatic of [secular] urban residents' rising fears of losing their intimate space' (2015: 6). In a city that for many years had been segregated along urban fault lines, including those between the devout and the secular but became increasingly mixed, ever more profane acts and symbols of everyday life took on a secular and Islamic meaning respectively. In the more recent past and with the increasingly authoritarian rule of the governing pro-Islamic Justice and Development Party (Adalet ve Kalkınma Partisi, AKP), the meaning of secularism changed once more as lifestyles, dispositions and spaces rendered as secular have come under ever more violent attack.[2] On the background of arrests on the grounds of 'secular propaganda' (*laiklik propagandası*) that prompted the main Kemalist opposition party to create a hashtag reading 'secularism is not a crime',[3] the sentiment among many self-described secularists, namely that secularism is under threat in Turkey, has been fuelled.[4]

As Kandiyoti (2012) has argued, changing constellations of power and a more popular movement of those concerned about an Islamization of everyday life have turned the once valid critique of secularism as a form of authoritarian rule in Turkey into a rhetoric of power, engaged in by new political actors seeking to consolidate their no longer marginal power positions in the state. After the re-election of the conservative Muslim ruling party in 2015 and the subsequent authoritarian turn of the political system, as well as a wave of terror attacks, some of which explicitly aimed at secular spaces and lifestyles, it is safe to say that secularism in Turkey is no longer the normative project of the ruling elite.

Methodology

This chapter is part of a larger research project on beauty, aesthetic body modification and the making of middle-class femininities in Istanbul that draws on fifteen months of anthropological field work in the city between April 2011 and March 2015. As part of field work I conducted some one hundred ethnographic guideline interviews with customers and patients of hair and beauty salons and clinics respectively, beauty therapists, salon owners, aesthetic surgeons and other experts, including tattoo artists and LGBTQ and feminist activists. I used multi-sited ethnography to follow beauty practices in different hair and beauty salons and clinics in the city, namely in the neighbourhoods of Başakşehir, Fatih, Nişantaşı, Beyoğlu, Moda/Kadıköy and Etiler. These were strategically chosen as highly contested urban areas, with some commonly regarded as Islamic and conservative, namely Başakşehir and Fatih, while others are regarded as rather secular. In these neighbourhoods, I regularly visited one or two hair and beauty salons or clinics each for interviewing and participant observation. The project also employs media analysis, including the systematic analysis of newspaper archives, online forums (*Kadınlar Kulübü* and *Fetva Meclisi*) and so-called makeover shows on private television. A questionnaire survey was conducted among visitors of the annual Istanbul Beauty and Care Fair and municipal training courses on make-up and facial care.

As elsewhere, the female body in Turkey is one of the key symbols in debates on national belonging and citizenship. Following the politicization of the headscarf in the 1990s in Turkey, much has been written on the continued role of women's bodies as a battleground between secularism and Islamism, modernity and tradition as well as the role of Islamic dress and sartorial styles in creating new, Islamic (elite) lifestyles.[5] For example, Sandıkçı and Ger have written on newly pious women's struggles to aestheticize pious fashion, carefully 'negotiating the tension between being faithful, modern, and nonreactionary' (2010: 10). This resulted not only in what has been labelled 'new Islamic' or 'conservative chic' but in what they call 'taste wars' between the 'old' secular elite and a newly emergent pious middle class.

In this chapter, I wish to contribute to this debate, however, by reversing the scholarly gaze to investigate the secular, rather than the Islamic, body and self. In contrast to the study of piety, secularism has only rarely been studied in its embodied and mundane aspects. The secular female body has long been the unmarked category in Turkey, against which pious women have been measured and found wanting, as a deviance from the norm. Moreover, there is a common association of the secular with the Sunni urban elite, which is rather problematic, because, needless to say, religious minorities, among them Alevi Muslims, activists of the left, working-class Sunni Muslims or those who live in rural areas may likewise self-identify as secular. The fact that this chapter focuses on the hegemonic norm of the Sunni, urban (upper) middle class is partly an outcome of my research in beauty salons and clinics in specific neighbourhoods of Istanbul, namely those considered central in the urban geography of beauty. Thus, it is important to note that 'the secular' has many meanings and does not constitute a homogenous group in Turkey, including in socioeconomic terms.

Drawing from this research, I wish to focus on the supposedly mundane acts of self-fashioning in everyday life, taking seriously Talal Asad's claim that in studying secularism, we should 'look to what makes certain practices conceptually possible, desired, mandatory – including the everyday practices by which the subject's experience is disciplined' (2003: 36). These acts, as Saba Mahmood (2004) shows in her ethnography of the ethical practices of self-fashioning by Egyptian women in the revivalist mosque movement, are not reducible to political tactics or strategies. Like forms of religiosity, Fadil and Fernando write, 'secularity too includes a range of ethical, social, physical, and sexual dispositions, hence the need to apprehend the secular via its sensorial, aesthetic, and embodied dispositions and not only its political ones' (2015: 64). While I agree with this, the following will show that within a highly charged atmosphere and in times of dramatic changes within the political system, even seemingly profane acts of 'care of the self' (Foucault 1984: 45) are traversed by webs of power and take on political meanings. The intimate and highly gendered space of beauty salons and clinics offered an excellent site to study such acts of bodily self-fashioning in their social embeddedness, political meanings as well as visible outcomes.

Republican women and the politics of intimacy in Turkey

In early May 2013, the national flagship airline Turkish Airlines (Türk Hava Yolları, THY) was in the headlines in Turkey, and indeed internationally, for what quickly came to be known as the 'lipstick ban'. The company had issued a guideline that called for plain make-up in pastel colours and banned certain shades of lipstick and nail polish, such as a bright red and darker colours, among flight attendants, claiming that 'the use of lipstick and nail polish in these colors by our cabin crew impairs visual integrity' (quoted from Yackley 2013). The case quickly went viral and countless critics took to the social media to voice their outrage. Yonca Tokbaş, a columnist with the Kemalist daily *Hürriyet*, framed the practice of wearing red lipstick within her family history of 'Republican Women Wearing Red Lipstick' (Tokbaş 2013), stating that '[a] mong the women of my family it was a tradition to wear Red Lipstick, with my mother leading the way'. Seeing the values that these women represented under attack, Tokbaş encouraged women to send in photos of themselves with red lipstick to start a 'Red Lipstick Movement'.

Within the debate, the THY administration became complicit with the attempts of the conservative government to redefine the role of women as pious mothers and housekeepers and aligned itself with it in what the secular media commonly labelled a 'culture war' between liberal secularism and authoritarian Islamism. While the THY quickly denied the charge of banning lipstick and backed down on the regulation, what is relevant for my argument here is how the public evolved, namely how something as mundane as the colour of lipstick or nail polish was captured as a case in point of the secular-religious divide. In a much-noticed column for the *Milliyet* daily, Mehveş Evin (2013) wrote:

> We will not be surprised if soon they ban high heels, eyeliners and the appearance of 'one strand of hair uncovered'. The actual problem is that they have defined flamboyance by red lipstick and dark colored nail polish. What lies beneath this is ... the efforts of the THY administration to re-design 'womanhood'. A woman who wears red lipstick and nail polish, in their eyes, is 'loose' or 'unsuitable'. This is the essence of the issue but indeed, they cannot say it openly.

Evin was one of several secularist men who took on the role of defending women's liberal 'right' to wear make-up by painting the grim picture of an Islamicizing Turkish Republic, where women, including flight attendants of the national flag carrier, would not be allowed to style themselves up and be required to wear pious dress. Revelling on the topic of red lipstick, typically illustrated with an image of a pair of slightly parted female lips painted in bright red, the international media widely reported on the 'Turkish lipstick ban' along similar lines. Reports and comments continued to be published even after THY backed down on the regulation on May 9, claiming that the company had 'no problem' with lipstick and the order 'was made by over-zealous junior managers who did not consult senior bosses about the initiative' (quoted from Faulconbridge 2013). Indeed, media coverage on the company continued to focus on the question of cosmetics even after on 15 May 2013 thousands of Turkish Airlines employees went on strike in a labour dispute over pay and the reinstatement of workers who had been sacked the previous year. The fact that their ongoing strike received little attention as compared to the 'lipstick ban' caused several hundred mostly young female flight attendants to publicly protest in early June 2013 (*Hürriyet Daily News* 2013).

The THY 'lipstick ban' was one of several cases in 2013 to 2014 with high levels of media attention in which embodied practices were linked to larger questions of gendered norms and appropriate behaviour for women. Other cases included, in October 2013, the sacking of a private TV channel moderator presumably for her low neckline (Hürriyet 2013), the debate on co-ed university housing in November 2013 (Arango 2013) or the declaration of Turkey's deputy prime minister, Bülent Arınc, in July 2014, that women should not laugh out loud and should remain chaste in public at all times (cf. Kandiyoti 2014). During interviews, secular interlocutors repeatedly referred to these cases as a clear sign of creeping Islamization. On this background, they narrated their own (aesthetic) practices and forms of secular self-fashioning as defiant or even rebellious acts of persistence. This raises the questions of why and how seemingly mundane and intimate matters such as the application and colour of lipstick or nail polish, ways of dressing or public female laughter could turn into heated debates on identity, belonging and secularism under threat in Turkey? Moreover, why do 'Republican women', as in the remarks of columnist Tokbaş, become a reference point for contemporary forms of self-fashioning? Thus, similar to Tokbaş, many of the secular middle-class women encountered as the customers and patients of Istanbul's central hair and beauty salons and clinics made a direct connection between their own and (early) Republican aesthetic norms and practices. In order to answer these questions, in the following I will briefly touch upon the making of secular femininities in early Republican Turkey to then move on to interlocutors' own forms of secular self-fashioning.

In her analysis of beauty contests in early Republican Turkey, Shissler (2004) shows the pivotal role played by the public presentation of 'beautiful Turkish women' in the state's attempts to project images of a modern and 'civilized' nation. On the background of contemporary teachings of biological racism and concurrent with hegemonic definitions of modernity, looks constructed as 'European' were favoured over 'Arab' looks, resulting in an appreciation of women with a light complexion, light eyes and a straight nose (cf. Özyürek 2004). The public presentation of 'honourable' (*namuslu*) women in state-sponsored beauty contests served to redefine patriarchal concepts of honour and shame, to 'secularize Islam' and 'normalize the female body' (Shissler 2004: 117). The outcome was an imaginary ideal of the secular Republican woman that a pious interlocutor in Jenny White's ethnography on the pious new middle class described as 'blond and modern, also honorable (*namuslu*), clean, sexually honorable (*iffetli*). ... [wearing] her skirt below the knees' (quoted from White 2013: 141).

Indeed, in trying to explain the meaning of beautification for them, many of my secular interlocutors started to talk about their Republican mothers or grandmothers as their personal ideals of beauty. Among them, Esra, a retired teacher and Kemalist born in 1953 to parents, who had likewise been teachers, described her mother as follows:

> My mother was born in 1923. They were the women of the Republic, the Republican women of Istanbul. They were very special. They used to go to coiffeurs, especially for haircuts and hair care. Perhaps not as often as I do [laughs], but nevertheless, they went. However, as far as make-up is concerned, my father was a very conservative man, a man of his time. That's why my mother put on lipstick for special occasions only. It took her 3–4 minutes to put it on, because her understanding of makeup was 'putting on lipstick.' Her hands and feet were well-groomed, and she used to get manicures and pedicures in her salon.[6]

Prompted by my question about the meaning of beautification for her, another interlocutor, Funda, a married housewife, aged sixty, in similar manner explained that she stemmed from a modern and 'European-type' family, who had helped establish the Turkish Republic. Going to hair and beauty salons had been part of the everyday routine for the women of her family for as long as she remembered, and she described her mother and grandmother as elegant, well-groomed and fashion-conscious 'Republican women' who put on make-up and had their sewing patterns and cosmetics imported from France.[7] Nehir, a retired English teacher in her mid-sixties, who was the daughter of early Republicans born and raised in Ankara, simply described her mother as 'a beautiful woman' (*güzel bir kadın*). When I asked her about the characteristics of a beautiful woman, she replied:

> First of all, she must take care of her body, her hair, face, nails, everything. She must look clean. And modern. Fully modern! Hair is important. Her hair must be coloured – not white like mine [laughingly points to the greys showing at her hairline]! A woman must take care of herself, must look clean, must look beautiful, and must look attractive.[8]

Like many self-identified secular women I encountered as part of my research, these women aligned their own, rather extensive beauty practices to those of their mothers, who, in their descriptions in the plural of Republican women, or as the generic 'beautiful woman,' became part of a vanguard of secular modernity in Turkey. For them, these women not only embodied the 'European look' that the young Republic strove to achieve in terms fashion and physiognomy to project itself as part of the Western world and in clear distinction from the recently abolished Ottoman Caliphate. For many secular middle-class women like Esra, Funda or Nehir, early Republican women also served as role models for being *aydın* (enlightened) or modern women during a time when this implied novel, and possibly risky, bodily practices such as unveiling or having one's hair touched and cut by non-related men such as hairdressers, not to speak of applying nail polish or lipstick, which required a societal redefinition of what was considered shameful and honourable/appropriate for middle-class women in Turkey. Not least, with their ascribed rigour and discipline, these women also functioned as shining examples of the ongoing gendered norm of women 'taking care of themselves' (*kendine bakmak*).

Taking care of oneself in this context refers to a particular feminine subject formation of becoming literate, self-sufficient and disciplined, while it also produced a concrete bodily outcome, namely feminine beauty (*güzellik*) and cleanliness (*temizlik*). According to common Turkish understandings, on a practical everyday level, this care of the self for women requires bodily techniques such as regular exfoliation (*kese*), the removal of body hair and the covering of grey hair, the shaping of eyebrows, manicures and pedicures, as well as, to a varying degree, certain feminine 'extras', such as the application of make-up and wearing of fashionable dress. According to their own understanding of themselves, Nehir, Esra and Funda each took great care of fulfilling this central gendered norm, investing much time, effort and financial resources in the consumption of beauty services. In their case, that of middle-aged women of economic means, this also included multiple cosmetic surgery (Nehir, Esra), regular Botox injections and other non-invasive aesthetic treatments (Funda, Nehir), wellness treatments such as regular massages or spa visits (Funda, Nehir), the highlighting or colouring of hair turned grey, as well as at least weekly beauty salon visits for manicures and/or the styling of hair – a rather common practice among a particular type of secular woman commonly nicknamed the *fönlü kadın* (woman with a blow-dry).

By referring to early Republican women by way of explaining their own beautification efforts, Nehir, Esra, Funda and many other self-identified secular women aligned themselves with those who had paved the way for them in terms of a particular self-fashioning. Moreover, by drawing a direct line from their 'Republican' mothers' and grandmothers' forms of self-fashioning to their own, these women ascribed a historical political role and mission to their costly beauty investments, some of which they felt were currently under threat. From talking to middle-aged, secular, middle-class women between 2011 and 2015, it became clear that many linked the value of 'taking care of themselves', as a particular form of beauty-intensive self-fashioning to their secular identity in a particular political moment. In this context, the narrative of standing in a line of self-identified modern, enlightened and European women taking care of themselves served as a form of social distinction from those who were unwilling (or unable) to afford the services this included. Moreover, within the socio-spatial landscape of Istanbul, it proved their belonging and indeed, as the following will show, their moral and historical claim to a particular urban space.

Claiming urban space as secular

In a much-noticed essay (2013), as well as her recent book (2015), Berna Turam describes spatial contestations and their implicit claims in Istanbul on the background of a neoliberal and authoritarian encroachment of the residents' right to the city. She also describes secular fears of 'mixing' in a city that is no longer segregated physically along the lines of socio-economic status and an 'Islamist-secularist axis', as a result of the massive rural-urban migration, which the city experienced from the 1960s onwards. Turam analyses how secular, urban elites 'alienated the pious in the slums' (*varoş*), due to their 'elitism' as well as the 'unfamiliarity' with them as newcomers in the city (2015: 28). The changes in the constellation of political power and the resultant rise of a new pious bourgoisie in the new millenium marked a change from 'mutually exclusive Islamic and secular neighborhoods into a contested proximity and integration between these groups' (2015: 30). This increased secular residents' fears that the conservative government and its cronies were 'taking their city away from them' (2015: 34).

Within the process, particular urban public sites, namely those commonly associated with secular lifestyles and non-religious activities, assumed a strong symbolic status as 'secular spaces' (Turam 2013: 410). For Istanbul's secular old-term residents, these spaces were associated with 'a sense of spatial belonging, intimate familiarity, and territorial entitlement' (2015: 8). Their readiness to defend these spaces against 'intruders', most visibly embodied by head-scarved women, created an atmosphere of 'microlevel urban contestations' (2015: 30). In the following, I will provide vignettes from fieldwork in beauty and fitness salons in Moda and Nişantaşı, urban neighbourhoods that clearly function as secular spaces within Turam's definition. By doing so, I will point to the gendered, embodied and affective aspects involved in the construction of everyday spaces as secular in present-day Istanbul.

In the autumn of 2013, I became a member of a women-only social club called World of Beauty in the central, middle-class neighbourhood of Moda, where I resided to attend a small mid-morning Pilates class three times a week as part of my fieldwork. Apart from me, there were ten to fifteen other women from the neighbourhood and adjacent area, some married housewives in their thirties or forties, some retired women in their fifties and sixties. Relationships between the women were close (*samimi*), with participants chatting and drinking tea after class and sometimes moving on to the hair salon or spa in the same building, or to have lunch together in the neighbourhood. All participants invested much efforts in their looks, fancied coloured or highlighted hair, nail polish and, so it became clear from interviews with some of them, in many cases had had cosmetic surgery and/or regularly consumed aesthetic treatments. They certainly recognised themselves and others in the neighbourhood as women, who took 'good care of themselves.'

In May 2014, for the first time ever, a young woman who covered her hair attended our Pilates class. At first, my classmates did not notice she was covered, because like me, she arrived late and entered the gym dressed in trendy sportswear, with her long, carefully highlighted hair pinned up in a bun. However, back in the changing room after the class, the small talk that had begun between the women ended abruptly when the newcomer started dressing in a long overcoat and covered her hair with a silky scarf, making room for an awkward silence. The woman did not return to the World of Beauty, and as far as I know, the incident was not mentioned again among the club members. Two days later, I conducted an interview with one of the participants, Nehir, a retired teacher in her mid-sixties (also mentioned above). It circled around Nehir's beauty practices – including a face-lift, cheek implants and blepharoplasty – as well as her life as the daughter of an army officer, the wife of a businessman and, more recently, a grandmother. Towards the end of the interview, seemingly unconnected to what we had just talked about, Nehir blurted out:

> But you know, those religious (*dinci*) women, they have no idea about looking beautiful, unfortunately. They don't know how to take care of themselves, also in terms of birth control. Also, they don't have any chance of wearing modern clothes and because of religion, they wear ugly clothes, you know. They look ugly, I mean, they make themselves look ugly, unfortunately.

> CL: You mean, because they are covering themselves?

> NH: Yes, yes. It is not natural – the way they dress and the way they behave, it is not natural, it goes against their own instincts. [They do that] because of social pressure, they wear [clothes] like that. But I think that a woman, wherever she lives, whoever she is, – God gave her the instinct that she must look clean, beautiful and attractive, even a little bit sexy. A woman has these feelings. Any woman who doesn't behave like this is under pressure. Because it is against creation (*tabiata karşı*). I mean, God created woman to be beautiful! But when you are under these clothes, you don't look beautiful.

Nehir's emotional outburst about the *dinci* ('religious') – a term that in contrast to 'Muslim' has a rather pejorative meaning and serves the (secular) speaker to distance themselves from the person signified – mixed up frustrations about the politics of the day with resentments on a deeper level. In a rather typical way, beauty here is associated not only with cleanliness and 'modern' looks but becomes a marker for a quasi-natural and 'instinctive' femininity based on attractiveness and a self-controlled ability and knowledge of how to take care of oneself. By violating the natural and even divine order of things with their sartorial choices, pious women were not only 'ugly' but ideologically fixated. This stood in stark contrast to Nehir's own 'natural' belief in God, which she, like many other self-identified secular (*laik*) women her age, regarded as in no way opposed to being secular. As *dinciler* the pious others were not supposed to look fashionable and attractive and if they did – like the woman who had recently entered the World of Beauty and who had obviously 'passed' as a club-mate until she put on her headscarf – this was clearly proof of them being hypocritical or, in Nehir's assessment, 'unnatural'.

Nehir's reference to the secular value of naturalness is contradictory, of course. First of all, and hardly surprising, it sets her own style of living, epitomized by the central value of taking care of oneself, as natural and, indeed, universal. This is reminiscent of Talal Asad's claim that liberal secularism is characterized by 'the claim to know what nature, including universal human nature, is' (Cannell 2010: 90). Second, it renders bodily practices of care of the self similar to those engaged in by herself as 'unnatural' when these are performed by pious subjects, an assessment which is informed by the secular knowledge of feminine beauty and attractiveness being problematic for pious women in public. The 'Islamic' or 'conservative chic' that some pious women have recently come to adopt in Turkey and that in the World of Beauty materialized in the visitor who covered her hair in public clearly irritates secular middle-class women like Nehir. Apart from occasional 'intruders' into 'their own' intimate spaces, this conservative chic has become increasingly visible in the urban space through a growing number of billboards promoting conservative fashion brands or the emergence of new Islamic fashion magazines such as *Ala*.

By creatively combining the consumption of beauty and fashion products and services with public notions of appropriateness and Islamic piety, the Islamic or conservative chic contradicts stereotypical images of the pious as *varoş* or rural, lower class, non-modern, 'ugly' and more generally 'backward'. It is a combination of what, in Nehir's definition, may, should and cannot be, namely of beauty and religious (*dinci*) identity. It points to the emergence of a new Muslim bourgoisie, who is able to afford such products and services, as well as to changing outlooks on feminine beauty among (younger) pious women, from an untouched beauty towards a carefully managed, new aesthetics. In her study on pious Turkish women in the Netherlands, Ünal points out that like secular women, these also draw on the beauty industry's current emphasis of 'naturalness', a kind of naturalness 'that can only be produced via cosmetics' (2013: 137). Instead of leading towards a more inclusive outlook of what it means to look modern, fashionable, attractive and 'natural' as a woman in Turkey today, for Nehir and many other secular middle-class women, the emergence of a fashion and beauty-conscious, pious, urban bourgoisie in 'their own' urban spaces confirmed an assessment of the non-secular as 'unnatural'.

Another, somewhat different example of the moral-spatial boundary-making in so-called secular urban neighbourhoods was provided by beauty salon workers who unveiled for work in the central upper-class neighbourhood of Nişantaşı. Among them was Saliha, a senior manicurist employed in an exclusive nail bar. Saliha and some of the other eight full-time beauty therapists employed in the nail bar removed their headscarves at the beginning of their shifts and changed from a more modest attire into pants and shirts at their workplace. They did so even though the nail bar was in no way a gender-segregated place and occasionally male customers requested their services. Saliha instead explained her decision to unveil as a 'strategic' attempt to avoid endless discussions with her ideologically secular customers, who, she reasoned, would certainly misunderstand her pious way of dressing as a sign of oppression or, even worse, her support for the ruling party, which they utterly hated. Instead, her job was to put her clients at ease (*rahat*), as she put it, a sensorium that would certainly be disrupted or spoilt for them by the sight of a headscarf in their favourite salon. Thus, apart from the visible outcomes, for Saliha's clients, the nail bar experience clearly included sensitive, affective and performative outcomes that she was utterly aware of: after their manicure treatments, customers visibly cheered up about the colourful beautification that materialized in their nails and frequently talked about the 'joy' they derived from their newly treated nails, a joy that continued to make their day.

Conclusion

In this chapter, I have followed Charles Hirschkind's call (2011) to study embodied practices and affective attachments in order to grasp what is unique to secularity. As we have seen, this uniqueness, in the case of Turkey, is gendered, affective and place-specific. On the background of a real and imagined loss of power by the Kemalist, urban elite, urban restructuring and the rise of a new pious middle class, Esra Özyürek (2004) observed that being secular and Kemalist became a question of identity carried into the intimate spaces of daily life. While Özyürek writes of Atatürk busts in living rooms and buttons pinned to coats and bags, my research illustrates that the fashioning of secular bodies also operates on a deeper level and may well include nail polish, lipstick and, indeed, Atatürk signatures inked into the skin.[9]

For the middle-aged, middle-class women I portrayed as the customers of beauty salons in two urban neighbourhoods, being secular includes a particular set of bodily practices that marks them as secular and is constitutive for their secular self-positioning. Not least, these bodily practices are tied to affective sensibilities – feelings of 'joy' and 'freedom' as well as gendered norms and ethical claims of what it means to be a 'proper' resident of Istanbul, namely a modern and European person. To repeat, for women, this condition was tied to a disciplined bodily care of the self best realized in particular parts of the city.

In accordance with the feminist analysis of femininity as constructed around ideals of beauty (cf. Bartky 1990), my research shows that acts of beautification play a crucial role in women's secular self-positioning. Whereas women sporting the Islamic headscarf have been found to emphasize notions of a '"healthy" and "well-groomed" look as the marker of proper care of self rather than a "beautiful" or "attractive" appearance' (Ünal 2013: 135), for many of the self-identified secular women portrayed in this chapter, the latter attributes were clearly also constitutional for their own care of the self. From their perspective, beauty practices such as the application of make-up or nail polish created a 'natural' kind of womanhood; not engaging in these practices, out of moral or religious concerns, in turn, resulted in an 'unnatural' form of femininity, as expressed by one interlocutor.

Donning nail polish and lipstick, among other forms of beautification, is not per se secular in Istanbul, where pious women have been creative in reconciling imaginings of themselves with public notions of appropriateness and Islamic piety. However, when pious women engage in beauty-intensive forms of care of the self that are similar to secular middle-class women's, this does not necessarily lead to a more inclusive perspective on what it means to be a proper woman in contemporary Istanbul, but, within a polarized political climate and amid the anxiety of losing ground in 'one's own' intimate social spaces, confirms stereotypical views of the pious other as 'unnatural'. Secular self-fashioning, the account has shown, permits and develops ways of being and living while disdaining and stunning others. While none of my interlocutors complied completely with the hegemonic ideal of femininity, the 'blond and modern' Republican woman described above (cf. White 2013: 141), each of them was deeply affected by the recent changes in this norm, whether real or imagined.

While constellations of power are clearly changing, it is important to note that the privileges of the former urban elite are not simply dissolving. In the case of the nail bar and beauty/fitness club described as secular spaces above, it can be said that the secular middle classes' anxiety about losing power makes them blind for their ongoing classed power positionings, not least in the social spaces they claim as their own: whereas Nehir and the other club members in Moda were seemingly alarmed by a veiled club member, they were not aware of and, arguably, not interested in knowing how their instructors dressed in their free time – just like the Nişantaşı nail bar customers did not (care to) know how their favoured manicurists dressed on their way home from the nail bar or why they dressed differently when they served them. Secular residents' anxieties over losing 'their' parts of the city are clearly directed towards those spatial intruders, who seem to challenge them in their positions of privilege, which is classed, but also tied to a particular, hitherto hegemonic, secular sensorium and feminine self-fashioning.

Finally, I would like to once again point to my limited view on the secular in Turkey that results from my research in central beauty salons and clinics, which tends to reproduce the stereotype of the secular as an urban (upper) middle class. Many of the interlocutors portrayed in this chapter belonged not only to a specific social class but also to a particular generation of women in Turkey, one that is commonly described as the '(self-)conscious menopausal woman' (*bilinç sahibi menopozlu kadın*). As such, they are the first generation of women in Turkey who were in their thirties and forties when Istanbul transformed into a global consumer city with an extensive beauty industry and who continue to claim a (sexually) active and younger-looking self through their ongoing consumption of beauty services after menopause. While they see themselves in a line of tradition with early Republican women, their practices of ageing stand in stark contrast to those of earlier women, who in older age tended to minimize feminine beauty and attractiveness. My interlocutors' ongoing consumption of beauty products and services may be related to changing ideas about femininity and naturalness in an age of body-centred consumption, but it may also be tied to the fact that within a polarized and hyper-politicized context these practices assumed a particular, affective 'secular' meaning.

Istanbul, this chapter has shown, is a conflictive terrain where women's consumption patterns and bodily self-fashioning have become a marker of the degree of their belonging to the urban space, the Republic and the wider world once more. The populist 'politics of ressentiment' (Kandiyoti 2014) that speaks from the anxious and belligerent voices of the women portrayed above have become characteristic of the political debate in Turkey; they are also employed by the conservative, pro-Islamic AKP regime against the metropolitan, secular middle classes. As such, Kandiyoti (2014: n.p.) analyses them as an attempt to obscure deepening 'class cleavages between the AKP ruling elite and their less advantaged followers'. Rather than emphasize the Islamist-secularist divide that some argue never truly existed in modern Turkey, it is the pointing out of the multiple contradictions implied in the labelling of others as 'secular' or 'religious', as well as of the unexpected coalitions and divides in a context such as Turkey that should be at the core of critical scholarship.

Love, War and Secular 'Reasonableness' among *hilonim* in Israel-Palestine

Stacey Gutkowski

In his 2002 lecture *How to Cure a Fanatic*, Israeli novelist and peace activist Amos Oz suggested that a combination of cool rationalism on both sides of the Israeli-Palestinian conflict, along with humour, imaginative empathy and the ability to feel comfortable with ambiguity, could sustain a two-state solution. He condemned the renewed rise of violent ethno-national 'religious fanaticism' among both Jews and Palestinians during the Second Intifada. The conflict is, he said, about 'real estate not religion' (Oz 2012: 43–81).

This emotio-political antidote resonated particularly with *hilonim*, secular Jewish Israelis, Oz's own religio-class constituency, after the collapse of the Oslo peace process.[1] It remains popular across the political spectrum, not just among leftists like Oz keen to see a two-state solution. It also resonates among Jewish Israelis on the right and centre who do not share the left's enthusiasm for Palestinian statehood, but who mobilize the formula of humour and empathy among Jewish Israelis towards, as they see it, cool, collective endurance of and solidarity in the face of Palestinian and Arab political violence.

Oz's emotio-political formula resonates because it taps into a shared *hiloni* habitus, a deep well of shared and individual epistemological, existential, ethical and emotional sensibilities, beliefs, identities and practices, of what it feels like to be a person living in a complex dialogue with both Western secular liberalism and Jewish tradition. For many who identify as *hiloni*, to be so is primarily to be a reasonable person, someone who uses her intellectual faculties for what Walzer (2002: 617–33) called 'dispassionate deliberation'. She appreciates her own passions but tries to gain critical purchase on and sometimes restrain her emotional impulses. Across the political spectrum, there is a strong connection between *hiloni* self-identity as 'rational' (Dalsheim 2007: 546)[2] and the framing of Israeli state policies they agree with as 'unfortunate but unavoidable' because they are 'rational'. Following three wars with Hamas-controlled Gaza since 2008 and the onset of what some call the 'knife intifada', Jewish Israeli society has increasingly found convincing government discourse that there is 'no [rational] partner for peace'. At the same time, despite this discourse of 'being rational' about the Palestinian conflict, *hilonim* are also shaped by the nationalist, emotional repertoires of Zionism. These draw on biblical symbolism such as return from exile in Egypt to the ancient land of Israel (*Eretz Israel*) for some of its most emotionally evocative themes. Ethnocratic Zionism defines the Jewish self who is entitled to sovereignty in the land against the non-Jewish other, who is welcome as a 'guest', only in limited numbers, only in particular spaces, whose public behaviour is regulated by the Israeli state.

Following Nussbaum (2003), I understand emotions as value-laden judgements about what is best for 'us'. Of the wider emotional ecology of the Israeli-Palestinian conflict (numbness, fear, worry, frustration, boredom, surprise, grief, envy, anger, shame, stoicism, joy, disgust, hatred), I choose to focus particularly on two types of love and the ways in which ethno-religious affinity does and does not shape these for 'secular Jews'. What the ancient Greeks called *philia* or 'brotherly love' is a critical component of the ethno-national, post-secular, emotional repertoires of Zionism. For *hilonim* on the political right and centre, what counts as ethical is judged primarily as being in accordance with *philia*, brotherly love: what is ethical will protect Jewish Israeli bodies from violence, post-Holocaust.

For some leftists, us or me is a more elusive concept, sometimes but not always going beyond the ethno-religious divide. For those on what is today called in Israel the 'hard left', a different kind of love, *agape*, governs emotional repertoires towards Palestinians. This is a charitable love for the emotionally and physically distant other whom one thinks of largely in the abstract, as opposed to *philia*'s intimacies. What is judged by these leftists as ethical and also reasonable is seen as in accordance both with *philia* and *agape*: what will protect Jewish and Palestinian civilians from violence. For *hiloni* leftists, that one can feel *agape* towards a broader 'us' is a demonstration of one's personal and political reasonableness, good judgement and ability to think 'rationally', but it requires conscious effort. However, for all varieties of *hiloni* leftists, these love repertoires are also quite complicated, determined sometimes but not always by one's political affiliation or the ethno-religious divide or the other's use of violence, rather than 'pure reason'. Contra Oz's dichotomy of secular reasonableness versus religious fanaticism (the Western stereotype of the fanatic illuminated by Toscano [2010]) the picture is more complex.

On the surface, it seems as though *hilonim* define themselves as 'reasonable' (rational plus ethical) people against a range of religious others, including Hamas and militant settlers from the national religious sector. However, post-secularity allows *hilonim* to implicitly grasp the often paradoxical dynamics of religio-politics among both Jews and Palestinians, even where the average young Israeli has little detailed knowledge. This post-secular intuition about religio-politics produces a complex three-way emotional ecology towards religious others: embarrassed and exasperated empathy for those violent settlers who see the land as given by God, effortful empathy for Gazan civilians who are 'religious' but not 'ideologues' and grim acceptance of Hamas as adversaries, rational 'like us'. Young *hiloni* understandings of themselves as 'reasonable people', able to think rationally and not be overwhelmed by emotion, holds this tenuous emotional ecology together (Sasson-Levy 2013: 40). They understand that Hamas are rational actors and not 'Islamic fanatics', however much its anti-Semitic rhetoric angers them. They try to feel pity for Gazan civilians, because they feel this is what a reasonable person 'should' do, though they feel torn because Palestinians do not naturally feel 'like family', requiring ongoing efforts to 'be reasonable'. And for violent settlers, against whom they most clearly define themselves as 'reasonable', they feel torn between anger and *phillu*. In tension with their liberal self-definition as 'rational' people, for young *hilonim*, post-secular empathy often defines what violence is 'reasonable', rather than cool, dispassionate assessment of 'evidence'. This chapter draws empirically upon qualitative analysis of over fifty in-depth semi-structured interviews with young secular Jewish Israelis aged twenty-five to forty-five from across the political spectrum from the self-described 'hard left' to 'hard right'.[3] These were conducted by the author between 2014 and 2016, starting in the aftermath of the 2014 Gaza War. This data is supplemented by an in-depth qualitative survey with ninety-five young *hilonim* conducted by the author over the same period, and this material is triangulated by other primary and secondary sources.[4]

This volume takes as its starting point the ways in which attention to the affective register helps scholars to understand the logics, practices and distinctions which are constitutive of the European secular. This chapter diverges from the book's starting point in two related ways. First, the constellation of ideas and conditions that make up the European secular tradition (cf Farman 2013) forms only part of the *hiloni* worldview. There is an intense debate in the literature as to whether and to what extent Israel's waves of inward migration have led its society to have a Western/European or Eastern/Arab character. While Ashkenazi cultural hegemony dominated society and governance during the first three decades of the state of Israel, today the case is best described as hybrid, taking into account the diversity of inward migration and settlement from the Euro-American, Latin American, former Soviet as well as the Arab-Mediterranean contexts. Second, while Hirschkind (2011: 634) described the secular as 'the water we swim in', this does not resonate for the Jewish Israeli case, for reasons described below. *Hilonim* borrow both from secular, Western, liberal culture and other influences, including Jewish religious influences, in order to constitute their worldview. The relationship between these resources is multi-directional, often an inverse one to the European story of the secular, with Jewish tradition shaping and governing the boundaries of liberalism in Israel. This chapter refers to Jewish Israeli society as a whole and also *hilonim* as 'post-secular' to take account of this complex borrowing. While the chapter diverges from the primary focus of the book, it does help provide critical purchase on the European secular as viewed through the affective register. How might these things work beyond the West? It also looks at violence, as an instance of visceral, emotionally-intense social practice to explore what may be distinctive about it vis-á-vis calmer times.

Post-secularity and the emotional repertoires of Zionism

The term 'Jewish secularism' is somewhat misleading and contested. To be *hiloni* (a 'secular Jew') is an identity marker. In the state of Israel, where Judaism shapes the cultural ethos as well as many aspects of state law, this has produced phenomena whereby Jews may live a non-Orthodox, 'secular' lifestyle; may simultaneously be theists, atheists or something in between; and still participate fully in national, collective, culturally Jewish ways of living. Judaism is typically understood by its adherents and analysts as defined by adherence to Jewish law (the *halakhah*) rather than by faith. There is no codified set of beliefs one must hold to be a Jew. To complicate matters further, Jewish religious identity is bestowed through matrilineal inheritance rather than adherence to the *halakhah* or a particular set of core tenets. One need not behave in accordance with Jewish law, nor believe in its divine mandate, nor indeed believe in God in order to be considered a Jew by the Orthodox rabbinate. While not adhering to (much of) the *halakhah*, those describing themselves as *hilonim* hold a series of non-Jewish (or not specifically Jewish) beliefs and commitments which may or may not be intertwined with implicitly or even explicitly Jewish commitments (Lahav 2016).[5]

In terms of behaviour and beliefs there is also much overlap between *hilonim* and *masortim*, traditionist Jews (Yadgar 2010). Religious belief and practice among Jewish Israelis lies along a spectrum, and boundaries between groups are blurred. Both groups engage in dialogue with Jewish religious tradition, engaging in a process of navigation and borrowing, individually, within families or among their immediate community. While Mizrahim, Jews from the Middle East, and Sephardim, Jews from southern Europe, identify most frequently as *masorti*, some in the younger generation, particularly those who are in Tel Aviv, discuss their identity as hybrid, periodically identifying more with a *hiloni* identity as a deviation from the *masorti* centre of gravity in which they grew up. Ashkenazi *masortim*, particularly *olim* migrants from Europe and North America, engage in some hybrid practices which are heavily influenced both by diaspora Judaism and by their Christian-majority, Western liberal origins. What distinguishes the groups, other than a discourse of boundary making which they police, is the extent to which individuals within the group borrow more or less heavily from Judaism or more or less heavily from Western liberal culture(s).

To signal multi-faceted rejection of the Western secularization paradigm in the Jewish Israeli case, some Jewish Israeli scholars use the term 'post-secular' to speak about *masorti* Jews or the Jewish Israeli case as a whole (Diamond 2004). They highlight the ways in which Judaism transcends binaries such as those between reason/knowledge/nature/secularity/the profane, on the one hand, and faith/belief/supernatural/spirituality/the sacred, on the other hand. Their conception of Jewish post-secularity is not so distant from Hirschkind's (2011: 633) definition of the secular as 'a concept that articulates a constellation of institutions, ideas, and affective orientations that constitute an important dimension of what we call modernity and its defining forms of knowledge and practice – both religious and nonreligious'.

While sympathizing with the impulse to problematize binaries, Furani rejects the term 'post-secular'. Furani (2015: 16) defines secularity as 'a subject's alertness to its finitude and worldliness'. For Furani (2015: 18), there are 'a plurality of secular ontologies, some religious, some nonreligious'. Furani's definition of secularity unpacks the binaries which scholars who use the term 'post-secular' also hope to – for example, Orthodox Jews' attention to worldly matters as well as their limits, as well as *hiloni* concerns with immanence and its boundaries. While I agree with Furani's impulse, for the purposes of this chapter I retain the term 'post-secular' to signal how this case differs from the European history of secularism.

Additionally, the case cannot be understood without attention to the continuities between Zionism as a national ideology and the Jewish religious symbolism from which it in part draws. Zionism developed in the eighteenth and nineteenth centuries in Europe through a complex conversation between national aspirations, the Jewish religion and (secular) socialism. This was provoked by a European context in which prospects for political emancipation and assimilation or alternatively isolation and anti-Semitism generated deep debate about 'what to do' among Jewish socialist intellectuals. Several strands among the first European Zionists, influenced by the *Haskalah* (Jewish Enlightenment), secularized the religious Messianic conception of redemption, seeing redemption as realized through human endeavour to build a state in *Eretz Israel* rather than transcendental means. In the pre-state (*Yishuv*) period, socialist Zionism dominated over other strands of Zionism. In this ideological context, the early settlers sought not to eschew religion entirely but to endow new, secular symbols of para-statehood with Jewish religious resonances. The socialist Zionist notion of redeeming the people by redeeming the land through hard agricultural labour is an example. In parallel, revisionist Zionism, the brainchild of Ze'ev Jabotinsky, developed as a response to the anti-religious character of early socialist Zionism. Though this was also a secular movement comprised predominantly of non-Orthodox Jews, including non-religious Jews, it also attracted the Orthodox. It affirmed 'not religion per se but the nationalist values inherent in respecting the religious commandments', combining these with romantic nationalism (Liebman and Don-Yehiya 1983: 70). Revisionist Zionism did not translate its ideology into real political power until the first electoral victory of the Likud party in 1977. This is the party of current Prime Minister Benjamin Netanyahu, which has again led the Israeli government since 2009.

With the establishment of the state of Israel in 1948, the first Israel prime minister David Ben Gurion's vision of statist Zionism was a secular, almost anti-religious, vision which simultaneously borrowed, secularized and reconfigured biblical symbols for nationalist purposes, a process which had begun during the Yishuv period (ibid.). Ben-Gurion himself was not religious and the majority of Jewish Israelis in this period also were not. However, this use of Jewish tradition was seen as a way of strengthening national cohesion among waves of new immigrants and more powerfully justifying why the state of Israel must be established on this particular piece of land.

After the Israeli Defence Forces captured the West Bank and Jerusalem during the 1967 war, including some of the holiest sites in Judaism, a new form of civil religion emerged in Israel, whereupon mainstream, state-led Zionism came to draw even more heavily upon religious symbolism. Lieberman and Don-Yehiya argue that Ben-Gurion's statism had failed to replace Jewish tradition with an equally ideologically potent force which could bind citizens to the state, to each other and to the land. In the 1970s, following the 1973 war, which was understood by Jewish Israelis as a loss for the existing political elites, Revisionist Zionism was able to emerge as a force to compete with other forms of Zionism which had not tied nationalism so tightly to respect for religious tradition. This culminated in Likud's electoral victory, but these shifts also made possible the emergence of the Religious Zionist strand of the settlement project Gush Emunim in the early 1970s. In the intervening decades, migration from the former Soviet Union (FSU) has strengthened and changed *hiloni* habitus in Israel from its early iterations. Additionally, power has become more multipolar in the Israeli system, with *haredi* (ultra Orthodox) and religious Zionist constituencies, both

Mizrahi and Ashkenazi, as well as Ashkenazi FSU constituencies vying for political, legal and social influence. The influence of the Orthodox rabbinate over state law and private life is one contested area.

This new multi-polarity as well as periodic violence since 2000 has also contributed to debates over the meaning and purpose of Zionism. Over the past decade, post-Zionists have questioned whether the state of Israel can be fully democratic when it privileges one ethnicity over others and while the Occupation of the West Bank continues. This strand of thought rejects the necessity of the Jewish character of state, populated by a Jewish majority, which Zionism implies, calling instead for a secular, democratic state in which citizenship is not hierarchized by ethnicity or religion. While post-Zionism has been criticized as a minority project of intellectuals, others on the left who consider themselves Zionists have gone through a decade of intense introspection over the purpose of Zionism in light of the Occupation. They have seen their influence over national politics diminish greatly and have refocused on legal and political battles to preserve liberal ways of life in Israel, often over addressing the Palestinian conflict. Where once *hilonim* formed the heart of the left, their political positioning and relationship to Zionism has diversified over the past decade.

Despite the political and intellectual contestation of Zionism, its emotional repertoires endure. Jewish Israelis across various cleavages in Israeli society (ethnic, religious, class, gender) engage with the emotional repertoires of Zionism, including its post-secular continuities with Judaism, expressed through national symbols which draw on the biblical history of the Jewish people in *Eretz Israel*. How do post-secular *hilonim* interact with the emotional repertoires of contemporary Zionism?

A full account of the development of collective emotio-political repertoires for Jews living in Israel today lies outside the scope of this chapter (Loeffler 2016). But it is helpful to point to a few sacred and secular vehicles of transmission. One is a cyclical calendar of national holidays, some of which are drawn from the Jewish religious tradition such as Yom Kippur and Purim and some of which are Zionist, nationalist creations such as Independence Day and May Day. Both types of holidays require public rituals of bodily practice and aim to inspire feelings of love, loyalty to and solidarity with the Jewish body politic in Israel. Other vehicles for transmission are the disciplining of the body and its emotions through schooling and army service.

For those Israeli Jews within the Orthodox and traditionist publics, there are additional collective emotional repertoires made possible by closer adherence to religious tradition. There are many ritual vehicles among these Israeli Jews for the channelling of emotion individually and collectively; the ecstatic group dancing of Orthodox Jews at the Western Wall in Jerusalem at sunset on Fridays is one example. *Hilonim* sometimes take part in these rituals – for example they also occasionally visit the Wall on Friday evenings, particularly if they are stationed in Jerusalem for army or police service, and most eat dinner with their families on Fridays, with or without the accompanying prayers. However, it is the national, Zionist ritual structure and emotional repertoire which most explicitly binds these Jewish publics together politically and to the state. A few specific vehicles of emotional transmission for the *hiloni* public exist as well, but are perhaps most (or even only) obvious in their intended divergence from the rhythms of the Orthodox life, particularly Shabbat.[6] For example, a *hiloni* family may gather to barbecue on Friday night, including cooking non-kosher food. Their *hiloni* practice is marked more obviously by the divergence from the *halakah*, but it also includes the formation of a distinctively *hiloni* family ritual, one which is familiar to us in the West but which retains the nationally, culturally and religiously Jewish chronology of *Shabbat* (Sabbath).

Critically, the national, Zionist vehicles noted above also serve to mark and reinforce the boundary between Jewish and Palestinian citizens of Israel. The Zionist repertoire is designed to generate within Jewish citizens an emotional attachment to what is often cited as the Jewish people's 4,000-year connection to *Eretz Israel* and to the Jewish people who endured 'exile'. While some commentators suggest that the Zionist repertoire is equally open to Palestinian citizens of Israel, in practice strict boundaries – legal, spatial, social, economic and emotional – remain in place.

Some individuals on the left have found ways to productively navigate and exempt themselves from the chauvinist aspects of emotive nationalism, forging friendships with Palestinians, expanding circles of intimacy. However, cycles of violence between Jews and those Arabs identifying as Palestinian on both sides of the Green Line largely serve to periodically, almost ritualistically, enforce national identification and intra-communal feelings of love and solidarity, while preserving a repertoire of fear, suspicion, hatred and confusion about the other side. This bears out Ahmed's (2014) argument that emotions 'do things' politically, especially in producing and maintaining political boundaries between groups. The experience of direct attack on Jewish Israeli citizens within the Green Line, both civilians and security services, mobilizes a shared, national emotional repertoire among Israeli publics regardless of their place on the religious spectrum. Using Ahmed's notions of the circulation and 'sticking' of emotion and its bodily manifestations, love circulates among the Jewish Israeli public through rituals of public kindness and helping other Jews while suspicion, fear and even hatred 'sticks' to those Palestinian bodies through rituals of security and public surveillance (cf. Ochs 2011).

Violence and the reasonable *hiloni* self

As other chapters in this volume have demonstrated, what constitutes the 'secular' is found within the emotional repertoires and performances within Jewish Israeli society. For example, the everyday rhythms of life in Tel Aviv, in Haifa and on some more *hiloni kibbutzim* and *moshavim* (types of rural settlements) – particularly on Shabbat – differ substantially from parts of the country where Orthodox or traditionist publics are the majority. Dress, food, movement around the home and across the community, celebration, even the experience of daylight and dark differ for these publics. What is 'secular', what is Orthodox, what is traditionist and the various gradations within and subtle and not-so-subtle differences between these categories are viscerally understood by those who participate in Jewish Israeli public and private life.

However, what differentiates this chapter from others in this book is its focus on the emotional phenomenology of violence. Kimmerling (1985) famously characterized Jewish Israeli society as a 'chronically interrupted system' which moves back and forth between war and peace. Plasse-Couture (2013) has argued that it makes little sense to differentiate peace from war; we should instead analyse the distribution and variable intensity of violence within Israel and the West Bank and the ways in which the Israeli government manages violence through neglect and strategic intervention against Palestinians. Lori Allen (2008) has pointed to the 'normalization everyday violence' which has come to define the complex relationships of resistance and occupation between Palestinians and Jewish Israelis since 1967. Allen (2012) also points to the 'scalar politics' of the Israeli-Palestinian conflict, which for Jewish Israelis makes it seem as though 'war' is anomalous, while for Palestinians the threat of violence is ever-present.

War is an emotionally intense arena of social practice. Against scholars who argue that war precipitates a radical break in social life, Lubkemann (2008) has argued that war does not suspend social processes but continues pre-existing dynamics, though sometimes temporarily altering aspects of these. Jewish Israelis' increased feelings of love and solidarity among the group during what they consider wartime have been widely cited in the literature (cf. Weiss 1997). This is evident in the display of flags, parades and, more recently, commentary on social media, within Israel and the Jewish diaspora. The emotional economy of Zionism becomes particularly pronounced during periods of political violence, temporarily rendering moot distinctions between Jewish Israeli social groups, including distinctions between religiosity, ethnicity, geography and social class.

My young *hiloni* interlocutors noted that during the three Gaza wars since 2008, in which many of the young men interviewed fought, they felt a strong emotional connection to the Jewish people as nation, though not to Judaism as a religion per se. Such emphasis on Jewishness as culture/ethnicity/nationhood is a feature of the *hiloni* worldview. While *hilonim* seem at first glance to draw on what Asad calls the Western grammar of secularism to distinguish nationhood from religion, another dynamic is at work. They are merely placing emphasis on one aspect of the bivalent nature of Judaism which is simultaneously both religion and also culture/ethnicity/nation (Gitelman 2009). A metaphor of a see-saw is useful for understanding the post-secular continuities between Judaism and Zionism as an ideology of Jewish nationalism. The weight on one end tilts the see-saw in one direction but it does not disrupt the structural integrity of the see-saw. For example, for my post-secular *hiloni* interlocutors, the biblical symbolism of the West Bank does not resonate overtly, but images of an ethno-religious group who has been violently persecuted from biblical times onwards are strongly salient.[7] *Hilonim* on both left and right describe an attachment to 'secular' nationalism, but because of the structural integrity of the see-saw, they cannot actually detach themselves from Zionism's emotionally evocative ethno-religious references.

Among my interlocutors there were some negative, monolithic reactions to violent ethno-religious nationalism which seem to echo what Toscano (2010) describes as the Western stereotype of fanaticism, associating 'excess' religion with unrestrained, emotionally driven violence. For example, in a conversation in July 2015 about rising tensions at the Haram al-Sharif/Temple Mount, David, an Ashkenazi, self-described political centrist former combat soldier from the north of Israel, matter-of-factly noted: 'Religion has a lot of power over people. There are billions of people interested in this place, in its sites. There's a lot of emotion. And as we know emotion can lead to war.' In describing himself, he distanced himself as a trained soldier from emotive outbursts by Palestinian and settler activists. For example, Gideon, an Ashkenazi centre leftist in his twenties from the centre of Israel, says, 'I think that the more religious you are the more extremist and ideological you are, especially in the Israeli-Palestinian conflict, and the more you adapt reality to your view of the world instead of understanding reality the way it is.'

Young *hiloni* narratives about settler and Hamas violence draw on and make reference to group constructions of the *hiloni* self as the reasonable, politically moderate centre of gravity, the index against which the actions of others are judged. This discourse, though found among Jewish Israelis across the religious spectrum, for *hilonim* stems genealogically from transformations in the European Jewish context during the nineteenth-century *Haskalah*. This was transmitted through the hegemonic Labour Zionist habitus which shaped Israeli national life during the first decades of the state and the statist ideology which underpinned it. This narrative of personal reasonableness draws on and reflects both Western, liberal narratives about the rational individualism as well as the Jewish rabbinical context, in which rational argument is valourized as the expression of the human duty to exercise her sovereignty as bestowed by God (cf. Soloveitchik 1994: 128).

For *hilonim* across the generations, narratives of personal reasonableness interact with and are contextualized by broader Zionist narratives of the state of Israel enduring near-continual security threats since its founding. Discourses of resilience and the cultivation of forbearance are common performances among Jewish Israelis, reflecting the longevity and cyclical nature of the conflict (Ochs 2011). State narratives of political resilience draw on three things: wider Jewish biblical notions of waiting for the Messiah and enduring exile from *Eretz Israel*; the Jewish historical experience weathering catastrophes such as the Holocaust, pogroms and periodic expulsions from the Arab world and Europe; and Zionist narratives about making the state of Israel 'bloom' in the arid desert.

Three things distinguish this generation's self-cultivation as reasonable. First, Israel's shift towards economic neoliberalism in the 1980s brought shorter working hours, more wealth and more leisure time to larger segments of the population. This opened opportunities for self-cultivation to members of the middle classes who came of age since this shift (cf Almog and Almog 2015). One outcome of this complex process observed by scholars has been religious, ethical and philosophical entrepreneurship among young Jewish Israelis, whereupon individuals draw from a range of resources, Jewish and non-Jewish. Many *hilonim* have capitalized on the opportunities afforded by a middle-class lifestyle and income to craft themselves as engaged, aware and critical individuals, drawing from resources such as science and Western philosophy, to shape themselves as sensible people living in dialogue with but beyond Judaism. Second, over the same period, a reconfiguration moved the centre of gravity in Jewish Israeli politics away from Ashkenazi *hilonim* towards a more multi-polar arrangement outlined above. Increasing political multi-polarity has prompted new forms of *hiloni* self-assertion in light of their relatively reduced influence (Shafir and Peled 1998). Self-assertion as the reasonable and responsible segment of society is part of a *hiloni* politics of boundary-making and alliance-building with rising groups.

Third, four wars with Hezbollah and Hamas since 2006 have contributed to feelings of solidarity with Western allies targeted by jihadism since 2001. As such, Jewish Israelis across the society (not just young *hilonim*) have also echoed popular Western political narratives about 'Islamic fanaticism', drawing connections to what they understand as similar threats faced by Israel. However, by and large, narratives of other and self and their accompanying emotional repertoires were more complex than this stereotype because of the ways in which post-secular intuition facilitates *hiloni* comprehension of Palestinian and Jewish religio-politics beyond Zionist boundaries of nationhood. It is to this nuance that we now turn.

Settler violence, *philia* and the Jewish body politic

In discussing the Israeli-Palestinian conflict, of all topics religious differences among Jewish Israelis elicited some of the greatest outpourings of feeling during interviews, including occasional outbursts of frustration or anger directed at settlers who committed violence against Palestinians. These interviews were conducted against a backdrop of a cycle of retaliation among Palestinians and some settlers in the West Bank, which in the summer of 2014 had culminated in war in Gaza and had continued after, with Palestinian attacks on Jewish Israelis spreading over the Green Line and army retaliation. For example, describing his encounters with 'hilltop youth' settlers during his army service in the mid-2000s, Oren, a formerly 'more religious', politically centre-right former combat officer, burst out, 'Those are crazy ass people! They are not people of God!' Scholars have noted that public display of emotion is valourized in *sabra* culture, tied to national constructions of the image of the 'tough Jew' among immigrants who fled Europe from the late nineteenth through the mid-twentieth century (Katriel 1986; Moscowitz 2015). Much has been written about how *hilonim* regularly engage in forms of boundary work between themselves and those they see as their significant others internal and external to the national collective: the religious right and Palestinians (Yaacov 2003).

My interlocutors argued that while some settlers may hold racist or politically extremist attitudes towards Palestinians, a minority commit physical violence in contravention of Israeli state law. (While they emphasized the minority nature of settler violence, only those furthest left on the political spectrum articulated the Occupation as a form of structural violence or referred to international law on West Bank settlements.) However, many, even those who described their politics as on the right, argued that the increasing political assertiveness of the right at national level gave succour to various religious nationalist projects, some of which were invoked to justify violence. They saw the small, ideologically driven component of the settlement movement as a negative and increasingly powerful political force, driving national politics and alternately forcing the hand of or being exploited by the Likud-led government. For example, Amir, a Mizrahi former combat solider in his thirties, noted that Netanyahu and senior politicians in the ruling coalition had started to use the phrase 'religious war' since the 2014 Gaza war. He scoffed dismissively, 'The Netanyahu followers love it. They are protecting the Temple Mount and the right of the Jews to go to pray. Nobody cared about it for 30, 40 years. Suddenly they found that it makes the situation go crazy and everybody cares about it. It's bullshit.' In an almost wistful tone, Ruth, a Jerusalem resident in her twenties who was born in the south of Israel, expressed her quiet frustration with the potency of ethno-religious symbols in the conflict and her own emotional detachment from them. She said, 'for religious people, when you look at the Wailing Wall, it's something I can't understand. For me it's a wall. If anything I feel kind of antagonistic because it causes so many problems and it looks like it's so easy to solve! … I'm kind of hopeless actually.'

Even where interlocutors described themselves as 'angry' or 'frustrated' with settler violence against Palestinians, they sought to express what they called 'tolerance' through mannerisms they had cultivated as reasonable – a calm tone of voice, detailed argument and performing the self as a rational subject. Nearly all my *hiloni* interviewees were highly reflexive about their conversational performance, proceeding carefully and with nuance, reflecting on the quality of their arguments, returning to a well-modulated and quieter tone following an outburst. They made reference to their identity as *hiloni*, tying this identity to a calm habitus and to political values of 'pragmatism' and moderation. The *hilonim* were not unique in presenting themselves to me this way in interview, as balancing passion with reasoned argument. My religious interlocutors also sought to conform to the social mores of academic interviews. But the *hilonim* were more self-reflexive about this, describing these mannerisms as a function of their *hiloni* identity, tied to their politics and to the other virtues they sought to cultivate.

My interlocutors grappled with the complexity of what they saw in the public sphere, particularly the media, with their personal, more nuanced experiences with Jews from other religious constituencies. These interviews were conducted between three months and one year after the 2014 Gaza War, during which a social media firestorm had erupted between Jews on the right and left. Mutual demonization continued after the war, including during the period of the interviews on social and mainstream media. Emotions were running high. *Hilonim* on the right politically saw themselves as standing up against a broader culture of emotional excess among leftists and vice versa.

My discussion with Rikva, a leftist, was paradigmatic. We discussed her experiences on Facebook during the last Gaza War, particularly her encounters with more right-wing friends. She said quietly,

This extremism [on social media] scares me sometimes. It makes me feel like why should ideology be connected to extreme violence or extreme feelings? That makes me angry. I'm really trying to keep in mind the differences. Not every person in my life who is right wing has these ideas. I have many right wing friends and many nationalist friends. Not all of them would call for violence against Arabs when things are inflamed. I try to remind myself that not all extreme ideologues would call for extreme violence but unfortunately in many, many cases I do see that. I think it's a pity. It's not what our society needs.

For Rikva, their views were more a function of their right-wing politics rather than religiosity, per se, though she noted, 'There's a spectrum. None would consider themselves secular. They practice religion in one way or another.' None of my interlocutors denied that there were many in Israel for whom right-wing politics and some level of religious politics go hand and hand. When I asked her if she thought secular people were somehow more politically reasonable than 'religious' people, Rikva observed,

> I don't think it has to do with religion in this case. In many cases it feels like it's linked directly. But I can think of many right wing nationalist religious friends that would not go to these extremes and they would even use their religious background to disagree with these kinds of ideas.

All my interlocutors drew connections between their personal experiences with individuals and their larger political views. For example, Rikva emphasized, 'I would respect anyone. This was strong in how I grew up.' This is not surprising. Before discussing contemporary politics, I began each interview by asking people to describe their earliest encounters with religion, from childhood through adolescence, in their families, neighbourhoods and schools. Most described childhoods ensconced within a nearly exclusively *hiloni* world, which the academic literature supports. Some described complex encounters with Jewish Israelis from other religious segments of society, many with warmth and humour, a few with discontent. A few were frustrated with the influence of the *haredim* (ultraorthodox) and the national religious on politics and law, fearing a reduction in their personal freedom. The majority presented themselves as intellectually and socially tolerant of religious difference. Describing with humour an exchange between a local group of *haredi* boys and his own friends (the *haredim* agreed to make up the numbers for a football match if the *hilonim* joined in a prayer), Noam calmly noted, 'My attitude is live and let live.' Many emphasized friendships, working relationships and family ties with more religious Jews, such as Dalia: 'We can laugh about each other but we give space and we give respect.' While differentiating settler violence against Palestinians in the West Bank and Jerusalem, many admired the religious nationalists for what they characterized as 'good morals' and political commitment of the modern Orthodox to the state. For example, Michael, a right-wing Ashkenazi and former combat solider argued, 'the *kippah surgah* [National Religious] are the Last Mohicans [defending] Zionism in Israel' since the left seems to him too willing to compromise on Israeli security in order to attain peace. Few shared Amnon's strongly secularist opinion about religion in general ('I think belief in God is a little bit ignorant'), which the literature on *hilonim* also supports (Jobani 2008).

Hiloni narratives were marked by a tension between trying to distance themselves ethically and politically from some settlers and feeling the post-secular, Zionist, centripetal emotional force of *philia*. In the Zionist logic of *philia*, their violence cannot be 'fanatical' in the Western stereotype, because they are also Jews. Such violence was described as illegal, unethical, dangerous, even stupid – but not outside the bounds of what *hilonim* could intuitively comprehend. By contrast, as will be detailed below, while three wars in six years bred emotional centrifugalism from Gazans, leftist *hiloni* narratives of reasonableness were marked by a tension between this centrifugalism and centripetal attempts to feel *agape* through rational consideration of the plight of Gazan civilians.

Palestinians, *agape* and political Islamism

Across the political spectrum, my interlocutors described a series of practices of self-cultivation which focused on developing their cognitive apprehension of the Palestinians and the political conflict: reading books and articles, avidly following the Israeli and international media, researching on the internet, taking academic degrees in political science and law, thinking deeply, most often in solitude, about the political and ethical issues raised by the conflict. This was a self-driven practice of entrepreneurship. Young Jewish Israelis generally have limited opportunities to learn about Palestinians in school, and the army curriculum for new recruits about Palestinian nationalism is geared towards securitization. Many came to 'know' the Palestinian other in an abstract, intellectual manner through practices associated with cultivating a reasonable sensibility – reading, and so on – rather than through face-to-face, emotional engagement with the other. Some combat soldiers described direct engagement with Palestinians in the West Bank and Gaza as provoking a deep-seated emotional reaction in them, one that drove them towards these practices of self-cultivation. A small number of interviewees described Palestinian colleagues at work or university, even fewer friendships.

While such projects of self-cultivation are not confined to *hilonim*, what was notable was the way in which my interlocutors drew links between their intellectual 'engagement' with the other and their *hiloni* identity and worldview. To be *hiloni*, in their view, was to use their human rationality to grapple intellectually with the numerous ethical and political paradoxes of the conflict and ongoing Occupation, to generate answers beyond faith in God's plan for the history of the Jewish people (cf. Dalsheim 2007).

They portrayed open-mindedness and open-heartedness as qualities they had actively cultivated in themselves as 'rational' *hiloni* people, with heart and mind given equal weight and value. For example, some of my interlocutors on the left emphasized their initial discomfort with 'Arabs', but then spoke of transformative moments, in which they, in their view, became more open to difference, intellectually and emotionally, some at work or university and several through civil society coexistence encounters. Others described the reverse, where their initial open-heartedness had led them to feeling hurt or angered by negative engagement with 'Arabs'. Those on the right politically saw these negative experiences not as a slight against openminded-ness as an intellectual practice but anger and embarrassment at being caught out as a soft-hearted *freier* (sucker or fool). Those on the hard left politically saw negative experiences as a test, a clarion call for them to cultivate further levels of intellectual open-mindedness and emotional open-heartedness.

Notably, self-conscious performance of reasonableness was most apparent among *hilonim* from across the political spectrum when we discussed Hamas and Hezbollah. These groups are the primary facilitators of attacks against Israeli civilians over the past decade, attacks that many of my interlocutors had lived through. Most interlocutors were keen to showcase their emotional distance, giving a nuanced, intellectual appraisal of these groups, carefully critiquing their impact on both Palestinian and Jewish Israeli societies. Others professed a lack of detailed knowledge. However, their efforts not to show intense emotion were noteworthy, where other, seemingly less politically sensitive topics provoked more animation. However, to call such performances of reasonableness 'stoicism' would not accurately capture the emotional landscape of these discussions, in which some quietly but visibly seemed to wrestle with distress.

I make an *etic* distinction between 'rationality' and 'reasonableness', terms often used interchangeably in English and in Hebrew. My young *hiloni* interlocutors used the term 'rational' in English to describe two types of judgement. To judge another person as reasonable meant to judge them (i) to be appropriately emotionally restrained when under pressure *and also* (ii) to have an inherently ethical character. To judge them as rational meant the other was seen as pursuing logical self-interest, even if unethically, with what is 'ethical' defined as in the interests of the Jewish majority in Israel. The most cited examples were Hamas military and political leaders; these young *hilonim* respected them militarily in an abstract sense.

Critically, while my interlocutors invoked the Western stereotype of the irrational, emotive, unrestrained 'Islamic' fanatic when discussing Islamic State, Al Qaeda or even the Taliban, such stereotypes were not applied to Hamas or Hezbollah. While the former groups were seen as operating outside the bounds of reason, Hamas was held to be a 'rational' actor, an anti-Semitic one who elicited anger and must be violently resisted for killing Jewish civilians, but ultimately a rational one, acting out of self-interest. For young *hilonim*, across the political spectrum, the politically Islamist origins of Hamas' and Hezbollah's ideologies did not matter per se; their propensity for violence committed against Jews for being Jews was what was at stake. For example ostensibly secular Marxist groups such as the Popular Front for the Liberation of Palestine were condemned as equally as Islamic Jihad for attacking civilians. Some on the right and centre stressed the anti-Semitic nature of Hamas, Islamic Jihad and Hezbollah ideologies, over and above their articulations of their ideologies as resistance. They argued that anti-Semitic ideology made these groups dangerous, but the imbalance of power between Israelis and Palestinians held fanaticism in check.

Across the political spectrum, young *hilonim* expressed a strong stereotype of pity for 'poor', 'uninformed', 'religious' Palestinian civilians, frustration with Palestinian elites and frustration with civilians who were either unwilling or unable to build a better political future by replacing current elites. Some on the left argued that Israel's policies play a role. Such leftist attitudes represent a form of *agape*, love for the distant other. While all expressed *philia* with deployed IDF and the Jewish Israeli communities hit by rocket fire, degrees of *agape* depended on the speaker's political orientation. A small number of my leftist interviewees described feeling sad and distressed by footage of IDF bombing of Gaza during the 2014 war.

My *hiloni* interlocutors stressed that Hamas, Hezbollah and other militant Palestinian factions were rational actors, not fanatical but not reasonable either (unreasonable for killing Jewish Israeli civilians and, in the case of Hamas, their Palestinian rivals). Palestinian civilians were seen as either reasonable (if emotionally distant and pitied) others or unreasonable stooges of Hamas, depending on the interlocutor's position on the political spectrum. While a few cited anti-Semitism in Palestinian school curricula, by and large interviewees across the political spectrum thought the religiosity or non-religiosity of Palestinian civilians was not an area in which they understood the social nuance. More importantly, they found it a point moot to the more pressing question of the killing of Jewish Israeli civilians.

Conclusion

What does this case suggest about further theorization of the affective dimension of the secular? Or, as Tina Turner sang, 'what's love got to do with it?' First, this case study suggests that even in instances where seemingly secular individuals seem to mobilize a component of a European grammar of secularism and liberalism (rationality), attention to the affective register and its associated discourses and practice may actually cause what is the secular to slip even further from our grasp as analysts. Though my interlocutors privileged rational thought in their self-fashioning, they did not do so not by mobilizing, in Hirschkind's (2011: 641) words, 'the secularist narrative of the progressive replacement of religious error by secular reason' per se. Instead of Oz's formula set out in the introduction, they mobilized a hierarchy of value based on others' violent actions against civilians, deploying language which echoed but did not draw its lifeblood from the secularist narrative. Refining Hirschkind, I suggest that post-secular self-fashioning may sometimes have little to do with individuals engaging the secular-religious boundary in a particular society. As argued previously, young *hilonim* borrow from the European cultural project to fashion themselves as reasonable, but not from this exclusively. In theorizing how 'the secular' is revealed through attention to affect, some account must be taken of post-secular cases as instances of partial, complex borrowing.

Second, attention to the affective dimension, with a particular focus on two forms of love in this case, suggests a fine-grained theoretical apparatus is necessary to take into account the distinctiveness of violence as a visceral threat to physical bodies and to the body politic. The relationship between violence, the secular and post-secular is in its theoretical infancy compared to a more developed literature on religion and violence (Gutkowski 2013). Attention to the affective dimension illuminates how violence in its emotional intensity and generative capacity collapses and reconstitutes relationships between religious and secular.

In this post-secular case, during times which are understood by Jewish Israelis as not 'war', *hilonim* engage in forms of self-cultivation recognizable in secular, European cases. Relationships between what counts as religious, traditional and secular for Jewish Israelis are constituted through a series of bodily practices, including dress, consumption of food, use of space and comportment. During 'war', these distinctions remain in place, but they are joined by additional, collective bodily and affectual demonstrations of Zionist nationalism, demonstrations which draw in part on Jewish religious symbolism. Soldiering is a good example. Differences in dress, food and comportment between religious (and other) constituencies which are routinely present in army life blur into a more homogenous figure of the IDF Soldier when the country is at war. 'War' is a chaotic, emotionally intensive event in which Israeli civilians and soldiers are asked by their state to behave in an orderly, emotionally restrained fashion for the good of the body politic. This seems to feed the *hiloni* habitus of reasonableness. This *habitus* is cultivated at peace, tested and problematized during war but reaffirmed post-war.

Even if associations like Oz's between claims to rationality and life lived on the less religious end of the spectrum seem familiar to a Western eye, its associated discursive practices are more complicated. In setting themselves up as reasonable, unlike what

Toscano describes as the Western stereotype, young *hilonim* do not valourize the reasonable, secular liberal in opposition to the Islamic fanatic (or even the settler religious fanatic). Rather this discourse of *hiloni* reasonableness sets up a complicated affectual regime whereby Hamas is hated for being anti-Semitic but retained as a rational figure; Gazan civilians are pitied for being poor but dismissed as too emotional or simply too weak to unseat Hamas; and violence committed by West Bank settlers is simultaneously angrily condemned but also induces feelings of guilt for leftists who see it as illegal and unethical but as something they can emotionally comprehend in the context of Jewish *philia*. This complexity can be ascribed both to post-secular repertoires of love and also to the long-term, spatially intense nature of the conflict.

Part Three

Making Secular Citizens

Secularizing Silent Bodies: Emotional Practices in the Minute's Silence

Karsten Lichau

As early as 1912, sociologist Émile Durkheim drew attention to the link between secularization and political assemblies that is at the centre of this chapter's examination of the minute's silence, a commemoration ceremony that was established few years later in the aftermath of the First World War. In his famous *Elementary Forms of the Religious Life*, Durkheim reflected on such a 'reunion of citizens commemorating … some great event in the national life', which he thought derived from a society's

> need of upholding and reaffirming at regular intervals the collective sentiments and the collective ideas which make its unity and its personality. Now this moral remaking cannot be achieved except by the means of reunions, assemblies and meetings where the individuals, being closely united to one another, reaffirm in common their common sentiments. (Durkheim 1915 [1912]: 427)

Durkheim's reference to 'collective sentiments' and 'unity' echoes similar calls by sociologists and philosophers of his time as well as the nationalist slogans that preceded the outbreak of the First World War. While such longings for (national) unity continued after 1918, by the end of the war, societal rifts had, if anything, deepened in nearly all of the warring countries. This is where the minute's silence intervened. Enabling individuals' remembrance of the war – a 'great event' that confronted the 'national life' of many countries with the deaths of millions of soldiers and civilians and the breakdown of political, religious, economic and cultural regimes – it also staged those individuals as being 'closely united to one another', whether by sensations of bodily proximity within huge crowds in public places, or in small groups meeting in private or peripheral locations, or even by isolated individuals tied into a collective body by sharing a common silence. The minute's silence, an acoustic phenomenon both virtual and real, conjured up a unified collective or 'political body' by means of concerted silence, even if the members of that body were dispersed all over the nation's territory.

Yet the minute's silence is not only intended to establish a more or less silenced soundscape (see Schafer 1994). It is by giving rise to appropriate feelings – to 'common sentiments' of mourning, reverence or glorification – that the minute's silence fills the fictitious political body with (emotional) life. The minute's silence is an acoustic and emotional staging of a unified political body, a body that is fictitious yet seems to demand corporeal enactment. And if acoustic unity is anything but easy to perform, so is the desired emotional coherence.

This chapter focuses on early historical stagings of the minute's silence in Britain and Weimar Germany, and asks how secular ceremonies draw on, transform or break with bodily gestures and practices that have been established by (mainly Christian) religion. In these countries, the institutions involved (churches, parties, social movements, the press, military organs or veterans' associations), the symbols applied, the cultural figures and fictions and the ideologies and 'guiding ideas' (Wohlrab-Sahr and Burchardt 2012: 881) of secularism varied. Yet we will discover in all of them one feature characteristic of secularity and secularism as macro-structures: an instability and ambivalence that is intrinsic to the secular. Several authors have argued that 'the secular will always be subject to a certain indeterminacy or instability … ensured by the in principle impossibility of bordering off the secular from the religious' (Hirschkind 2011: 643), but there have been few studies that examine how this instability plays out at the micro-level in bodily practices deemed secular. The minute's silence allows us to trace the instability of secularism's discursive macro-structures down to the body, for it is only by their being enacted and embodied through corporeal practices that the powerful, yet unstable, 'formations of the secular' (Asad 2003) are affirmed, promulgated, challenged, disputed or contested, that they fail or succeed.

In order not to endlessly reiterate the complexity and fluidity of the secular and its formations, it seems important to me to complement and operationalize Asad's theory with other concepts and methods. Yet, the elements that come to be taken as secular must not be mistaken for fixed notions of what the secular is, but as contingent elements of the complex, interwoven and often-changing configurations that the secular (and, hence, the religious) might assume. Framed by discourses and other practices, these contingent elements might, at one moment or another, take on relative stability and meaning and stand for the secular, while in others they might not. As a bodily performance of the nation's fictitious political body, the minute's silence enacts political, social and cultural macro-structures while addressing numerous individual bodies that it wants to perform gestures of mourning, reverence, glorification or thanks; such performances may also give rise to other less expected or desirable feelings. A practice-theory approach to the history of 'emotional practices' as elaborated by Monique Scheer (2012a) enables scrutiny of how these macro- and micro-dimensions intertwine and interact with one another, how they build upon or counter each other. Emotional practices encompass all the different acts of organizing, preparing and fostering feelings, the complex set of actions creating a mood that is favourable to the emergence of such feelings and their affective interpretation, and without which emotions could neither germinate nor be identified in body and mind.

> Access to emotion-as-practice – the bodily act of experience and expression – in historical sources or ethnographic work is achieved through and in connection with other doings and sayings on which emotion-as-practice is dependent and

intertwined, such as speaking, gesturing, remembering, manipulating objects, and perceiving sounds, smells, and spaces. I have termed these 'doings and sayings' 'emotional practices', which build on the embodied knowledge of the habituated links that form complexes of mind/body actions. (Scheer 2012a: 209)

Recent research has pointed out not only the dynamic and instable character of secularity and secularism but also the multiplicity of routes taken by the emergence, functioning and establishment of secularist structures. Monika Wohlrab-Sahr and Marian Burchardt (2012), for example, have put forward the concept of 'multiple secularities', comprising four different ideal types meant to be heuristic rather than definitive or stable categories (889–90). The first type, 'secularity for the sake of individual liberties', proposes guiding ideas such as individuality and freedom, but is less interested in social cohesion or the concerns of social groups; these are highlighted by the second type, 'secularity for the sake of balancing/pacifying religious diversity'. Here, guiding ideas of tolerance, respect and non-interference are most valued. In the third type – 'secularity for the sake of societal or national integration and development' – guiding ideas of progress, national unity, enlightenment or modernity dominate over concerns with the freedom of groups or individuals. The fourth type – 'secularity for the sake of the independent development of institutional domains' – also places societal interests above those of the individual, but with regard to functional differentiations in a society (law, science, education, art, religion), following guiding ideas such as rationality, efficiency or autonomy. Although all four categories join in the secular project, they may give rise to tensions between secularist issues such as freedom (of individuals or groups), national unity and balance between societal groups or domains.

Though I am wary of classifying whole nations under one of these categories, no matter how heuristic they are meant to be, in the following, I will take them as hinting at four forces at work in each nation's continuing, dynamic struggle over secular issues; one or two eventually take on a dominant position, while always running the risk of being overtaken by the others. This is an especially useful approach for the time around the First World War, a period of fierce quarrels between old and new political, cultural, religious and secular protagonists and institutions. And while dealing with stagings of a nation and its political body might tend to adopt a methodical nationalism, strengthened by national policies' attempts to reaffirm national identity, stagings of the minutes' silence in different countries show numerous traces of transnational and entangled histories, which become manifest in acoustic symbols and signals or the duration of the respective silences (cf. Lichau 2014).

A short history of a short(ened) silence

The acoustical-emotional programme of staging a national political body is evident in King George V's appeal – published on 7 November 1919 in nearly all major newspapers of the British Empire – to all his people for a 'Two Minutes' Pause from Work'. This was to commemorate the 'Glorious Dead' on the anniversary of the armistice:

To all my People. Tuesday next, November 11, is the first anniversary of the Armistice which stayed the world-wide carnage of the four preceding years and marked the victory of Right and Freedom. I believe that my people in every part of the Empire fervently wish to perpetuate the memory of the Great Deliverance, and of those who have laid down their lives to achieve it. To afford an opportunity for the universal expression of this feeling it is my desire and hope that at the hour when the Armistice came into force, the eleventh hour of the eleventh day of the eleventh month, there may be for the brief space of two minutes, a complete suspension of all our normal activities. During that time ... all work, all sound, and all locomotion should cease, so that, in perfect stillness, the thoughts of every one may be concentrated on reverent remembrance of the Glorious Dead ... At a given signal, which can easily be arranged to suit the circumstances of each locality, I believe that we shall all gladly interrupt our business and pleasure, whatever it may be, and unite in this simple service of Silence and Remembrance. (George R. I. 1919: 12)

The two minutes' silence that would follow this call four days later was not the first moment of silence that had ever been observed. There had already been a similar moment in the United States, staged on 9 February 1919, in memory of President Theodore Roosevelt, who had died on 6 January of that year. Preliminary forms of such a ceremony had been observed on the occasion of King Edward VII's burial (20 May 1910) and in April 1912 commemorations of the victims of the *Titanic*'s sinking; however, these varied in length from several minutes to two hours and did not yet – as the November 11 'Two Minutes' Pause from Work' did – involve nationwide coordination and synchronization.

The British format, which was to become paradigmatic,[1] took up a proposal from Australian ex-soldier George Edward Honey, who, in a letter to the London *Evening News* published on 8 May 1919, asked 'for five minutes, five little minutes only. Five silent minutes of national remembrance' (Foster [i.e. Honey] 1919: 4). Honey's participation in a rehearsal of a five-minute silence in early November testifies to the importance of his proposal, but since the population was deemed incapable of keeping silent for five minutes, the length was finally reduced to two minutes. A second, decisive initiative came from Sir Percy Fitzpatrick, who on 4 November of the same year submitted a memorandum to the War Cabinet asking for a moment of silence in remembrance of the dead soldiers.

In both Honey's and Fitzpatrick's texts, the complex alliance between Christian tradition and an ostensibly secular event is already evident. Fitzpatrick describes his wish for 'the moving, awe-inspiring silence of a great Cathedral where the smallest sound must seem a sacrilege' to be staged anywhere, in order to have 'a multitude moved suddenly to one thought and one purpose' (Fitzpatrick, cited in Gregory 1994: 9). Honey goes even further. He is willing to contemplate '[c]hurch services, too, if you will, but in the street, the home, the theatre, anywhere, indeed, where Englishmen and their women chance to be, surely in this five minutes of bitter-sweet silence there will be service enough' (Foster [i.e. Honey] 1919: 4). The proposals do not exclude religious – or more precisely church – ceremonies, but grant them only minor importance. Honey emphasizes the non-religious and incidental character of the profane locations in which potential participants may 'chance to be and speaks of the 'service' of the nation, which is semantically opposed to the religious 'church services' and is distinguished by a 'bitter-sweet' taste, rendering other (religious) services unnecessary ('there will be service enough').

The initial conceptualization of the moment of silence displays the residual attachment of secularism – which Asad (2003) defines as the strategic, discursive and practical formations establishing, perpetuating and ruling over the secular-religion divide – to religion (specifically, Christianity): The decisive move is not against religious practices, but towards practices that fit with secularism's norms and concepts (and against those practices that do not fit with it). As long as they avoid the verdict of adhering to 'bad' religion, religious practices can 'pass' in secularism's regime, their religious quality being obfuscated or considered tolerable.

Ambiguities of silence

As we have seen from George V's appeal, as well as from Honey's letter and Fitzpatrick's memorandum, the secular question is an obvious, yet highly complex, dimension of the minute's silence. Since the generic model of the minute's silence and some of its crucial elements are themselves deeply marked by ambivalence – by an overlapping of the secular and religious – I will first analyse the secularity of some general features of the ceremony before proceeding to specific cases.

First, there is the ceremony's spatial dimension. When suggesting that a minute's silence be performed in chance locations, Honey explicitly situated the proposed silence in everyday places, whether work, school, leisure or transport, whether public or private. They could also be religious places, but they did not have to be: for Honey, the minute's silence was about falling silent wherever people 'chance to be', hence in places that could hardly be more ordinary. Honey implies an equivalence between these everyday places (as opposed to sacred ones) and the secular when he contrasts the incidental space and 'church services'.

But if the space is marked as ordinary, and hence secular, the moment is not. The temporal dimension of the silent moment is established through its auditory experience, provoked by an extraordinary soundscape. Acoustically speaking, the minute's silence is anything but a pure absence of sound. With the assembled crowd falling more or less silent, a whole set of low, usually inaudible micro-sounds comes to people's ears – the silenced bodies find their ambience suddenly changed from the 'lo-fi soundscape' characteristic of large modern cities, where 'individual acoustic signals are obscured in an overdense population of sounds', to a 'hi-fi soundscape ... in which discrete sounds can be heard clearly because of the low ambient noise level' (Schafer 1994: 43). If this 'hi-fi soundscape' is far from being a total absence of noise, it is clearly distinct from everyday acoustics, and from the noisy lo-fi soundscapes of the modern city. Thus, the silence introduces a break into the continuous, even monotone, linear flow of time, not only by the call for corporeal immobilization but also by the sudden change in the acoustic environment.

The minute's silence, then, takes place in an ordinary space – that the initiators take to be secular – and unfolds in an extraordinary suspension of time. Numerous reports on the first minute's silence allude to this break in time as numinous, sacred or even religious: 'It was the minute that touched me most, reaching down to the deepest ground of my own being ... the great, the sublime, the superhuman minute of silence and of devotion' (Pagès 1922: 1). Here, religious notions of time are confronted with the profanity of the locations, which, conversely, are coded as secular, a situation that testifies to the inherent instability of the secular/religious divide within formations of the secular.

Moreover, instability and ambivalence lurk not only in the paradoxical intertwinement of (mostly) profane place and sacral time but also in the enigmatic acoustic medium of silence itself. Even though there are several cultural spheres in which silence plays an important role – the court, the bourgeois home, the military, the school, the hospital – the practices of silent moments proposed in 1919 heavily drew on a bodily knowledge of religious practice: taking up and transforming century-old gestures from silent prayer and silent worship, monastic and anchoritic vows of silence and mythic silence, the minute's silence bore promises of re-enchantment, inverting what was deemed the *disenchanted, noisy* and *accelerated* life-world of secular modernism into a *sacral aura, silence* and *standstill.*

Yet while it is impossible to ignore the religious attitude vibrating in the sounds of silence, we should also lend our ear to some profane undertones that fall into that silence and give it a different timbre, such as the synchronization effect, eminently important to the staging of an acoustically unified national body. The locally assembled crowds not only have to be transformed into silent members of this body but also have to be linked *simultaneously* with others, who have to fall silent throughout the whole country at the same second if there is to be real silent unity. For the minute's silence is not simply about silence; it is about synchronizing collective silence. To achieve this, the minute's silence relies on the technical devices and media of modern, rationalized and disenchanted civilization and its uniform, linear time model, such as newspapers, a crucial medium for synchronizing the members of the political body.[2] The installation of modern town clocks and the process of synchronizing them are equally crucial, given that the beginning and end of the minute's silence had to be signalled at exactly the same time throughout the entire nation, a task that often failed (cf. Gregory 1994: 42).

The model of the minute's silence proves to be highly ambiguous: it is a sacred moment, staged in profane places, heavily drawing on Christian tradition to invoke a numinous atmosphere, yet enabled only by rational, mechanistic time management. And it is precisely by participating in this ritual and thus enacting these ambiguities that the production of secular bodies and emotions is set into motion.

Resonating silence: The British Armistice Day 1919

Arguably, the UK in this period was hardly secular, the king being the head not only of the British Empire's political body but also of the established Church of England, a fact inconsistent with the secular separation of church and state. Yet British culture and politics after the First World War were deeply marked by the various processes that have been subsumed under the notion of 'secularization'. At the time when the minute's silence was being introduced, there was no clearly dominant type of secularity in Britain, with three or all four of the above-mentioned types implicated in historical and contemporary problems. Obviously, secularity for the sake of national integration and progress had long been part of the British colonial and imperial project, and the war had surely not put an end to this, as is evident in George V's call for his people's unity. But due to a long history of violent confrontations between Anglicanism, Roman Catholicism and Puritanism, the need to balance and pacify religious groups within society was also an important feature of British secularity, with the Irish War of Independence reviving the political implications of a divergent religious denomination. There was also a strong tradition of secularity committed to individual freedom, owing much to the political and cultural heritage of Puritanism. All this accounts for the lack of any reference to religious or Christian practices in the king's call for a two minutes' silence, as well as for the secular attitude in Honey's and Fitzpatrick's initiatives; it may also account for the general success of the two minutes' silence in Britain. The balance between the different types of secularity, especially the influence of secularity for the sake of individual freedom, may partially explain the absence of major disturbances in the British two minutes' silence, in contrast to numerous such incidents in France and Germany. To better understand this discrepancy, I will now discuss a specific emotional practice in the British two minutes' silence that allowed for performances of non-disrupting refusal.

Anger, fully interiorized: Enlarging the spectrum of silent emotions

On 11 November, the *Daily Herald* – at that time the most important independent left-wing newspaper – published an article calling for readers to participate in the two minutes' silence. The beginning of the article does not stand out from those published in mainstream newspapers:

> You are asked to be silent for two minutes to-day, to be silent and to pause in your labours, to remember this day and this hour last year. At 11 a.m. a year ago this day the guns that had made the days hideous and the nights hell ceased firing along all the Western front. The war that seemed endless had come suddenly to an end … And to-day, at the same hour, you are to be silent for two minutes; you are to stand bareheaded wherever you be; you are to remember the Glorious Dead. ('Remembrance Day' 1919: 1)

Yet in following this call, the *Daily Herald* encourages its readers to perform a remarkable emotional practice that differs from the officially requested one, adding to the emotional spectrum an affect far from the aims of the organizers. The article does so by drawing up its own list of what was to be remembered, but also of what was likely to be forgotten:

> What will you remember and what will you forget? You will remember, mothers, the gay sons you have lost; wives, you will think of the husbands who went out in

the mist of the winter morning – the mist that sent cold chills round the heart – never to come back. And brothers will think of brothers, and friends of friends, all lying dead to-day under a tortured alien soil. But what will you forget? The crime that called these men to battle, or the fond, glorious and tragic delusion under which they went. The war that was to end the war, and that in bitter reality did not? The lies, the hatred, the cruelty, the hypocrisy, the pride; and the agony, the tears of the innocent, the martyrdom of the weak, the hunger of the poor? Make the most of this day of official remembrance. By the sacred memory of those lost to you, swear to yourself that never again, God helping you, shall the peace and happiness of the world fall into the murderous hands of a few cynical old men. ('Remembrance Day' 1919: 1)

By recalling past feelings and sensations, the unknown author seeks to spark emotion in the present. Although not expressed directly, the emotions supposed to result from this invocation reach far beyond respect, grief and mourning to encompass rage and hatred. But these affects are detached from the bodily gestures they usually combine with – gestures that tend towards outward expression by means of external, often agitated facial or bodily movements, words or cries, not to mention aggressive and violent acts. None of these are appropriate or even possible for a participant of a minute's silence, and the article does not allude to visible or acoustic articulations of the anger-and-hatred spectrum of emotions.

This performance of silent and motionless anger builds on emotional practices of interiorization and privatization, which are characteristic of the modern secular self and its isolation from the outer world[3] and which originated in Christian religion. In this case, however, it is remarkable that the *Daily Herald* recommends this interiorization practice for anger and rage, feelings that one would expect to be eliminated, tamed or suppressed, while here they are provoked only to be interiorized.[4] The practice it aims for does not devalue or counter anger, but welcomes it, while cutting it off from any exterior expression. This is a rather difficult and complex task and is perhaps only conceivable under the harsh emotional regime of 'Edwardian stoicism' (see Cook 2012) that admonished Englishmen and women – not only those from the upper classes – to keep one's feelings to oneself and avoid any display of emotion.

For theorists of secular bodies, gestures and emotions, the text offers not only this baffling yet instructive effort to incite anger while keeping it inside the body; this practice may also indicate a possibly secular feature of the collective body. For if the *Daily Herald*'s call for fully interiorized anger (whether or not it was followed) points to the diversity of emotional practices and feelings that were articulated and interiorized by a large collective body, this diversity might be seen as a specific quality of a *secular* collective body. Given that the secular is ambiguous and indeterminate 'all the way down', from its institutional, discursive and ideological formations to individual bodies, we can assume that secular bodies felt ambiguous. Charles Hirschkind argues that the comparatively strong visual, acoustic, discursive and cognitive regimes ruling over the education of religious habitus and bodies make us easily accept the idea of religious bodies, whereas asking about 'a particular configuration of the human sensorium – of sensibilities, affects, embodied dispositions – specific to secular subjects, and thus constitutive of what we mean by "secular society"' (Hirschkind 2011; 633), arouses some unease. Drawing on Hirschkind's intuition, I would argue that it is precisely this unease that might be characteristic for bodies under a secular regime. If this regime is mainly implemented by highly dynamic, flexible and unstable discursive and strategic processes, then a diversification of gestures and emotions is likely to result. Yet such diversification does not make it impossible to conceive of 'a' secular body: perhaps we only need to change our concepts and categories of emotional practices and dispositions when approaching secular bodies.[5]

The emotional practice encouraged by the *Daily Herald* enlarges the spectrum of emotions addressed by George V and illustrates the diversity of affects that can be found in the silent minute's political body as it performs 'perfect unity'. This diversity highlights two points interesting for the study of secular bodies, gestures and emotions. First, it testifies to the manifold techniques of interiorization that secularity is built upon (and that weigh heavily on both non-religious and religious practices under secularism's regime) by proposing a remarkable, even extreme form of interiorization practice. Second, our case accounts for a large diversity of emotional practices performed during the two minutes' silence. I would propose that this diversity is based on the type of secularity committed to individual freedom.

This combination of the emotional style of Edwardian stoicism and secularity for the sake of individual freedom may have provided many participants with a bodily disposition favourable to the performance of silence and immobility and may therefore have contributed to the remarkable resonance of the British two minutes' silence. Finally, the case presents some evidence that individual members of a collective body, 'doing emotions' under secularist regimes, are likely to perform particularly diverse emotional practices; accordingly, some of those actors' bodies might feel uneasy with choosing which performance to stage. Hirschkind's unease therefore resonates with the specific configurations within which secular bodies act and may be regarded as a specific attitude of a secular body. We will encounter similar kinds of unease throughout the next cases.

'Moved by an uncontrollable impulse': Learning the minute's silence

My second example is also drawn from the first ever British two-minute silence, performed on 11 November 1919, or, to be more precise, from the discursive context surrounding, interpreting and commenting on this performance. Two points in the description by an anonymous British journalist on his own experience of the event are of special interest for exploring secular bodies. First, his report – published in the *Times* on 12 November – hints at a certain unease and reticence with regard to the impending ceremony of silent remembrance. Second, it reveals a gap between the gestures and feelings that the participants in a minute's silence may desire (or the practices applied to achieve them) and the feelings actually performed in the situation. This gap also testifies to an indeterminacy in what is supposed to be the practice of a collective secular body and to a lack of familiarity with the situation and the emotional style to be applied, since some of the actors performing the ceremony prove unaware of the appropriate emotional practice or are not particularly skilled at it.

The *Times* article is also a fine example of the corporeal and social dimensions of the performance of emotion-as-practice, showing that emotional practices are invested with the body's complex social knowledge (Scheer 2012a: 196–97). The social competence and intelligence of learned, culturally shaped bodies can even run counter to intentions.

The reported episode took place in a secular locale, where the participants 'chance to be': 'When the hour struck for the great tribute to the fallen four of us were on the top of an omnibus climbing a steep hill in South-West London. A minute or two before we had been discussing, with a forced cynicism of which each of us was secretly ashamed, some supposedly humorous sides of the proposed standstill' ('Cynics Confounded' 1919: 16). The description of the young men joking at the impending two minutes' silence exemplifies a performative strategy of discursive utterances (jokes, humorous discussion) and bodily signs (smiling, laughing); the young men claim to feel amused. This joviality results from their intention of opposing themselves to the call for respect and mourning by the hegemonic emotional regime (which nevertheless manifests itself in their alleged feelings of secret shame). This attempt initially seems to be successful, but then comes the moment of silence:

> Our conversation was interrupted by the stoppage of the omnibus. It stopped opposite a small factory … [T]he Union flag was lowered to half-mast. Facing it were 10 or a dozen of the factory workers, wearing their working overalls but not their caps, and standing rigidly at attention. Glancing along the road, we saw at irregular intervals perhaps 20 people, mostly women, some with children in perambulators, others laden with the morning's shopping purchases. Without exception they stood still, while the maroons boomed near and far. All was motionless and silent. ('Cynics Confounded' 1919: 16)

This is the moment when the young men's bodies, as if guided by some secret force, counter their disrespect for the impending two minutes' silence and switch to another emotional practice:

> It was then that we four cynics on the omnibus top realized that we, too, were on our feet and our heads were uncovered. None of us could say by what process of thought he came to that position; looking back on the action, we would all confess that we did it half-unconsciously, as though moved by an uncontrollable impulse. For the full two minutes we, and the women, and the line of factory workers, stood, as myriads of others stood, to do homage to the immortal dead. ('Cynics Confounded' 1919: 16)

It would be too easy to classify this practice as the four young men's bodies succumbing to their social surroundings by pure corporeal contagion as a passive process of obedient bodies, triggered and overwhelmed by external processes (cf. Scheer 2012a: 206). The seemingly instantaneous emotional 'overwhelming' described by the journalist is the result of long-term emotional refinement and learning that made these bodies capable of analysing and interpreting, in a very short time, the social situation and the performance taking place and of avoiding the impending social sanctions that would probably have followed had the four continued to mock and joke at the other passengers' performance of sincere (or feigned) mourning and reverence for the dead soldiers. Consequences could have ranged from the young men appearing ridiculous, to 'killing' glances of disapproval, or even open aggression in word or deed. The four young men's bodies prove their habitus' social and corporeal knowledge, which is at once subject to and the subject of emotional practices:

> We are subjected by and through emotions – the fact that they 'overcome' us and are outside our control is the embodied effect of our ties to other people, as well as to social conventions, to values, to language. Emotions do not pit their agency and autonomy against ours; they emerge from the very fact that subjectivity and autonomy are always bounded by the conditions of their existence, by the fundamental sociability of the human body and self. (Scheer 2012a: 207)

Looking at the narrative structure of the article, there is a small element that – doubts as to its real or fictitious nature notwithstanding – sets the stage for the allegedly unforeseen change in behaviour by a hidden inner impulse: the brief remark that the men are 'secretly ashamed' of their own cynicism serves a narrative strategy of authentification. It qualifies the reverent emotional practice finally adopted by the 'four young cynics' as stemming not only from pure external contagion but also from an inner impulse. In doing so, it both attributes emotional agency to the subjects and, in line with the traditional dichotomy of true inner feelings and false outer appearance, gives their acts an authentic quality.

By identifying an inner as well as an outer source of the resulting emotional practice, the text grasps the complex, intertwined structure of the silent gestures: their performance in a collective staging makes them at once inwardly and outwardly oriented, since the gestures aim for devotion, reverent remembrance and mourning (emotional practices that only become 'sincere' when addressing and reaching the bodies' 'interior'), which are then intensified by the public performance, which is to say, by an external dimension.

In this respect, the silent gestures are evidence of the complex process of learning emotional practices, in which body, subject and social environment engage and intertwine. The four young men's ability to make such a sudden commitment to the performance they had just mocked must stem from a much longer process of incorporating the complex hegemonic structures and normative emotional practices of a society, since they would surely not have been able to change their minds so quickly by means of rational discourse (as the author himself admits: 'None of us could say by what process of thought he came to that position'). The ability to adapt immediately to the social situation is dependent on social knowledge incorporated by the 'mindful body'. The metamorphosis in the young men's bodily and emotional gestures follows 'an intentionality not necessarily based on propositional thought. Emotions can thus be strategic without implicating conscious goal-orientation – they can even be at odds with conscious wills and desires, but nevertheless be oriented toward goals presented by social scripts' (Scheer 2012a: 203).

Nevertheless, the gap between these 'social scripts' and the mockery emotive uttered in the bus scene accounts for the feelings of unease or reticence that I take to be a specific attitude of secular bodies and that I will examine in more detail in my next case study.

Silence, reticence and the motley crowd: How to deal with secular bodies?

In Weimar Germany, the cultural and political contexts of secularity were particularly complex, with regard to both the relations between secular and religious institutions and the reconfiguration of the churches' positions and cultural influence.

Although the Weimar constitution clearly broke with the 'state church' principle of the regional churches, the legacy of a 'sometimes confusing overlap and co-mingling of church and state responsibilities at the institutional level' (Habermas 2011: 458) continued to influence the cultural and political sphere. Things became even more confusing when the Catholic Church found its way back into public recognition, because it was – despite its enthusiasm for the war – far less identified with and thus compromised by the collapsed Wilhelmine state than was Protestantism. In consequence, the relationship to democracy and state politics of both Christian churches remained marked by instability, reticence and strategic interests, and support for the republican state's public ceremonies was not very strong in either Protestantism or Catholicism.

This contributed to making the remembrance of the war dead a difficult task in Weimar Germany. When Edwin Redslob, the Weimar Republic's *Reichskunstwart*, or 'Imperial art protector', finally succeeded in arranging a *Gedenkfeier des Deutschen Volkes zu Ehren der Opfer des Weltkriegs* (Commemoration by the German people to honour the victims of the World War) on 3 August 1924, with a 'two-minute-commemoration pause' as its emotional highlight, the churches remained reluctant. And so did other institutions involved in memory politics. Political parties, regional governments and Veterans' Associations – especially the very influential militaristic and right-wing league for the care of German war graves, the *Volksbund Deutsche Kriegsgräberfürsorge*, whose participation was crucial for any war-remembrance project – dissented on what was to be remembered and how: the soldiers' bravery or their misery, only German soldiers or all soldiers, the fight for Germany or for the Kaiser, glory or mourning. And there was also dissent regarding the date, some of the institutions insisting on their own commemoration days in November (for the churches) or March (for the *Volksbund*). This added to a general lack of political support for Redslob's *Gedenkfeier* and left it open to political attacks, as reported in the *Vossische Zeitung*:

The two minutes' commemoration pause in remembrance of the dead had just begun and profound silence lay suddenly upon the square. This was the moment that a few communist groups among the participants had chosen to disturb the ceremony. Pamphlets were thrown in the air, and some agitators tried to start speeches. In most cases, the other participants did not tolerate this, and the police also intervened immediately. There were a few attempts to sing the *Internationale*, but these were countered by dissenting groups singing *Die Wacht am Rhein* and also the *Flaggenlied* [two emblematic songs of the right-wing movements, K,J,], and finally they came to a poor end when the two-minute commemoration pause was over. (Z_R 1924: 4)

The *Vossische Zeitung*, known as Republic-friendly, does not emphasize what the lines make evident: not only did the attempts to disturb the minute's silence come to 'a poor end' but so did the official ceremony itself, and it would never again make an appearance in Weimar Germany's official remembrance politics (see Lichau 2014).

This acoustic incident and its echoes in the newspapers surely had a negative impact on Redslob's project of establishing a commemorative ceremony for the war dead, but another article shows more subtle forms of reticence and unease. In the August 3 issue of the *Vossische Zeitung*, Erdmann Graeser, a writer known for his popular dialect novels about Berlin's lower classes, ponders the forthcoming 'two-minute commemoration pause', during which 'the whole of Berlin transport [will] pause from 12 o'clock to 12.02 pm' (Graeser 1924: 5). Graeser imagines the impressive acoustic and emotional effect of 'standstill and silence, suddenly in the roaring song of the big city – two minutes only. And yet, an endless time span for him who will emotionally go through its gravity and mourning, if we consider that one can relive one's whole life in the last second of one's existence' (Graeser 1924: 5).

Graeser emphasizes the temporal state of exception and the break with the perception of linear time, conjuring up a strange atmosphere never yet experienced by the German and Berlin population:

Is there any familiarity with being seized by standstill and silence? Well, there is in other countries, but to us, this kind of ceremony is entirely new. The Berlin people have already set their clocks for various goals, for solar and lunar eclipses, but never for such a commemorational pause in silent remembrance of those who gave their lives for us. (Graeser 1924: 5)

Mentioning the familiarity with this atmosphere 'in other countries' demonstrates a vivid interest in other nations' cultural and memorial politics – something that we find in France as well, where the British and Belgian ceremonies on 11 November commanded much attention and more admiration than the French event. But the crucial point in Graeser's meditations is a kind of uneasiness with or reticence towards the secular dimension of the minute's silence, notably when he comes to reflect on the places where the performance is to be staged and on their socially coercive nature:

Maybe in one or another person something might protest against revealing, on demand, the concerns of his heart in a chance location. Usually, one keeps aloof with grief; often the wounds begin to burn by themselves, suddenly, in the silence of the night. How shall we now – amid a motley crowd of total strangers – handle this situation? (Graeser 1924: 5)

Graeser's reflections on an inner 'protest against revealing' feelings in public attest to the importance of modern self and its bodily capacity to interiorize emotions (which we already found at work in the *Daily Herald*'s call for fully interiorized anger), as well as to the importance of learning how to feel 'inner emotions' (Scheer 2012a: 200). Interiorization is an emotional practice crucial to secularism's capacity to establish secular religion as a practice 'passing' as compliant with the norms that secularism imposes on cultural practices, religious ones included (see Asad 2003: 52–56). This modern and secularist cultivation of interiority has mostly admonished the self to keep its 'inner' emotional practices not only inside the body but also inside the 'private realm' – places that are 'familiar' in the strict sense and do not belong to the public sphere. This is what matters in Graeser's unease with the notion of inner feeling on external demand: it is an emotional practice that is to be ostentatiously displayed in a public composed of 'total strangers'.

In other words, whereas the silent setting and the accompanying immobilization of the participants' bodies are favourable to the interiorization processes called for ('the imparting of the desired emotional response involves imparting the requisite bodily disposition, for example in the silent, reverent postures and minimal movements that support interiorization' [Scheer 2012a: 216]), the *place* in which this setting is to be applied is, though clearly marked as secular, at odds with the culturally required conditions of interiorization practices. The cultural script of secular emotions withdraws feelings from the public sphere and relegates them to the realm of the interior.

There is something we can learn from this when considering the secular body. Graeser's reflections illustrate that the performance of inner feelings might be at odds with their public staging. And yet, this conflict may be resolved by a new shift in the ever-dynamic discursive regime of secularism, even if that shift would take some time to be incorporated. The emotional practice that I want to draw attention to, however, is not merely interiorization, but Graeser's feeling of reticence and unease.

Perhaps most striking is the element of discomfort and hesitation in the author's imagination of the sudden confrontation with the situation, a situation that calls for public performance of a feeling deemed to belong to the private realm. Might we not take this unease as a bodily manifestation of the indeterminacy and ambivalence inherent to secularist regimes and epistemologies? If formations of the secular are haunted by an instability that is not only 'a condition of its exercise' (Hirschkind 2011: 643) but also a dilemma hinting at the need for an incessant subjection of practices to the discursive regulation of the secular/religious distinction, then I would argue that secularism as a discursive regime is likely to leave the body somewhat alone.

I agree with Hirschkind that a certain '*reticence* to speak about the embodied capacities and dispositions of a secular subject is not just the result of scholarly prudence, but … reflects, rather, something about the concept of the secular' (Hirschkind 2011: 641; emphasis added). But does this not also point to a dilemma or 'reticence' that might viscerally affect historical bodies? Might some of these bodies not, due to their historically and socio-culturally refined knowledge, come to be affected by this secularist indeterminacy? And might this not give rise to corporeal processes that are not necessarily expressed in well-defined signs or easily decoded gestures, but rather in undetermined and blurred emotional practices of reticence and unease? Finally, if 'the secular will always be subject to a certain indeterminacy or instability' (Hirschkind 2011: 643), could we not take Graeser's text as suggesting such a corporeal manifestation of unease, an emotional trace hinting at the underlying secular regime's 'indeterminacy or instability'?

This is not, of course, to say that feelings of unease or reticence are unknown to 'religious bodies', which according to Hirschkind are much easier to conceive of. Hegemonic religious cultures just as much as minoritarian or heretic religious cultures and the emotional regimes or styles they establish are subject to historical change and political struggle, which also alter these emotional regimes. But such historical changes give rise to religiously inflected gestural and emotional practices that are, if not stable, still considerably more identifiable than are those of the secular period. We might thus ask whether emotional 'moods' such as uneasiness or reticence should be interpreted as implicit or indirect manifestations of secularist constellations, making secular bodies 'speak' in a tacit way that differs from the more overt ways in which religious bodies speak, but that is nevertheless sometimes put into words by a subtle author (such as Graeser or Hirschkind).

We can also pose the question of the secular body in another way: If there is no secular body, then who is to perform ceremonies in secular times? Hirschkind insists that the dynamic interpretations of secularism's regime are 'a condition of its existence', and such interpretations also comprise bodily training and staging. This is emphasized by Durkheim's reference to 'reunions, assemblies and meetings where the individuals, being closely united to one another, reaffirm in common their common sentiments' (Durkheim 1915 [1912]: 427), but also by Bourdieu's theory of practice.[6]

When dealing with the question of the secular body, we may need to adapt our concepts and perceptions of bodies, affects and emotions. If there is no stable and identifiable secular body, it is the bodies trained in traditional roles that perform such ceremonies. Or, if the repertoire of gestures and emotions to be performed does not itself pose a problem, the question of whether that repertoire is appropriate to the actual place and situation might still do so. Due to the effect of *hysteresis* that makes bodies persist in corporeal habits and practices to which they have long been accustomed, Christian gestures survive under secular rule. But bodies also learn where these are appropriate and where they are not. From the nineteenth century on, the

> interiority of the soul produced in this way was mirrored by the drawing of sharp boundaries between private and public in the social sphere. The bourgeois home as a refuge was the principal location where 'sympathetic feelings' – the distinguishing feature of private bourgeois relationships … amongst family members or friends – could be experienced and become habituated. Part of this set of emotional practices was religion, or rather belief, held to be highly private … and introverted. (Scheer 2012b: 183)

Indeed, this is what puzzles Graeser when he asks how to 'handle this situation', a situation that wants his body to perform gestures of interiorization and display emotions of mourning, usually practised in private – where one is not supposed to be amid 'total strangers' – in public places (such as the proverbial street or an omnibus) that do not belong to the religious or private realm.

There may, then, be a secular body (or several of them). But if we want to understand that body and follow its traces in emotional practices, we may need to shift our perspective and not search for clearly distinguished gestures and signs. Instead, the secular body lurks in vague and blurred practices, as indeterminate and instable as are the powerful formations of the secular by which it is forged. Drawing on Hirschkind's striking metaphor of the secular as 'the water we swim in', I would like to take this fluid, dynamic element not only as an instructive illustration of the instable, dynamic and ever-changing quality of the secular *around us* but also of the secular *inside us*. As human bodies consist mainly of water, I would argue that the secular is not only the 'water we swim in' but also the water that swims in us, in our bodies – troubled water that is not calmed even by standstill and silence.

Required Romance: On Secular Sensibilities in Recent French Marriage and Immigration Regulations

J. A. Selby

'Fatima': Three days after [I delivered my son] – imagine – the police came to our home. The police came to our house to see if we were really married. They looked at photos. They questioned my mother who was visiting [from Algeria] for the birth. So, they saw my mother, they looked at the photos, and my son, and my husband. So, yeah, there was an investigation [*une enquête*] about it [our relationship], to see if we were really married.

JS: Did they let you know in advance?

F: Not at all. They don't warn you. They knock at the door. And you have to be ready.

Pascal Clément, French Minister of Justice: Marriage has, in effect, become a major stake in migration. ... Joining a spouse has become the main motive of family immigration ... We must recognize that the number of frauds reported by mayors and consular and diplomatic agents to the public prosecutor have not stopped rising. (Ministère de la Justice 2006)[1]

This chapter considers the effects of post-2006 governmental attention to the marriages of transnational couples, focusing on Muslim French of Algerian origin who live in a northwestern Parisian suburb.[2] Imagined as an impediment against foreign nationals who gain legal entry into France through 'love fraud with a migratory goal' (*escroquerie sentimentale à but migratoire*), new laws were introduced in 2006 and 2011, as well as a governmental memorandum in 2010. I situate these changes amid a broader French legal climate that, since 2004, has increasingly restricted visible expressions of Islam. I argue that scrutiny of transnational marriages reveals a dovetailing of the state's surveillance of sexuality with its protection of *laïcité* (French secularism).[3]

Whether or not it is officially mandated as such, most of my interlocutors experience the citizenship project of France as intimately tied to a 'secular' one. For this reason, I examine a 'sexual-secular-citizenry' constellation through consideration of how it appears in their marriage partner preferences and marriage ceremonies and experiences. Because the state controls civil marriage ceremonies[4] and has articulated concern that transnational marriages are increasingly undertaken for duplicitous non-romantic purposes, I see the French state's protection of access to civil marriage as a form of border control, and as reflecting secular sensibilities for both genders (Scott [2018] has brilliantly focused on the constellation's continuing impact on women). Drawing on ethnographic data and considering factors of postcoloniality and racialization, I therefore show how my participants navigate the state's expectations of 'romantic love'.

The first passage, above, is excerpted from an interview with Fatima, thirty-two, born in Algeria. Fatima currently lives next to my field-site of Petit-Nanterre, a suburb fifteen kilometres northwest of Paris.[5] She wears her long black hair pulled back in a high ponytail and dresses in trendy sports clothes (I too describe her body as revelatory of her immigration and religious politics). She is an Arabophone fluent in French. She recounts the police investigation of her transnational marital union to a distant French-born cousin after their wedding in Algeria and her migration to this suburb where he grew up. As she points out, police visits are unannounced to preclude rehearsed romance.[6] These visits can take place at any point in the first four years of marriage.

The second passage is an excerpt from a March 2006 speech delivered by then French minister of justice Pascal Clément to defend the beginning of a new series of family regroupment immigration-focused laws that effected non-EU marriage partners.[7] Clément describes a rising tide of familial-based immigration where one gains residency and then citizenship through marriage. This kind of family-based immigration has been the most common legal entryway into France since the early 1970s, and in recent history, has been pejoratively characterized by Presidents Chirac and Sarkozy (among others) as *immigration subie* (imposed) and not *choisie* (chosen, meaning selective or economy based). To curb this 'major migration issue', Minister Clément argues for greater scrutiny of these 'imposed' transnational unions, perceived as a loophole for legal settlement in France. Clément notes how, in 2005, one of every three marriages in the Republic was 'mixed', or a French national marrying a non-French non-EU individual. Indexed as threatening the 'purity and integrity of French citizenship', transnational civil marriage has become a site of increasingly rigidified surveillance of love with *laïque* scripts and sensibilities. Racialized and non EU-nationals in 'traditional' arrangements are most vulnerable. What counts as 'appropriate love' indexes desired constructions of race, immigration and *laïcité*.

Drawing on theoretical developments in secularism studies, on my own ethnographic data and on French political and legal documents, following some contextualization, the next three sections examine how my participants navigate the discretionary power of French administrators in their assessment of emotional and bodily displays of intimacy in civil marriage-related procedures. In this analysis I make two assumptions: that secular-articulated legal projects are always necessarily linked to the framing of religiosity and that the secular entails 'a framework of corporeal experience and struggle' (Warner 2008; see also Asad 2003; Selby and Fernando 2014; Amir-Moazami 2016). This framework can be seen in how the sincerity of transnational marrying couples is questioned: Do they display 'proper' intimacy and sexuality?

"My interlocutors' experiences with the evaluation of their 'proper' comportment evidence liberal notions of individualism and their so-called emancipatory power to 'protect' against patriarchy."

Background and context

Scholars have long shown how governmental jurisdiction on sexuality – particularly of foreign encultured subjects – is heightened amid colonial politics, where its control is 'a fundamental class and racial marker implicated in a wider set of relations of power' (Stoler 2002: 45; see also MacMaster 1997; Dobie 2001). In the French case, others have argued that the 'end' of colonialism further entrenched the Republic's putative sexual freedoms (see Clancy-Smith 1998; Shepard 2012; Surkis 2010). Beyond colonial politics, all marrying couples are socialized into socially desirable performances of wedding ceremonies; today these typically privilege capital consumption and visible amorousness. The French state arguably holds a privileged role in the regulation of marriage given that, even as its social meanings and legal contours continue to shift,[8] all state-recognized ceremonies take place in a city hall and, if they take place abroad, are legitimized by a French consulate, which must apply the same directives (*Le Monde* 2006).

As social values about marriage shift, so too do those related to *laïcité*, which today is increasingly positioned as a lynchpin of the nation state's *vivre ensemble* (living well together), with a distinctly anti-Muslim tenor. Mapped on the body, in the German context, this secular discourse, says Schirin Amir-Moazami (2016: 149), 'gains currency *through* the discursification of the Muslim body'. Indeed, constructing its undesirable religious counterpoint is central to the secular's role. In France, the banning of visible religious signs in public schools and government offices in 2004 mobilized this language of living well together, which re-emerged when niqabs and face-covering veils were prohibited in the public sphere in 2011 and in public debates on the appropriateness of burkinis in 2016. The sociologist Éric Fassin describes this period as espousing a new Republican regime of 'sexual democracy' (2006, 2010), akin to the historian Joan Wallach Scott's appellation of 'sexularism' (see also Fernando 2014: 689). After 2004, 'Frenchness', notes Fassin, becomes 'primarily about sexual freedom and equality' (Fassin 2010: 512; see also Scott 2018: 175). Body-covering garments were thus legally expunged from an imagined shared public sphere because they violate the sexual-secular-citizenry constellation: they are too conservative, too patriarchal, too Muslim, too foreign, too conspicuous. It is therefore no accident that, within this same period (2006–2011), the 'purity and integrity' of citizenship with transnational unions became flagged as a vulnerable entry point.

This post-2004 period is noteworthy. Recent theoretical examinations of the secular body including Talal Asad's (2011; see also Connolly 2011; Hirschkind 2011; Selby and Fernando 2014) locate the secular's ordering mechanisms as expressed through and on bodies, pointing to the 'hidden transcript' of these machinations (cf. Scott 1990). Asad (2011: 661), for instance, argues that the secular body's normativity and invisibility are what grants it power: 'you couldn't tell whether she was a believer or not'. William Connolly (2011) similarly contends that the secular body's expectations are concealed and therefore immunized from challenge, appearing through 'dress codes, regularized gestures, public vocabularies, strategies of justification, and styles of walking' (2011: 272). In contrast, my findings suggest that secular bodies and sensibilities in post-2004 France are neither invisible nor concealed. Legal projects since 2004, including those I discuss related to transnational marriage, are increasingly prescriptive and demanding of a secular legibility. Unlike Asad's notion of a 'repressed' secular body, Connolly's subtle 'filtered' one or Charles Hirschkind's (2011: 634) description of the secular body as 'the [invisible] water we swim in,' all must wade through the state's secular prescriptions to different degrees, in ways that for many of my interlocutors, demand visible emotional and bodily work. For example, we will see how, despite holding French citizenship, Nawel, 28, who emigrated from Algeria to a Parisian *banlieue* for her studies, expressly worries that because her marriage is not a romantic 'love match,' the French consulate in Algiers might not validate her and her husband's papers. Nawel knows her performance at the consulate could have significant implications: if not deemed sincere, she may not later receive a *livret de famille* ('family book,' a formal record of marriage, children's births and other 'family records,' required in France when enrolling children into school, applying for state benefits, purchasing property and so on). In this moment of contact (cf. Linke 2006), Nawel enacts what she feels are preferred postures and comportment, namely by performing her freedom from the supposed clutches of Islamic patriarchy. Even if symbolically facile, her purposeful chignon hairstyle worn to the French consulate in Algiers is one marker to this end, as are how she chose to apply her make-up and how she consciously censored the arranged beginnings of her marriage in conversation.

The aforementioned laws and political discourses focus on transnational marriage, but its logic is particularly concretized in a 2010 memorandum on *mariages gris* (grey marriages) that followed the 2006 legislation, concerned by fake (*blanc*), fraudulent (*gris*) and forced (*forcé*) marriage.[9] In order to impede the fraud and heartache of a *mariage gris*, then minister of immigration, integration, national identity and co-development Eric Besson granted more discretionary power to marriage administrators to determine and report marriage fraud. The twenty-three-page 22 June 2010 memorandum lists two pages of questions to be asked by officiants to couples separately to assess their knowledge of one another. It suggests that officiants note details about the ceremony (the atmosphere, mood, who paid for the rings), as well as the couple's living situations. According to this document, marriage is 'primarily' about 'living together and sharing family life' (*Ministère de la Justice* 2010), so that unions contracted with an eye to other benefits, including citizenship, can be considered fraudulent and then impeded or annulled (see Robledo 2011).[10] A handful of scholars have examined these laws (see Cole 2014; Fassin 2010, 2014; Robledo 2011), but there was little governmental debate or media attention prior to their passing (*Le Monde* 2006). In addition to segregated questioning at mayors' offices and in French consulates, surveillance extends to unannounced follow-up visits to couples' homes. As Fatima explains, above, these visits focus on non-French nationals and are meant to surveil intimacy. I now turn to how this logic plays out in the experiences of individuals of Algerian origin, beginning with Ilias' take on romantic and religious rationales.

The irrationality of religion (read: Islam)

'Ilias': But, in the end [*en fin de compte*], dating wasn't working for me. So, ummm, I preferred to proceed by other means. And, umm, proceed religiously. And so, there you have it [*voilà*]. So I started to read [online] and see who was interested in this approach. And, in fact, I found it really interesting to see how reason takes precedence over love. And that's, that was what I was looking for, actually. That a religious approach is more rational.

Ilias, twenty-five, grew up in the Parisian suburb where my field research has been based since 2004. At the time of our formal interview in 2014, I had known him for ten years (and had interviewed his grandmother about her marriage migration in 2006), but we had never spoken privately about personal matters, like his marital decisions. Tall and good-humoured, he is a third-generation, Algerian-origin full-time waiter who dreams of becoming an actor. Ilias married Zara, also twenty-five, a little more than a year ago. Ilias has dual French and Algerian nationality. Perhaps owing to the fact that I knew his grandmother well, in our interview he speaks at length about how he has been influenced by his paternal grandparents' migration and marital lives. In speaking about their marriage, he notes:

For me, my « method » [of living, of finding love] is my grandmother ... I found all of that [referring to his grandparents' marriage] very, very beautiful. Very, very simple. Very natural and ... I was really supported by that. That was ... those were real commitments [*des vrais engagements*].

Ilias' grandmother migrated from Algeria in the late 1950s following his grandfather's arrival to work in a neighbouring factory. His grandparents had had an arranged marriage in their hometown, and she had then waited, with the first of their five children, for her husband to settle before joining him in a shack and then apartment in this Parisian suburb. Skipping over his parents and their influence is no accident. Like a good number of youth of that generation, as a young man in the early 1980s, Ilias' French-born ethnic Algerian father became involved in the suburb's drug trade. His father married his mother, who migrated from Algeria for the arranged marriage, and who was unaware that he had a drug addiction and was embroiled in crime. Her 'traditionalism' and virginity offered him a fresh start. A social worker in a community association explained to me that women like Ilias' mother relied upon family networks in their migration and often hoped for glamour and new opportunities in France.

Unfortunately, Ilias' functionally illiterate mother encountered neither glamour nor opportunity in Petit-Nanterre and died from complications of HIV-AIDS, contracted from his father through his intravenous drug use; his father died by suicide. When it looked like Ilias might also fall into the local trade, at fourteen, his grandparents sent him to live with relatives in rural Algeria for three months. Although he had visited on vacation with his parents a handful of times, this trip impacted him: the *Bled* (Arabic for 'home country'; see Selby 2014a, 2017) has become a place for *ressourcement* (meaning both 'returning to one's roots' and 'rejuvenation'). As he explains in the opening passage of this section, after years of casually dating women of different backgrounds, he decided he wanted to *procéder autrement … procéder religieusement* (proceed differently … proceed religiously) in seeking a suitable marriage partner after the death of his grandmother.

Zara was born in Algeria and migrated with her family to a northeastern Parisian suburb when she was ten years old. For Ilias, Zara's upbringing was ideal: she had absorbed notions of modesty and religiosity but had attained French residency status, removing the suspicion of duplicitous motivations. Zara wears hijab but removes it everyday for her job at the Roissy airport. Also unlike his mother, Zara speaks French fluently and is well socialized in French culture, skills Ilias saw as handicapping his 'traditional' and religiously practising mother's short life. At the same time, Zara understands his 'grandmother method' of seeking an arranged match. Aware of the 2006 and 2011 laws on transnational marriage, and with the acute knowledge of his parents' failed union, Ilias states plainly, 'I preferred not to be bothered by all the paperwork [to sponsor a transnational bride].' Governmentality lingers in their union in so far as Ilias knew paperwork for a transnational union would be burdensome. Still, referring to the legacies of two previous generations of transnational marriages, Zara's virginity and the religious parameters of the match, he concludes, 'it's good to start cleanly [*proprement*]'.

This shift in attitude could be related to Ilias' newfound more regular religious practice. Like many young men in Petit-Nanterre (Selby 2014a), Ilias has practised Ramadan since his teens, but recently began praying on Fridays and has grown a beard. Yet even if religion is part of his approach, his grandparents' example anchors his marital choices. In his narrative, Ilias incisively understands what is at stake when he imagines marriage in a way he thinks his grandmother would have understood and encouraged. He is fully aware of the competing pressures of French 'secular' and 'traditional' forms of love and how they are constructed as such. He believes that because he and Zara have had a traditional arranged marriage which members of their families supported (as well as Allah), when they inevitably face challenges, they will have a better chance than those holding the individualizing conceptions of love implicitly upheld by the French state. This traditional 'grandmother method' Ilias describes is in large part what the French state subtly aims to curtail.

Ilias' negotiation of marriage partner sheds some light on how the state has impacted his marital aspirations in ways that are not immediately perceptible. Concerned with the Muslimness of his bride, he nevertheless sought to protect himself from a *mariage gris*. More notably, Ilias astutely rejects the logic undergirding these laws: that romance and individual choice safeguard against love fraud, and that 'traditional' arranged marriages are anathema to love and rational choice. On the contrary, after conducting his own research on what was Islamically appropriate, Ilias references his religiously framed marital arrangement as wholly 'rational'. From his perspective, this rationality is superior to an imagined romantic love sought after in state-sanctioned transnational weddings. In other words, Ilias indicates the compatibility of arranged, religious marriages with love. He has taken measures that he thinks will give his marital life greater longevity than the state-favoured parameters. He has thus destabilized the prevailing notion of the French state, which conceives of a 'proper' marriage in secular terms. Ilias reframes the logic undergirding the legislation against transnational marriage. For him, to be religious and traditional is to be entirely modern and rational.

Secular scripts and sensibilities

> '*Nawel*': It wasn't a love marriage. We didn't know each other. And we didn't have a lot of time to get to know one another because the marriage came together really really quickly: two months from the proposal to the wedding. So, we weren't, we didn't know what to expect [at the French consulate in Algiers, validating their marriage].

Nawel was born in Tlemcen, a small Western Algerian city, approximately forty kilometres west of Morocco. She already held French citizenship when she married 'Khalid', a neighbour in her hometown, who also held two passports. Nawel and Khalid's marriage took place two years before we met at their apartment in a rented hall in Tlemcen one day and featured eight dresses and a feast and party with both of their extended families and friends present. As aforementioned, citizenship was not at stake, but their wedding certificate needed to be legitimized at the French consulate for their *livret de famille*. A helpful way to frame the prescriptions of individualism and sexual emancipation laden in these secular mores and embodiments is with Nadia Fadil's (2009: 444) notion of the 'dominant sensitivities' latent in liberal-secular regimes. Fadil examines a different register: her participants express concern with managing others' affects more than gaining access to rights and citizenship. Her analysis of Muslim Belgian Maghrebi female informants shows how they manage emotionally laden and potentially socially transgressive practices (see also Jouili 2015: 101). This section considers how two young women – Nawel and Fatima – take on secular sensibilities in their marriage-related engagement with the French state.

At the time of our interview, Nawel and Khaled lived in a small bright, newly built fifth-floor one-bedroom rental apartment, north of Paris, furnished with Ikea furniture and packed tight with baby equipment and toys for their eighteen-month-old son. At the time of their engagement, they knew of each other from Tlemcen, but they had never met in France. They agreed to the marriage in Algeria arranged by their parents. As with a number of my second- and third-generation participants, Nawel's mother, Maria, also had a transnational marriage, in this case slightly different because Maria was born in France. Maria's father had emigrated from Algeria in the 1940s and worked as a nurse at the Avicenne Hospital, north of Paris. Maria met Nawel's father while on summer holiday in Tlemcen. She studied English in Canada and the UK, and Nawel proudly notes that she once travelled solo to the United States. Nawel smiles as she tells these stories about her mother's premarital travel, but later admits that she too questioned her mother's agency in marrying and migrating from France, which she sees as a far more desirable place to live and love than Tlemcen:

> She [my mother] chose to return [*de rentrer*] to Algeria to marry. There you have it [*voilà*]. When I asked her if it was forced, she said, 'Oh no, no. Not at all. It was my choice ... I decided. I chose. And I returned [to Algeria].'

Nawel's parents had three children and run an export business. At nineteen, Nawel left Tlemcen to complete her baccalaureate degree in French at Université Paris III; due to health concerns, she returned a few years later to regroup and work in the family's business. When she turned twenty-five, she says she had had enough of the *mentalité* in her hometown and returned to France for studies in Arabic language literature. She was ready for marriage. Within four months of living in outside of Paris with a maternal aunt, Nawel returned home to marry Khalid, then thirty. She says she appreciated that Khalid had a good job, had lived outside of Paris for eleven years and, most importantly, had had his French nationality papers for five years. She explains:

> That's a huge fear when one has French citizenship. We're afraid that another Algerian or a Maghrebian marries us just for that. *Voilà*. So then, in this case, that wasn't a worry, so that was good.

Even if citizenship was not at stake for her, Nawel knew she wanted to remain and be *tranquille* [untroubled or calm] in France in her adult life. The couple would need French paperwork to validate their Algerian marriage. At the time of their wedding Nawel did not yet wear hijab, as she has done since the birth of her son. She conjectures that veiling would have surely negatively impacted her chances with the consulate visit in Algiers. She describes feeling most anxious about the arranged element of their union. To deal with this stress, she reminded herself that their union was *mektoub* (destined), like her mother's marriage before her. God would surely help them.

Nawel's description of how she took a great deal of care to do her hair and make-up in 'French styles' when they visited the Algerian consulate, effectively, I suggest, depicts her internalization of the French secular sensibilities and how she rendered her union 'legible'. Nawel consciously refashioned her body, emotions and social comportment to render herself a 'good' (read: moderate and 'secular') Muslim. Even if minor hairstyle and cosmetic choices, Nawel's interpretation of how these secular sensibilities should be apparent sheds light on a central intent of the laws: that they are, in fact, less interested in displays of love or romance and more about displaying secularity. Perhaps because she marked her body as 'secular' (free to choose and free from Islam) or perhaps because she had overestimated the consulate's scrutiny of their arrangement, but Nawel and Khalid were not subject to separate questioning on their emotional and sexual intimacy, as implied by the 2010 officiant directives. They received their French family book and settled in France, where their son was born.

So too for Fatima, whom we met in this chapter's opening passage, her arranged marriage evolved into what she calls a 'love match'. For her, the fear of not performing appropriately, of not incorporating romantic ideals of love in the presence of police, is real. Proof of marital intimacy in an unannounced visit includes wedding photos on display, wearing a diamond engagement ring and the physical presence of the spouse and their shared children. The couple can be questioned on their partner's favourite colour; his or her literary, film or musical tastes; and the timing of their last sexual encounter (Robledo 2011: 5). In our conversation at a McDonald's in the large *La Défense* shopping centre outside of Paris, Fatima describes this fifteen-minute police visit, which she had completely forgotten would happen. She says the three police officers asked about the couple's day-to-day activities and requested to see photos of them together since the wedding, as they were not displayed. They also questioned Fatima's French-speaking mother, who had been visiting from Algeria to help her in the baby's first month. Despite her exhaustion upon returning home after giving birth, Fatima says she was relieved at the police's timing: their newborn son was proof of their sexual intimacy.

For Fatima, the larger effect of the recent legislation on transnational marriage was knowledge that she could not leave her husband for any period or her French citizenship possibilities could vanish. This knowledge was particularly challenging in their first year of marriage. After their wedding in her hometown, they had lived for six months in his parents' apartment before securing their own one-bedroom apartment. Fatima says that when they moved into their own place, having never lived away from his parents' supervision, her husband fell into *niaiseries* (foolishness). When, for instance, he began staying out all night with his friends without consulting her, she explains that she could not move out for fear the police could find out and interpret it as a marital separation, which could mean losing her chance at citizenship. Because she did not want to involve her in-laws and had little other recourse to curb his behaviour, she notes, *Heureusement, il s'est beaucoup calmé depuis* ('Thankfully, he's calmed down a lot since then'). Even a temporary separation could have meant interrogation, an annulment and the end of French citizenship.

Both Fatima and Nawel's narratives shed light on how marriage-related surveillance of their unions become manifest on their bodies and externalized comportment. These women are relatively privileged in comparison with other women I have interviewed. Nawel grew up speaking French as a second language and visited Paris half a dozen times on family vacations, both of which influenced her confidence and goal of settling permanently. Fatima and Nawel also completed university degrees in French and Arabic and have French-language literacy, tools that give them relative advantages. Of the two, as a foreigner, Fatima is more vulnerable. In their arranged marriage, she knows that her actions are under greater scrutiny than her French-born husband's. Nawel held French citizenship prior to marriage but remained hyperaware that theirs is not a desirable 'romantic love' match.

The secular's individualism and 'sexual freedom'

Nicolas Sarkozy: Women, in France, are free like men. Free to circulate. *Free to marry.* Free to divorce (cited in Daumas 2007; my emphasis).

'Rachida': He ['Farid'] was looking for a woman who didn't have a past [who was a virgin]. Who was modern, who was … everything you want. Who came from a good family. There you have it [*voilà*]. Who hasn't dated. Who's serious. So they [Franco-Algerians looking for transnational partners] like to test this [Rachida says it was important for Farid that she had first refused his invitation to meet for a coffee, to demonstrate her modesty and sexual reluctance].

Thus far, I have examined how my interlocutors tacitly and strategically manoeuvre amid secular sensibilities in relation to marriage ceremonies and partner choices, particularly when citizenship or other state-sanctioned paper work is at stake. In this section I argue that these sensibilities index state expectations about individualism and the female body's sexual emancipation. These notions relate to French secularism in so far as its definition typically hinges on a similar notion of individual-based freedom and, in France, the visual accessibility of the female body (a discourse prevalent in the law against full-face veils; see Selby 2011). An underlying equation can be traced: to be visibly secular is to be an emancipated liberal and sexual subject, and, relatedly, to be a modern democratic citizen. Widespread assumptions about religious bodies' lack of autonomy and individuality (and in France, lack of femininity and sexual autonomy) have been recurrent since the Enlightenment.[11] In describing the contemporary French context, where Muslim women are most vulnerable to this assumption about religious bodies, Jocelyne Cesari (2016: 54) notes how because 'the religious individual is [perceived as] restricted by the ideas of discipline, restraint and asceticism', she 'cannot follow through on all personal motives or desires'. The secular body is thus articulated as individualized and autonomous from a religious-cultural community compulsion. Romantic love serves as a facile marker of this sexual-secular-citizenry constellation. In the French context, the rationale delivered prior to the legislation passed in 2006 and 2011, and the 2010 memorandum is that freely and individually chosen marital unions offer women greater sexual freedom and protection from conjugal violence. Unsurprisingly, my ethnographic data suggest that 'traditional' marriage matches do not necessarily promote domestic violence.[12]

The protection of encultured women and concurrent defence of the Republic's borders is echoed in Clément's 2006 speech (cited at the beginning of this chapter) on the problem of transnational marriages and Sarkozy's equation of freedom with a woman's choice to marry (above). Performance of a certain kind of romance at wedding ceremonies marks this individualism and serves as evidence of emancipation from compulsion. Absence of sexual intimacy can be read as indicating community pressure and the absence of female choice. Clément's 2006 speech supporting the initial legislation and Sarkozy's comments, above, also shows how concern for the sexual emancipation of a migrating and marrying individual is feminized. The capacity of supposedly religiously encultured women like 'Rachida', above, to freely choose her marriage partner is therefore questioned, particularly when the marriage means access to French citizenship.

Rachida's narrative depicts an alternative way governmental surveillance of the body and its individualism surface. She ostensibly performs 'romantic love' and modernity in ways that differ from the other participants featured here. Rachida, forty-five, migrated to France from Algeria through family regroupment following her marriage to 'Farid', who had immigrated to France with his parents when he was eight. In our conversation on a Saturday afternoon in her apartment, Rachida describes meeting her husband as 'spontaneous' and as a love match several times, presumably to distance herself from stigmatized stories of forced and/or opportune transnational weddings. Rachida may also use this gloss as a way to translate her relationship as legible to her perception of my own values. Rachida lives in a well-kept social housing low-rise apartment with Farid and their four young children and works part-time in a community association where she assists other immigrants. She has a no nonsense way about her; her hair is cut short and coloured blond. Rachida and Farid met in the street when Farid was on holiday in Algiers. At the time she worked for an ad agency and she describes how he persistently tried to woo her. She explains in the opening passage to this section why she thinks he was drawn to her: she did not have a past and was 'pure'. Three months after their first meeting, Farid returned to Algiers to surprise her and they agreed to marry. She was twenty-four and he was more than ten years older. The signing of the religious marriage or *fatiha* took place several months later at her parents' apartment in Algiers in Farid's absence.[13]

Having heard rumours of problems at the French consulate in Algiers and in France in translating marriage acts (even before the 2006 laws), Farid insisted that they marry civilly in France. A few days after her arrival with a tourist visa to an adjacent suburb where Farid lived at that time, they married at the local city hall, with his sister and work colleague as their witnesses. Rachida's parents were unable to obtain tourist visas in time and Farid's mother had recently passed away, so they celebrated their French civil union alone in an inexpensive restaurant. Rachida frowns as she recalls the 'sadness' of their civil ceremony and celebration in France. They were away from family and friends, there was no fanfare and it was a grey January day. In retrospect, Rachida wishes they had married in Algeria:

> Back home [*au pays*], when you're there, you don't need to tell anyone to do this or that. Everyone knows things go like this and not like that. But here, you have to explain why. Here [in France], a wedding is a debate.

For Rachida it is impossible to find the right 'ingredients' and guests for their wedding party in France. Unfamiliar with many of its cultural codes, for her, a wedding in France ensured 'debate' and no supportive community. She ate at a *greque* for her post-wedding meal, not a delicious multi-course dinner she imagines she would have dined in Algiers. But, she admits Farid was right about holding the civil wedding in France: she received her *carte-de-séjour* (residency card) quickly and without hassle.

Farid's desire for Rachida's 'purity' and other interlocutors' ties to and understanding of the *bled* and *mektoub* are marital rationales that, on the surface, differ from motivations of romantic love and individualism implied in the 2010 memorandum for marriage officiants. The handful of participants I have introduced do not describe seeking to offend liberal romantic sensibilities. They have alternative concerns at stake. A number of women like Rachida and Nawel are impelled to translate their sense of a religiously destined match into a heteronormative love idea. Desirable and surveilled performances of romantic love as the basis of marital legitimacy stand in contrast to the marriages common among my interlocutors. In expressly seeking marriage partners in

Algeria, their 'dominant sensitivities' (cf Fadil 2009) appear to counter those presumed by the required legible French secular sensibilities. Love, often deemed as 'destined by God' (and imbued by love to God) as in Nawel's case, or 'spontaneous', like in Rachida's, or 'rational', like Ilias', recurs in these unions. Yet, *mektoub*, or looking for a good spouse on religious grounds, is illegible in marriage officiant guidelines because it is not on part of a 'secular' scripted romance and does not ensure pre-marital sexual intimacy.

Despite significant differences in the socio-economic backgrounds of my interlocutors, in monitoring their wedding partners and their *habitus* at the moment of their legal union, these sensibilities make blanket assumptions regarding their individuality, sexual politics and religiosity in relation to their or their spouse's foreignness. Equally problematic are the implications for the safety and sexual emancipation of newly immigrant women to France, particularly those who do not have French-language fluency. Promoting legible secular cues, bodies and romantic gestures in civil marriage become markers of women's freedom in ways that further entrench patriarchal values, rather than untethering women from them. Are Nawel's chignon and make-up necessarily emancipatory? Women's bodies remain central to how they are valued and assessed. Lastly, more pressingly, these laws appear to have little impact in curtailing and supporting women who are victims of domestic violence, which affects both religious and non-religious women.

Conclusion

To consider central expressions of the contemporary sexual-secular-citizenry constellation in France, I have drawn on 2006 and 2011 laws and a 2010 memorandum that aim to curb fraudulent, fake and forced transnational marriage and immigration and, through the lens of governmentality, have considered how these laws translate into how my interlocutors negotiate their marriage-partner preferences and civil marriage experiences. I have argued that these laws serve to promote secular sensibilities that parallel more overt delineations since 2004 that require hyper-legible cues (for Fatima, post-marital photos on the display and the presence of the couple's newborn son) that increasingly also signal the state's purview to trespass into the so-called private intimate realm. Significantly, few marriages have been annulled.[14] Still, I suggest, the impacts of these laws on civil marriage are not in their enforcement; their force is subtler and more powerful. Despite a divorce rate in France of more than 50 per cent, these series of laws and concerns around them serve to articulate secular sensibilities and locate marriage as a key moment for the state to assess access to citizenship. The monitoring of bodies in marriage ceremonies and, for some, in subsequent unannounced home visits is mainly oriented towards policing a *vivre ensemble* or a national body that hinges on a narrow secular script. Certain bodies require more disciplining than others. In the French context, this governmentality of the body and of displays of sexuality is disproportionally felt and embodied by non-EU marriage partners, especially those who are women, racialized and visibly Muslim.

I have argued that these secular sensitivities in the contemporary French context are increasingly present (and not invisible, as some scholars of secular studies like Asad and Connolly have suggested), are necessarily tied to Islam and construct and regulate a specific homogeneous and pejorative version of Islam. Not only does this characterization of Islam not correspond to my interlocutors' religiosity, but it also narrowly characterizes the intentionality of religion, here related to marriage choices, as primarily about sexuality and the family. It particularly entrenches visibly religious women in particular as unagentic and as undesirable citizens with a strict protocol of female sexuality.

In conclusion, these laws are worthy of pause because they implicitly delineate who is part of the 'national body' – that is who 'can participate in the *idea* of the nation' (Hall 1996: 612) – and, who cannot. My interlocutors' stories index how their bodies can be precarious, as evidenced by the state's overstepping into their private lives, and the necessary public performance of sexual freedom in civil marriage ceremonies. The surveillance of the social comportment and the bodies of transnational marriage partners becomes a shortcut to ostensibly protect women's rights and the values of the nation state, in ways that are reminiscent of colonial-era logic of protecting foreign women from their patriarchal religious families and the state from these values. The individuals examined here at times conform and at other times reconfigure and transform this corporal version of the sexual body politic that references limited versions of individualism and sexual freedom. Far from a neutral framework, their narratives usefully show the prescriptiveness of this surveillance, so we might begin to question what it means to be acceptable in sexual and citizenry terms in contemporary France.

Quantitative Knowledge Production on Muslims in Europe as a Practice of 'Secular Suspicion'

Birgitte Schepelern Johansen and Riem Spielhaus

In 2008, 17 per cent of Muslims in France have been somewhat or strongly opposed to 'the principle of a separation of state and religion'.[1] In a survey carried out in 2008 in the UK, almost one in three (29 per cent) Muslim students said they were unsure whether Islam is compatible with the separation of religion and government and over half of non-Muslim students (55 per cent) said that Islam and the separation of religion and government were incompatible.[2] A study in six European countries from 2013 found that 65 per cent of Muslim respondents affirm that 'religious rules are more important than secular law',[3] and in a 2016 poll, 29 per cent of French Muslims 'rejected secular law'.[4] Numbers like these surface regularly in the media, policy reports and governmental investigations, testifying to a continuous interest in quantitative knowledge on Muslims. How should we understand such numbers? What kind of work are they doing, and what needs do they respond to? Quantitative knowledge has since the nineteenth century increasingly served as a means to provide factual, ideally incontestable, grounds for governance as well as public debates. Numbers served this political purpose well because they, as Nikolas Rose has convincingly argued, 'conferred certainty, they contributed to knowledge, they revealed regularities, they created regularities. And, in doing so, numbers could be thought of as fostering detachment from feeling, passion and tumults' (Rose 1999: 225). By seeking to settle questions of public concern and interest, namely questions pertaining to the compliance or non-compliance of Muslims with secularist claims, polls and surveys offer to contribute knowledge and thereby potentially inform and qualify public discussions and political decision-making processes in a context of heated debate.

However, numbers do more than that. The seeming detachment from 'feeling, passion and tumults' that numbers convey potentially obscure the way they also function as technologies for imagining and representing a population composed of 'Muslims' and 'non-Muslims', just as they contribute to the production and maintenance of particular feelings about and between the two categories. These feelings, we will argue, can be understood as intrinsically secular, in the sense that they feed on or emerge from particular narratives about religion and its proper role in society. So, we may ponder, why are Muslims questioned about their attitudes towards the relationship between religion and politics in the first place? How are they questioned and how does such questioning create particular emotional economies between Muslims and non-Muslims? In this chapter, we seek to engage these questions and entangle some of the implications of the practice of questioning Muslims through quantitative surveys. The aim of this investigation is twofold. First, we want to qualify, at a more principled level, in what ways it makes sense to trace a nexus between numbers, emotions and the secular. Second, we aim to exemplify these points through an empirical analysis of selected polls and surveys. Here we show how certain notions of the secular are entrenched in these surveys, linking issues of freedom, gender equality and political loyalty with the ability to recognize the proper place of religion in societies. Muslims apparently continuously need to be tested on these matters, and the polls and surveys thereby (also) become part of a broader interrogative, perhaps even accusatory, conversation that produces Muslim subjects as potentially suspicious citizens. In doing so, we argue, the surveys contribute to cultivating and managing appropriate secular feelings about the Muslim presence in Europe.

We should emphasize that our concern here is not the quantitative methodology as such, that is, its strengths and weaknesses. Rather, the polls interest us as a discursive venue. Our focus is on how the questions they ask aim to disclose the convictions of Muslims and how the questions, in this process, offer particular, limited (and sometimes troubling) subjectivities to Muslim respondents. In pursuing our inquiry, we investigate polls and surveys with Muslim respondents conducted during the last decade in Germany, France, Denmark, Norway and the UK, plus different multi-national surveys on Muslims in several European countries, a total of approximately one hundred publications based on fifty different surveys. The polls and surveys included in the study range from short media polls to large-scale academic integration surveys, and they reflect a growing interest in and call for more factual knowledge about Muslim populations in Western Europe: how they live, what they think, what their interests and concerns are and, not least, how well integrated they are (see Johansen and Spielhaus 2012 for overview). So they are part of a particular political formation in which concerns about Islam and Muslims are continuously intertwined with concerns about immigration, integration, national cohesion and security (Sunier 2012). This again implies that the polls and surveys display some regularity regarding their composition, for example that they tend to address Muslims within particular nation states (Johansen and Spielhaus 2012). Further, in the actual questions, the categories of Muslim and immigrant are often intertwined, which implicitly positions Muslims as outsiders, regardless of whether they are converts, immigrants or their descendants. However, the way this foreignness is configured in public and political discourses is not arbitrary. The 'otherness' of Muslims is related to them embodying Islam, which again in a European context figures as a sub-category of the general category *religion*: being Muslim means to be religious in a particular way. Hence, the presence of Muslims is also to be understood within the context of political and cultural idea(l)s of what religion is or ought to be – a context that, as we lay out in more details below, intelligibly can be labelled as secular. In this chapter, we wish to pay special attention to the aspects of the more general surveying of Muslims that pertain to their position as a certain kind of religio-political subjects, defined and potentially problematized against a domain of secular norms, values and attitudes.

The chapter from here falls in four parts. First, we situate the current practice of polling Muslims as part of a longer history of enumerating populations and thereby imagining the social body as an object of governance. Here we also explain our take on the polls and surveys as techniques for producing and managing public emotions. Then follows a section on our approach to the secular as a cultural grammar, while the third part contains the empirical analysis of the ways secular concerns are entrenched in the polls and surveys and the kind of affectively loaded relations they create. Finally, we conclude with a discussion of the potential implications of questioning Muslims in this particular way.

Numbers, bodies, governance

The current production of polls and surveys on Muslims continues a longer tradition of delimiting and quantifying assumed deviant categories of people. As, among others, Michel Foucault (2007 [1978]), Ian Hacking (1991) and Nicolas Rose (1999) have shown, the growth in the production of population statistics during the nineteenth century went hand in hand with the emergence of a particular form of governance. This form of governance enshrined from the central idea 'that one can improve – control – a deviant subpopulation by enumeration and classification' (Hacking 1991: 3), with the ultimate aim of improving the quality of the social body. It is probably not a coincidence that the invention of the statistical notion of normality in the late nineteenth century was coterminous with the discovery of the bacteria predicated upon the invention of the microscope. As historian Alexandra Minna Stern (1999) has brilliantly argued, both of these techniques made it possible in radically new ways to 'see' a reality that has hitherto been hidden beneath the surface of immediate experience. They both shared 'a disdain for the perception of the naked eye, representing new techniques of visualization and spatialization for categorically determining who was sick or healthy, normal or abnormal' (Stern 1999: 589). While the microscope made it possible to investigate the tissue of the physical body, population statistics became one of the prime tools for drawing forth the conditions of the social body, creating a new kind of visibility of all sorts of deviancy.[5] For this purpose, categories of people had to be made distinct and recognizable; hence the mad, the unemployed, the divorced, the criminals, the suicidal, the sick, the retarded, to mention but a few, emerged as objects of enumeration and governance during the late nineteenth and early twentieth century. The popularity of statistics as a tool for state governance went hand in hand with their promise of providing factual, indisputable and therefore dispassionate knowledge – something that easily fitted in with emerging ideals of politics, more precisely liberal democratic politics, as demanding a rational basis. Knowledge, rather than tradition, dogmas or passions, should govern public deliberation (Rose 1999), and hence the birth of modern statistics is an intrinsic part of the historical developments and conceptual reconfigurations that constitute the secular.

Today, the avalanche of numbers has in no way disappeared, but pervades most aspects of modern life. And as the times change, so do the categories of people suitable for enumeration, as seen in the increasing attention paid to various forms of immigrants and, not least, to their descendants within the overall political framework of 'integration'. The current focus on Muslims as an object of quantification can be approached as a continuation and expansion of this integration agenda. The production of quantitative knowledge is here typically connected with political and legal practices either as part of providing a legitimate basis for decision-making or as a means to measure subsequent outcomes and consequences of legislative practices (Rose 1993; Supik 2014). And in some cases, they serve rather straightforwardly as preparation for regulating religious expressions (see for example Brems 2014 on the recent mappings on the number of women wearing niqabs and burqas in several Western European countries) or for facilitating the practice of religion (see for example Fuess 2011 on the introduction of Islamic religious instruction in German schools).

But the production of numbers is more than a technique for imagining and governing the social body – its needs, disruptions and deviations. The survey, especially the opinion poll or the exit poll, has also in the context of representational democracy increasingly become a means, alongside the election, for people to gain representation, to raise their voice and to express their opinions on various issues in the public sphere (Burchard and Mar this volume, also Asad 2003: 14ff.). Thus the polls and surveys also co-construct the parties engaged in public debates (in this case Muslims and non-Muslims) and they frame what we supposedly ought to debate. They are, we argue, in these various respects part of an ongoing public conversation, where questions are asked and answers (sometimes) given – a conversation that often takes place between uneven parties and in a mediated and disrupted form. And, as is often the case with conversations, this one too holds the capacity for having certain emotional import. Questions are rarely innocent, and to pose a question is, as Pia Lauritzen has emphasized, exactly to pose: to position oneself and the other in a certain way (Lauritzen 2016). Further, questions, at least serious questions, are dictated by the border of our knowledge, and they are directed at resolving not any uncertainty but a 'certain uncertainty' (Fales 1943: 61). Thus, they point back towards what is already known (or thought to be known), and as such they open a limited space for answering. Such spaces may be of many different sorts, for example factual (asking for direction), empathetic (asking how someone is feeling), curious (asking what goes on) and so on. But they may also be more or less implicitly accusatory, expressing a worry or concern. Questions have the capacity to create potentialities, thus asking whether someone is beating his or her children situates the one who is being asked as someone who potentially could perform such an act, even if he or she is allowed the possibility to deny it. Hence, the question not only invites a response but also in some sense holds the one being asked *respons*ible for what is evoked in the question. Asked in a context where child beating is considered immoral and harmful, such questioning obviously has moral implications: it voices doubt about the other's affirmation of a norm. To the extent that emotions are habituated bodily arousals that involve judgements (that something is threatening, joyful, disgusting, pleasant, admirable and so on), such questioning has emotional imports as well.[6] It is not surprising, then, that certain types of questions (e.g. accusatory ones) may elicit frustration, fatigue or even resentment on behalf of those invited to answer. And for those posing the questions, they may be imbricated with a hope of relief from one's worries or confirmation of one's assumptions.

Obviously, questions are – as any communication – overdetermined, and their exact meaning and implications are settled by the context in which they are raised as well as their reception. So too is their emotional import. When we in the following make suggestions about the emotional implications of the practice of questioning, at stake are two different levels of analysis. The first, and primary, level pertains to a formal reading of the context of questioning, the cultural conventions and assumptions that are likely to undergird the questions and their place in the aforementioned public conversation. Thus, the level of analysis here is the collective bodies that emerge in the surveys ('Muslims' and 'non-Muslims') and the kind of relationship and emotional dynamics that becomes possible between them. The other, secondary, level of analysis pertains to the probable emotional effects of such questioning on actual, living bodies. Due to the available material for this chapter, which does not entail interviews or field studies, this secondary level is inevitably more speculative and tentative. Thus, what we offer here is merely an invitation to think through the possible implications of the questioning.

Approaching the secular

The occupation with producing quantitative knowledge on Muslims has, as mentioned, emerged in response to an increasing politicization of the Muslim presence in Europe. As Göran Larsson (2012) and Brian Jacobsen (2007, 2012) have shown, demographic arguments have become crucial for many critics of Islam, especially those attracted to the 'Eurabia' thesis: the idea that Europe – as a spatiotemporal unit as well as a certain kind of people – is facing a 'demographic time bomb', where Muslims due to immigration and higher fertility rates will outnumber the European populations within a few generations (Larsson 2012: 148). Thus, one important domain of quantitative interest is to assess the number of Muslims living in Europe, and the current scholarly work on quantification of Muslims has mainly engaged with this aspect. The focus of our work is somewhat different, since we do not engage with the estimations of the size of the Muslim populations in Europe. Rather, we probe the attempts to figure out who or what these Muslims are. And often this interest relates to secular norms and the worry that Muslims potentially deviate from them.

What do we mean, more precisely, when we speak of the secular as something that can be entrenched in the questions of polls of surveys? The awkward words here are obviously 'more precisely', because the 'secular' is, as discussed in detail in the introduction to this volume, an immensely broad and slippery term. Here we approach the secular first and foremost as a particular historical-cultural context in which categories such as religion, politics, private and public, body and surroundings, citizenship, rights and democracy are structuring social reality in specific ways (Asad 2003, Fernando 2014, Taylor 2007). More precisely, the guiding assumption is that the separation (partially or completely) of religion from the realms of politics and public reason is a necessary step towards a realization of a modern, democratic state with its associated freedom rights (Asad 2003: 13; Taylor 2007: 580ff). This assumption is given meaning and credibility through a cluster of grand narratives, which according to Taylor can be subsumed under the heading 'subtraction': that religion withdrew or was gradually expelled from the realm of immanent reality, leaving open for rational investigation 'the social' or 'the historical'. It is thus a story of emancipation, of science from dogma and of the individual from religious morality and tradition. It is also a story of an emerging human maturity, assigning the prime authority in matters of life to humans, and humans only. The subtraction story thus implies or invites a continuous drama on the frontier zone between religion and other domains – e.g. science, politics, law – a drama that, as Hussein Agrama explains, establishes the secular also as a particular problem space. The secular is thus

> a historical ensemble of questions and attached stakes; the question that anchors this historical ensemble is where to draw the line between religion and politics and what the limits of religion in society ought to be; the attached stakes are those rights and liberties typically identified with liberalism – such as equality, tolerance, and freedom of belief. (Agrama 2012b: 27)

The emergence and consolidation of the secular is simultaneous to the birth of certain notions of religion that support and sustain the story and the drama. These ideas have gradually since the late seventeenth century put more and more emphasis on proper religion as related to inner convictions, faith, ethics and individual choice, while improper religion – pathetically or dangerously – insists on its prior glorious status as reality and communal framework for the good life (Taylor 2007).

It is within such narratives that the production of quantitative knowledge on Muslim attitudes should (also) be understood and interpreted, and much of the public discussions about the presence of Muslims in Europe have revolved around the potential impossibility of Islam and Muslims to conform to the secular distinctions, thereby potentially rejecting the promises of the good life and the good society they carry (Cesari 2004: 44, also Asad 2006). Our approach in the following analysis is to distinguish between three main forms of questions that seek to grasp Muslims' attitudes towards secular arrangements and values. The first form is direct questions that test the respondent's allegiance to the doctrinal separation of church and state, or religion and politics. The second is questions on attitudes that in reports analysing, summarizing and presenting survey results are understood as indicators of an allegiance with the separation. This would for example be questions regarding the status of sharia vis-à-vis national legislation, or questions on the status of religious authorities vis-à-vis legal or political authorities. Third, polls and surveys ask about a range of other topics that can be seen as secular concerns in more indirect ways. These questions might not present themselves as being about religion or secularity, but they are often articulated in public debates as the kind of social goods that are secured only when religion has found its proper place and scope. The allegiance to democracy, freedom and equality are, pace Agrama, the most prominent examples. The call for allegiance to these values and attitudes can therefore be approached as an example of what Talal Asad refers to as 'shadows' of the secular (Asad 2003: 16), in the sense that their reference to the doctrinal separations is implicit.

The separation of religion and state

In the following analysis, we take as our point of departure a specific survey entitled *Islam on Campus: A Survey of UK Student Opinions*, investigating Muslim students in twelve British universities. This study lays out a pattern of interrogation that we find in several other surveys. A more comprehensive presentation of this survey allows us to trace how the secular logic is entrenched not only in particular questions but in the wider composition of the questionnaire and in how the responses are analysed and presented. Examples from other surveys will help us to circle in on the major secular concerns and show that *Islam on Campus* reveals a recurring pattern. *Islam on Campus* is compiled by the independent think tank Centre for Social Cohesion, which since 2011 has been part of the right-wing think tank Henry Jackson Society. It is based on a YouGov survey of 600 Muslim and 800 non-Muslim university students, and as many polls and surveys, the introduction of the report frames its questions within the context of growing radicalization. While only few Muslims have committed terrorist attacks, the 'issue is', as the report states, 'bigger than terrorism. The ideas, people and groups that individuals come into contact with during their university years inevitably help shape the rest of their lives'. Hence, from the outset the questions asked in the survey are inscribed in a story of a potential violent threat and hence a story that is imbricated with fear, worry and aggression. While the potential for radicalization may reach across the Muslims/non-Muslims divide, the specific target of the investigation is the potential radicalization among the *Muslim* students, who are positioned as probable objects of the fear, worry and aggression. This framing, it should be mentioned, is far from evident in all the polls and surveys in our material. Some are rather inscribed in a story about Muslims as a minority struggling with marginalization (e.g. the survey series 'Muslims in Europe' from Open Society Foundation), thereby suggesting a rather different emotional import, such as empathy, tolerance or indignation. However, such polls and surveys rarely question Muslim secularity. *Islam on Campus* dedicates a chapter to 'Islam and secularism', which is introduced like this:

> Respondents were then asked if they felt Islam is compatible with the separation of religion and government. Findings indicate divided opinion on the separation of religion and state. Over two fifths (43%) of Muslim students polled said the two were compatible – almost a fifth (8%) felt very so and a quarter (25%) fairly so. Almost three in ten (28%) said they were incompatible – 8% fairly so and one in ten (10%) very so. Almost one in three (29%) – the largest single group – were unsure. ... By contrast, over half (55%) of non-Muslim students polled said that Islam and the separation of religion and government were incompatible. A fifth (20%) felt they were compatible and a quarter (25%) were unsure. (Thorne and Stuart 2008: 55–56)

The precise wording of the question is 'And how compatible, if at all, do you think Islam is with the separation of religion and government?' The question does not explain what such a separation may imply, and this lack of explicitness concerning what the separation means is symptomatic of the direct questions. Do respondents think that Islam is compatible with an arrangement in which the state does not fund religious institutions, with a parliamentary system in which religious arguments cannot be used in political debate or that the government cannot decide anything on matters of religion – or the other way around? The reader has no way of finding out. Neither do we get any explanation of what is meant by religion, but we could assume that Islam is taken to be an instance of the category religion. Hence the actual question is whether Islam and politics can be separated, and implicitly whether the Muslim respondents are capable of keeping Islam out of the shared, public decision-making process.

A similar way of defining secularity we find in a French opinion poll 'Islam et citoyenneté', commissioned by the newspaper *Le Monde*. 'Are you quite favourable, somewhat favourable, somewhat opposed or strongly opposed to secularism, that is to say, the principle of separation of state and religion?' (CSA 2008: 26). Different possible interpretations of a separation do not seem to be the target of these questions. In both cases, through the use of the definite article '*the* separation' and '*the* principle', the questions probe a subscription to something which, however empty or unspecified, appears to be immediately intelligible. Asked in a context where the merits of 'the separation' is largely hegemonic[7] and where Muslims' ability to comply with this is continuously problematized and connected with radicalization and extremism, such 'empty'[8] questions, we argue, become more a test of loyalty than actually providing knowledge about the respondents' attitudes on a complex issue. Thereby the question becomes somewhat parallel to the equally frequently asked question 'Do you feel mostly Muslim or British?'[9] In that sense, even though the pollsters may not themselves be fearful, worried or suspicious, the very composition of the question and the accepted view that this is an important question to ask people tap into and reproduce a formal anxiety about the (non)conformity of Muslims to something considered fundamentally good. The question is then also an occasion for the respondents to confirm their allegiance to this good and hence potentially pave the way for relief of the anxiety as well as an aspiration for recognition and trust (we are like you). However, as we will return to in the conclusions, this potential is a rather precarious one.

Separation of religion and law

Both surveys define secularism in the direct question (as the 'separation of religion and government' and as 'the principle of separation of state and religion'). However, as mentioned these direct questions are rather few, typically limited to this one question in a survey. Yet several surveys contain batteries of questions that do not mention secularism or secularity but are concerned with associated relations, for example between religion and law or religion and law making.[10] These questions mostly focus on respondents' attitudes towards Sharia and they mainly seem to express a concern about loyalty towards different kinds of authorities. Thus, it is telling that in our material all definitions of Sharia emphasize the concept's legal implications. For example, *Islam on Campus* dedicates a chapter to the separation between secular and religious law. The chapter is introduced by a definition of Sharia as 'Islamic principles commonly laid down as legal codes' that is derived from the Quran, in addition to the 'recorded sayings and deeds attributed to Mohammed' and 'from centuries of precedent laid down by diverse – and sometimes competing – Muslim jurists' (Thorne and Stuart 2008: 38). However, as several scholars have argued, the understanding of Sharia is widely contested among European Muslims and there are intense discussions on whether Sharia is a fixed system of law or a flexible ethics among Muslim scholars in Europe (Crone 2010: 142). Thus, even though Sharia cannot easily be reduced to a legal concept (also Nielsen 2010), other interpretations of Sharia are not an option in most of the questionnaires.

The insistence on a narrow legal understanding of Sharia situates again the answers from the Muslim respondents in a potential conflict of loyalty, this time between potentially competing legal systems (see also Shah 2010). Further, the emphasis on Sharia as law can be seen as an attempt to fit Sharia into standing secular categories of religion, law and politics – an attempt where Sharia, however overdetermined, ends up in the legal category. Yet, it is exactly through this attempt to settle its meaning that Sharia becomes a troublesome and worrying hybrid between two things that – within a secular logic – ought to be separated: religion and law. As such, the continuous need to question Muslim attitudes towards Sharia could be read in the context of a more fundamental anxiety, namely what Zygmunt Bauman (with due reference to Freud) calls the anxiety of the 'undecidables'. That is, the emotional tension that emerges from objects that through our available classificatory systems comes out not as reassuring 'either-or' (either law or religion) but as worrisome 'neither-nor' or, in this case, 'both-and' (both law and religion).

The section contains three questions regarding Sharia: one about the respondent's personal acceptance of interpreting Sharia in context, one about the legitimacy of such interpretation according to Islam and the final one about their support for an introduction of Sharia law into UK law for Muslims (Thorne and Stuart 2008: 38–40). Again, there is no specification of the rules that could be introduced with Sharia law, and the broader concern could also here be the (in)compatibility between Islam and British society. However, the questions are also asked in the context of a genuine debate about possible changes in British law that provides for the possibility of different communal laws – that is the public debate on the introduction of Sharia councils as part of family law arbitration (Korteweg and Selby 2012; Shah 2010). So in this case, the questions are not only testing formal allegiance but probing the respondents' support for an actual possible change in the legal system. Yet, questions on Sharia also abound in surveys carried out in countries without such debates. This points towards broader concerns about competing legal systems and the securing of rights in a democratic context. For example, the following quote from a report of a survey among Muslims in Denmark situates the question on Sharia more explicitly in the context of democracy and freedom rights.

In this note we focus on the new Danes' attitudes to Sharia law, interferences with freedom of expression and personal freedom. The results point in different directions, and thus add nuances to our knowledge of new Danes value policy positions. The results indicate, first, that there is little support for the introduction of Sharia law through legislative channels in Denmark, which almost eight out of ten immigrants oppose. But new Danes support for democratic norms of freedom of expression and personal freedom is not as strong as the rejection of Sharia. Every second is in favour of banning books and films that attack religion, and more than one in four are in favour of a ban on homosexuality. (CEPOS, Denmark 2009: 1)

In the Danish survey the possibility of introducing Sharia is not conceived of as a test case for religious freedom (as in the UK discussions), but as something that potentially stands in opposition to other freedom rights (freedom of expression, personal freedom and sexual freedom). Testing the respondents' position on Sharia is seen as a way of testing their positions on these freedom rights, defined as democratic norms, which is the main underlying aim of the survey. Thus, there might be rather uniform concepts at stake in the different surveys (here Sharia understood as religious law); however, these concepts are multivalent: they can unfold into particular, differently situated discussions.

Despite these differences, in both surveys the question of Sharia ties in with the issue of freedom of religion. In the Danish survey, Sharia is perceived as potentially at odds with secular freedom rights, and in the UK debates on Sharia, those sympathetic to the introduction of Sharia courts have typically invoked freedom of religion as a crucial secular right (Shah 2010). This bifurcation of arguments (Islam is a threat to secular freedoms versus secular freedoms protect Islam) and the continuous impossibility of settling them resonate across a wide variety of controversies, such as the debates about prohibiting particular Islamic dresses or the discussions about freedom of expression and blasphemy. Here we want to bring in Hussein Agrama's notion of secular suspicion in order to unpack this impasse (Agrama 2012a, b). Secular suspicion, which we might also see as fundamentally a liberal suspicion, is according to Agrama characterized by a distinctive structure of doubt and anxiety. It is emblematic to the freedom rights promoted in liberal, secular states and it emerges from a perceived gap between the law as principle and its practical application (Agrama 2012a: 130). The legal protection of religious freedom (and any right-based freedoms) implies a certain loss of control over the domain that is emancipated. Such a loss then tends to be accompanied by heightened attempts to control peoples' capacity for handling the freedom granted, eliciting various extra-legal activities (e.g. education, investigation) in order to secure that the principled liberties are not 'misused' in their actual application. 'What this suggests', Agrama points out, 'is that, under a liberal secular legal regime, suspicion of religion is the flip-side of the freedom of religious belief' (Agrama 2012c). As an effect the very process of investigation, through which transparency is sought, will tend to distribute suspicion among legal subjects, creating an atmosphere of distrust. Thus, the suspicion entails a process where the values and principles at stake continuously undermine themselves: control undermines freedom, and doubt undermines trust.

Secular shadows: Democracy and equality

The Danish survey from CEPOS shows how the Sharia questions tie in with the topic of democracy as the proper mode of governance. Such a connection recurs in several surveys, and it is in these connections between the topics – where the doctrinal separation slides into the background – that we move into the shadow of the secular. For example, *Islam on Campus* asks about the compatibility of Islam with democracy: 'To what extent if at all do you think Islam is compatible with the Western notion of democracy?' (Thorne and Stuart 2008: 54). This question does not mention anything about separations between religion and X, and it does not exclude the possibility of the respondents imagining a non-secular democracy. Yet, Western notions of democracy are usually tied in with the premise of its secularity, for example based on the demand that it is the sovereign people who govern in a democracy – not God (e.g. Taylor 2007). Thus, democracy, even though it was categorized by Weber as a form of charismatic leadership and hence potentially shortsighted, opportunistic and unpredictable, is often inscribed in a story about the progressive emancipation of the political decision-making process from dogma, passion and tradition – a process in which representational democracy (itself a quantitative and statistical construct) is a current highpoint. We do not know whether such assumptions undergird the question, but to the extent that it does, and to the extent that it is assumed that Islam challenges the doctrinal separations, such 'compatibility-questions' pit two potentially incompatible foundations against each other. So even though the conflict in some sense can be annulled through the respondents' answer (if they answer yes), the logic of the conflict is still there entrenched in the question. The answer 'yes' therefore becomes one that appears intuitively odd and in need of explanation, which again feeds the suspicion.

Another secular shadow is equality. This is one of the most frequently raised topics in polls and surveys, and it is mostly addressed in terms of *gender* equality. The reappearance of this topic is not surprising given its prominent position in public discussions about the presence of Muslims in many European countries. These discussions mainly revolve around the proposition that Muslim women are oppressed and that Islam generally promotes inequality between the sexes, thus positioning Islam in opposition to a general norm of gender equality and the liberation of women from patriarchal, religious patterns in society (Scott 2009, see also the introduction of this volume). Surveys test this assumption in different ways, and let us return to the *Islam on Campus* survey's questions as an example:

- 'From your understanding of Islam are men and women considered equal in the eyes of Allah?' (Thorne and Stuart 2008: 67).
- 'And in your experience of Islam in your local community are men and women treated equally?' (Thorne and Stuart 2008: 69).
- 'Do you believe that men and women should be treated equally?' (Thorne and Stuart 2008: 71).
- 'In your understanding how acceptable is it for men and women to associate freely in Muslim society?' (Thorne and Stuart 2008: 72).

Three of the four questions ask about the respondent's principled opinion on how things are ('in the eyes of Allah') or should be (in society). As with the other questions presented here, we do not get any substantial information about what such equality would amount to, leaving them open for different interpretations of what equality means. This is evident in the very different answers provided by the Muslim and the non-Muslim respondents: the vast majority of Muslims answer the first and third question in the affirmative, while a slightly smaller majority of non-Muslims answer the first question in the negative. It is also evident from the high affirmative response rate on the third question that gender equality, across the respondent groups, has a hegemonic status as valuable. However, the agents potentially responsible for (un-) equal treatment remain remarkably vague (treated equally by whom?), and the questions leave gender equality in British society more generally out of the picture. This is emphasized by a question posed only to non-Muslim respondents: 'And in your experience of British society are Muslim men and women treated equally? (Non-Muslims only)' (Thorne and Stuart 2008: 70).

This topos, according to which Muslims in particular need to be questioned about equal treatment, but not the larger society or its government, has been described well by Sarah Bracke (2011) and Schirin Amir-Moazami (2011) in their work on the interrogating interactions between governmental bodies and Muslim representatives – cases where the larger society is presented as 'flagships' of gender equality. One implication is that the emotional import of the questioning differs between the categories 'Muslim' and 'non-Muslims', since 'Muslims' – and thereby by association the Muslim respondents – from the outset are in a defensive position. This is different from the non-Muslim respondents who are not questioned about their own attitudes or experiences on gender (in)equality, but can take the position as the observers and judges of Muslim behaviour. This discrepancy ties in with another recurring voice in the public conversations about Islam and Muslims, namely that Muslims are being treated unfairly and that 'the majority' society navigate according to double standards.[11] Such perceived unfairness, regardless of whether it is well founded or not, is likely to be a prime driver of resentment and scepticism towards the ideals that supposedly should apply equally to everyone. Consequently, resentment and scepticism may emerge as the flip side of the secular suspicion described by Agrama.

Secular norms – Suspect Muslims

Obviously, one does not need to consult polls and surveys in order to discover that there are concerns, anxieties and aggressive attitudes towards Islam and Muslim in a European context. This is confirmed on an almost daily basis through the media. Our point has been to show how the polls and surveys are not neutral, factual means to illuminate and ideally settle these heated political debates by making visible 'the Muslim population'. Rather they are intrinsic parts of a conversation – curious as well as accusatory and defensive – about who they/the Muslims really are. When we study surveys on Muslims as a genre and try to understand the affective tropes entrenched in them, their role as a tool of 'interrogating' Muslim subjects as potentially suspicious citizens becomes apparent. During the interviews for these surveys, through the questions asked, individuals of Muslim belief and background are offered subjectivities imbricated with doubt about their allegiance to the fundamentals of Western societies. Off hand, the problematizing potential in the questions may be rejected by the respondents' answers. But the norms, and the confirmation of Muslim subjectivity as potentially failing to acknowledge them, are reproduced each time Muslim respondents are asked these questions. Do Muslims submit to the idea of doctrinal separation and the promises attached to it? This seems a condition for being recognized as loyal and integrated citizen. However, this manifest articulation of the secular appears mainly to be an empty signifier, and therefore it seems that what is expected from Muslims is not an alignment with a concrete version of secularity. What is expected is an identification with and declaration of loyalty to a general principle, and perhaps even more: to the community that allegedly is founded upon this principle. In this way, the secular suspicion becomes more than a general effect of a secular, liberal legal regime, as outlined and discussed by Agrama. The suspicion becomes part of what we might call a secular 'body politics', through which the population is refashioned through a consistent differentiation between 'trustworthy' and 'not-so-trustworthy' agents.

Consequently, a self-perpetuating logic seems to be at stake in the practice of polling Muslims: the surveys seek to provide factual knowledge that aims to settle 'public concerns' about Muslims' attitudes and loyalties, while simultaneously (re)producing a continuous suspicion that Muslims are not loyal and that they hold problematic attitudes. In other words, they (co-)create the emotional drive that they aim to settle. This circularity is an inevitable feature of the kind of social polarization materialized in the 'empty questions'. What they seek is a final reassurance and closure of the social body, through an absolute determination of the other (are they truly like us or not?). Such a confirmation can obviously never be given in a satisfactory and final way. Muslims (like non-Muslims) do not and will never make up one, unified body that can be made legible. They have varied and multi-faceted opinions, just as the questions in the surveys themselves are overdetermined in their possible meanings. Illustratively, the *Islam on Campus* survey has to conclude that

> The results show that Muslim students hold opinions and attitudes, which are broad and varied, giving cause both for hope and concern.
> (Thorne and Stuart 2008: ix)

Hope and concern – and so the suspicion – continue for the unspecified, worried (secular) reader.

Finally, we may also probe the possible emotional effects of this mode of questioning on actual persons. As mentioned initially, we can within the methodology of this study only speculate about such effects. Yet, it is fairly easy to imagine that the suspicion may 'travel' and leave its mark on actual meetings in the street, the metro, the workplace and so on, where people through particular visible traits become associated with the categories of suspect Muslim and suspicious non-Muslim. It may also have a more direct effect on the respondents participating in the surveys, depending on the extent to which the respondents experience the questions as intelligible and the possibilities for answering them as meaningful. 'Empty' questions, questions that test compatibility and loyalty, and questions that simplify or misrepresent central Islamic concepts (e.g. Sharia as law), are, we suggest, more likely to elicit frustration or discontent than questions that aim to specify or nuance various possible understandings of the themes and concepts at stake. Further, it is most likely that respondents will hear/read the survey questions as part of the public debate on Islam and Muslims. To the extent that respondents know what answers will provide 'hope' rather than 'concern', these surveys implicitly become an invitation to choose sides. This may provide an opportunity for respondents to align themselves with the majority, thereby trying to relieve themselves from the suspicion and anxieties that circulate in the public debates. However, since it is not likely that such an alignment will change the dominant public perceptions of Muslims, the risk of building up resentment or anger towards those asking the questions, or those who come to represent the unspecified subject driving the interrogation, is also present. The same may apply for those who do not accept the polarization and its implicit accusation, just as it may be an occasion to confirm, to varying degrees, one's active alignment with the 'worrying' side.

This is of course not the only way to interview Muslims as Muslims, and suspicion is not an unavoidable feature of the quantitative methodology. It is rather the suture of the specific questions with broader political discourses that determines whether a survey and its interviews turn into interrogations or not. Surveys that cover religiosity as a constitutive aspect of daily life in contemporary societies (Religionsmonitor 2008), that ask for experiences of discrimination among religious and other minorities (FRA 2008) or that aim to show the material needs for Muslim communities, for example Islamic burial spaces and so on (Haug et al. 2009) do not in the same way create and disseminate suspicion. Rather they seem to engage respondents as religious subjects, subjects of discrimination or subjects of rights rather than as potentially suspect citizens. These latter examples may of course still be intelligibly analysed as secular, in so far as they probe concepts and create subjectivities that gain their meaning from a secular grammar (such as 'religion', 'recognition', 'rights', 'discrimination', 'politics'). But they do not to the same extent mobilize the secular as constitutive of a threatened, majoritarian identity. So, to the extent that surveys and polls play an important part in crafting a public sphere in which social agents can be imagined and conversations between them take place, perhaps suspicion is not the most fruitful *modus operandi*. Perhaps the important move would be to consider what secular trust might look like?

Secular Affect and Urban Exclusion: Feelings about Burkas in Public Spaces

Marian Burchardt and Mar Griera

This chapter examines the imaginaries, ideas and sentiments that shape public discourses on Islamic face-veils in an urban context in Southern Europe. Through a qualitative case study on the regulatory politics of face coverings in public space, we explore the repertoires of justification employed and mobilized by local actors to legitimate (or contest) the ban. Our aim is to go beyond an analysis anchored in the religious-secular divide and offer a more nuanced and complex understanding of the causes and implications of the controversy by discussing its relationship with secular affect, urban dynamics and historical trajectories. In particular, we discuss the notion that Islamic face-veils disturb the sense of tranquility of other urban residents and explore how the (perceived) Islamization of urban space is related to other kinds of urban disturbances such as nudity and prostitution.

Controversies on face-veils have gained momentum in Europe during the last decade. Former French president Nicolas Sarkozy created an 'expert commission' to deliberate over face-veils in 2009. The commission's final report called on the French parliament to adopt a resolution declaring the incompatibility between the wearing of the face-veil and the 'values of the Republic'[1] and paved the way for the passing of a national ban on face coverings in France (French: *LOI n° 2010–1192: Loi interdisant la dissimulation du visage dans l'espace public*). However, even before France, some Italian cities prohibited the wearing of face-veils through local by-laws. This was, for instance, the case of Azzano Decimo, which passed an edict that banned the use of face-veils in the public space in July 2004.[2] The ban was replicated in many other towns in Northern Italy (Piatti-Crocker and Tasck 2015) but was later deemed illegal by the Italian Council of State.[3]

In the case of Spain, the controversy started in the city of Lleida in 2010 when the mayor mobilized the city council to ban the face-veil (Burchardt et al. 2015). The initiative quickly spread to other nearby towns. No less than twelve Catalan municipalities passed regulations on the wearing of face-veils, while only in a few of them public debates actually prompted these regulations. There were also several initiatives aimed at implementing a national or regional ban of face-veils in public space against which human rights activists appealed in courts and which were finally rejected. In the city of Reus, which is in the focus of this chapter,[4] the face-veil was prohibited in 2014 after several previous attempts and amid a bitter public controversy. The banning of facial veiling occurred through a municipal by-law on *civismo* (civil participation) aimed at regulating a series of public practices that were considered 'undesired': covering one's face, nudity and visible forms of prostitution. The by-law was strongly resisted by radical leftist parties and finally modified in 2016 after a change of the composition of the local assembly. All of the bans mentioned above have been abandoned in the meantime due to a decision by the Spanish Supreme Court in 2013.

Face-veil debates are part of a post–9/11 situation where Islam has been securitized and Muslim women's bodies are under permanent public scrutiny. Variously addressed as a religious symbol, an expression of piety and a particular form of spirituality (Parvez 2011), face covering is often embedded in debates about the role of religion in the public sphere (Ferrari and Pastorelli 2013). In these debates, the religious-secular distinction forms the fundamental analytical grid over and against which institutional responses to new religious manifestations in the public sphere are explored and claims to religious rights adjudicated. As we will show, however, secularity and secularism are not only 'cognitive frames' (Taylor 2007) and 'principles of statecraft' (Casanova 2009) but have an affective dimension that shapes routine practices of being in public space in everyday life (Wohlrab-Sahr and Burchardt 2012).

Thus far, only few anthropologists and sociologists (Brems 2014) have addressed controversies over Islamic face coverings from an empirical angle. By and large, the debate has been dominated by legal scholarship and political theorists concerned with the normative dimensions of these new regulations (Giffen 2011; Grillo and Shah 2016). While welcoming this scholarship, in this chapter, by contrast, we aim to address the particular cultural, emotional and political meanings attached to face-veil wearing that are mobilized in public discourse. We will describe the local dynamics and show that contestations around face-veils emerged from the ways in which arguments over it drew on the mobilization of sentiments and affective states. These sentiments articulated urban memories of earlier contentious politics around Islam, secular notions of urban space and social practices that codify the ethics of urban conviviality.

Theorizing secular emotions

European debates about the Islamic face-veil, especially the discourses of those favouring regulations or even bans, seem to provide evidence for the idea that controversies around Muslim practices are expressions of militantly secularist visions of society, borne by historical secularization processes and driven by secular emotions. As, or to the extent that, European societies are construed as secularized, the political and legal measures that aim at curbing religious minority practices must be secularist in inspiration (Bader 2010; Calhoun 2008; Casanova 2009). In this vein, they are often perceived in continuity with other controversies such as those surrounding the publication of the cartoons ridiculing the prophet Muhammad in Denmark. According to dominant views, such controversies pit particular religious expressions and beliefs against secular liberalism and that, in defending liberal principles and values such as free speech, individual freedom and gender equality against 'religion fanaticism', secular activism acquires itself a strong emotional quality (Duyvendak 2011: 80). Indeed, scholars such as Göle (2010), Özyürek (2006) and Navarro-Yashin (2002) have pointed to the fact that secularism is not only an abstract principle of statecraft but that it carries affective force that plays out in aesthetic practices and social relationships in everyday life. Conversely, Saba Mahmood (2009), while not directly addressing the question of secular affect, usefully pointed to the affective and embodied ways in which religious subjects attach themselves to and 'cohabit' with religious signs such as icons or images, which Protestant and liberal semiotic ideologies may render unintelligible as they construe relationships between objects and signs through models of representation.

In this chapter, we suggest that the view from Spain complicates assumptions about secular emotions as the drivers of the so-called 'burka debates' and as a dominant outcome of secularization processes. While experiencing accelerating secularization processes during the last decades, especially following the transition to democracy in 1975 (Perez-Agote 2010), Spain is still one of the most religious countries in contemporary Europe. At the same time, because of the deep historical legacies of Roman Catholicism as the dominant religion, Spain is not easily assimilated to theoretical concepts that cede much explanatory power of secular emotions on the impact of Protestantism such as those of Mahmood (2009).

This becomes especially clear with a view towards the history of anticlerical violence that marked much of the history of the nineteenth and the first half of the twentieth century. As many historical studies show, one peculiar aspect of Spanish anticlericalism was that it was directed not only against priests, monks, nuns and other religious people but specifically against things: churches and convents were burnt down, statues destroyed and Catholic symbols desecrated. If Roman Catholicism in Spain does not adhere to a 'representational model' of piety (Mahmood 2009: 847), neither does anticlericalism for that purpose. In fact, anticlerical violence was animated by and shared with Roman Catholic devotion, the assumption that religious objects were authoritative presences, and embodiments, not 'symbols' of the sacred (see also Belting 1994). As a result, we argue in the following that the sensibilities that feed into current 'anti-burka' initiatives in countries as diverse as France, Spain and Lithuania have other historical sources than the semiotic misrecognition of Muslim women's forms of piety.

Moreover, as anthropologist Manuel Delgado shows in great detail anticlerical violence in Spain rarely followed a political logic despite official declarations to the contrary, that is, as necessary steps of revolutionary change. Anticlerical action was profoundly shaped by what he calls 'sacred ire' (Delgado 1992), in other words, an emotional regime that was fundamentally an inversion of people's emotional attachment to the Catholic Church and a mirror of the latter's strength. According to most observers, anticlerical violence often reached levels of grotesque brutality and was driven by pure rage. Yet importantly, it would be a mistake to construe anticlerical sentiments as secular, in the sense of unreligious. As Delgado (1992) argues, anticlerical violence was itself religious, and thus based on religious feelings. Anticlericalism therefore did not promote secularization; it was neither instrumentally related to any revolutionary project nor to liberal-republican efforts to secularize the state. Anticlerical violence lacked a unified purpose, drove wedges into popular social alliances and thus often undermined revolutionary struggles.

Against this backdrop, we suggest that in the Spanish context, secularization was not only about the disenchantment of Roman Catholicism but about the parallel disenchantment of anticlericalism as its Siamese twin. This complicates and has several implications for our understanding of secular emotions as well as for how they play into face-veil politics. First, secular emotions articulate not so much anti-religious sentiments as *distance* from religion. As we will show, it was the lines of action of ban *opponents* that were sustained by secular emotions but they were hardly anti-Islamic. Second, those promoting the face-veil ban were Catholic conservatives and they carried positive emotional attachments to religion and its public presence as long as this presence remained within limits defined by the current 'secular settlement' (Mayrl 2016). And third, we suggest that it is important not to explore secular and religious emotions as if they existed in isolation from the concrete circumstances that elicit them. In the following analysis, we show how they take shape in relation to contestations over regimes of public space and how regulatory practices serve to sanction certain emotional states, in particular 'tranquility', that people are presumably entitled to.

Immigration, religion and local conflicts

Reus is a city located in the south of Catalonia in the province of Tarragona and has around 104,000 inhabitants, more than 20 per cent of which are foreign-born[5] (IDESCAT 2015). In 2000 the proportion of foreigners in Reus was less than 2 per cent but strongly increased in the first decade of the twenty-first century – and slightly decreasing from 2010 due to the economic crises. Moroccans are the first major immigrant group (43.06 per cent), followed by Romanians (17.08 per cent), Bolivians (4.6 per cent) and Colombians (3.9 per cent).

Debates on the integration of migrants have long pervaded the local political scene. Especially remarkable are long and bitter controversies around the opening of mosques. The first mosque was inaugurated in 1999 and provoked the protest of the neighbours who argued that the mosque led to an increase in crime and a sense of insecurity in the surrounding area.[6] Despite these polemics, the mosque was opened but soon became too small to accommodate the increasing Muslim population. However, each time the Muslim community tried to open a new place, opposition of local residents started anew. The conflict had episodes of special virulence, especially when neighbours organized several marches and public assemblies to protest (in 2001, 2004 and 2011).[7]

The case of Reus is not an exception in the region. As Astor (2012: 46) puts forward, 'in recent years, contention surrounding mosques has become an increasingly common occurrence in Spain, particularly in Catalonia .... Since 1990, residents of 31 different Catalan municipalities have mobilized in protest of the presence of mosques in their neighborhoods. The high level of opposition elicited by mosques in the region has had important social, political, and legal ramifications'. The Catalan religious landscape has been profoundly reshaped in recent years due to this rise of international migration.[8] The growth of religious diversity, and especially of the Muslim population, has generated increased media and political attention. This has fostered the institutionalization of new policy programmes aimed at accommodating religious diversity at the national and, to a lesser extent, local level (Burchardt 2016; Griera 2012). However, policy actions in this terrain have not been uniform – ranging from very inclusive and accommodationist policies to much less-friendly approaches towards religion, and especially religious minorities.

Two controversies have been especially salient in recent years: the controversies on the opening of places of worship (especially Muslim but also Pentecostal) that we already mentioned and the local regulations on face-veils. In both cases, the origin of the controversy lies at the local level, and while the Catalan and the Spanish government have usually fostered measures to tone down the polemics and facilitate the accommodation of new populations, local authorities have not always worked in this way. Indeed, in most of the controversies around the opening of mosques or the prohibition of face-veils, local authorities have if not fostered, at least permitted, local residents' heated expressions of hostility. This has entrenched many of these conflicts and has hampered the success of Catalan state policies designed to solve it. To some extent, local policies on Islam have been greatly influenced by the emergence of political parties and far-right movements at the local level, especially the party Platform for Catalonia with its markedly anti-Islamic discourse (Hernandez-Carr 2011). Despite its lack of electoral success, this party has had a crucial influence in shifting the discourse of conservative parties towards populist positions.[9]

Disputes concerning the opening of places of worship have been ongoing more or less constantly since 2000 but have been slightly reduced in recent years. However, controversies over the face-veil are mainly concentrated from 2010 onwards. The face-veil controversy initially exploded in the northern city of Lleida when mayor Angel Ros decided to issue a by-law regulating the wearing of the face-veil in public spaces with fines up to 600 € for violations. The by-law was approved by the Lleida local plenary assembly on 28 May 2010 and was widely covered by the local and national press. The approbation of the by-law –popularly known as the 'burka ban'– took place amid the European (especially French and Belgium) controversies on the issue and was largely framed as a tool to stop Islamic radicalism in local contexts. The Lleida debate was the catalyst for the emergence of new proposals to regulate the wearing of the face-veils in many other Catalan cities,[10] such as Reus. Amid these local debates, the major conservative party (*Partido Popular, PP*) presented a motion in the Catalan parliament to regulate the face-veil at the Catalan level, which was rejected by simple majority.[11] Importantly, some of the parties that voted against the regulation at the Catalan level were promoting the banning of wearing of the face-veil in local contexts.

Judicially, the process was also complex and long (Burchardt et al. 2015, 2018). After some legal uncertainty, the judicial conflict ended when the Spanish Supreme Court determined that city governments had no competence to regulate the wearing of the face-veil and added that 'there were no sociological grounds that justified the ban and deemed it to be contrary to the principle of religious freedom'. However, this did not prevent some city councils, such as Reus, from introducing new local regulations on the matter.

Face-veils, public nudity and prostitution in Reus

The story of the face-veil ban in Reus is not straightforward but contains many twists and turns. The initial idea of the prohibition emerged amid Lleida's controversy and by a 'contagion effect'. The regulation of the wearing of face-veil was debated in a Reus plenary session in June 2010 – only one month after the Lleida prohibition. However, unexpectedly, the proposal was rejected. Most of the local parties were in favour of prohibiting the wearing of face-veils in the public space, but they did not agree on the terms used to justify the prohibition. On the one hand, centre and conservative parties (CiU and PP) opted for framing the prohibition as an act for protecting the 'dignity of woman' and by directly signalling the burka and the niqab at the centre of the regulation. On the other hand, centre and left-wing parties – who were in power at that moment – submitted a proposal to regulate the wearing of the face-veil through a generic ban against the covering of the face in public spaces (and without the specific mentioning the face-veil). According to the socialist mayor, 'the motion seeks to avoid stigmatizing the Muslim community' and 'if anyone cares to rule on the need to go with the face uncovered in public buildings, we regulate it, but we don't want to mix this with religious motives'. Because of the impossibility to agree on the terms of the prohibition, the by-law was not approved. However, some months later, in December 2010 the mayor decided to release a decree prohibiting the use of face-veils in public buildings. Conservative parties were not satisfied with the initiative: 'We do not want a decree, but an ordinance to extend the ban on public space.' The ordinance became a reality when the Catalan conservative party CIU won the municipal elections in 2011. After a long process of discussion, the plenary approved the so-called *Ordenança de civisme* (ordinance on civil life) in February 2014 with the conservative vote in the following terms :

> The main purpose of this ordinance is to preserve public space as a place of coexistence where all people can freely develop their activities to free movement, leisure, meeting, entertainment and expression, with full respect for the dignity and the rights of others ... The purpose of this ordinance is to maintain a climate of civility, mutual respect and social coexistence that promotes relations of solidarity, tolerance and respect among citizens, determining mechanisms to correct and, if necessary, sanction the anti-social behavior, negligent and irresponsible that impair quality of life.[12]

The by-law is a twenty-page-long document that regulates public behaviour down to the last detail. Activities and forms of appearance such as nudism, drinking in the street, begging and playing football in public space are carefully regulated and in most of the cases banned. Article 10 of the by-law, which focuses on 'rules of conduct', has a specific section devoted to prohibit the wearing of 'full veil, burka, niqab, balaclava, helmet (except for general traffic regulations) or other clothing or accessories that prevent or hinder identification'.

At first sight, the trajectory of the regulation reveals three significant elements. First, the necessity to justify the ban on Islamic face-veiling through a 'second order category' that equates face-veiling with other practices such as wearing a helmet or a balaclava. As a consequence, it is not a religious practice per se but a more generic behaviour such as non-identifiability that is criminalized and inscribed in the legal order. In the case of Reus, the construction of a 'second order category' was a strategic move aimed at avoiding overtly discriminatory regulations. In addition, it was openly recognized as a 'legitimate trick' by some ban proponents but not for others. The same structural logic was evident during the French hijab discussions, which translated the debate on the hijab into a formulation against 'ostentatious religious symbols'.

Second, local political debates also made evident the elective affinity between negative attitudes towards pious Muslims wearing face-veils and an exclusionary conception of public space characterized by an increased punitivism (Garland 2001). The fact that the wearing of face-veils, nudity and the act of drinking and eating on the street were regulated together reminds us of what German sociologist Norbert Elias called the 'standards of outward bodily propriety', which he considered 'good markers of social changes' (Górnicka 2016: 144). Importantly, Reus is in no way unique in tightening regulations of street drinking or nudity, which has become an increasing trend in Catalan cities. The banning of the face-veil has been integrated in this already existing policy agenda on the 'fight against incivility' (Delgado 2006; Fernández González 2014), which has facilitated the process of policy framing and regulation. Together with other measures that are part of this agenda, it serves to strongly expand the existing scope of the state's control over behaviour in public spaces.

Third, the trajectory of the regulation shows that despite the disagreements on the terms of the adequate protocol through which to regulate face-veiling in public space, only the radical left party actively opposed the ban. Most political actors agreed on the need to take action on this matter. As Nadia Fadil (2014: 13) also recounts for the case of Belgium, face-veiled women seemed to 'trigger a visceral reaction and to touch upon a sense of "human dignity" that is seen to be under threat' and that seemed to generate consensus on the issue across the lines of political difference.

Two questions emerge from these considerations: First, what exactly are the emotions that the face-veil engenders and that have been able to produce such a consensus among political actors? And, how are these emotions related to the broader agenda of policing public space? As we already mentioned, most of the literature addressing face-veil bans in Europe interprets the prohibition as a consequence of a 'secular agenda' in which the wearing of the face-veil appears as threatening the 'secular order'. While not denying these statements, the case of Reus shows that the analysis can benefit from analysing the 'elective affinity' between face-veil bans and the policing and sanctioning of respectable behaviour, and by scrutinizing the emotional repertoire that binds together practices such as face-veiling, nudism and begging.

The micropolitics of urban space: Shame, nudity and face-veils

Goffman (1971) understood public space as the realm of unfocused interactions between strangers. From his perspective, public space is characterized by being governed by the rule of 'civil inattention', that is, to carefully avoid direct interaction with co-present others while showing that we have no hostile intentions. The following of the rule of 'civil inattention' is what permits the street passers-by to feel 'safe and sound to continue on with the activity at hand with only peripheral attention given to checking up on the stability of the environment' (1971: 283). However, 'civil inattention' cannot be considered a completely spontaneous or untaught behaviour but is the result of enculturation, socialization and the naturalization of social norms. Therefore, the dramaturgical stage of streets is not a power-free space but a place governed by certain normative standards that mirror cultural hegemonies. For those belonging to dominant social groups, norms governing street interaction become embodied and thereby experienced as natural or unquestionable. 'Civil inattention' rules largely remain invisible and only become visible when they are violated. Ban proponents perceive Islamic face-veiling as an infraction that put in peril the stability of the environment and their assumptions about behaviour in public space. However, what kind of infraction they see in it is not self-evident.

There are two ways to approach this question from a theoretical point of view: first, in philosophy Levinas (1969) explored in a phenomenological perspective the significance of the face. From his understanding, it is in the face-to-face encounter with the other where the foundation of ethics lies. What he calls the 'defenseless nudity' of the face affects us in a pre-reflective form, and engenders a feeling of self-identity and of responsibility towards others. Schütz (1967) introduced phenomenological methods into sociological theory, arguing that face-to-face interactions, the reciprocity of perspectives based on the idealization of exchangeability and the congruence of systems of relevance allow social actors to suspend and neutralize inevitable differences in their perspectives on social situations. We suggest that the visibility of the other's face is, for Schütz and Goffman, unproblematic and given, but it does indeed play a critical role that only comes to the fore when the other's face is not visible. From the perspective of Western sociological theory, face-veiling introduces new forms of face-to-non-face interactions, which cannot but disrupt assumptions about the visual reciprocity of the actors' perspectives: one sees without being seen.

Our local interlocutors in Reus interpreted face-veiling by drawing on different semantics. According to the discourse of ban proponents, showing the face is fundamental to social life, and an essential attribute of contemporary societies. Seeing and showing one's face is conceived as a means of mutual identification and as a requirement for assessing one's intentions, moods and desires. The cultural grounding of these ideas was succinctly expressed by the mayor of Reus, who argued:

> At least, in our culture the visage shows the face and the face is the mirror of the soul. If you are happy one can see it in your face. If you feel hate it is reflected in the face. In conversations, through the eyes and the expressions you show what you think and whether what you say is true or whether you cheat.

Therefore, to be able to see the other's face in interaction is perceived as crucial for fostering social trust and maintaining rituals of communication.

The notion, however, that was to shape contestations in Reus and subsequent legal claims-making most powerfully was that face-veiling disturbs one's *tranquility* in public space. Interestingly, this was argued to be slightly different from a security concern.

From the mayor's point of view, 'You can be safe but your tranquility can be disturbed'. Then, what is at the stake is one's feeling of tranquility, which appears as autonomous to the objective level of (in)security. Tranquility emerges as an emotional state that is seen as not only desirable when being in public space but that one is entitled to and that should be preserved. As one of the ban proponents mentioned, 'We do not want people with their faces covered in the street because it gives a feeling of insecurity'. And when questioned about the reasons that engender these feelings of insecurity, he attributed them to the fact that 'in our culture we show the face'. For him, seeing and being seen in public space produces a familiarity that allows for tranquility.

Significantly, in the Spanish context complaints against the disturbance of tranquility have so far mainly referred to noise disturbances engendered by third parties, for example through construction activities or late-night pubs. Since the face-veil, as any other element used for face-covering, does not produce noise in the same way, there is obviously a semantic shift whereby the 'disturbance of tranquility' is rendered an emotional state that, as we will discuss in detail below, appears as the normalized substrate of routine urban encounters. Correspondingly, a pro-ban activist from the *Partido Popular* argued that 'we did not aim actually to persecute the burka, we are simply preserving our conviviality'. And in order to do so there was a need, in her own words, for a strategy of 'zero tolerance'. Stemming as it does from the vocabulary of crime control and urban recovery, this rendition raises crucial questions about the ways in which the (perceived) Islamization of public space is articulated with other urban disturbances.

We suggest that the key to understanding urban contestations around face-veil wearing really lies in the fact that it was regulated together with public nudity and publicly visible forms of prostitution in one and same municipal by-law. Doing so constitutes face-veil wearing as part of a wider category of 'obscene' practices that are seen to deny hegemonic codes of public conduct. Importantly, these codes also include ideas about normal emotions that run along with encounters in urban space, and emotions that are to intolerable extents undesirable and disturbing. For local conservatives, the central emotional import of face-veil wearing is shame. Onlookers feel, or are viewed to feel, ashamed because of the supposedly denigrating nature of hiding, or having to hide – depending on one's view – one's face: a practice that is viewed to eradicate one's individuality.

As mentioned, the by-law suggests that both face covering and nudity produce this shame in a comparable, if not similar fashion. A front-line anti-face-veil activist from the conservative party corroborated this understanding by pointing to the (presumed) detrimental effects on children of having to see burka-wearing women. 'You just don't want children to see that', she said, in the same way that young children should not be exposed to nudity. Another interlocutor justified the ban saying that there were complaints from the school principals who considered it not pertinent to 'give' the children to a face-veiled mother. Banning the practice of face-veil wearing from playgrounds or schoolyards was thus justified as a form of protecting people's sentiments from emotional damage and harm.

The production and regulation of shame is a strong mechanism of social control. The generation of social conformity comes along with the production of shame, which becomes an affective and effective tool for self- and social regulation (Elias 1969; Goffman 1971). According to sociologist Thomas Scheff, shame can be defined as 'a large family of emotions that includes many cognates and variants, most notably embarrassment, humiliation, and related feelings such as shyness that involve reactions to rejection or feelings of failure or inadequacy. What unites all these cognates is that they involve the feeling of a threat to the social bond' (2000: 97). In his definition Scheff points to the relationship between the production of shame and the maintenance of social bonds. Disruptive elements produce embarrassment or shame because they are seen as threatening the maintenance of the community. Through this perspective, the Goffmanian micro-sociological approach reveals how micro-social interaction becomes the locus for the reproduction of social structures.

In this perspective, the idea of face-veiling as a disruptive practice that generates shame reflects broader social processes of community foundation and reproduction. 'Undesirable' practices such as wearing face-veils – but also eating in the street or nudism – are constructed as threatening the maintenance of social cohesion: a community that is imagined as consisting of individuals who are able to perform in a normal way (Goffman 1971) and being able to carry 'safe' social interactions, and thus avoiding feelings of embarrassment and shame. All these practices – begging, visible forms of prostitution or wearing face-veil – are considered (and felt) as disruptive patterns that menace the desired uniformity of the community. Thus, it becomes clear that face-veil regulations stand in continuity with an exclusionary conservative policy agenda based on policing social, economic and cultural differences not fitting into hegemonic conceptions of the community.

However, the production of shame does not follow a stable pattern but is subject to historical, social and cultural changes. As Elias (1969) observed, the 'standards of outward bodily propriety' have considerably changed in the course of the 'civilizing processes'. In a more concrete fashion, Górnicka (2016) shows how the social perception and regulation of nakedness has evolved in the last century, by relating this transformation with broader social processes that also shape perceptions of face-veils as a 'disruptive practice'. The judging gaze of users of public space is not neutral but mediated by particular urban memories, collective perceptions and aspirations. Importantly, however, the inclusion of face-veiling in the by-law draws on arguments, which are different from those related to nudity, street drinking or begging, as it condenses ideological narratives and metaphors that have served to stigmatize Muslim populations across Europe.

Across Europe (Moors 2009), as well as in our own interviews, people have used the prison metaphor to express their emotional response to face-veils and described it as a publicly visible incarceration that is all the more scandalous and ultimately unintelligible, since it was presumably self-chosen. Importantly, what links face-veiling, nudity and prostitution is the sense of shame it produces in them. According to this discourse, as a form of self-chosen imprisonment, face-veil wearing thus produces the same kind of shame in our local conservative interlocutors as does the public confrontation with sexual submission. To understand face-veil wearing as a self-imposed form of piety and humble submission to god as the French women Parvez (2011) talked to does not unsettle but affirms such emotions since for ban proponents this is just another way of stating the case: a practice incompatible with the existing emotional regime of public space. From the point of view of emotional regimes, to insist, as civil rights activists have done in numerous national contexts, that the face-veil was not forced upon women by their patriarchal husbands but freely chosen does not so much counter than compound 'anti-burka' sentiments. As Fadil shows there is a central paradox in the veil ban: 'whereas defenders of the law often argue that such a regulation is needed to "liberate" women, several studies have documented and shown that Muslim women who decide to face-veil actually "chose" to do so, and that a ban thereby limits their freedom and autonomy' (2014: 22). We may speculate that conservatives feel a greater familiarity with gender-based subordination than with the hyper-individualist religious subjectivity, which according to many activists and anthropologists face-veil wearing illustrates and which for conservatives can only appear as irrational in the face of their anxieties, fear and shame.

The conservative councillor from the PP justified the inclusion of the face-veil in the following terms: 'The aim was to give a message, a social message to the people of Reus and people who came from outside that immigration has to be integrated, legal and organized. Not everything is acceptable.' She added: 'The burka is the most visible and most radical sign of this Islam ... and we are not going to tolerate this, we need to put some limits.' In this regard, the face-veil can be considered as an available symbolic resource in the global arena that can be strategically used to play politics in the local scene. The hyper-visibility[13] of the face-veil epitomizes fears of Islamization, and its capacity to arouse strong and visceral emotions affords greater public visibility to the prohibition. The ban's efficacy in mobilizing support rests on its ability to mobilize the same kind of emotions in the populace that have motivated it in the first place. We concur with Mazzarella that 'any social project that is not imposed through force alone must be affective in order to be effective' (2009: 299).

Legislating 'secular bodies'? Gender, Islam and the politics of secularism

The analysis of the discourses mobilized around face-veil in Reus shows the need to go beyond the simplistic reading of the controversy through the religious-secular dichotomy. If we understand secularity as the lack of religious attachments, it seems difficult to describe the face-veil controversy as directly emerging from a secular affect. In fact, in Reus, those mobilizing against the prohibition mainly described themselves as 'secularist' and as distanced from religion. Radical left activists who declared themselves to be 'far from religion' vigorously contested the ban and organized the opposition. In this case, Muslim actors were almost invisible in the media debates as the defence of the right to wear the face-veil in public was carried by a small leftist party (CUP) and social activists. Their arguments were not built on concerns over religious freedom but based on notions of cosmopolitanism and the 'right to the city'. While animated by the face-veil ban, they protested against the more general securitization of urban space. 'When you want to hang a poster for instance', one CUP party activist told us in this context, 'this poster first has to be approved by the city council responsible for public space, and once it is approved you get a stamp for it. This is really like in the times of the Dictatorship of Franco'. Again, we see how the political aspects of control and surveillance of public space are foregrounded, and indeed placed not in debates about religious diversity but in the context of the struggle against authoritarianism. The driving force behind their involvement was the fight against an exclusivist conception of the public space and of what they perceived as a neo-liberal and neo-conservative agenda. Thus, the analysis of this case reveals that the configurations of the actors' positions in relation to the face-veil do not directly correspond to the traditional secular-religious divide, since the defenders of the ban were not 'secularists' but rather (mainly) Catholics.

However, it is worth noting that defenders of the ban also built their argument by placing the wearing of the face-veil beyond the religious realm, by stating that this practice had nothing to do with Islam. One of our interlocutors affirmed: 'Islam does not say that it is necessary to go with the face covered'. While considering the headscarf as a 'legitimate' religious practice to be respected for the sake of the freedom of religion, he questioned the religious character of the face-veil. In a similar fashion, another interviewee argued: 'We were studying this and we realized that this is a pre-Islamic issue, it has nothing to do with Islam. I think that the origin lies in the desert of Pakistan, they started to wear it in order to protect themselves from the wind and the sand'. Therefore, there is a conscious effort by ban proponents to construe the face-veil as cultural, not religious. The reason is that most of them do not identify as 'secularist' and don't feel at ease with secularist repertoires of argumentation because they associate 'assertive' secularism (Kuru 2009) with historical forms of anticlericalism. Indeed, most ban proponents are self-declared Catholics, count with the support of Catholic voters and perceive secularists as their political and cultural enemies, not allies. Construing the face-veil as cultural, instead of religious, is part of an effort to *sanitize* religion, to expel its presumably illiberal expressions or components and to buttress the notion of religion as socially valuable. In line with this goal, they also defend the headscarf as a respectable practice of piety and denounce the face-veil as an alien practice that contaminates the 'good' reputation of Islam. Denying the religious character of the face-veil reveals itself as a strategy to protect the existing negotiated order of secularism, to show the compatibility between religion and secularism, and thus to foster an image of religion (whether Catholic or Muslim) as compatible with Western modernity. The 'unintelligibility' (Amiraux 2013) that the face-veil produces and the visceral emotions it engenders could threaten their claim about the harmonious conviviality (and adaptability) between religious and secular citizens in contemporary society. Thus, paradoxically, the banning of the face-veil is better understood as an act aimed to 'redeeming' religion rather than as a secularist attempt to ban religion from public space.

These observations have implications for the question of the 'secular body' posed by Charles Hirschkind (2011). What does it mean to talk of a 'secular body'? Hirschkind asked, and more fundamentally, 'What is a secular body?' If we understand secularity as distance to religion and the lack of religious attachments, it seems difficult to describe the face-veil controversy as a secular contestation. In fact, in Reus, those who self-described as 'secularist' and read themselves as distanced from religion were those mobilizing against the prohibition.

Conclusion

If we construe secularity as the symbolically and culturally anchored form in which religion and the secular are related to one another (Wohlrab-Sahr and Burchardt 2012: 881), the face-veil controversy is surely an instance in which the human, especially the female, body becomes a site where religious-secular distinctions are redrawn. In this view, and similarly in the work of Asad (2003) and Hirschkind (2011), the religious and the secular are co-constituted and co-implicated in the construction of liberal modernity. Understanding secularism in terms of disciplining and domesticating religion helps us to construe the face-veil controversy as a new stage on which the boundaries between religion and the secular as well as the limits of 'legitimate religion' are contested, defined and authorized.

Likewise, the empirical analysis of the face-veil controversy in Reus shows the relevance of understanding that the religious and the secular are reframed in relation to other instances of power in society. More specifically, our argument is that the analysis of the affective registers in the face-veil controversy speak to both the governance of public space and about the governance of religion and must address both sets of power relations in conjunction. Secular and religious affects do not unfold in a vacuum but in relation to certain regimes of power. In this chapter, we have analysed how 'secular affect' intersects with particular conceptions of the public space, which complicates the reading of the controversy as a direct effect of the religious-secular cleavage.

At a micro-sociological level, the contentious nature of face-veil polemics mainly lies in the fact that they intersect with what Spencer (1878) identified as the most general kind of government that is the 'government of ceremonial observance'. The face-veil is perceived as breaching the ritual organization of social encounters (Goffman 1971) by disrupting taken-for-granted routines of everyday life. As Tonkiss (2005: 71) argued, 'The street … is not an abstract space of social encounter, but a thicket of social codes and potentially risky contacts', and there are multiple occasions in which the 'normal' order of interaction is challenged, and the delicate moral framework that sustains the public order has to be renegotiated. As a 'universal indicium of civilization' (Fournier 2013: 689), showing one's face is turned into a marker of belonging and renders citizenship a matter of bodily performance. Indeed, the practice of face-veiling is articulated to a set of three different bodily gestures that Muslim behaviour is viewed to deny and that are perceived as potentially disruptive: seeing one's face, shaking hands and drinking wine. Many informants mentioned several anecdotes and specific episodes associated with these elements, which are identified as symbolic gestures marking the boundary between 'us' and 'them' and as defining minimal standards of assimilation. These 'convivial disturbances' dramatize difference by disrupting the routinized flow of local social life. They signal insufficient deference (Goffman) as the ceremonial means of showing appreciation of participants.

There is an interesting way to look at public spaces as infrastructures of conviviality and the notion of the ideal consumer or user they envisage, or on which their functioning is premised (Burchardt and Höhne 2015). And it may seem that the very existence of such images of 'ideal users' homogenizes populations according to standards and subjects them to processes of normalization. Emotional regimes of public space thus contribute to the graded regimes of urban inclusion that articulate one's abilities to enjoy and be in urban space, with economic resources and class status. The outcomes of these articulations may fashion graded regimes of infrastructural urban citizenship – a form of citizenship that occludes many of the categories of people with which it operates. As Sonesson (2014: 7) suggested, 'Urbanity originates as a scene on which the gaze, well before the word, mediates between the sexes, the classes, the cultures, and other avatars of otherness.'

From this perspective the prohibition of the face-veil serves to articulate a vision of public space as regulated, uniform and as producing a predictable set of desirable, or at least tolerable emotions. The micro-politics of the controversy are therefore better understood if seen in the light of the exclusionary nature of contemporary public space (see also Cook and Whowell 2011). We suggest that the boundaries between religion and the secular acquire meaning and social force through the ways in which they are afforded emotional force, which is in turn spatially mediated. Interestingly, as a cultural habitus and emotional disposition secularity shaped the views and practices not primarily of those who mobilized on behalf of more rigid behavioural regimes of public space but of the progressive groups who routinely rally against the control of public space.

Afterword: Getting Hold of the Secular

Matthew Engelke

How could you read this rich collection of essays and come away with any other conclusion? *Of course there are secular bodies.* And affects, and emotions.

True, they can be limned in a variety of ways. There are the intentional acts of marking them as such, which we can see in everything from the application of lipstick in Istanbul (Liebelt); to the crafting of humanist wedding vows in Britain (Aston); to the impassioned project of a nineteenth-century Italian revolutionary, for whom cremation was a marker of science, reason and progress (Kosuch). And admittedly, none of these can be seen as clear-cut. But then, what kinds of bodies, affects and emotions ever are? Are embodiments ever singular?

So we have to take account of the ways in which secular bodies get recast, refit and even rejected. The body of a woman on birth control is not always finally, or even initially, secular (Klassen), while the laic of Quebec can have Catholic sensibilities (Mossière). In Israel, *hiloni* (secular Jewish citizens) strain to communicate their reasonableness by making sure not to get emotional when the conversation turns to Hamas or Hezbollah (Gutkowski). In still other instances, the manifestations of secularity aren't a question of either self-conscious embrace or deeply ingrained structures of feeling. Sometimes, their embodied and emotive aspects settle and lift with all the qualities of a fog, prompting cynical men on a London omnibus to find themselves standing up, hats off, to commemorate the war dead (Lichau). In France, on the other hand, these aspects can come in the form of a short, sharp knock on the door as the police seek to uncover – which is to say, name – the 'real' reasons for marriage between Muslims/migrants (Selby).

And yet, if the conclusion is so clear, why is it not offered by any of the contributors? None of the authors in this volume end up making unequivocal claims, and where some come close to a firm position, it tends to be in the opposite direction – with the refusal of secular embodiments. Nearly all of the authors say something along the lines of the following: *In some instances, and in some respects, some of the time, we could make an argument that bodies, affects and emotions are secular.*

The inconclusive conclusion is driven by more than the requisite caveat, of nothing ever being singular or one dimensional. Taking their cue from a short thought-piece by Charles Hirschkind (2011), most of the authors here emphasize a particular issue when it comes to secular matters, which is that secularity in itself resists demarcation.

By its very logic, we might say, the secular is everything and nothing. It is the object that doesn't exist, the disembodied body, the enervated emotion.

In their introduction to the book, Birgitte Schepelern Johansen, Nadia Fadil and Monique Scheer sum this up by writing of 'the impossibility of the secular as a substantially independent entity' (p. 4). In part what they mean is that the secular can never be understood outside of its relations to religion. This is now accepted wisdom in the human sciences, and is often expressed in terms of the secular and religious being 'mutually constitutive'. I want to come back to this. But another part of what they mean concerns secularity's everything-and-nothing character, which is well worth exploring in more depth. For the secular does not want bodies to be secular.

The editors provide an excellent sketch of this point in their introduction, drawn from the work of several key philosophers, anthropologists and others. Other contributors add to the sketch, which I would like to take the opportunity here to frame. In doing so, I want to argue, we can consider how certain combinations of sensibilities, ideas and regimes of value have come to prevail in the modern era. Taken together, the chapters in the book reveal these sensibilities, ideas and regimes of value to be part of a story, a kind of 'Enlightenment story', in which bodies, affects and emotions are supposed to play minor roles.

The Enlightenment story

To situate their analyses, many of the contributors to this book refer to what Webb Keane (2007) calls 'the moral narrative of modernity'. This is 'a story of human liberation from a host of false beliefs and fetishisms that undermine freedom' (2007: 5). The moral narrative is a core feature of the larger Enlightenment story I want to recount. As J.B. Schneewind writes, we can also think of this in terms of 'the invention of autonomy', of progression from 'morality as obedience', which dominated the West up through the seventeenth century, to 'morality as self-governance', which, from that time on, made increasing allowance for 'a social space in which we may each rightly claim to direct our own actions without interference from the state, the church, the neighbors, or those claiming to be better or wiser than we' (1998: 4).

The autonomy has correlates. One has to do with the importance of interiority, or 'modern inwardness', to our conceptions of the self (Taylor 1989: 111–207). In the moral narrative of modernity, freedom requires the material chains of the external world to be removed – or, at least, loosened according to our wishes. Even more than this, freedom is realized through the workings of individual minds. First, in the use of reason: as Immanuel Kant charges, 'dare to know!' And second, in the exercise of our conscience: as Polonius says in William Shakespeare's *Hamlet*, 'to thine own self be true'. No one's thoughts must be coerced, no one else's beliefs should be accepted as one's own and the moral compass is to be found within. In a manner of speaking, this story of being modern puts mind over matter.

Individuality, interiority and inwardness have a further correlate, too: their immaterial quality. And this brings us to another strand of the moral narrative, which is the emphasis on thoughts and ideas over things. The Protestant Reformation is often recognized as a major catalyst for this shift, especially in those instances of reform that led to a 'stripping of the altars' (Duffy 1992). 'Freedom, in this light, seems to depend on the dematerialization of what is most definitive of humans, whether that be understood as the soul, thoughts, belief, or, say, the meanings of words' (Keane 2007: 7). It is the light of Christian moderns. Over time, however, the soul was increasingly challenged by the mind as 'the only locus of thoughts, feelings, spiritual élan' (Taylor 2007: 30). Christian moderns gave ground to secular moderns. The self became more and more contained – 'bounded', as Charles Taylor puts it, such that humans alone could be seen as agents in the world (not gods, or tree spirits, or amulets, or fragments of bone). By the 1920s, Rainer Maria Rilke could write of a wholly interior, immaterial relationship:

> Nowhere, Beloved, will world be but within us. Our life
> passes in transformation. And the external
> shrinks into less and less. Where once an enduring house was,
> now a cerebral structure crosses our path, completely
> belonging to the realm of concepts, as though it still stood in the brain.
> Our age has built itself vast reservoirs of power,
> formless as the straining energy that it wrests from the earth.
> Temples are no longer known. It is we who secretly save up
> these extravagances of the heart. Where one of them still survives,
> a Thing that was formerly prayed to, worshipped, knelt before –
> just as it is, it passes into the invisible world.
> Many no longer perceive it, yet miss the chance
> to build it *inside* themselves now, with pillars and statues: greater.
> (Cited in Taylor 1989: 501–02)

The disembodied, dispassionate side of secular life, along with certain forms of Protestant life that parallel and precede it, has often led to mixed judgements. Rilke, clearly, has not lost passion, yet the bigger Enlightenment story that helps animate his words tends to play down passion. Max Weber spoke of this in terms of a disenchantment of the world, a process in which poetic wonder is crowded out and replaced with the principle that everything is subject to calculation. Weber was a strong advocate of reason and rationality, yet his writings on science and disenchantment also contain hints of nostalgia – or, at least, respect – for the meaning in magic and integrity of the priest's 'intellectual sacrifice'. More recently, Taylor's account of the secular age has turned on the loss of a certain kind of 'fullness', by which he means a source of order and meaning that exists beyond human thought and action. Tinged by a mix of nostalgia and biting (if always polite) criticism, Taylor argues that one of the problems with Enlightened culture is the extent to which it is subject to 'the dominance of instrumental rationality' (2007: 542). Throughout his work on the modern self, Taylor often speaks of 'disengaged reason' (see Taylor 1989, 2007). In doing so, he tries to underscore how dispassion and disembodiment are central to the constitution of this self. Taylor is not entirely opposed to this mode of reason; he thinks it has brought much good. Yet its 'dignity' is offset by the extent to which 'expressive fulfillment … has been savaged in its name' (1989: 502).

In some versions of the push against the Enlightenment story, the coldness of reason, science and secularity make it not only unsatisfying but uncompelling. For William Connolly, what gets lost in the enlightened mode of statecraft and civic engagement is a 'visceral register of being' (1999: 21). No gut. No passion. For Jane Bennett, the moral narrative of modernity is a disenchantment story that can only lead to glazed eyes and laggard responses, so dull and dead is the scripted ending. As she sees it, the issue is 'whether the very characterization of the world as disenchanted ignores and then discourages affective attachment to that world' (2001: 3). Still others have pushed for finding 'the joy of secularism' (Levine 2011), in some cases claiming that the counter-narrative of affective wonder ends up killing off what it then seeks to resurrect (Robbins 2011: 93). Some of these joyous secularists also bristle at Taylor's refusal to grant them a truly expressive fulfilment. In any case, we seem to find an insistence that life is not yet totally dull and dead.

Is there a secular body?

Concerns with an enlightened push toward 'excarnation' (as Taylor puts it) are, in the end, what provide the impetus for this book. And here we can come back to the essay by Hirschkind (2011), and, more specifically, the bald question he poses therein: Is there a secular body? If we can say that the Enlightenment story promotes freedom and autonomy, and if the specific cant to this combination of values helps foster a modern identity defined by its individuality, inwardness and immateriality, what room is there for bodies – what room is there, really, for anything base in the world?

What more do we need to answer this question than what we find (or don't find, as the case may be) in Lois Lee's chapter? She writes of the 'Atheist temple', commissioned by the philosopher (of course a philosopher) Alain de Botton. And she argues how the building 'manifests certain body pedagogics' (p. 117). But then, we might note that *this temple does not exist*, except on the page. It has never been built. Rilke, again, comes to mind: 'Where once an enduring house was,/now a cerebral structure crosses our path, completely/belonging to the realm of concepts, as though it still stood in the brain.' More of nothing, here, in the so-called Atheist temple.

Such emptiness or absence is also expressed through acts of evacuation and desensitization. Karsten Lichau's work on the Minute's Silence, as developed in the wake of the Great War, shows this well. Even the King of England sought to legitimize and authorize such commemoration as secular. And what are its characteristics? Stilling movement, sound and the rush of life. By producing such absence, or erasure, and forcing the inward focus, the Minute's Silence is a perfect instantiation of secularity. It gives a whole new layer of meaning to the idea of secularization as a 'subtraction story' (see Taylor 2007).

There is even a sense in which the subtraction and negation take place irrespective of materiality per se. Take the museum, that modern institution which, in key respects, seems to buck the trend to de-materialization. Museums are modern and they are often used to illuminate key aspects of modernity's secularity (even as they cultivate senses of the sacred). But museums are also all about stuff. What Judith Dehail seems to suggest, in her research on music history museums, is how a certain process of disenchantment takes place within them — certainly from the perspective of the curators and restorers. The life of the instrument, its agency and personality, gets shorn. 'This new relationship that takes place in the museum involves considering the image or the object exclusively for its symbolic value and therefore abstracting it from the concrete "realm of life"' (Dehail, p. 151).

Yet this does not completely still the passions. The museum workers we find in Dehail's work are still affected by the wonder of the objects. Her chapter is a good reminder that reason and passion are not wholly opposed or incommensurable. In certain renderings of the Enlightenment story, this is often the impression given – or, at least, taken for granted. We forget about the joy of secularism. Laïcité and revolution aside, though, even the French state wants to see passion in the world. We should therefore not see it as ironic but, rather, unsurprising that French bureaucrats and security personnel insist that marriage is only 'really' marriage where they can find evidence of romantic love. In the cases described by Jennifer Selby, the state-produced stereotype is of the Muslim as the instrumental actor, someone for whom calculation is the order of the day.

Almost as soon as Hirschkind asks his question, he pulls back. It *is* bald; maybe even ribald. Posing the question seems to furrow brows, to refuse resolution. When we try to find 'the embodied capacities of secular subjects' (2011: 634), he suggests, we are often stymied, because even in those places where we might expect to find them – the gym, maybe, or a training course for advertising executives – it's not easy to make a case for why we should understand those subjects, and their bodies, as 'secular', as opposed to 'modern', say, or 'liberal'. This is partly because when we highlight the quality of secularity, what we are highlighting is another kind of negation: a not-religiousness. So often – as most of these chapters remind us – to be secular is to be not religious. To extend one of Hirschkind's examples: in order for that training course for advertising executives to be producing 'secular' subjects, it is almost as if we would expect some of the training to involve an explicit denunciation of God. *Make sure you really listen to the client; and, oh, by the way, remember all that stuff you learned in church about salvation by grace? What nonsense!* It's an unlikely scenario. It's not enough for God to be absent or in the shadows. His absence must be noted, the shadows purposefully dispelled. And that doesn't happen in many corporate training rooms or gyms.

This negative relation is drawn out well by some of the contributors to this volume. For the *hilonim* discussed by Stacey Gutkowski, the dispositions and views of 'religious' Jews (especially conservatives) provide a constant point of contrast. 'Nearly all my *hiloni* interviewees were highly reflexive about their conversational performance, proceeding carefully and with nuance, reflecting on the quality of their arguments, returning to a well-modulated and quieter tone following an outburst', she writes. 'They made reference to their identity as *hiloni*, tying this identity to a calm habitus and to political values of "pragmatism" and moderation' (p. 293–94). In her chapter, Carolin Kosuch also points to such positions. It was held by the German physician Friedrich Küchenmeister, whose advocacy of cremation was in explicit opposition to religious beliefs, 'a form of mental obtuseness which had to be "cut open with the scalpel of reason"' (p. 88).

More than the negative relation to religion, however, what Hirschkind's example of gyms and corporate training highlights is that aspect of secularity's character that insists on self-denial. But I am not so sure this makes it impossible to recognize their secularity. For in the shadows of such places, religious subjects often poke about. When I was conducting fieldwork on a Christian charity in England (Engelke 2013), it was not at all unusual for the Evangelical advocates I got to know to speak of such sites as the gym and the corporate office as 'secular'. Because they are. For the Evangelical Christian, the fact that body builders and chief operating officers don't engage in God-bashing as body builders or COOs is not the point; it's simply that they don't do what they do as Christians. This is, for them, just another sign of secularity's embeddedness, which turns on what the sociologist Courtney Bender has expressed in a simple maxim: 'we can be secular without knowing it' (2012: 286). Certainly many of the Christians I have studied understand this to be true.

Scalpels of reason aside, the cremation movement in nineteenth-century Europe is a very good example of the partial truth of secularity's negative relationality. For one thing, Paolo Gorini and Küchenmeister were only one type of advocate for cremation. They told the Enlightenment story in a particular style. Others told it in slightly different ways, including Protestant clergy, who used the scalpel of reason in their own fashion (science and faith have never always been incompatible). In Britain, one of the strongest advocates for cremation was a druid (Laqueur 2015: 533), with whom I doubt Gorini and Küchenmeister would have found much else in common.

In her chapter on contraception, Pamela Klassen charts this instability to secularity particularly well. Despite what such scholars as Charles Taylor suggest, Klassen argues, increasing access to the birth control pill in the 1960s is not necessarily the hallmark of a secular body, or autonomous 'secular actor' (p. 35). John Rock, a Catholic and physician in Canada, made theological arguments in favour of the pill; he was joined by some high-ranking clergy in North America. So 'the concept of the secular is not up to the task of encapsulating the complexity of a woman's decision to use contraception to control her fertility' (Klassen, p. 59).

It is not up to the task of encapsulating the positions of laic Quebecois, either. For them, being secular (even in the anti-religious sense) is not anti-thetical to being Catholic. One of the key points to take away from Geraldine Mossière's chapter, then, is how secular sensibilities recast certain aspects of 'religion' as 'cultural'.

Instability and partiality seem to be the case in Spain, where Marian Burchardt and Mar Griera have been conducting work on political controversies over the banning of face-veils. On the one hand, Burchardt and Griera argue that these controversies index specific understandings and experiences of secular emotions, above all a highly prized sense of 'tranquility'. On the other hand, this secularity is shaped by the conjunction of two related but distinct commitments. The first is (for some) an Islamophobia. The second is (for others) an ideal of the public square, through which the burka is linked to other disruptive elements, including even loud music. The emphasis on tranquility in this case also links well to the everything-and-nothing aspects of the secular character, of thinking of it as 'the water we swim in' (Hirschkind 2011: 634). And those waters ought to be calm.

At least most of the time, or in the normative rendering. Take the use of number, for example. Statistical sciences bear the mark of secularity in several respects, not least the ways in which they disembody authority. Numbers are absolutely everything and nothing: objective, pure, neutral. As Birgitte Schepelern Johansen and Riem Spielhaus show in their analysis of think-tank polls conducted across Europe, however, quantitative research, with all its dull and disenchanted calculation, serves as a very good ladle with which to stir the pot of 'secular suspicion' over Islam. In their innocence, and in the secular conceit of speaking only for themselves, numbers become all the more significant. Critics in the human sciences have long recognized the fictive nature of such conceits, of course. What Johansen and Spielhaus document so carefully is just how much such 'neutral' technologies can craft secular emotions and affects within the publics they reach. Like an M.C. Escher sketch, in which two hands draw each other, in these cases secularist sensibilities are shaped by secular epistemologies – and vice versa.

Beyond mutual constitution

The negative aspect of secularity's not-religious or other-than-religious character is partial in another sense, because we do see secular ontologies and epistemologies emerging on their own terms, putting forward specific combinations of values, emotional sensibilities and affective registers. This is perhaps the least explored avenue in this book, but it is one we ought to pursue more in future work.

As in so many things, the dead teach us a lesson here. For whether or not it makes sense to speak of a secular body and its states of being, it is becoming increasingly possible to imagine a secular *dead* body. The relationship between life and death might in fact be a particularly useful one to consider when it comes to the embodied and impassioned aspects of secularity – the very qualities which the secular wants to downplay or even outright deny.

Consider cryonics. This is the practice of having one's body (or, in some cases, just one's head) frozen in liquid nitrogen after being declared legally dead, in the hope that, someday, one might live again. So the frozen body is a secular body, too. As Abou Farman (2013) puts it, it becomes 'speculative matter', by which he means the object through which we reflect on and redefine the meaning and limits of life, death and personhood. What makes this secular body interesting is its status as a 'quasi-person' or, in an even more telling phrase, 'personless body'. But if the body is personless, how can personhood be restored? Where does personhood go? Cryonicists are materialists; like good secular moderns, they deny the existence of the soul, or anything else that might flout the laws of nature. So personhood has to be there. At the same time, what makes personhood – what makes the secular self – are the values of freedom, autonomy and reason, as we set them out earlier, in relation to Shakespearean and Kantian sensibilities. Consciousness is other than material. 'The secular body, then, is the body produced by materialism, in order to be "real," at the same time as it is the body that must escape it, in order to be "autonomous"' (Farman 2013: 753).

The dead body, then, forces us to confront an awkward aspect to the moral narrative of modernity, certainly as fashioned into the strongest renderings of the Enlightenment story: the difficulty of fully reconciling materialism with rationalism – each of which are central to the story's telling. Farman pinpoints the tension:

> To the extent that in the West the secular arose through the materialist elimination of the soul as a condition of the real, it committed itself to a determination of personhood based on physical laws, rather than transcendent, idealist, or nonmaterial ones. To the extent that it arose through rationalist conceptions, it advocated for the separability of personhood from its physical container. The latter risks being accused of cultivating mysteries unless it manages to ground some of its assumptions in a materialist science; the former is grounded in the material but has trouble accounting for such mental features as autonomy, intentionality, and consciousness, that constitute the secular subject. (2013: 752)

One of the more intriguing points that Farman makes in his work on cryonics and 'immortalism' is that we can by now understand the 'secular' not only as a relative term – tied always to its other, religion – but as something which can be approached as a tradition in itself, with its own 'rules and tensions ... that can be examined partly on their own terms' (2013: 738). When it comes to the medico-legal regimes that set the definitions of life and death, there may be some truth to this. Farman's point isn't that religious traditions and sensibilities play no role in how we can understand the personless body; it is only that the secular framings of materialism and rationalism are sturdy enough on their own to shape specific social and institutional definitions of life, death, consciousness and personhood.

Judges and doctors may be able to provide this sturdiness; clearly though, many of the communities, individuals and technologies of concern to the authors in this volume cannot. They still depend on 'a negative gesture whereby the forms of knowledge and practice posited as religious are continuously overcome' (Hirschkind 2011: 644). When it comes to the contemporary practice of humanist weddings, for example, as discussed by Katie Aston, 'religion' is always part of the picture, always something which, in one way or another, has to be reckoned with. 'Non-religious weddings' are just that: they perform some kind of negation. Of course, this does not mean that nothing positive or constructive gets done. The same could be said about the application of red lipstick by certain women in Istanbul's beauty parlours. As Claudia Liebelt explains, such practices are intentionally coded as secular. So are face-lifts and cheek implants. These acts of self-fashioning are part of an embrace of beauty and pleasure that get cast as hallmarks of secular modernity. (This ties in well with historian Roy Porter's observation that 'the Enlightenment's novelty lay in the legitimacy it accorded to pleasure' [2000: 260].) Yet even this doesn't mean they lack connection to a life of faith. Indeed, many of the women Liebelt got to know understood themselves to be *laik* (secular) and Muslim – but notably, not *laik* and 'religious'. To call someone religious, or *dinci*, is derogatory. 'Those religious (*dinci*) women', says one of her informants, 'they have no idea about looking beautiful, unfortunately. They don't know how to take care of themselves ... ' (p. 263). 'Religion' is so often the dirty word in a secular imaginary, at once other and an inescapable part of the self.

All the same, we are starting to get hold of the secular – not only in its relation to religion, and not only as something with its own rules and tensions, but also something embedded and embodied. We are starting to articulate the ways in which the resistance we encounter in our attempts to answer the question of secular body comes from the body itself, from its being-in-the-world and other material – often lively – manifestations. As a volume, *Secular Bodies, Affects, and Emotions* takes us some way forward in this understanding, in this grasp. And we should not, I think, mistake partiality, resistance, elusiveness and the many other contingencies that seem inherent in the logic and workings of the secular as indicative of its immateriality. We need to be wary, in these emerging discussions, of making the secular into a black hole. And we can certainly say, in a sincerely complimentary spirit, that this volume gives us more of nothing than we ever thought we had.

Notes

Chapter 1

1. For an overview of the discussion in anthropology, see Cannell 2010; an approach in sociology also interested in varieties of secularism is Wohlrab-Sahr and Burchardt 2012. See also Verkaaik and Spronk 2011 for a call to research secularism from a practice-oriented perspective.
2. See Connolly 1999 for discussions of such exclusions in politics and Sullivan et al. 2011 with regard to law.
3. An early overview of 'embodied cognition' is presented by Wilson 2002. A related area of research is referred to as 'grounded cognition' (see Barsalou 2008).
4. The literature on the anthropology of the body is vast, coming from areas as wide-ranging as the anthropology of sports and of dance, the anthropology of religion as well as medical anthropology. To mention only a few important works, in which the relationship of emotions and 'the body' are particularly emphasized (as opposed to the anthropology of emotions, which emphasized language): Scheper-Hughes and Lock 1987, Leavitt 1996, Lyon 1997.
5. Asad 2011, also Tønder 2013 for a discussion of the implication of such understanding of pain for political toleration.
6. For critiques and discussion see also Asad 2011; for how this scheme is translated into the various terms for emotions, from affect to passion to sentiment, see Scheer 2014.
7. See Schaefer 2015 for a useful discussion of different approaches to affect that divides them, broadly, into Deleuzian (e.g. Massumi's concept) and phenomenological approaches (to which, for example, Sara Ahmed's work belongs).
8. On the performance of a 'European body', see Lewicki 2016.
9. See Luehrmann 2011 and Pelkmans 2017 for explorations at the interface of atheism and religion with some attention to embodied and emotional dimensions.

Chapter 2

1. In this chapter, I discuss 'men' and 'women' as these are the categories predominantly in use in contexts about which I write. The question of what access to contraception means for trans and gender-fluid people is worth considering but is beyond the bounds of this chapter.
2. Writing about debates regarding Christianity and contraception in 1960, the Irish labour historian Flann Campbell used a similar metaphor of 'the strange borderland where sex and metaphysics meet' (Campbell 1960: 147).
3. The spiritual politics of the condom, especially with the onset of HIV/AIDS, require a different analysis, in part because they are used for preventing both pregnancy and sexually transmitted diseases.

4 I thank the editors and anonymous reviewers for their very helpful comments
   on this chapter. I am also grateful to Magdalene Klassen and Suzanne van Geuns
   for their careful readings of this chapter, and especially for sharing with me their
   interpretations of *Lemonade*.

Chapter 3

1 I would like to thank Ana Cristina Vargas and Laura Ranni (Biblioteca Fondazione
   Fabretti Turin) for their constant support during my archival research. Thank you
   also very much to Monique Scheer for her careful reading and helpful comments,
   and to Diana Madden for an excellent editing. If not indicated otherwise, all
   translations from French, German and Italian are the author's.
2 On cremation in general, see Davis and Mates 2005; in Germany: Ameskamp 2008,
   Fischer 1996, in Italy: Conti et al. 1998.
3 Modern cremations in Europe were first conducted on a regular basis in Italy
   (beginning in Milan in 1876) and Germany (beginning in Gotha in 1878). For the
   majority of the nineteenth century these two countries led the (admittedly very
   small) movement in terms of the total number of cremated corpses, crematories and
   cremation societies (see Davis and Mates 2005: 433–37).
4 On Italian and German liberalism, see Carter 2010 and Sheehan 2011.
5 The difficulties physicians were faced with in trying to implement their theories and
   gain social recognition are analysed by Bynum 1994 and Hardy 2005. On physicians
   becoming substitutes for priests, see Foucault 2010: 36.
6 On the nineteenth century's widespread anticlericalism, see also Clark and Kaiser 2003.
7 Pope Pius IX and his successors accepted neither the national unity achieved during
   the *Risorgimento* nor Freemasonry, which they regarded as its emblem. Freemasons,
   for their part, used cremation as leverage against a papacy that was consolidating
   its position (Syllabus Errorum, 1864/Non Expedit, 1874). Cremation was declared
   to be incompatible with Catholicism by Leo XIII in 1886. This decision was echoed
   in many articles and books on the topic and led to long-lasting disputes. See also
   Novarino 2005 and Borutta 2010.
8 On the negative image of 'the south', see Moe 2006.
9 See on the overreaching topic of traditional cemeteries spreading contagion e.g.
   Thompson 1884: 5, 22.
10 See for the Italian case Pogliano 1984.
11 I rely on Charles Hirschkind's definition of 'the secular' (2011: 633).
12 For biographical information, see Carli and Stroppa 2010.
13 The Milanese uprising marked one of the peaks of the revolution of 1848 in the run-
   up to the First Italian War of Independence. See also Monti 2004.
14 See for further reading Westphal 2016.
15 See for example Soper 2013.
16 See for example the Masonic principle of the 'architect of the universe' as God, which
   reappears in Gorini's writings.
17 On Monism, see Weir 2012.
18 See Cozzi 2010.
19 In his analysis, Dalmas speaks of an existing 'Anglomania italiana' (Cozzi 2010: 68), which
   could explain Gorini's comparison and his sense of being in competition with the British.

20   This famous dictum stems from Italian anthropologist Alfredo Niceforo. See Moe 2001.
21   Gorini even expressed hopes of one day reanimating the preserved bodies with the
     help of infusions of warm blood (Gorini 1871: 540f.).
22   See 'Bericht aus Wien über die XXII. ordentliche Generalversammlung des Vereins
     der Freunde für Feuerbestattung "Die Flamme" Wien' (1907: 245).
23   On cremationist's corresponding attempts to reform and even abolish the earth
     burial-based Christian cemetery, see Malone 2014.
24   See for example 'Aufbewahrung der Toten in Sizilien' (1894: 1470), and 'Ueber die
     Beerdigungsverhältnisse in Italien' (1895: 1844). See also Nussbaum 2004, where she
     describes feelings of disgust in the sociocultural setting of modern times as 'magical
     ideas of contamination, and impossible aspirations to purity that are just not in line
     with human life as we know it' (Nussbaum 2004: 14).
25   For example, cremation was discussed in Florence (Second Medical International
     Congress 1869), in Dresden (First Cremation Conference 1874) and in Milan (as
     branch of the International Hygiene Conference 1880).
26   See 'Zum internationalen Kongreß für Hygiene und Demographie in Verbindung mit
     dem Verbandstage der Vereine für Feuerbestattung' (1894: 1613).
27   On the intense debates regarding cemeteries and hygiene in Italy, see Conti, Isastia
     and Tarozzi 1998: 109–27.
28   The German Protestant church and its stance towards cremation are analysed by
     Heike-Gmelin 2013.
29   See Goppelsroeder 1890: 61, who speaks of the dead body as 'a horrible, repulsive
     counterpart'. See also Trusen (1855: 101): 'foul mass', and Wernher (2013: 84): 'The
     abhorrence death evokes and the disgusting impression the rotten corpse makes on
     our senses.'
30   'Just think of the macabre image of a large family in one bed with the body of the
     dead once so close to them, and you will witness something quite common.' Trusen
     1855: 200. On mortuaries, see Trusen 1855: 198–211.
31   Küchenmeister 1875: 47–50.
32   See also Macho 1990: 327–407.
33   Küchenmeister 1875: 58.
34   Funeral ceremonies in Italy were often held by leading members of local cremation
     societies; in the German case, however, for Protestants often by a pastor. Cremation
     in these cases did not necessarily indicate a withdrawal from religion; on the
     contrary, German cremation press claimed the new way to deal with human remains
     to be consistent with Christianity. (See for example 'Die Regelung der religiösen
     Trauerfeier in den württemberg. Krematorien' (1905: 4556f).)
35   Küchenmeister 1875: 180. See for a recent similar observation, Engelke 2015: 43.
36   For the overstrung debate on apparent death among nineteenth-century
     cremationists, see Wernher 2013: 158–62, and Trusen 1855: 127–81. See also Ariès
     2005: 504–18.
37   The regulation of emotions as an aspect of the civilizing process is described by Elias
     1994: 414–20 (on shame).
38   Reclam spoke of the solemn poetry of the columbarium as being equal to that
     of a church. He emphasized that it invites the visitor to remember the deceased,
     contemplating the precious remains in serious reflection. In cremation discourse,
     emotions were expressed in the realm of aesthetics, of art and poetry, which were
     printed in almost every issue of *Die Flamme* (e.g. 1894: 1553). On the general
     tendency to aestheticize death in the nineteenth century, see Ariès 2005: 715–70.

39 Küchenmeister 1874: 145.
40 This worldliness was specific to the modern history of death in general. See Ariès 2005: 519–602.
41 Küchenmeister 1874: 144.
42 Grimm exaggerated the historical significance of cremation and, to a certain extent, invented a tradition in the sense of Hobsbawm.
43 On Moleschott in general, see Cosmacini 2005.
44 A critical argument against the quasi-religious 'materialism of the urn' is expressed in Goppelsroeder 1890: 61. On Ernst Haeckel, see Gregorio 2004.
45 Because the brains of higher animals contain high levels of phosphorus, Büchner argued, drawing on the large quantities of phosphorus stored in corpses, cremation and the fertilization of fields with ashes would secure cultural, scientific and even moral progress. The moral character of a people, he concludes, depends on the composition of the soil and vegetation in their environment.
46 On the relation of modernity and the secular, see Hirschkind 2011: 633.
47 For a description of cremationist funeral rituals, see Isastia 1998: 76–78.
48 While the Evangelical-Lutheran churches in Germany officially opposed cremation and, until 1934, declared it to be a non-Christian custom, pastors were in fact often given permission to act according to their conscience. However, in Prussia for example, they were not allowed to wear their official attire during funeral services for the cremated, and permissions in general were restricted and conditional.
49 E.g. instead of 'Peace to his soul!' the words 'Peace to his ashes!' were spoken during the funeral service (Heike-Gmelin 2013: 117f.).
50 The numbers in Italy are still very low today, with 7 per cent (2002) of all the deceased being cremated, especially when compared to Great Britain's 72 per cent (2002) and Germany's 40 per cent (with regional differences) (1999) (Davis and Mates 2005: 454f.).

Chapter 4

1 I have greatly appreciated the opportunity to develop this work as part of the 'Secular Bodies, Affects and Emotions' workshop held in Tübingen in 2016. Thank you to Monique Scheer, Birgitte Schepelern Johansen and Nadia Fadil for including me in this event, and to participants for their helpful comments on earlier versions of this chapter. Particular thanks to Birgitte Schepelern Johanse for her detailed, insightful and stimulating comments. Thank you also to Tom Greenall for allowing me to use images of the Temple to Perspective in this chapter. This chapter was also made possible through the support of grants from the John Templeton Foundation (grant numbers 59544 and 60624); the opinions expressed in this publication are those of the author and do not necessarily reflect the views of the John Templeton Foundation.
2 De Botton is also known as the founder of the School of Life (SoL), an organization that is frequently identified alongside the Sunday Assembly and New Atheism as a key example of organized non-religion (or, in the United States, 'organised secularism' [Cragun et al. 2017]). The SoL uses religious language and formats such as Sunday sermons to provide metaphysical, existential and psychological guidance (at a price), via its six sites around the world and a successful series of YouTube lectures with approaching 3 million (2,763,363) regular subscribers as well as other viewers at the time of writing. (https://www.youtube.com/user/schooloflifechannel, accessed 1 September 2017).

3   See Bullivant and Lee 2012 and Lee 2016 for overviews.

4   As well as my own work (e.g. Lee 2015), Wohrlab-Sahr and Burchardt 2012 and Burchardt et al. 2015 are significant exceptions.

5   I do not observe these conventions for reasons set out in Lee 2015 (also Lee 2012, 2014). In short, applied in this way both concepts are best seen as emic terms arising from particular Western traditions, despite being frequently taken up by (Western) academics as etic, analytic terms.

6   This work is of course motivated by many other factors too. These include, for example, the emancipatory agendas of non-religious scholars working in contexts where non-religion is marginalized; the growth, sometimes rapid, of non-religious populations and non-religious cultures in several parts of the world; and egalitarian concerns about the many differential ways that traditionally religious, alternatively spiritual, non-religious and areligious actors are often understood by political regimes and in everyday social settings.

7   Cf. Luehrmann's (2015: 141–51) approach to transcendence (after Luckmann), which sees religious and non-religious transcendence as distinct, echoing distinctions between 'horizontal' and 'vertical' transcendence in contemporary psychology of religion and non-religion.

8   Existential humanism involves humanity-centred understandings of reality and human life and can be differentiated from ethical humanism, which sees the flourishing of humanity and individuals qua humans as a good. Ethical humanism is not only compatible with existential humanism but with diverse existential orientations, including theistic ones.

9   http://www.tomgreenall.co.uk/project.php?sel=7, accessed 4 September 2017.

10 Johannes Quack's major collaborative project on the Diversity of Nonreligion is a major example. See Lee 2016 for an overview.

11 In the British context (as in many others), 'atheism' is usually seen as non-religious, since theism is viewed as integral to religion (Lee 2015).

12 As well as Dawkins, other examples of those contesting the premise of the Atheist Temple were fellow public Atheist John Gray (2012), and a blog piece which included it in a list of 'construction projects we're kind of glad were never built' (http://www.citymetric.com/skylines/6-terrible-construction-projects-were-kind-glad-were-never-built-654, accessed 4 September 2017).

13 See also Luehrmann 2015: 145 on the 'small transcendence' that building walls are able to create, and which are harnessed in religious ritual practice.

Chapter 5

1   As shown (inter alia) by Mary Bouquet and Nuno Porto 2005, numerous other types of museums can be used to illustrate this analysis, not just art museums.

2   Duncan criticizes the generally accepted opposition between the categories of secular and religious truth using the idea that 'the museum is not the neutral and transparent sheltering space that it is often claimed to be'. She points out that this institution, by fulfilling its declared missions (preserving and displaying objects), also 'carries out broad, sometimes less obvious political and ideological tasks'. The supposedly 'objective and universal' knowledge (i.e. the secular truth, rooted in experience) that the museum claims to be presenting and that is generally conceptualized as

different from the religious truth (i.e. subjective belief, magic and other irrational transformations and events) is actually an exercise of control of the representation of a community and its highest values and truths' (1991: 90). She writes indeed: 'Those who are best prepared to perform its ritual – those who are most able to respond to its various cues – are also those whose identities (social, sexual, racial etc.) the museum ritual most fully confirms' (1995: 474). Far from disinterested and 'objective' knowledge, what is presented in the museum therefore echoes who constitutes the community and who defines its identity. It is essential, according to Duncan, that we 'recognize the ideological character of our Enlightened vocabulary and the claims made for the secular – that its truths are lucid, rationally demonstrable and objective' (1991: 91).

3   See notably Chaumier 2010; Deloche 1985; Davallon 1986, 2000; Desvallées and Mairesse 2010, 2011; Gob and Drouguet 2014; Pomian 1987; Rivière 1989.

4   Paine 2013: 2.

5   Paine notes how, in some cases, religious objects in museums can still be worshipped. Most of the time, however, the worshipping is framed and controlled by the museum itself. See Paine 2013: 37–44.

6   About this practice in the *Musée Instrumental* in Paris, see Gétreau 1993: 147–148.

7   It was in this same perspective that the Galpin Society had been created in 1946 in the United Kingdom.

8   Interview with curator in the musée de la Musique, Paris, 23 June 2009 (my translation from French). This research is based on several in-depth interviews held with visitors and museum professionals in the musée de la Musique in Paris and in the Grassi Museum für Musikinstrumente der Universität Leipzig. A total of 112 interviews were conducted with visitors between May 2011 and August 2013 and 24 interviews with various museum professionals (curators, conservators, guides, directors etc.) between June 2009 and August 2013.

9   Interview with conservator in the Grassi Museum in Leipzig, 9 August 2011 (all translations into English from German or French are mine).

10 Ibid.

11 Interview with instrument maker, per Skype, 4 August 2011.

12 Ibid.

13 Interview with conservator in the Grassi Museum in Leipzig, 8 July 2011.

14 Interview with instrument maker, per Skype (in English).

15 Interview with conservator in the Grassi Museum in Leipzig, 11 August 2011.

16 Interview with museum visitor in the musée de la Musique in Paris, 31 July 2013.

17 Interview with museum visitor in the musée de la Musique in Paris (in English), 6 August 2013.

18 The showcase contains only Stradivarius instruments.

19 Interview with museum visitor in the Grassi Museum in Leipzig, 19 July 2011.

20 Le Marec has argued that the specificity of this relationship is largely overseen by museum theorists (or more generally, institution theorists) and therefore tends to be abused. She notably denounces the way the marketing approach – increasingly used in museums – fails to grasp the complexity of this relationship and tends to reduce it to a mere commercial exchange (Le Marec 2007).

21 Interview with museum visitor in the Grassi Museum in Leipzig, 29 July 2011.

22 In Leipzig, the exhibition is composed of clearly distinguished spaces. The historical instruments are exhibited on the ground floor, in a chronological manner,

throughout sequenced rooms. One floor up, in a separate room called the 'Sound Laboratory', the visitors can try out modern instruments or copies of historical instruments.

23 Interview with museum visitor in the Grassi Museum in Leipzig, 29 July 2011.
24 Interview with museum visitor in the musée de la Musique in Paris, 27 July 2013.
25 According to the Freudian approach, these conflicting feelings illustrate the interactions between the id and the super-ego of the visitors.

Chapter 6

1 This concept of 'self-mastery' is not unique to the secular or only a product of liberal thought. There are many religious traditions and ascetic practices which rely on the notion of 'self-realization', but as Saba Mahmood points out. liberalism's unique contribution is to link the notion of self-realization with individual autonomy, wherein the process of realizing oneself is equated with the ability to realize the desires of one's 'true will' (Mahmood 2011: 11).
2 This number was closer to 3000 in Scotland where humanist ceremonies are legal, and are the third most popular choice for wedding ceremonies (Copson, personal correspondence, 2014).
3 People often referred to their civil ceremony as the 'legals' and the humanist ceremony as the 'real' event.

Chapter 7

1 I want to thank Charles Hirschkind, Jennifer Selby, Rebekka Habermas and Nadia Fadil for their thoughtful comments that significantly helped to build the argument of this chapter as well as Samuel Victor for editing the article.
2 The project's title is 'Religious trajectories and identity challenges among Francoquébécois born Catholic: An ethnography of meaning paths'. It is funded by the Fonds Québécois de Recherche sur la Société et sur la Culture (FQRSC), programme young professors-researchers (2014–2017). The project started in 2014 and it is still underway.
3 The Council Vatican 2 that took place from 1962 to 1965 was followed by a politics of aggiornamiento in the Catholic Church that resulted in a dramatic change in liturgy and social and political interventions of the institution in public matters.
4 Interviews were conducted by me and a team of research assistants to whom I express my gratitude for their thorough work: Ariane Bédard-Provencher, Guillaume Boucher, Charlotte Guerlotte, Véronique Jourdain, Isabelle Kostecki, Simon Massicotte, Annie-Claude Piché, Gilles Saucier and Maryse Trudel.
5 Corresponding to a gross revenue ranging from $60,000 to $100,000/year.
6 'Emotions are about the ways in which the social world is one in which we are involved' (Rosaldo 1984: 143).
7 Available online: http://monumenttotransformation.org/atlas-of-transformation/html/n/nostalgia/nostalgia-svetlana-boym.html (accessed 2 August 2017).

Chapter 8

1   This chapter is part of a larger study supported by the German Research Foundation (No. LI 2357/1–1), the Chair for Social Anthropology at the University of Bayreuth, and the Department of Sociology of Boğaziçi University. I am grateful to the participants of the preparatory workshop for this volume and the editors of this volume for their insightful comments. I would also like to thank Esra Özyürek for her reading of and feedback on this chapter.

2   For example, on New Year's Eve 2016, a gunman walked into a renown Istanbul nightclub, killing thirty-nine and wounding many others. The attack, for which the Salafi militant group Islamic State of Iraq and the Levant (ISIL) later claimed responsibility, was commonly interpreted by the liberal media, government critics and the opposition as directed against secularism and a secular lifestyle in Turkey.

3   In early January 2017, a young journalist was arrested on the grounds of 'secular propaganda' after a video emerged on social media that showed her participating in a social centre meeting where an anonymous speaker had called for 'the flag of secularism' to be raised against 'reactionary forces' (cf. *Hürriyet Daily News* 2017).

4   See for example the online daily *Birgün* (available online: http://www.birgun.net/ haber-detay/chp-li-tanrikulu-laikligi-savunmak-ne-zamandir-suc-141623.html [accessed 14 February 2017]) or the independent online communication network *Bianet* (available online: https://bianet.org/bianet/hukuk/182279-tanrikulu-ndan-soru-onergesi-laiklik-propagandasi-suc-mu [accessed 14 February 2017]).

5   See for example Çınar 2005; Gökarıksel 2009, 2012; Gökarıksel and Secor 2009, 2010; Göle 1997; Navaro-Yashin 2002: 78–113; Secor 2001; White 2002: 29–76 and 212–241, 87–89 and 136–162.

6   Interview with Esra, 24 February 2014.

7   Interview with Funda, 6 November 2013.

8   Interview with Nehir, 19 May 2014.

9   In concurrence with a global trend, there is a recent tattoo boom in Istanbul with more and more middle-class women sporting tattooed skin in public. During my research, I found that tattoos became increasingly visible on women's bodies, including tattoos of Atatürk signatures, often inked for free by Kemalist tattoo artists on 10 November, the public holiday commemorating Atatürk's death. Interlocutors often explained their tattoos as an aesthetic choice that also spoke of their secular disposition, given the fact that tattoos are commonly seen as 'un-Islamic' in Turkey.

Chapter 9

1   This orientation also has multiple complicated genealogies among Jewish Israelis from other religious constituencies, but that lies beyond the scope of this chapter.

2   In Hebrew, my interlocutors invoked the senses of *rationali* (action with rational thought), *hedioni* (logical), *nadvuti* (intellectual) and *savel* (feasible or likely to happen).

3   The left/right distinction denotes attitudes towards the Israeli/Palestinian conflict.

4   Interviewees were sought through public advertisement and snowball-sampling for hard-to-reach individuals. Fifty-two *hilonim* were selected through random-

purposeful criterion sampling for age, *hiloni* identity and gender, with an additional sample to seek maximum variation in political orientation, and geographic diversity and some variation in class and ethnic origin. Fourteen orthodox and traditionist Jewish Israelis and a sample from transitional generation XY were also interviewed for critical purchase. Interviews were analysed using a modified Stevick-Colaizzi-Keen method for phenomenological analysis. Data were collected in Israel/Palestine over three months, including participant observation in urban and rural areas within the Green Line, and nine interviews were conducted with Jewish Israeli migrants in London. Interview and survey data were contextualized with results from public opinion polls. Civil society and government reports, memoirs and secondary literature lend further context, authenticity and credibility to the study, as does a qualitative textual analysis of three major newspapers with a *hiloni* readership representing diverse points on the political spectrum (the *Jerusalem Post*, *Haaretz* and *Yedioth Ahronoth*, 2005–16).

5   I am also grateful to Dr Lahav for related conversations on these points.
6   A beach drum circle in Tel Aviv at Friday sundown (versus the Jewish tradition of lighting Shabbat candles at home with family) is one explicitly *hiloni* ritual.
7   For example, Avigdor, who describes his politics as 'hard Right', explained, 'Judea and Samaria is the place where the Jewish people were formed …. If you take from me Judea you take from me my whole existence. Even me as a secular person, this is something I cannot accept because once I decide to let them have it I let them have my whole DNA as a Jew. From that moment to the moment we cease to exist as a Jewish state before 1967 will be a very short time …. I consider the Bible as a secular text… I don't know if God gave us the land or not but I refer to the Bible as *my* historical document.' Like Avigdor, a majority of Leftist participants in the study believed in a Jewish moral-historical claim to the West Bank and East Jerusalem, though one which could be over-ridden politically, dismantling the settlements.

Chapter 10

1   During the 1920s, the minute's silence was taken up in a similar format by other countries, such as France and Belgium in 1922 and Poland in 1925, often becoming an important element in national memorial cultures. In 1924, an attempt to take up the ceremony in Weimar Germany failed, making the minute's silence a rather marginal and rare element in German remembrance practices.

After the Second World War, the minute's silence also spread into political cultures as different as the Soviet commemoration of soldiers killed in the 'Great Patriotic War' with the *minuta molčanija*, broadcast on radio each 9 May from 1965 onwards and mockingly called 'the prayer' due to its heavy use of religious sounds and symbols. The Israeli tradition has the silence in reverence to the victims of the Shoah 'sounded' by sirens wailing at 10 o'clock on *Yom Ha-Shoah*, a tradition that began in the early 1960s, and a second silence on *Yom Hazikaron* to commemorate soldiers and civilians killed by war and political violence.

On the transnational level, minute's silences have become more and more popular, especially in the context of highly mediated events like Princess Diana's funeral, and notably since 9/11 and recent European experiences of terrorism.

2 On the crucial role of newspapers in the emergence of 'imagined communities' and their 'apprehensions of time', see Anderson 2006 [1983]: 22–36.

3 On the influence of Protestantism in the establishment of bourgeois interiority, see Scheer 2012b: 181–84.

4 On distinctions between interiorized 'feelings' and exteriorized 'affects' and the ideologies around them, see Scheer 2012b; on the history of hate and its locations in the body, see Johansen 2015; on the history of anger and American ideas about eliminating it, see Stearns and Stearns 1986.

5 I would like to thank Nadia Fadil for drawing my attention to the need for such a shift in conceiving of secular bodies.

6 '... the attention paid to staging in great collective ceremonies derives not only from the concern to give a solemn representation of the group (manifest in the splendour of baroque festivals) but also, as many uses of singing and dancing show, from the less visible intention of ordering thoughts and suggesting feelings through the rigorous marshalling of practices and the orderly disposition of bodies, in particular the bodily expression of emotion, in laughter or tears' (Bourdieu 1990: 69).

Chapter 11

1 Translations from French are my own. All informants' names have been anonymized. I gratefully acknowledge the organizers of the authors' workshop in Tübingen, research support from the Social Sciences and Humanities Research Council, legal advice from Pierre Chaudet, thoughtful feedback from Nadia Fadil and the generosity of my interlocutors in France and Algeria.

2 Petit-Nanterre has a population of approximately 8,800, of which 30.8 per cent are first-generation immigrants (INSEE 2011). It is a ZUS (Sensitive Urban Zone) with a high unemployment rate (in 2013, 42.5 per cent of Nanterre was unemployed; INSEE 2013), likely higher in Petit-Nanterre, the suburban city's poorest neighbourhood. Owing to family regroupment and migratory patterns, this neighbourhood is primarily of Algerian origin. I do not assume these interlocutors are Muslim. But, in more than 150 interviews I have conducted in the neighbourhood since 2004, I have met one Algerian Christian who was a recent convert. Islam remains an important referent among a majority of *croyants* (believers) who are not *pratiquants* (practitioners) (see similar national data in Selby 2014b: 42).

3 I define the secular as a regulating discursive mechanism that delineates, among others, the so-called public from the private sphere within a contingent series of legal and political projects, all of which are deeply implicated in the definition and management of religion (see Hurd 2012: 955).

4 Michel Foucault's work on governmentality and the regulation of sexuality through 'biopower' is a useful framework with which to consider the French state's preference for signs of romantic love (Foucault 2003; see Fassin 2006: 123–31).

5 I interviewed more than 60 adults about their marriage partner choice arrangements in Petit-Nanterre, France (3 stays over 15 months total between 2011 and 2016) and another 30 over the course of two transnational weddings in 2011 and 2016 in Algeria. Compared to non-Algerians, Algerian French marry more often, seek out heteronormative unions and often do not cohabitate before marriage (at least officially; Hamel et al. 2010: 85–87).

6 Also remarkable is Fatima's husband's desire for a transnational bride, despite knowing how her residency requests will be scrutinized by the state.

7 The *loi de 2006 relative au contrôle de la validité des mariages* (2006 law on the validity of marriage) introduced a five-year prison and 15,000 euro fine to deter fraudulent marriage. An amendment in 2009 escalated these penalties for groups organizing marital fraud, to ten years in prison and a €750,000 fine, suggesting that marriage fraud has become more pervasive and organized.

8 Same-sex marriage was legally recognized in France in 2013 and followed the PACS (*Pacte civil de solidarité*), a legal contract between two people signed at the prefecture, which did not offer couples adoption or reproductive rights (Segalen 2003: 83). Fassin (2014) shows how the same-sex debate, which centred on concern for adoption and reproductive rights, emphasized protecting the 'national body', a discourse I see in the perceived threat of transnational marriage.

9 A *mariage forcé* is based on non-consensual force. In a *mariage blanc*, the two parties mutually agree to marry primarily so that one of the spouses obtains citizenship, while in a *mariage gris*, one person (typically imagined as the foreigner) takes advantage of the other, luring them into marriage by pretending to be in love. The assumption is that once the person (again, often depicted as foreign and racialized) receives his or her paper work, he or she divorces.

10 Subsequent laws in 2011 doubled down on "grey" marriages and set a longer period for marriage prior to making citizenship requests (from four to five uninterrupted years), allowed officials up to thirty years to annul a marriage deemed fraudulent and granted more discretionary power to administrators to determine, report and annul them (*Ministère de la Justice* 2011).

11 See also Saba Mahmood's classic *Politics of Piety* (2005), based on an ethnographic analysis of religiously conservative Cairene women, which astutely disaggregates secularism from liberal Western feminism to show how they buttress one another (see also Scott 2007: 148).

12 A handful of the women I have interviewed in Petit-Nanterre of Algerian origin were married by force (the category can be sometimes difficult to parse in relation to arranged or wished unions); and, while my interviews did not focus on conjugal violence, several women living in Petit-Nanterre have shared their experiences of domestic abuse (see examples in Selby 2012: 101–02, 152–57).

13 Farid had just started a new job outside of Paris with a rare permanent contract and could not yet request time-off. His mother and his Algerian relatives attended the celebration at Rachida's parents' apartment that featured sixteen dresses and 'even the matches, as they say'. He phoned immediately after the contract was signed to participate from a distance.

14 The Ministry of Justice suggests that less than 2 per cent of the 737 marriages annulled in 2006 were forced marriages (see Belmokhtar 2006). Reasons for annulment include the absence of consent, bigamy, being a minor, non-appearance, lack of intention to marry, forced marriage and misrepresenting the essential qualities of an individual.

Chapter 12

1 Conseil Sondage Analyses (CSA): 'Islam et citoyenneté', 26. The main part of the research for this chapter was carried out at the Centre for European Islamic Thought at the University of Copenhagen with the support of the Danish National Research Foundation (DNRF). We would also like to thank Monique Scheer and Nadia Fadil

as well as good colleagues at the Centre for Advanced Migration Studies, University of Copenhagen, for their insightful comments on earlier versions of this chapter.

2 Thorne and Stuart 2008: 55–56.

3 SCIICS survey on Turkish and Moroccan immigrants and descendants 2013, reported in Koopmans 2014: 11.

4 Institute Montagne 2016: 19.

5 Stern writes in the context of the late-nineteenth- and early-twentieth-century United States; however, similar analysis addressing the European history can be found in the work of Foucault 2007, Hacking 1991 and Rose 1999.

6 We here draw on an understanding of emotions that foregrounds intentionality (Goldie 2012). Emotions imply cognition and judgements in the sense that they direct us against objects or persons in the world in ways that, through our bodily arousals, tells us something about the object of the emotion (that it is dangerous, that it is repulsive, that it is good etc.). Thus, we use the term 'emotions' to grasp those bodily arousals that are picked up, signified and organized according to available cultural script, norms for proper conduct, biographical memory and so on.

7 In the European value survey, the questions that address separations between religion and politics gain overwhelming positive responses in favour of a separation.

8 Here we draw on Laclau's notion of the empty signifier as social and political mobilizers (1996).

9 In this respect, it is interesting that 25 per cent of the respondents in 'Islam on Campus' answer the question with 'don't know' or 'no answer', which often in quantitative research points towards either an uncertainty regarding what the question implies or some kind of dissatisfaction with available possibilities for answering (Thorne and Stuart 2008: 55).

10 Examples of such questions are: 'Should we introduce Sharia in Norway?' (TNS Gallup, Norway 2006), 'If I could choose, I would prefer to live in Britain under sharia law rather than British law' (Mirza et al. 2007), 'I would approve of, if in my country of origin certain offences would be sentenced, like in Islamic law, with flogging' (Brettfeld and Wetzels, Muslime in Deutschland, Germany 2007: 141), 'Which statement do you agree with most? Sharia law should be applied fully/partly, Islamic law (sharia) should be applied fully, regardless of the country in which you live, Islamic law (sharia) should be applied in part, it can adapt to the rules of the country where you live, Islamic law (sharia) does not apply in non-Muslim countries' (CSA, Islam et citoyenneté, France 2008: 9).

11 This has, for example, been a recurring point in debates about the niqab, where critics of a ban has argued that European governments are promoting women's liberation while simultaneously putting restrictions on Muslim women's choice of dressing.

Chapter 13

1 See http://www.loc.gov/law/help/france-veil.php (accessed February 2017).

2 See http://www.telegraph.co.uk/news/worldnews/europe/italy/1468885/Italian-mayor-fights-terror-threat-with-ban-on-Muslim-veils.html (accessed February 2017).

3 See http://religaredatabase.cnrs.fr/spip.php?article129 (accessed February 2017).

4   The study is based on a case study research design (Yin 1989) and developed through qualitative interviews with key actors involved in the controversy (politicians and civil society) and document analysis (media statements, reports) carried out between 2013 and 2014. The chapter is focused on the case of the city of Reus but is also informed by previous research conducted by the authors in the city of Lleida (Burchardt et al. 2015).

5   The category of foreigner includes those that do not have Spanish nationality. Therefore, those that are foreign-born but have become Spanish citizens are not included.

6   See http://elpais.com/diario/2004/01/12/catalunya/1073873246_850215.html (accessed 15 January 2015).

7   Ibid.

8   From 2000 to 2012 the percentage of foreigners living in Catalonia increased from 2.9 per cent to almost 16 per cent of the population (Climent-Fernando 2012). This substantial growth of the foreign population has shaken the Catalan religious scene. More than 250 Muslim worship places have been built in the last two decades (ISOR 2015), and currently Muslims accounts for the 7.3 per cent of the population (CEO 2015).

9   In some cases, as it was in the case of Reus in 2005 and 2014, neo-fascist movements have gone beyond the realm of the discourse and have staged violent actions as racist painted on the walls of mosques or throwing Molotov cocktails and other artefacts to the mosque.

10 In a less than three months, seven new local governments passed by-laws to prohibit the wearing of full face-veils, while two other cities adopted the ban by mayoral decree without debate. In addition, face-veils bans were debates in other five Catalan municipalities but proposals were rejected in the local plenaries.

11 The PP tried again to get support to approve a motion in this regard in June 2011 but it also failed. In 2013, a new centre-right party brought it again into the Catalan Parliament and demanded a change in the law on religious freedom, which recognizes face-veil wearing as discriminatory against women and as security threat. The proposal was rapidly rejected again.

12 See http://www.naciodigital.cat/delcamp/reusdiari/noticia/4548/ordenanca/civisme/ reus (accessed 15 January 2016).

13 This hyper-visibility is more 'mediated' by TV images than by real personal experiences with face-veiled women. We don't count with exact data about the number of face-veiled wearers living in Reus or in Catalonia. As Warburg et al. 2013 note political debates on the face-veil in Europe have not been based on factual knowledge but on vague information.

References

Chapter 1

Agrama, H. (2012), *Questioning Secularism: Islam, Sovereignty and the Rule of the Law in Modern Egypt*, Chicago, IL: Chicago University Press.

Anidjar, G. (2003), *The Jew, the Arab. A History of the Enemy*, Stanford, CA: Stanford University Press.

Asad, T. (1979), 'Anthropology and the Analysis of Ideology', *Man*, 14 (4): 607–627.

Asad, T. (1982), 'Anthropological Conceptions of Religion: Reflections on Geertz', *Man*, 18 (2): 237–259.

Asad, T. (1993), *Genealogies of Religion: Discipline and Reason of Power in Christianity and Islam*, Baltimore: Johns Hopkins University Press.

Asad, T. (2003), *Formations of the Secular: Christianity, Islam, Modernity*, Stanford, CA: Stanford University Press.

Asad, T. (2011), 'Thinking about the Secular Body, Pain, and Liberal Politics', *Cultural Anthropology*, 26 (4): 657–675.

Barsalou, L. W. (2008), 'Grounded Cognition', *Annual Review of Psychology*, 59: 617–645.

Bear, L. and N. Mathur (2015), 'Introduction. Remaking the Public Good: A New Anthropology of Bureaucracy', *Cambridge Journal of Anthropology*, 33 (1): 18–34.

Beckford, J. and A. P. Hampshire (1983), 'Religious Sects and the Concept of Deviance: The Mormons and the Moonies', *British Journal of Sociology*, 34 (2): 208–229.

Berger, P., ed. (1999), *The Desecularisation of the World: Resurgent Religion and World Politics*, Washington: Ethics & Public Policy Center.

Berlant, L. (2011), *Cruel Optimism*, Durham, NC: Duke University Press.

Beyer, P. (1994), *Religion and Globalisation*, London: Sage.

Binder, S. (2017), 'Total Atheism: Making "Mental Revolution" in South India', PhD diss, Utrecht University.

Bourdieu, P. (2006 [1977]), *Outline of a Theory of Practice*, Cambridge, UK: Cambridge University Press.

Brown, W. (2006), *Regulating Aversion: Tolerance and Identity in the Age of Empire*, Princeton, NJ: Princeton University Press.

Brown, W. (2013), 'Introduction', in T. Asad, W. Brown, J. Butler and S. Mahmood (eds), *Is Critique Secular? Blasphemy, Injury, and Free Speech*, 7–19, New York, NY: Fordham University Press.

Bubandt, N. O. and M. van Beek, eds (2012), *Varieties of Secularism in Asia: Anthropological Explorations of Religion, Politics and the Spiritual*, London: Routledge.

Burkitt, I. (1997), 'Social Relationships and Emotions', *Sociology*, 31 (1): 37–55.

Cannell, F. (2010), 'The Anthropology of Secularism', *Annual Review of Anthropology*, 39: 85–100.

Cantwell Smith, W. (1978), *The Meaning and End of Religion*, London: SPCL.

Casanova, J. (1994), *Public Religions in the Modern World*, Chicago, IL: University of Chicago Press.

Connolly, W. E. (1999), *Why I Am Not a Secularist*, Minneapolis, MN: University of Minnesota Press.

Connolly, W. E. (2002), *Neuropolitics: Thinking, Culture, Speed*, Minneapolis, MN: University of Minnesota Press.

Csordas, T. J. (1990), 'Embodiment as a Paradigm for Anthropology', *Ethos*, 18: 5–47.

Dobbelaere, K. (1999), 'Towards an Integrated Perspective of the Processes Related to the Descriptive Concept of Secularization', *Sociology of Religion*, 60 (3): 229–247.

Dobbelaere, K. (2002), *Secularization: An Analysis at Three Levels*, Brussels: P.I.E. Lang.

Douglas, M. (1980 [1969]), *Purity and Danger: an Analysis of Concepts of Pollution and Taboo*, London: Routledge and Kegan Paul.

Elias, N. (1998), 'Homo Clausus: The Thinking Statues', in N. Elias (ed.), *On Civilization, Power, and Knowledge: Selected Writings*, 269–292, Chicago, IL: University of Chicago Press.

Engelke, M. (2014), 'Christianity and the Anthropology of Secular Humanism', *Current Anthropology*, 55 (S10): S292–S301.

Fadil, N. (2014), 'Asserting State Sovereignty. The Face Veil Ban in Belgium', in E. Brems (ed.), *The Experience of Face Veil Wearers in Europe and the Law*, 251–262, Cambridge, UK: Cambridge University Press.

Fernando, M. (2012), 'Belief and/in the Law', *Method and Theory in the Study of Religion*, 24 (1): 71–80.

Fernando, M. (2014), *The Republic Unsettled: Muslim French and the Contradictions of Secularism*, Durham, NC: Duke University Press.

Gregg, M. and G. Seigworth, eds (2010), *The Affect Theory Reader*, Durham, NC: Duke University Press.

Greil, A. L. and D. Bromley, eds (2003), *Defining Religion: Investigating the Boundaries between the Sacred and the Secular*, Bingley: Emerald Group.

Gutkowski, S. (2012), 'The British Secular Habitus and the War on Terror', *Journal of Contemporary Religion*, 27 (1): 87–103.

Habermas, J. (2008), 'Notes on Post-secular Society', *New Perspectives Quarterly*, 25 (4): 17–29.

Hirschkind, C. (2011), 'Is There a Secular Body?', *Cultural Anthropology*, 26 (4): 633–647.

Hurd, E. S. (2008), *The Politics of Secularism in International Relations*, Princeton, NJ: Princeton University Press.

Jakobsen, J. R. and A. Pellegrini, eds (2008), *Secularisms*, Durham, NC: Duke University Press.

Johansen, B. S. (2011), '"Doing the Secular": Academic Practices in the Study of Religion at Two Danish Universities', *Arts and Humanities in Higher Education*, 10 (3): 279–293.

Keane, W. (2013), 'Secularism as a Moral Narrative of Modernity', *Transit: Europäische Revue*, 43: 159–170.

Lauwers, J. (1974), 'Les théories sociologiques concernant la sécularisation: Typologie et critique', *Social Compass*, 20 (4): 523–533.

Leavitt, J. (1996), 'Meaning and Feeling in the Anthropology of Emotions', *American Ethnologist*, 23: 514–539.

Lewicki, P. (2016), 'European Bodies? Class and Gender Dynamics among EU Civil Servants in Brussels', *Anthropological Journal of European Cultures*, 25 (2): 116–138.

Leys, R. (2011), 'The Turn to Affect: A Critique', *Critical Inquiry*, 37 (1): 434–472.

Luckmann, T. and P. Berger (1991 [1966]), *The Social Construction of Reality: A Treatise in the Sociology of Knowledge*, London: Penguin.

Luehrmann, S. (2011), *Secularism Soviet Style: Teaching Atheism and Religion in a Volga Republic*, Bloomington: Indiana University Press.

Lutz, C. (1988), *Unnatural Emotions: Everyday Sentiments on a Micronesian Atoll and Their Challenge to Western Theory*, Chicago, IL. Chicago University Press.

Lutz, C. and L. Abu-Lughod, eds (1990), *Language and the Politics of Emotion*, Cambridge, UK: Cambridge University Press.

Lyon, M. L. (1997), 'The Material Body, Social Processes and Emotion: "Techniques of the Body" Revisited', *Body & Society*, 3: 83–101.

Mahmood, S. (2006), *Politics of Piety: The Islamic Revival and the Feminist Subject*, Princeton, NJ: Princeton University Press.

Mahmood, S. (2009), 'Religious Reason and Secular Affect: An Incommensurable Divide?', *Critical Inquiry*, 35 (4): 836–862.

Mahmood, S. (2016), *Religious Difference in a Secular Age: A Minority Report*, Princeton, NJ: Princeton University Press.

Martin, D. (1969), 'Towards Eliminating the Concept of Secularisation', in D. Martin (ed.), *The Religious and the Secular: Studies in Secularization*, 9–22, London: Routledge and Kegan Paul.

Martin, D. (1978), *A General Theory of Secularization*, Oxford: Basil Blackwell.

Massumi, B. (1995), 'The Autonomy of Affect', *Cultural Critique*, 31: 83–109.

Massumi, B. (2015), *Politics of Affect*, London: Polity.

McCarthy Brown, K. (1991), *Mama Lola: A Vodou Priestess in Brooklyn*, Berkeley, CA: University of California Press.

McDannell, C. (1995), *Material Christianity: Religion and Popular Culture in America*, New Haven, CT: Yale University Press.

Merleau-Ponty, M. (1962), *Phenomenology of Perception*, New York, NY: Humanities Press.

Meyer, B., ed. (2009), *Aesthetic Formations: Media, Religion and the Public Sphere*, New York: Palgrave.

Moors, A. (2009), 'The Dutch and the Face-Veil: The Politics of Discomfort', *Social Anthropology*, 17 (4): 393–408.

Morgan, D., ed. (2010), *Religion and Material Culture: The Matter of Belief*, London: Routledge.

Navaro-Yashin, Y. (2012), *The Make-Believe Space: Affective Geography in a Postwar Polity*, Durham, NC: Duke University Press.

Orsi, R. (1985), *The Madonna of 115th Street: Faith and Community in Italian Harlem*, New Haven, CT: Yale University Press.

Pelkmans, M. (2017), *Fragile Conviction: Changing Ideological Landscapes in Urban Kyrgyzstan*, Ithaca, NY: Cornall University Press.

Pellegrini, A. (2009), 'Feeling Secular', *Women and Performance*, 19 (2): 205–218.

Plamper, J. (2015), *The History of Emotions: An Introduction*, Oxford: Oxford University Press.

Proudfoot, W. (1985), *Religious Experience*, Berkeley, CA: University of California Press.

Quack, J. (2012), *Disenchanting India: Organized Rationalism and Criticism of Religion in India*, New York, NY: Oxford University Press.

Reckwitz, A. (2012), 'Affective Spaces: A Praxeological Outlook', *Rethinking History*, 16 (2): 241–258.

Reddy, W. (2001), *The Navigation of Feeling: A Framework for the History of Emotions*, Cambridge, UK: Cambridge University Press.

Rosaldo, M. Z. (1984), 'Toward an Anthropology of Self and Feeling', in R. Shweder and R. A. LeVine (eds), *Culture Theory: Essays on Mind, Self, and Emotion*, 137–157, Cambridge, UK: Cambridge University Press.

Rosenwein, B. H. (2002), 'Worrying about Emotions in History', *American Historical Review*, 107 (3): 821–845.

Schaefer, D. (2015), *Religious Affects: Animality, Evolution, and Power*, Durham, NC: Duke University Press.

Scheer, M. (2012), 'Are Emotions a Kind of Practice (And Is That What Makes Them Have a History)? A Bourdieuian Approach to Understanding Emotions', *History and Theory*, 51 (2): 193–220.

Scheer, M. (2014), 'Topographies of Emotion', in U. Frevert et al. (eds), *Emotional Lexicons. Continuity and Change in the Vocabulary of Feeling 1700-2000*, 32–61, New York, NY: Oxford University Press.

Scheper-Hughes, N. and M. M. Lock (1987), 'The Mindful Body: A Prolegomenon to Future Work in Medical Anthropology', *Medical Anthropology Quarterly*, 1: 6–41.

Scott, D. and C. Hirschkind (2006), *Powers of the Secular Modern: Talal Asad and His Interlocutors*, Princeton, NJ: Princeton University Press.

Scott, J. W. (2009), 'Sexularism', *RSCAS Distinguished Lectures, Ursula Hirschmann Annual Lecture on Gender and Europe*, Florence: European University Institute. Available online: cadmus.eui.eu/bitstream/handle/1814/11553/RSCAS_DL_2009_01.pdf (accessed 15 October 2017).

Stark, R. (1999), 'Secularization R.I.P.', *Sociology of Religion*, 60 (3): 249–274.

Streicher, R. (2016), 'Imperialism, Buddhism, and the Secular in 19th-Century Siam: Notes on Provincializing Secularism', *TRAFO, Blog for Transregional Research*. Available online: trafo.hypotheses.org/3941 (accessed 15 October 2017).

Sullivan, W. F. (2009), *Prison Religion: Faith-Based Reform and the Constitution*, Princeton, NJ: Princeton University Press.

Sullivan, W. F., R. Yelle and M. Taussig-Rubbo, eds (2011), *After Secular Law*, Stanford, CA: Stanford University Press.

Taylor, C. (1992), *The Ethics of Authenticity*, Cambridge, MA: Harvard University Press.

Taylor, C. (2007), *A Secular Age*, Cambridge, MA: Harvard University Press.

Tønder, L. (2013), *Tolerance: A Sensorial Orientation to Politics*, Oxford: Oxford University Press.

Tschannen, O. (1992), *Les théories de la sécularisation*, Genève: Librairie Droz.

Turner, B. (1984), *The Body and Society*, Oxford: Basil Blackwell.

Verkaaik, O. and R. Spronk (2011), 'Sexual Practice: Notes on an Ethnography of Secularism', *Focaal*, 59: 83–88.

Wetherell, M. (2012), *Affect and Emotion: A New Social Science Understanding*, London: Sage.

Wilson, M. (2002), 'Six Views of Embodied Cognition', *Psychonomic Bulletin and Review*, 9: 625–636.

Wohlrab-Sahr, M. and M. Burchardt (2012), 'Multiple Secularities: Toward a Cultural Sociology of Secular Modernities,' *Comparative Sociology*, 11: 875–909.

Chapter 2

Allitt, P. (1995), *Catholic Intellectuals and Conservative Politics in America, 1950–1985*, Ithaca, NY: Cornell University Press.

Anderson, K. (2011), *Life Stages and Native Women: Memory, Teachings, and Story Medicine*, Winnipeg, MB: University of Manitoba Press.

Anderson, M. A., R. L. Fastiggi, D. E. Hargroder, J. C. Howard and C. W. Kischer (2011), 'Ectopic Pregnancy and Catholic Morality', *The National Catholic Bioethics Quarterly*, 11 (1): 65–82.

Appleby, B. M. (1999), *Responsible Parenthood: Decriminalizing Contraception in Canada*, Toronto, ON: University of Toronto Press.

Bagge, P. (2013), *Woman Rebel: The Margaret Sanger Story*, Montreal, QC: Drawn & Quarterly.

Beisel, N. K. (1998), *Imperiled Innocents: Anthony Comstock and Family Reproduction in Victorian America*, Princeton, NJ: Princeton University Press.

Benbow, C. (2016a), 'Lemonade Syllabus', *Lemonade Syllabus*, May 6. Available online: http://www.candicebenbow.com/lemonadesyllabus (accessed 10 September 2016).

Benbow, C. (2016b), 'Beyoncé's "Lemonade" and Black Christian Women's Spirituality', *Religions and Politics*, June 28. Available online: http://religionandpolitics. org/2016/06/28/beyonces-lemonade-and-black-christian-womens-spirituality (accessed 10 September 2016).

Bender, C. (2010), *The New Metaphysicals: Spirituality and the American Religious Imagination*, Chicago, IL: University of Chicago Press.

Beyoncé (n.d.), *Lemonade*. Available online: http://www.beyonce.com/album/lemonade-visual-album (accessed 10 September 2016).

Bradley, R. and D. Hampton (2016), 'Close to Home: A Conversation about Beyoncé's "Lemonade"', *NPR.Org*, April 26. Available online: http://www.npr.org/sections/ therecord/2016/04/26/475629479/close-to-home-a-conversation-about-beyonc-s-lemonade (accessed 10 September 2016).

Brown, C. G. (2012), *Religion and the Demographic Revolution: Women and Secularisation in Canada, Ireland, UK and USA since the 1960s*, Woodbridge, UK: Boydell Press.

Cady, L. E. and T. Fessenden (2013), *Religion, the Secular, and the Politics of Sexual Difference*, New York, NY: Columbia University Press.

Cahill, J. F. (1966), 'Contraception and Eve', *New Blackfriars*, 47 (553): 466–483.

Campbell, F. (1960), 'Birth Control and the Christian Churches', *Population Studies*, 14 (2): 131–147.

Christie, N. (2002), 'Sacred Sex: The United Church and the Privatization of the Family in Post-War Canada', in N. Christie (ed.), *Households of Faith: Family, Gender and Community in Canada, 1760–1969*, 348–376, Montreal, QC and Kingston, ON: McGill-Queen's University Press.

Critchlow, D. T. (1999), *Intended Consequences: Birth Control, Abortion, and the Federal Government in Modern America*, New York, NY: Oxford University Press.

Davis, T. (2005), *Sacred Work: Planned Parenthood and Its Clergy Alliances*, New Brunswick, NJ: Rutgers University Press.

Day, M. (2012), 'Church Attacks Nun's Book on Sexual Ethics', *The Independent*, 5 June. Available online: http://www.independent.co.uk/news/world/europe/church-attacks-nuns-book-on-sexual-ethics-7815172.html (accessed 1 March 2013).

Delaney, C. (1991), *The Seed and the Soil: Gender and Cosmology in Turkish Village Society*, Berkeley, CA: University of California Press.

Delgado, T. (2014), 'Beyond Procreativity: Heterosexuals Queering Marriage', in M. Larrimore, K. T. Talvacchia and M. F. Pettinger (eds), *Queer Christianities: Lived Religion in Transgressive Forms*, 91–102, New York, NY: New York University Press.

D'Emilio, J. and E. B. Freedman (1988), *Intimate Matters: A History of Sexuality in America*, Chicago, IL: University of Chicago Press.

DeRogatis, A. (2014), *Saving Sex: Sexuality and Salvation in American Evangelicalism*, New York, NY: Oxford University Press.

Dion Fletcher, V. (2016), '#MenstrualAccessory', *Vanessa Dion Fletcher*. Available online: http://www.dionfletcher.com/ (accessed 10 September 2016).

Dion Fletcher, V. (2018), 'Vanessa Dion Fletcher', *Vanessa Dion Fletcher*. Available online: http://www.dionfletcher.com (accessed 1 June 2018).

Dobbelaere, K. (2002), *Secularization: An Analysis at Three Levels*, Brussels: Peter Lang.

Duncan, C. B. (2005), 'Hard Labour: Religion, Sexuality and the Pregnant Body in the African Diaspora', *Journal of the Motherhood Initiative for Research and Community Involvement*, 7 (1): 167–173.

Eveleth, R. (2013), 'Lysol's Vintage Ads Subtly Pushed Women to Use Its Disinfectant as Birth Control', *Smithsonian*, September 30. Available online: http://www.smithsonianmag.com/smart-news/lysols-vintage-ads-subtly-pushed-women-to-use-its-disinfectant-as-birth-control-218734/ (accessed 10 September 2016).

Farley, M. A. (2006), *Just Love: A Framework for Christian Sexual Ethics*, London: Continuum International Publishing Group.

Fessenden, T. (2007), *Culture and Redemption: Religion, the Secular, and American Literature*, Princeton, NJ: Princeton University Press.

Flood, C. M. (2006), *Just Medicare: What's In, What's Out, How We Decide*, Toronto, ON: University of Toronto Press.

Fogel, S. B. and L. A. Rivera (2004), 'Saving Roe Is Not Enough: When Religion Controls Healthcare', *The Fordham Urban Law Journal*, 31 (3): 725–749.

Foster, A. M., A. Dennis and F. Smith (2011), 'Do Religious Restrictions Influence Ectopic Pregnancy Management? A National Qualitative Study', *Women's Health Issues: Official Publication of the Jacobs Institute of Women's Health*, 21 (2): 104–109.

Fraser, G. J. (1998), *African American Midwifery in the South: Dialogues of Birth, Race, and Memory*, Cambridge, MA: Harvard University Press.

Frazer, J. G. (2012 [1890]), *The Golden Bough: A Study in Comparative Religion*, Cambridge, UK: Cambridge University Press.

Gaskin, I. M. (1990), *Spiritual Midwifery*, 3rd rev. edn, Summertown, TN: Book Publishing Company.

Gedicks, F. M. (2015), 'One Cheer for Hobby Lobby: Improbable Alternatives, Truly Strict Scrutiny, and Third-Party Employee Burdens', *Harvard Journal of Law and Gender*, 38 (1): 153–176.

Geuns, Suzanne van (2016), 'Grieving June Cleaver: Fifties Nostalgia in Biblical Womanhood Blogging', M.A. thesis, Utrecht: Utrecht University.

Ginsburg, F. D. and R. Rapp (1995), *Conceiving the New World Order: The Global Politics of Reproduction*, Berkeley, CA: University of California Press.

Gordon, L. (2002), *The Moral Property of Women: A History of Birth Control Politics in America*, Urbana and Chicago, IL: University of Illinois Press.

Gostin, L. O. (2014), 'The Aca's Contraceptive Mandate: Religious Freedom, Women's Health, and Corporate Personhood', *JAMA*, 312 (8): 785–786.

Griffin, L. C. (2003), 'What Might Have Been: Contraception and Religious Liberty', *University of St. Thomas Law Journal*, 1 (1): 632–646.

Griffin, L. C. (2015), 'The Catholic Bishops vs. the Contraceptive Mandate', *Religions*, 6 (4): 1411–1432.

Griffith, R. M. (2012), 'American Religion's Fascination with Sex', in S. J. Stein (ed.), *The Cambridge History of Religions in America*, 471–487, Cambridge, UK: Cambridge University Press.

Griffith, R. M. (2017), *Moral Combat: How Sex Divided American Christians and Fractured American Politics*, New York, NY: Basic Books.

Gustafson, D. L. and J. A. Selby (2016), 'Theorizing De-Christianization in Women's Reproductive Lives in Newfoundland and Labrador, Canada', *Women's Studies International Forum*, 59 (Supplement C): 17–25.

Haberski, R. (2012), 'Machinations of Religious Liberty', *U.S. Intellectual History Blog*, 10 February. Available online: http://s-usih.org/2012/02/machinations-of-religious-liberty.html (accessed 10 September 2016).

Hale, A. O. (2007), 'Practices and Attitudes toward Contraception in the Black Community', in H. Pipes McAdoo (ed.), *Black Families*, 297–316, Thousand Oaks, CA: SAGE.

Hannah, W. (1965), 'Protestants Query a Priest on Essential Birth Control', *United Church Observer*, March 1.

Harrison, J. E. (1922), *Prolegomena to the Study of Greek Religion*, Princeton, NJ: Princeton University Press.

Hobson, J. (2016), 'Lemonade: Beyoncé's Redemption Song', *Ms. Magazine*, 29 April. Available online: http://msmagazine.com/blog/2016/04/29/lemonade-beyonces-redemption-song (accessed 10 September 2016).

Holscher, K. (2016), *Religious Lessons: Catholic Sisters and the Captured Schools Crisis in New Mexico*, New York, NY: Oxford University Press.

Hoyt, R. G. (1967), 'Birth Control! The Catholic Church's Most Explosive Issue Reviewed by One of Its Most Outspoken Laymen', *United Church Observer*, November 1.

Jakobsen, J. R. and A. Pellegrini (2008), *Secularisms*, Durham, NC: Duke University Press.

Jay, N. (1992), *Throughout Your Generations Forever: Sacrifice, Religion, and Paternity*, Chicago, IL: University of Chicago Press.

Johnson, K. and J. Rock (1964), 'Longer Interview with Dr. John Rock on the Pill and the Church', *This Hour Has Seven Days*, Toronto, ON: CBC. Available online: http://www.cbc.ca/archives/entry/longer-interview-with-dr-john-rock-on-the-pill-and-the-church (accessed 1 June 2018).

Kalbian, A. H. (2014), *Sex, Violence, and Justice: Contraception and the Catholic Church*, Washington, DC: Georgetown University Press.

Klassen, P. E. (2001), *Blessed Events: Religion and Home Birth in America*, Princeton, NJ: Princeton University Press.

Klassen, P. E. (2011), *Spirits of Protestantism: Medicine, Healing, and Liberal Christianity*, Berkeley, CA: University of California Press.

Klassen, P. E. (2015), 'Fertile Blood: A Review of Gil Anidjar's Blood: A Critique of Christianity', *The Marginalia Review of Books*, March 2. Available online: http://marginalia.lareviewofbooks.org/fertile-blood-pamela-klassen (accessed 1 June 2018).

Lira, N. and A. M. Stern (2014), 'Mexican Americans and Eugenic Sterilization: Resisting Reproductive Injustice in California, 1920–1950', *Aztlan: A Journal of Chicano Studies*, 39 (2): 9–34.

Lofton, K. (2017), *Consuming Religion*, Chicago, IL: University of Chicago Press.

Maguire, D. C. (2001), *Sacred Choices: The Right to Contraception and Abortion in Ten World Religions*, Minneapolis, MN: Fortress Press.

Manian, M. (2014), 'The Consequences of Abortion Restrictions for Women's Healthcare Roe at 40: The Controversy Continues: Session 5', *Washington and Lee Law Review*, 71 (2): 1317–1338.

Marcotte, J. (2016), 'The Agnotology of Abortion: A History of Ignorance about Women's Knowledge of Fertility Control', *Outskirts*, 34 (May): 1.

Marks, L. (2010), *Sexual Chemistry: A History of the Contraceptive Pill*, New Haven, CT: Yale University Press.

McGreevy, J. T. (2004), *Catholicism and American Freedom: A History*, New York, NY: W. W. Norton.

McLaren, A. and A. T. McLaren (1997), *The Bedroom and the State: The Changing Practices and Politics of Contraception and Abortion in Canada, 1880–1997*, Oxford: Oxford University Press.

Meehan, P. (2011), 'The Lesser of Two Evils? Archbishop Philip Pocock, Vatican II, and the Birth Control Controversy', in M. S. Attridge, G. Routhier and C. E. Clifford (eds),

Vatican II: Experiences Canadiennes – Canadian Experiences, 209–225, Ottawa, ON: University of Ottawa Press.

Noonan Jr., J. T. (1986), *Contraception: A History of Its Treatment by the Catholic Theologians and Canonists*, enlarged edn, Cambridge, MA: Harvard University Press.

Our Bodies Ourselves (n.d.), 'History', *Our Bodies Ourselves: Information Inspires Action.* Available online: http://www.ourbodiesourselves.org/history (accessed 3 July 2015).

Paul VI (1968), 'Humanae Vitae: Encyclical Letter of His Holiness Paul VI on the Regulation of Birth', July 25. Available online: http://www.vatican.va/holy_father/paul_vi/encyclicals/documents/hf_p-vi_enc_25071968_humanae-vitae_en.html (accessed 1 June 2018).

Pellegrini, A. (2015), 'Everson's Children', in W. F. Sullivan, E. Shakman Hurd, S. Mahmood and P. G. Danchin (eds), *Politics of Religious Freedom*, 253–261, Chicago, IL: University of Chicago Press.

Petchesky, R. P. (1990), *Abortion and Woman's Choice: The State, Sexuality, and Reproductive Freedom*, Boston, MA: Northeastern University Press.

Raiss, L. (2017), '3 Art History Experts Explain Beyoncé's Epic Grammys Performance', 15 February *MTV News.* Available online: http://www.mtv.com/news/2983457/art-history-experts-explain-beyonce (accessed 22 September 2017).

Rapp, R. (1999), *Testing Women, Testing the Fetus: The Social Impact of Amniocentesis in America*, New York, NY: Routledge.

Robinson, K. (2001), 'Government Agency, Women's Agency: Feminisms, Fertility, and Population Control', in M. Jolly and K. Ram (eds), *Borders of Being: Citizenship, Fertility, and Sexuality in Asia and the Pacific*, 36–57, Ann Arbor, MI: University of Michigan Press.

Rodgers, S. (2002), 'The Legal Regulation of Women's Reproductive Capacity in Canada', in *Canadian Health Law and Policy*, 2nd edn, 331–365, Markham, ON: Butterworths.

Schneider, P. and J. Schneider (1995), 'Coitus Interruptus and Family Respectability in Catholic Europe: A Sicilian Case Study' in F. D. Ginsburg and R. Rapp (eds), *Conceiving the New World Order: The Global Politics of Reproduction*, 177–194, Berkeley, CA: University of California Press.

Scott, J. W. (2017), *Sex and Secularism*, Princeton, NJ: Princeton University Press.

Sepinwall, A. J. (2015), 'Corporate Piety and Impropriety: Hobby Lobby's Extension of RFRA Rights to the For-Profit Corporation', *Harvard Business Law Review*, 5 (2): 173-204.

Sered, S. S. (1996), *Priestess, Mother, Sacred Sister: Religions Dominated by Women*, New York, NY: Oxford University Press.

Shachar, A. (2001), *Multicultural Jurisdictions: Cultural Differences and Women's Rights*, Cambridge, UK: Cambridge University Press.

Sheridan, E. F. (ed) (1991), *Love Kindness!: The Social Teaching of the Canadian Catholic Bishops (1958–1989)*, Toronto, ON: Jesuit Centre for Social Faith and Justice.

Stern, A. M. (2015), *Eugenic Nation: Faults and Frontiers of Better Breeding in Modern America*, Berkeley, CA: University of California Press.

Sullivan, W. F. (2007), *The Impossibility of Religious Freedom*, Princeton, NJ: Princeton University Press.

Sullivan, W. F. (2015), 'The World That Smith Made', in W. F. Sullivan, E. Shakman Hurd, S. Mahmood and P. G. Danchin (eds), *Politics of Religious Freedom*, 231–239, Chicago, IL: University of Chicago Press.

Taylor, C. (2007), *A Secular Age*, Cambridge, MA: Harvard University Press.

Tentler, L. W. (2004), *Catholics and Contraception: An American History*, Ithaca, NY: Cornell University Press.

Toates, F. (2014), *How Sexual Desire Works*, Cambridge, UK: Cambridge University Press.
Tone, A. (2006), 'From Naughty Goods to Nicole Miller. Medicine and the Marketing of American Contraceptives', *Culture, Medicine and Psychiatry*, 30 (2): 249–267.
Tone, A. (2012), 'Medicalizing Reproduction: The Pill and Home Pregnancy Tests', *The Journal of Sex Research*, 49 (4): 319–327.
United States Conference of Catholic Bishops (2009), *Ethical and Religious Directives for Catholic Health Care Services*, 5th edn, Washington, DC. Available online: http://www.usccb.org/about/doctrine/ethical-and-religious-directives (accessed 1 June 2018).
Weiner, I. (2017), 'The Corporately Produced Conscience: Emergency Contraception and the Politics of Workplace Accommodations', *Journal of the American Academy of Religion*, 85 (1): 31–63.
Wenger, T. (2017), *Religious Freedom: The Contested History of an American Ideal*, Chapel Hill, NC: University of North Carolina Press.
Westoff, C. F. and N. B. Ryder (1977), *The Contraceptive Revolution*, Princeton, NJ: Princeton University Press.

Chapter 3

'Aufbewahrung der Toten in Sizilien' (1894), *Die Flamme*, January: 1484.
'Beerdigung und Feuerbestattung' (1894), *Die Flamme*, September: 1617.
'Bericht aus Wien über die XXII. ordentliche Generalversammlung des Vereins der Freunde für Feuerbestattung "Die Flamme" Wien' (1907), *Phoenix*, 6: 245.
'Die Regelung der religiösen Trauerfeier in den württemberg. Krematorien' (1905), *Die Flamme*, May: 4556.
'Eine Stätte der Todten' (1895), *Die Flamme*, May: 1746.
The Referee, 9 March 1884, in B. Parsons (2005), *Committed to the Cleansing Flame. The Development of Cremation in Nineteenth-Century England*, Reading: Spire Books: 114.
'Ueber die Beerdigungsverhältnisse in Italien' (1895), *Die Flamme*, October: 1844.
'Urnenhaine' (1899), *Die Flamme*, December: 2875.
'Zum internationalen Kongreß für Hygiene und Demographie in Verbindung mit dem Verbandstage der Vereine für Feuerbestattung' (1894), *Die Flamme*, September: 1613.
Ameskamp, S. (2008), 'Fanning the Flames. Cremation in Late Imperial and Weimar Germany', in A. Confino, P. Betts and D. Schumann (eds), *Between Mass Death and Individual Loss. The Place of Death in Twentieth-Century Germany*, 93–112, New York, NY: Berghahn Books.
Angenendt, A. (1994), *Heilige und Reliquien. Die Geschichte ihres Kultes vom frühen Christentum bis zur Gegenwart*, Munich: Beck Verlag.
Ariès, P. (2005), *Geschichte des Todes*, 11th edn, Munich: Deutscher Taschenbuch Verlag.
Asad, T. (2003), *Formations of the Secular. Christianity, Islam, Modernity*, Stanford, CA: Stanford University Press.
Baginsky, A. (1874), *Die Leichenverbrennung vom Standpunkte der Hygiene*, Berlin: Denicke.
Beales, D. and E. Biagini (2002), *The Risorgimento and the Unification of Italy*, London: Routledge.
Bernstein, S. (1874), *Ueber Pietät gegen die Todten*, Berlin: Denicke.
Borutta, M. (2010), *Antikatholizismus. Deutschland und Italien im Zeitalter der europäischen Kulturkämpfe*, Bürgertum Neue Folge vol. 7, Göttingen: Vandenhoeck und Ruprecht.

Büchner, L. (1864), *Force and Matter. Empirico-Philosophical Studies, Intelligibly Rendered*, London: Trübner and Co.

Burchardt, M. and M. Wohlrab-Sahr (2013), 'Multiple Secularities. Religion and Modernity in the Global Age – Introduction', *International Sociology*, 28 (6): 605–611.

Bynum, W. F. (1994), *Science and the Practice of Medicine in the Nineteenth Century*, Cambridge, UK: Cambridge University Press.

Carli, A. and A. Stroppa, eds (2010), *Paolo Gorini. Autobiografia*, Villasanta: Limina Mentis.

Carter, N. (2010), *Modern Italy in Historical Perspective*, London and New York, NY: Bloomsbury.

Clark, C. and W. Kaiser, eds (2003), *Culture Wars. Secular-Catholic Conflict in Nineteenth-Century Europe*, Cambridge, UK: Cambridge University Press.

Coletti, F. (1866), 'Sulla incinerazione dei cadaveri', *Gazzetta medica italiana*, 9 (229–232): 237–240.

Conti F., A. M. Isastia and F. Tarozzi, eds (1998), *La morte laica. Storia della cremazione in Italia (1880–1920)*, Turin: Paravia Scriptorium.

Cosmacini, G. (2005), *Il medico materialista. Vita e pensiero di Jakob Moleschott*, Roma: Laterza.

Cozzi, B. (2010), 'L'opera museale di Paolo Gorini nel contesto del suo tempo e in una prospettiva storica', in A. Carli (ed.), *Paolo Gorini (1813–1881): Storia di uno scienziato*, 17–36, Bergamo: Bolis.

Cranston, M. (1994), *The Romantic Movement*, Oxford: Blackwell.

Cucaro, F. (1883), *I tempi, i popoli, la cremazione. Considerazioni critiche*, Bologna, Milan and Naples: Vallardi.

Dalmas, D. (2012), '"Libero paese," "slavery of superstition." Viaggio letterario nei miti dell'Inghilterra e dell'Italia', *Bollettino della società di studi valdesi*, 33: 67–78.

Davis, J. D. and L. H. Mates, eds (2005), *Encyclopedia of Cremation*, Aldershot and Burlington: Ashgate Publishing.

Douglas, M. (1966), *Purity and Danger. An Analysis of Concepts of Pollution and Taboo*, London and New York, NY: Routledge.

Elias, N. (1994), *The Civilizing Process*, Oxford: Blackwell.

Emsley, J. (2000), *The Shocking History of Phosphorus. A Biography of the Devil's Element*, London: Macmillan.

Engelke, M. (2015), 'The Coffin Question. Death and Materiality in Humanist Funerals', *Material Religion*, 11 (1): 26–48.

Fischer, N. (1996), *Vom Gottesacker zum Krematorium. Eine Sozialgeschichte der Friedhöfe in Deutschland seit dem 18. Jahrhundert*, Kulturstudien vol. 17, Cologne: Böhlau.

Foucault, M. (2010), *The Birth of the Clinic. An Archaeology of Medical Perception*, London: Routledge.

Ginsborg, P. (2011), 'European Romanticism and the Italian Risorgimento', in S. Patriarca and L. Riall (eds), *The Risorgimento Revisited. Nationalism and Culture in Nineteenth-Century Italy*, 18–36, Basingstoke: Palgrave Macmillan.

Goppelsroeder, F. (1890), *Ueber Feuerbestattung. Vortrag gehalten am Abende des 13. Februars 1890, in Verbindung mit Experimenten und unter Vorweisung von kolorierten Bildern im Naturwissenschaftlichen Vereine zu Mühlhausen im Elsasse*, Mühlhausen: Wenz und Peters.

Gorini, P. (1871), *Sull'origine dei vulcani. Studio sperimentale*, Lodi: E. Wilmant.

Gorini, P. (1873), *La conservazione della salma di Giuseppe Mazzini. Notizie fornite*, Genoa: Tipografia del R. Istituto Sordo-muti.

Gorini, P. (1876), *Sulla purificazione dei morti per mezzo del fuoco. Considerazioni, sperimenti e proposte*, Milan: Battezzati.

Gorini, P. (1879), *First Crematory in England and the Collective Crematories*, London: Henry Renshaw

Gregorio, M. A. Di (2004), *From Here to Eternity. Ernst Haeckel and Scientific Faith*, Göttingen: Vandenhoeck und Ruprecht.

Gregory, F. (2012), 'Proto-Monism in German Philosophy, Theology, and Science (1800–1845)', in T. Weir (ed.), *Monism. Science, Philosophy, Religion, and the History of a Worldview*, 45–69, New York, NY: Palgrave Macmillan.

Grimm, J. (1850), *Ueber das Verbrennen der Leichen. Eine in der Academie der Wissenschaften am 29. November 1849 von Jacob Grimm gehaltene Vorlesung*, Berlin: Akademie der Wissenschaften.

Hardy, A. L. (2005), *Ärzte, Ingenieure und städtische Gesundheit. Medizinische Theorien in der Hygienebewegung des 19. Jahrhunderts*, Frankfurt am Main: Campus Verlag.

Heike-Gmelin, A. (2013), *Kremation und Kirche. Die evangelische Resonanz auf die Einführung der Feuerbestattung im 19. Jahrhundert*, Berlin: LIT Verlag.

Hirschkind, C. (2011), 'Is There a Secular Body?', *Cultural Anthropology*, 26 (4): 633–647.

Isabella, M. (2009), *Risorgimento in Exile. Italian Emigrés and the Liberal International in the post-Napoleonic Era*, Oxford: Oxford University Press.

Isastia, A. M. (1998), 'La laicizzazione della morte a Roma. Cremazionisti e massoni tra Ottocento e Novecento', *Dimensioni e problemi della ricerca storia*, 2: 55–96.

Kristeva, J. (1982), *Powers of Horror. An Essay on Abjection*, New York, NY: Columbia University Press.

Küchenmeister, F. (1874), *Über Leichenverbrennung: Vortrag gehalten am 8. April 1874 zum Besten des Neustädter Gymnasial-Stipendienfonds*, Erlangen: Enke.

Küchenmeister, F. (1875), *Die Feuerbestattung. Unter allen zur Zeit ausführbaren Bestattungsarten die beste Sanitätspolizei des Bodens und der sicherste Cordon gegen Epidemien*, Stuttgart: Enke.

Laqueur, T. (2015), *The Work of the Dead. A Cultural History of Mortal Remains*, Princeton, NJ: Princeton University Press.

Lueger, O., ed. (1908), *Lexikon der gesamten Technik und ihrer Hilfswissenschaften*, 2nd edn, vol. 6, Stuttgart and Leipzig: Deutsche Verlagsanstalt.

Luzzatto, S. (2001), *La mummia della republica. Storia di Mazzini imbalsamato (1872–1946)*, Milan: Rizzoli.

Macho, T. (1990), *Todesmetaphern. Zur Logik der Grenzerfahrung*, 2nd edn, Frankfurt am Main: Suhrkamp.

Malone, H. (2014), 'Secularisation, Anticlericalism and Cremation within Italian Cemeteries of the Nineteenth Century', *Modern Italy*, 19 (4): 385–403.

Mantegazza, P. (1989), *Lezioni di antropologia (1870–1910)*, Firenze: Società Italiana di Antropologia e Etnologia.

Mantegazza, P. (2010), *The Year 3000. A Dream*, trans. N. Pireddu and D. Jacobson, Lincoln: University of Nebraska Press.

Margarita, E. N. (1876), 'Cremazione e sentimento', in M. De Cristoforis and G. Pini (eds), *Bollettino della società per la cremazione dei cadaveri di Milano*, 34–38, Milan: Fratelli Rechiedei.

Metzger, F. (2011), *Geschichtsschreibung und Geschichtsdenken im 19. und 20. Jahrhundert*, Bern: UTB.

Moe, N. (2001), 'This Is Africa. Ruling and Representing Southern Italy, 1860–61', in A. R. Ascoli and K. v. Henneberg (eds), *Making and Remaking Italy. The Cultivation of National Identity around the Risorgimento*, 119–145, Oxford: Bloomsbury.

Moe, N. (2006), *The View from Vesuvius. Italian Culture and the Southern Question*, Studies on the History of Society and Culture vol. 46, Berkeley, CA, Los Angeles and London: University of California Press.

Moleschott, J. (1855), *Der Kreislauf des Lebens. Antworten auf Liebig's Chemische Briefe*, Mainz: Verlag Victor von Zabern.

Monsagrati, G. (2004), 'Al servizio della libera scienza', in C. Canonici and G. Monsagrati (eds), *Carlo Maggiorani. Politica e medicina nel Risorgimento*, 125–149, Rome: Gangemi.

Monti, A. (2004), *Il 1848 e le cinque giornate di Milano. Dalle memorie inedite dei combattenti sulle barricate*, Genoa: Fratelli Frilli.

Municipal Archive of Gotha (1884), *Statuto della società per la cremazione dei cadaveri di Milano*, 2/3631, 51 (105a), Gotha.

Novarino, M. (2005), 'Freemasonry', in J. D. Davies and L. H. Mates (eds), *Encyclopedia of Cremation*, 207–210, Aldershot and Burlington: Ashgate Publishing.

Nussbaum, M. (2004), *Hiding from Humanity. Disgust, Shame, and the Law*, Princeton, NJ: Princeton University Press.

Pini, G. (1885), *La crémation en Italie e à l'étranger de 1774 jusqu'à nos jours*, Milan: Hoepli.

Pogliano, C. (1984), 'L'utopia igienista (1870–1920)', in F. Della Peruta (ed.), *Storia d'Italia vol. 7: Malattia e Medicina*, 589–631, Turin: Einaudi.

Reclam, K. (1874), 'An die Gegner der Feuerbestattung', *Die Gartenlaube*, 38: 608–610.

Sheehan, J. J. (2011), *German Liberalism in the Nineteenth Century*, New York, NY: American Council of Learned Societies.

Società per la cremazione dei cadaveri di Milano, ed. (1880), *La cremazione della salma del professore Giovanni Polli*, Milan.

Soper, S. C. (2013), *Building a Civil Society. Associations, Public Life, and the Origins of Modern Italy*, Toronto, Buffalo and London: University of Toronto Press.

Thompson, H. S. (1884), *Cremation. The Treatment of the Body after Death*, 3rd edn, London: Smith, Elder, and Co.

Trusen, J. P. (1855), *Die Leichenverbrennung als die geeignetste Art der Todtenbestattung. Darstellung der verschiedenen Arten und Gebräuche der Todtenbestattung aus älterer und neuerer Zeit*, Breslau: W. G. Korn.

Weir, T., ed. (2012), *Monism. Science, Philosophy, Religion, and the History of a Worldview*, Basingstoke: Palgrave Macmillan.

Weir, T. (2014), *Secularism and Religion in Nineteenth-Century Germany. The Rise of the Fourth Confession*, New York, NY: Cambridge University Press.

Wernher, A. (2013), *Die Totenbestattung in Bezug auf Hygiene, geschichtliche Entwicklung und gesetzliche Bestimmungen*, Hamburg: Severus.

Westphal, J. (2016), *The Mind-Body Problem*, Cambridge, MA: MIT Press.

Chapter 4

Asad, T. (2003), *Formations of the Secular: Christianity, Islam, Modernity*, Stanford, CA: Stanford University Press.

Baker, J. O. and B. G. Smith (2015), *American Secularism: Cultural Contours of Nonreligious Belief Systems*, New York, NY: New York University Press.

Beckford, J. A. (2012), 'SSSR Presidential Address Public Religions and the Post-secular: Critical Reflections', *Journal for the Scientific Study of Religion*, 51 (1): 1–19.

Bender, C. (2016a), 'How and Why to Study Up: Frank Lloyd Wright's Broadacre City and the Study of Lived Religion', *Nordic Journal of Religion and Society*, 29. 100–116.

Bender, C. (2016b), 'Rethinking the "Technological Sublime": Wright's Urban Planning and Secular Uses of Religion', Scientific Study of Nonreligious Belief Lecture Series, UCL (University College London), 26 July 2016.

Booth, R. (2012), 'Alain de Botton Reveals Plans for "Temple to Atheism" in Heart of London', *The Guardian*, 26 January 2012. Available online: https://www.theguardian.com/books/2012/jan/26/alain-de-botton-temple-atheism (accessed 6 August 2018).

Bullivant, S. (2010), 'The New Atheism and Sociology: Why Here? Why Now? What Next?' in A. Amarasingam (ed.), *Religion and the New Atheism: A Critical Appraisal*, 109–124, Leiden: Brill.

Bullivant, S. and L. Lee (2012), 'Introduction: Interdisciplinary Studies of Non-religion and Secularity: The State of the Union', *Journal of Contemporary Religion*, 27 (1): 19–27.

Burchardt, M., M. Wohlrab-Sahr and M. Middell (2015), 'Multiple Secularities beyond the West: An Introduction', in Marian Burchardt, Monika Wohlrab-Sahr and Matthias Middell (eds), *Multiple Secularities beyond the West*, Berlin and Boston, MA: De Gruyter.

Campbell, C. (2013 [1971]), *Towards a Sociology of Irreligion*, No place: Alcuin Academics.

Connolly, W. E. (2011), 'Some Thesis on Secularism', *Cultural Anthropology*, 26 (4): 648–656. doi: 10.1111/j.1548-1360.2011.01117.x.

Cragun, R. T., L. L. Fazzino and C. Manning, eds (2017), *Organized Secularism in the United States: New Directions in Research*, Berlin and Boston, MA: De Gruyter.

Davie, G. (2013), 'Belief and Unbelief: Two Sides of a Coin', *Ecclesiastical Law Journal*, 15: 259–266.

Day, A. (2017), *The Religious Lives of Older Laywomen: The Last Active Anglican Generation*, Oxford: Oxford University Press.

de Botton, A. (2013), *Religion for Atheists: A Non-Believer's Guide to the Uses of Religion*, London: Penguin.

Gray, J. (2012), 'Alain de Botton's Atheist Temple Is a Nice Idea, but a Defunct One', The *Guardian*, 2 February 2012. Available online: https://www.theguardian.com/commentisfree/2012/feb/02/alain-de-botton-atheist-temple-defunct (accessed 4 September 2017).

Gutkowski, S. (2012), 'The British Secular Habitus and the War on Terror', *Journal of Contemporary Religion*, 27 (1): 87–103.

Hall, A. (2017), 'Evolution on the Small-Screen: Reflections on Media, Science and Religion in Twentieth-Century Britain', Conference presentation at Science and Religion: Exploring the Spectrum, June 2017.

Hervieu-Leger, D. (2000), *Religion as a Chain of Memory*, New Brunswick, NJ: Rutgers University Press.

Hirschkind, C. (2011), 'Is There a Secular Body?' *Cultural Anthropology*, 26 (4): 633–647. doi: 10.1111/j.1548-1360.2011.01116.x.

Keane, W. (2007), *Christian Moderns: Freedom and Fetish in the Mission Encounter*, Berkeley, CA: University of California Press.

Keane, W. (2013), 'Secularism as a Moral Narrative of Modernity', *Transit: Europäische Revue*, 43: 159–170.

Knott, K. (2005), *The Location of Religion: A Spatial Analysis*, London: Equinox.

Kuppinger, P. (2017), 'At Home in the Multicultural City: Islam and Religious Place-making in Stuttgart, Germany', in D. Garbin and A. Strhan (eds), *Religion and the Global City*, London: Bloomsbury.

Lee, L. (2012), 'Talking about a Revolution: Terminology for the New Field of Nonreligion Studies', *Journal of Contemporary Religion*, 27 (1): 129–139.

Lee, L. (2014), 'Secular or Nonreligious? Investigating and Interpreting Generic "Not Religious" Categories and Populations', *Religion* 44 (3): 466–482, doi.org/10.1080/0048 721X.2014.904035.

Lee, L. (2015), *Recognizing the Non-religious: Reimaging the Secular*, Oxford: Oxford University Press.

Lee, L. (2016), 'Nonreligion', in M. Strausberg and S. Engler (eds), *The Oxford Handbook of the Study of Religion*, 84–94, Oxford: Oxford University Press.

Lee, L. (2017), 'Godlessness in the Global City', in D. Garbin and A. Strhan (eds), *Religion and the Global City*, 135–152, London: Bloomsbury.

Luehrmann, S. (2011), *Secularism Soviet Style: Teaching Atheism and Religion in a Volga Republic*, Bloomington: Indiana University Press.

Luehrmann, S. (2015), 'Was Soviet Society Really Secular? Undoing Equations between Communism and Religion', in T. T. T. Ngo and J. B. Quijada (eds), *Atheist Secularism and Its Discontents: A Comparative Study of Religion and Communism in Eurasia*, 134–154, Basingstoke: Palgrave Macmillan.

Mahmood, S. (2005), *Politics of Piety: The Islamic Revival and the Feminist Subject*, Princeton, NJ: Princeton University Press.

Meek, J. (2011), 'In Broadway Market', London Review of Books, 9 August 2011. Available online: http://www.lrb.co.uk/blog/2011/08/09/jamesmeek/in-broadway-market/ (accessed 9 August 2011).

Mellor, P. A. and C. Shilling (2010), 'Body Pedagogics and the Religious Habitus: A New Direction for the Sociological Study of Religion', *Religion*, 40: 27–38.

Mumford, L. (2015), 'Living Non-Religious Identity in London', in L. G. Beaman and S. Tomlins (eds), *Atheist Identities: Spaces and Social Contexts*, 153–170, New York, NY: Springer.

Quack, J. (2014), 'Outline of a Relational Approach to "Nonreligion"', *Method and Theory in the Study of Religion*, 26 (4–5): 439–469.

Schmidt, L. E. (2000), *Hearing Things: Religion, Illusion and the American Enlightenment*, Cambridge, MA: Harvard University Press.

Sheard, M. (2014), 'Ninety-Eight Atheists: Atheism among the Non-elite in Twentieth Century Britain', *Secularism and Nonreligion*, 3 (6): 1–16. doi: http://dx.doi.org/10.5334/snr.ar.

Shillitoe, R. (2017), '"Why Are We Talking about Religion?" Reimagining Non-religion in Collective Worship', Conference paper, British Sociological Association Sociology of Religion Study Group Annual Conference, 12–14 July 2017.

Strhan, A. (2015), *Aliens and Strangers: The Struggle for Coherence in the Everyday Lives of Evangelicals*, Oxford: Oxford University Press.

Taves, A. (2016), *Revelatory Events: Three Case Studies of the Emergence of New Spiritual Paths*, Princeton, NJ: Princeton University Press.

Taylor, C. (2007), *A Secular Age*, Cambridge, MA: Harvard University Press.

Vásquez, M. A. and K. Knott (2014), 'Three Dimensions of Religious Place Making in Diaspora', *Global Networks*, 14 (3): 326–347.

Wohlrab-Sahr, M. (2011), 'Multiple Secularities and Their Normativity as an Empirical Subject', *Immanent Frame*, 13 December 2011. Available online: https://tif.ssrc.org/2011/12/13/multiple-secularities-and-their-normativity-as-an-empirical-subject/ (accessed 4 September 2017).

Wohlrab-Sahr, M. and M. Burchardt (2012), 'Multiple Secularities: Toward a Cultural Sociology of Secular Modernities', *Comparative Sociology*, 11 (6): 875–909.

Chapter 5

Asad, T. (2003), *Formations of the Secular: Christianity, Islam, Modernity*, Stanford, CA: Stanford University Press.

Association des amis de Georges Henri Rivière (1989), *La Muséologie selon Georges Henri Rivière: cours de muséologie, textes et témoignages*, Paris: Dunod.

Belting, H. (1994), *Likeness and Presence: A History of the Image before the Era of Art*, Chicago, IL: University of Chicago Press.

Belting, H. (2007), *La Vraie Image*, Paris: Gallimard.

Bennett, T. (1995), *The Birth of the Museum: History, Theory, Politics*, London: Routledge.

Bouquet, M. and N. Porto, eds (2005), *Science, Magic, and Religion: The Ritual Processes of Museum Magic*, Oxford and New York, NY: Berghan Books.

Candlin, F. (2010), *Art, Museums and Touch*, Manchester: Manchester University Press.

Chaumier, S. (2010), 'L'objet de Musée', *dossier documentaire réalisé dans le cadre de l'exposition L'objet collectionné, au Musée de la vie bourguignonne de Dijon*, 23 avril-20 septembre 2010.

Christin, O. (1991), *Une révolution symbolique. L'iconoclasme Huguenot et la reconstruction catholique*, Paris: Editions de Minuit.

Christin, O. (2002), 'Du culte chrétien au culte de l'art: la transformation du statut de l'image (XVe–XVIIIe siècles)', *Revue d'histoire moderne et contemporaine*, 2002/3 (49–3): 176–194.

CIMCIM (1960), 'Comité de l'Icom pour les musées et collections d'instruments de musique', *ICOM News*, 13 (4–5): 17–20.

CIMCIM (1967), *Preservation and Restoration of Musical Instruments. Provisional Recommendations*, Paris: ICOM.

CIMCIM (1985), *Recommandations pour réglementer l'accès aux instruments de musique dans les collections publiques*, Paris: ICOM (Also published in: *Les Nouvelles de l'ICOM* (1986), 39 (3): 5–8.

CIMCIM (1993), *Recommendations for the Conservation of Musical Instruments: An Annotated Bibliography*, CIMCIM Publications (1).

Classen, C. (2007), 'Museum Manners: The Sensory Life of the Early Museum', *Journal of Social History*, 40: 895–914.

Classen, C. and D. Howes (2006), 'The Museum as Sensescape: Western Sensibilities and Indigenous Artefacts', in E. Edwards, C. Gosden and R. Philips (eds), *Sensible Objects: Colonialism, Museums and Material Culture*, 192–222, Oxford: Berg.

Davallon, J. (1986), *Claquemurer pour ainsi dire tout l'univers*, Paris: Centre Georges Pompidou, Centre de Création Industrielle.

Davallon J. (1992), 'Le musée est-il vraiment un média', *Publics et musées*, 2: 99–124.

Davallon, J. (2000), *L'exposition à l'oeuvre. Stratégies de communication et médiation symbolique*, Paris/Montréal, QC: L'harmattan.

Deloche, B. (1985), *Museologica: Contradictions et logiques du musée*, Paris: J. Vrin.

Deloche B. (2010), *Mythologie du musée, de l'uchronie à l'utopie*, Paris: Le Cavalier Bleu.

Desvallées, A. and F. Mairesse, eds (2010), *Concepts Clés de Muséologie*, Paris: Armand Colin.

Desvallées, A. and F. Mairesse, eds (2011), *Dictionnaire Encyclopédique de Muséologie*, Paris: Armand Colin.

Duncan, C. (1991), 'Art Museums and the Ritual of Citizenship', in I. Karp and S. D. Lavine (eds), *Exhibiting Cultures: The Poetics and Politics of Museum Display*, 88–103, Washington/London: Smithsonian Institution Press.

Duncan, C. (1995), *Civilizing Rituals: Inside Public Art Museums*, London and New York, NY: Routledge.

Duncan C. (1998), 'The Art Museum as Ritual', in D. Preziosi (ed.), *The Art of Art History: A Critical Anthology*, 473–485, Oxford: Oxford University Press.

Elkins J. (1998), *On Pictures and the Words that Fail them*, Cambridge, UK: Cambridge University Press.

Fontana, E. (2008), 'Copie di strumenti musicali storici della raccolta dell'Università di Lipsia. Copies of Historic Musical Instruments in the Collection of the University of Leipzig', in G. Rossi Rognoni (ed.), *Restauro e conservazione degli strumenti musicali antichi. La spinetta ovale di Bartolomeo Cristofori. Restoration and Conservation of Early Musical Instruments. The spinetta ovale by Bartolomeo Cristofori*, 53–92, Florence: Nardini editore.

Gétreau, F. (1993), 'Restaurer l'instrument de musique. L'objet sonore et l'instrument sont-ils conciliables ?', *Geschichte der Restaurierung in Europa. Histoire de la Restauration en Europe*, 2: 145–154.

Gétreau, F. (1995), 'L'instrument de musique comme objet de patrimoine: Quels objectifs de restauration ?', in C. Périer-d'Ieteren and A. Godfrind-Born (eds), *Conservation – Restauration Technologie*, Cycle de conférences – Débats, 57–75, Brussels: Université Libre de Bruxelles.

Gob, A. and N. Drouguet (2014), *La muséologie. Histoire, Développements, Enjeux actuels*, Paris: Armand Colin.

Greenblatt, S. (1990), 'Resonance and Wonder', *Bulletin of the Academy of Arts and Sciences*, 43 (4): 11–34.

Hirschkind, C. (2011), 'Is There a Secular Body?', *Cultural Anthropology*, 26 (4/2011): 633–647.

Hooper-Greenhill, E. (1992), *Museums and the Shaping of Knowledge*, London and New York, NY: Routledge.

Jay, M. (1993), *Downcast Eyes: The Denigration of Vision in Twentieth-Century French Thought*, London: University of California Press.

Jeanneret, Y. (2011), *Where Is Mona Lisa, et autres lieux de la culture*, Paris: Le Cavalier Bleu.

Kirshenblatt-Gimblett, B. (2000), 'The Museum as Catalyst', *Museum 2000: Confirmation or Challenge*, Vadstena. Available online: https://www.nyu.edu/classes/bkg/web/vadstena.pdf (accessed 19 January 2016).

Le Marec, J. (2007), *Publics et musées: La confiance éprouvée*, Paris: L'Harmattan.

Le Marec, J. (2013), 'Le public, le tact, et les savoirs de contact', *Communication & Languages*, Issue 175, 3–25.

Morgan, D. (1998), *Visual Piety: A History and Theory of Popular Religious Images*, Berkeley, CA: University of California Press.

Noordegraaf, J. (2004), *Strategies of Display. Museum Presentation in Nineteenth and Twentieth-Century Visual Culture*, Rotterdam: NAi Publishers.

O'Doherty, B. (1986), *Inside the White Cube, the Ideology of the Gallery Space*, Santa Monica and San Francisco: The Lapis Press.

Paine, C. (2013), *Religious Objects in Museums: Private Lives and Public Duties*, London and New York, NY: Bloomsbury.

Pomian, K. (1987), *Collectionneurs, amateurs et curieux, Paris-Venise XVIe–XVIIIe siècle*, Paris: Gallimard.

Preziosi, D. (1996), 'Brain of the Earth's Body: Museums and the Framing of Modernity', in P. Duro (ed.), *The Rhetoric of the Frame: Essays on the Boundaries of the Artwork*, 96–110, Cambridge, UK: Cambridge University Press.

Rees Leahy, H. (2012), *Museum Bodies, the Politics and Practices of Visiting and Viewing*, London: Ashgate.

Sachs, C. (2003), 'La signification, la tâche et la technique muséographique des collections d'instruments de musique', *Cahiers d'ethnomusicologie*, 16 (2003). 11 41. (Article first published in *Mouseion*, 27–28 [1934]: 153–184.)

Van Mensch, P. (1990), 'Methodological Museology', in S. Pearce (ed.), *Objects of Knowledge*, 141–157, London: The Athlone Press.

Chapter 6

Asad, T. (2003), *Formations of the Secular: Christianity, Islam, Modernity*, Stanford, CA: Stanford University Press.

Aston, K. (2015), *Living without God: Nonreligious Alternatives in the UK*, unpublished Doctoral thesis, Goldsmiths College, University of London.

Bauman, Z. (2013), *Liquid Love: On the Frailty of Human Bonds*, London: Polity Press.

British Humanist Association (2013), 'Amendment to the Marriage (Same Sex Couples) Bill NC15 Briefing from the British Humanist Association for Commons Report Stage', 21 May. Available online: http://humanism.org.uk/wp-content/uploads/BHA-Briefing-humanist-marriage-amendment-to-the-Marriage-Same-Sex-Couples-Bill-Commons-Report-Stage.doc (accessed 23 August 2013).

Campbell, C. (1971), *Towards a Sociology of Irreligion*, London: Macmillan Press.

Carter, J. and Duncan, S. (2017), 'Wedding Paradoxes: Individualized Conformity and the "Perfect Day"'. *The Sociological Review*, 65 (1): 3–20.

Charsley, S. R. (1991), *Rites of Marrying: The Wedding Industry in Scotland*, Manchester: Manchester University Press.

Engelke, M. (2014), 'Christianity and the Anthropology of Secular Humanism', *Current Anthropology*, 55 (10): 292–301.

Engelke, M. (2015a), 'The Coffin Question: Death and Materiality in Humanist Funerals', *Material Religion*, 11 (1): 26–48.

Engelke, M. (2015b), 'Humanist Ceremonies: The Case of the Non-religious Funeral', in Copson, A. and A. C. Grayling (eds), *The Wiley Blackwell Handbook of Humanism*, 216–233, John Wiley & Sons.

Funeralcare, Co-operative (2011), *The Ways We Say Goodbye*.

Hirschkind, C. (2011), 'Is There a Secular Body?', *Cultural Anthropology*, 26 (4): 633–647.

Humanist UK (2018), 'Revealed: How Many Marriages Each Religious Group and Humanists UK Do'. Available online: https://humanism.org.uk/2018/05/09/revealed-how-many-marriages-each-religious-group-and-humanists-uk-do/ (accessed 20 May 2018).

Keane, W. (1997), 'From Fetishism to Sincerity: On Agency, the Speaking Subject, and Their Historicity in the Context of Religious Conversion', *Comparative Studies in Society and History*, 39 (4): 674–693.

Keane, W. (2002), '"Sincerity," "Modernity," and the Protestants', *Cultural Anthropology*, 17 (1): 65–92.

Keane, W. (2006), *Christian Moderns: Freedom and Fetish in the Mission Encounter*, vol. 1. Berkeley, CA, Los Angeles and London: University of California Press.

Keane, W. (2013), 'Secularism as a Moral Narrative of Modernity', *Transit*, 159–170.

Latour, B. (2010), *On the Modern Cult of the Factish Gods*, Durham, NC: Duke University Press.

Lee, L. (2012), 'Research Note: Talking about a Revolution: Terminology for the New Field of Non-religion Studies', *Journal of Contemporary Religion*, 27 (1): 129–139.

Lee, L. (2015), *Recognizing the Non-religious: Reimagining the Secular*, Oxford: Oxford University Press.

Mahmood, S. (2001), 'Rehearsed Spontaneity and the Conventionality of Ritual: Disciplines of Ṣalat', *American Ethnologist*, 28 (4): 827–853.

Mahmood, S. (2011), *Politics of Piety: The Islamic Revival and the Feminist Subject*, 2nd edn, Princeton, NJ: Princeton University Press.

Moore, S. (2013), 'Flowers, Fire, Dylan – and the Jabberwocky', *New Humanist*, 128 (4): 15.

Office of National Statistics (2012), 'Religion in England and Wales 2011'. Available online: http://www.ons.gov.uk/ons/dcp171776_290510.pdf (accessed 20 May 2018).

Office of National Statistics (2018), 'Marriages in England and Wales 2015'. Available online: https://www.ons.gov.uk/peoplepopulationandcommunity/ birthsdeathsandmarriages/marriagecohabitationandcivilpartnerships/bulletins/marria gesinenglandandwalesprovisional/2015#main–points (accessed 20 May 2018).

Royle, E. (1980), *Radicals, Secularists, and Republicans: Popular Freethought in Britain, 1866–1915*, Manchester: Manchester University Press.

Schwartz, L. (2010), 'Freethought, Free Love and Feminism: Secularist Debates on Marriage and Sexual Morality, England c. 1850–1885', *Women's History Review*, 19 (5): 775–793.

Schwartz, L. (2013), *Infidel Feminism: Secularism, Religion and Women's Emancipation, England 1830–1914*, Manchester: Manchester University Press.

Taylor, C. (2007), *A Secular Age*, Cambridge, MA: Harvard University Press.

Chapter 7

Anderson, B. R. O'G. (1991), *Imagined Communities: Reflections on the Origin and Spread of Nationalism* (revised and extended edn), London: Verso.

Benhadjoudja, L. (2017), 'Laïcité narrative et sécularonationalisme au Québec à l'épreuve de la race, du genre et de la sexualité', *Studies in religion/Sciences religieuse*, 46 (2): 272–291.

Bilge, S. (2012), 'Mapping Québécois Sexual Nationalism in Times of "Crisis of Reasonable Accommodations"', *Journal of Intercultural Studies*, 33: 303–318.

Bilge, S. (2013), 'Reading the Racial Subtext of the Québécois Accommodation Controversy: An Analytics of Racialized Governmentality', *South African Journal of Political Studies*, 40: 157–181.

Bilge S., P. Hamel and B. Thériault (2010), '… alors que nous, Québécois, nos femmes sont égales à nous et nous les aimons ainsi', *Sociologie et societies*, 42: 197–226.

Boym, S. (2001), *The Future of Nostalgia*, New York, NY: Basic Books.

Burchardt, M. (2017), 'Recalling Modernity: How Nationalist Memories Shape Religious Diversity in Quebec and Catalonia', *Nations and Nationalism*, 23 (3): 599–619.

Davie, G. (2000), *Religion in Modern Europe – A Memory Mutates*, Oxford: Oxford University Press.

Dillon, M. (2012), 'Habermas and Post-secular Appropriation of Religion', in P. S. Gorski, D. K. Kim, J. Torpey and J. VanAntwerpen (eds), *The Post-secular in Question: Religion in Contemporary Society*, 249–278, New York, NY and London: New York University Press.

Farris, S. (2017), *In the Name of Women's Rights: The Rise of Femonationalism*, Durham, NC: Duke University Press.

Ferrari, A. (2009), 'De la politique à la technique: laïcité narrative et laïcité du droit. Pour une comparaison France/Italie', in B. Basdevant-Gaudemet and F. Jankowiak (eds), *Le droit ecclésiastique de la fin du xviiie au milieu du xxe siècle en Europe*, 333–343, Leuven: Peeters.

Fortier, A.-M. (2016), 'Afterword: Acts of Affective Citizenship? Possibilities and limitations', *Citizenship Studies*, 20 (8): 1038–1044.

Foucault, M. (2001), *L'herméneutique du sujet*, Paris: Gallimard.

Habermas, J. (2008), 'Notes on a Post-secular Society', *signsandsight.com*, 18 June. Available online: http://www.signandsight.com/features/1714.html (accessed 2 August 2017).

Hervieu-Léger, D. (2008), *La religion pour mémoire*, Paris: Les Éditions du Cerf.

Isambert, F.-A. (1976), 'La sécularisation interne du christianisme', *Revue française de Sociologie*, 17 (4): 573–589.

Jenkins, J. H. (1991), 'The State Construction of Affect: Political Ethos and Mental Health among Salvadoran Refugees', *Culture, Medicine and Psychiatry*, 15 (2): 139–165.

Klassen, P. E. (2015), 'Fantasies of Sovereignty: Civic Secularism in Canada', *Critical Research on Religion*, 3 (1): 41–56.

Lutz, C. A. and L. Abu-Lughod (1990), *Language and the Politics of Emotion*, Cambridge, UK: Cambridge University Press.

Mahmood, S. (2009), 'Religious Reason and Secular Affect: An Incommensurable Divide?', *Critical Inquiry*, 35 (4): 836–862.

Masuzawa, T. (2005), *The Invention of World Religions, Or, How European Universalism Was Preserved in the Language of Pluralism*, Chicago, IL and London: University of Chicago Press.

Özyürek, E. (2006), *Nostalgia for the Modern: State Secularism and Everyday Politics in Turkey*, Durham, NC: Duke University Press.

Reddy, W. M. (1997), 'Against Constructionism: The Historical Ethnography of Emotions', *Current Anthropology*, 38 (3): 327–351.

Ricœur, P. (1988), 'L'identité narrative', *Esprit*, 7: 295–305.

Rosaldo, M. (1984), 'Toward an Anthropology of Self and Feeling', in R. A. Shweder and R. A. LeVine (eds), *Culture Theory: Essays on Mind, Self and Emotion*, 137–157, Cambridge, UK: Cambridge University Press.

Scott, J. W. (2017), *Sex and Secularism*, Princeton, NJ: Princeton University Press.

Taylor, C. (2002), *Le malaise de la modernité*, Paris: Les Éditions du Cerf.

Wilkins-Laflamme, S. (forthcoming), 'De nouveaux enjeux dans le paysage religieux québécois', in J.-P. Perreault and D. Koussens, *Actes du colloque de l'ACFAS 2016*.

Chapter 8

Arango, T. (2013), 'After a Break, Turkey's Prime Minister again Courts Controversy', *New York Times*, 7 November. Available online: http://www.nytimes.com/2013/11/08/world/europe/turkey-coed-dormitories-.html?_r=0 (accessed 18 June 2015).

Asad, T. (2003), *Formations of the Secular: Christianity, Islam, Modernity*, Stanford, CA: Stanford University Press.

Babayan, K. and A. Najmabadi (2008), 'Preface', in K. Babayan and A. Najmabadi (eds), *Islamicate Sexualities: Translations across Temporal Geographies of Desire*, vii–xiv, Cambridge, MA: Harvard University, Center for Middle Eastern Studies.

Bartky, S. L. (1990), *Femininity and Domination: Studies in the Phenomenology of Oppression*, New York, NY: Routledge.

Cannell, F. (2010), 'The Anthropology of Secularism', *Annual Review of Anthropology*, 39: 85–100.

Çınar, A. (2005), *Modernity, Islam and Secularism in Turkey: Bodies, Places and Time*, Minneapolis, MN: The University of Minnesota Press.

Erol, M. (2011), 'Neoliberalism's Second Spring: The Social Construction of the Menopause in Turkey' [Neoliberalizmin İkinci Baharı: Türkiye'de Menopozun Toplumsal İnşası], in C. Özbay, A. Terzioğlu and Y. Yasın (eds), *Neoliberalizm ve Mahremiyet: Türkiye'de Beden, Sağlık ve Cinsellik*, Istanbul: Metis [Turkish].

Evin, M. (2013), 'Red Lipstick', *Hürriyet Daily News*, 3 May (originally published in Turkish in *Milliyet*, 2 May). Available online: http://www.hurriyetdailynews.com/red-lipstick-.aspx?pageID=238&nID=46120&NewsCatID=396 (accessed 26 September 2016).

Fadil, N. and M. Fernando (2015), 'Rediscovering the "Everyday" Muslim: Notes on an Anthropological Divide', *HAU: Journal of Ethnographic Theory*, 5 (2), Available online: http://dx.doi.org/10.14318/hau5.2.005 (accessed 12 December 2016).

Faulconbridge, G. (2013), 'Turkish Airlines Backs Down on Lipstick Ban', *Reuters*, 9 May. Available online: http://www.reuters.com/article/us-turkey-airlines-lipstick-idUSBRE9480HQ20130509 (accessed 9 January 2017).

Foucault, M. (1984), *The Care of the Self, History of Sexuality*, 3, London: Penguin Books.

Gökarıksel, B. (2009), 'Beyond the Officially Sacred: Religion, Secularism and the Body in the Production of Subjectivity', *Social and Cultural Geography*, 10 (6): 657–674.

Gökarıksel, B. (2012), 'The Intimate Politics of Secularism and the Headscarf: The Mall, the Neighborhood, and the Public Square in Istanbul', *Gender, Place & Culture*, 19 (1): 1–20.

Gökarıksel, B. and A. J. Secor (2009), 'New Transnational Geographies of Islamism, Capitalism, and Subjectivity: The Veiling-Fashion Industry in Turkey', *Area*, 41 (1): 6–18.

Gökarıksel, B. and A. J. Secor (2010), 'Between Fashion and Tesettür: Marketing and Consuming Veiling-Fashion', *Journal of Middle East Women's Studies*, 6 (3): 118–148.

Göle, N. (1997), *The Forbidden Modern: Civilization and Veiling*, Ann Arbor, MI: University of Michigan Press.

Greenblatt, S. (1980), *Renaissance Self-fashioning*, Chicago, IL: University of Chicago Press.

Hirschkind, C. (2011), 'Is There a Secular Body?', *Cultural Anthropology*, 26 (4): 633–647.

Hürriyet (2013), 'Gözde Kansu neden gönderildi' [Why was Gözde Kansu dismissed?], 9 October. Available online: http://www.hurriyet.com.tr/gozde-kansu-neden-gonderildi-24877005 (accessed 23 January 2017).

Hürriyet Daily News (2013), 'Turkish Airlines Flight Attendants on Strike Join Gezi Park "Marauders" with Parody', 5 June. Available online: http://www.hurriyetdailynews.com/turkish-airlines-flight-attendants-on-strike-join-gezi-park-marauders-with-parody.aspx?pageID=238&nID=48307&NewsCatID=345 (accessed 26 September 2016).

Hürriyet Daily News (2017), 'Woman Detained after Appearing on Viral "Secularism" Video', 2 January. Available online: http://www.hurriyetdailynews.com/woman-calling-for-secularism-in-istanbul-detained-after-isil-attack-on-nightclub.aspx?PageID=238&NID=108046&NewsCatID=34 (accessed 13 January 2017).

Kandiyoti, D. (2012), 'The Travails of the Secular: Puzzle and Paradox in Turkey', *Economy and Society*, 41 (4): 513–531.

Kandiyoti, D. (2014), 'No Laughing Matter: Women and the New Populism in Turkey'. Available online: https://www.opendemocracy.net/5050/deniz-kandiyoti/no-laughing-matter-women-and-new-populism-in-turkey (accessed 18 June 2015).

Low, S. (2003), 'Embodied Space(s): Anthropological Theories of Body, Space, and Culture', *Space & Culture*, 6 (1): 9–18.

Mahmood, S. (2004), *Politics of Piety: The Islamic Revival and the Feminist Subject*, Princeton, NJ: Princeton University Press.

Navaro-Yashin, Y. (2002), *Faces of the State: Secularism and Public Life in Turkey*, Princeton, NJ: Princeton University Press.

Özyürek, E. (2004), 'Miniaturizing Atatürk: Privatization of the State Imagery and Ideology in Turkey', *American Ethnologist*, 31 (3): 374–391.

Özyürek, E. (2006), *Nostalgia for the Modern: State Secularism and Everyday Politics in Turkey*, Durham and London: Duke University Press.

Sandıkçı, Ö. and G. Ger (2010), 'Veiling in Style: How Does a Stigmatized Practice Become Fashionable?', *Journal of Consumer Research*, 37 (June): 15–36.

Secor, A. J. (2001), 'Toward a Feminist Counter-geopolitics: Gender, Space and Islamist Politics in Istanbul', *Space and Polity*, 5 (3): 191–211.

Sehlikoglu, S. (2016), 'Exercising in Comfort: Islamicate Culture of Mahremiyet in Everyday Life', *Journal of Middle East Women's Studies*, 12 (2): 143–165.

Shissler, H. (2004), 'Beauty Is Nothing to Be Ashamed Of: Beauty Contests as Tools of Women's Liberation in Early Republican Turkey', *Comparative Studies of South Asia, Africa and the Middle East*, 24: 107–122.

Tambar, K. (2009), 'Secular Populism and the Semiotics of the Crowd in Turkey', *Public Culture*, 21 (3): 517–537.

Tokbaş, Y. (2013), 'Let's Put on Red Lipstick' [Kırmızı ruj sürelim sürdürelim]. *Hürriyet News*, 29 April. Available online: http://www.hurriyet.com.tr/kirmizi-ruj-surelim-surdurelim-23162286 (accessed 9 January 2017).

Turam, B. (2013), 'The Primacy of Space in Politics: Bargaining Rights, Freedom and Power in an İstanbul Neighborhood', *International Journal of Urban and Regional Research*, 37 (2): 409–429.

Turam, B. (2015), *Gaining Freedoms: Claiming Space in Istanbul and Berlin*, Stanford, CA: Stanford University Press.

Ünal, R. A. (2013), 'Wardrobes of Turkish-Dutch Women: The Multiple Meanings and Aesthetics of Muslim Dress', M.A. diss, University of Amsterdam, Amsterdam.

White, J. B. (2002), *Islamist Mobilization in Turkey: A Study in Vernacular Politics*, Seattle and London: University of Washington Press.

White, J. B. (2013), *Muslim Nationalism and the New Turks*, Princeton, NJ and Oxford: Princeton University Press.

Yackley, A. J. (2013), 'Secular Turks See Red over Airline's Lipstick Ban', *Reuters*, May 3. Available online: http://uk.reuters.com/article/us-nt-turkey-airlines-lipstick-idUKBRE94209M20130503 (accessed 26 September 2016).

Chapter 9

Ahmed, S. (2014), *The Cultural Politics of Emotion*, 2nd edn, Edinburgh: Edinburgh University Press, 2014.

Allen, L. (2008), 'Getting by the Occupation: How Violence Became Normal during the Second Intifada', *Cultural Anthropology*, 23 (3): 453–487.

Allen, L. (2012), 'The Scalar Politics of Occupation: "Operation Cast Lead and the Targeting of the Gaza Strip"', *Critique of Anthropology*, 32 (3): 261–284.

Almog, O. and T. Almog (2015), *Generation Y – Research Report*, Haifa: The Samuel Neaman Institute for Policy Research Press [Hebrew].

Dalsheim, J. (2007), 'Deconstructing National Myths, Reconstructing Morality: Modernity, Hegemony and the Israeli National Past', *Journal of Historical Sociology*, 20 (4): 521–554.

Diamond, J. S. (2004), 'The Post-secular: A Jewish Perspective', *Cross Currents*, 53 (4): 580–606.

Farman, A. (2013), 'Speculative Matter: Secular Bodies, Minds and Persons', *Cultural Anthropology*, 28 (4): 737–759.

Furani, K. (2015), 'Is There a Post-secular?', *Journal of the American Academy of Religion*, 83 (1): 1–26.

Gitelman, Z., ed. (2009), *Religion or Ethnicity: Jewish Identities in Evolution*. Piscataway, NJ: Rutgers University Press.

Hirschkind, C. (2011), 'Is There a Secular Body?', *Cultural Anthropology*, 26 (4): 633–647.

Jobani, Y. (2008), 'Three Basic Models of Secular Jewish Culture', *Israel Studies*, 13 (3): 160–169.

Katriel, T. (1986), *Talking Straight: Dugri Speech in Israeli Sabra Culture*, Cambridge, UK: Cambridge University Press.

Kimmerling, B. (1985), *The Interrupted System: Israeli Civilians in War and Routine Times*, Virginia: Transaction Publishers.

Lahav, H. (2016), 'What Do Secular Women in Israel Believe In?', *Journal of Contemporary Religion*, 31 (1): 17–34.

Liebman, C. S. and E. Don-Yehiya (1983), *Civil Religion in Israel: Traditional Judaism and Political Culture in the Jewish State*, Berkeley, CA: University of California Press.

Loeffler, J. (2016), 'When Hermann Cohen Cried: Zionism, Culture and Emotions', in I. Bartal and R. Jojansky (eds), *Zionism as a Cultural Movement*, Leiden: Brill.

Lubkemann, S. C. (2008), *Culture in Chaos: An Anthropology of the Social Condition in War*, Chicago, IL: University of Chicago Press.

Moscowitz, D. (2015), *A Culture of Tough Jews: Rhetorical Regeneration and the Politics of Identity*, Bern: Peter Lang.

Nussbaum, M. C. (2003), *Upheavals of the Thought: The Intelligence of Emotions*, Cambridge, UK: Cambridge University Press.

Ochs, J. (2011), *Security and Suspicion: An Ethnography of Everyday Life in Israel*, Philadelphia: University of Pennsylvania Press.

Oz, A. (2012), *How to Cure a Fanatic*, London: Vintage Books, 2012.

Plasse-Couture, F. (2013), 'Effective Abandonment: The Neoliberal Economy of Violence in Israel and the Occupied Territories', *Security Dialogue*, 44 (5–6): 449–466.

Sasson-Levy, O. (2013), 'A Different Kind of Whiteness: Marking and Unmarking the Social Boundaries in the Construction of Ethnic Hegemony', *Sociological Forum*, 28 (1): 27–50.

Shafir, G. and Y. Peled (1998), 'Citizenship and Stratification in an Ethnic Democracy', *Ethnic and Racial Studies*, 21 (3): 408–427.

Soloveitchik, J. B. (1994), *Halakhic Man*, Philadelphia: Jewish Publication Society.

Stacey Gutkowski, Secular War: Myths of Religion, Politics and Violence (London: IB Tauris, 2013).

Toscano, A. (2010), *Fanaticism: On the Uses of an Idea*, London and New York, NY: Verso.

Walzer, M. (2002), 'Passion and Politics', *Philosophy and Social Criticism*, 28 (6): 617–633.

Weiss, M. (1997), 'War Bodies, Hedonist Bodies: Dialectics of the Collective and Individual in Israeli Society', *American Ethnologist*, 24 (4): 813–832.

Yaacov, Y. (2003), 'Between "the Arab" and "the Religious Rightist": "Significant Others" in the Construction of Jewish-Israeli National Identity', *Nationalism and Ethnic Politics*, 9 (1): 52–74.

Yadgar, Y. (2010), *Secularism and Religion in Jewish-Israeli Politics: Traditionists and Modernity*, London: Routledge.

Chapter 10

Anderson, B. (2006 [1983]), *Imagined Communities: Reflections on the Origin and Spread of Nationalism*, revised edn, London: Verso.

Asad, T. (2003), *Formations of the Secular: Christianity, Islam, Modernity*, Stanford, CA: Stanford University Press.

Bourdieu, P. (1990), *The Logic of Practice*, trans. R. Nice, Stanford, CA: Stanford University Press.

Cook, H. (2012), 'Emotion, Bodies, Sexuality, and Sex Education in Edwardian England', *The Historical Journal*, 55 (2): 475–495.

'Cynics Confounded: The Force of Collective Emotion' (1919), *The Times*, 12 November: 16.

Durkheim, É. (1915 [1912]), *The Elementary Forms of the Religious Life*, trans. J. W. Swain, London: G. Allen & Unwin.

Fitzpatrick, Sir P. (1919 [1994]), 'Memorandum Submitted to Lord Milner for the Attention of the War Cabinet', in A. Gregory (ed.), *The Silence of Memory: Armistice Day 1919–1946*, 9, Oxford and Providence: Berg.

Foster, W. (i.e. Honey, George Edward) (1919), 'Five Minutes' Silence. On Peace Day to the Memory of the Dead', *The Evening News*, 8 May: 4.

George, R. I. (1919), 'The Glorious Dead. King's Call to His People. Armistice Day Observance. Two Minutes' Pause from Work', *The Times*, 7 November: 12.

Graeser, E. (1924), 'Stille und Stillstand. Die Zwei-Minuten-Gedenkpause', *Vossische Zeitung*, 3 August: 5–6.

Gregory, A. (1994), *The Silence of Memory: Armistice Day 1919–1946*, Oxford and Providence: Berg.

Habermas, R. (2011), 'Piety, Power, and Powerlessness: Religion and Religious Groups in Germany, 1870–1945', in H. W. Smith (ed.), *The Oxford Handbook of Modern German History*, 453–480, Oxford: Oxford University Press.

Hirschkind, C. (2011), 'Is There a Secular Body?', *Cultural Anthropology*, 26 (4): 633–647.

Johansen, B. S. (2015), 'Locating Hatred: On the Materiality of Emotions', *Emotion, Space and Society*, 16: 48–55.

Lichau, K. (2014), '" … während dessen auf zwei Minuten jeder Ton und jede Bewegung aussetzt". Die akustische Inszenierung politischer Einheit in der Schweigeminute', in G. Paul and R. Schock (eds), *Sound der Zeit. Geräusche, Töne, Stimmen – 1889 bis heute*, 506–512, Göttingen: Wallstein.

Pagès, L.-A. (1922), 'L'anniversaire de l'Armistice. A l'Arc de Triomphe, l'hommage au Soldat Inconnu a été particulièrement émouvant', *L'Ouest-Eclair*, 12 November: 1.

'Remembrance Day. Will You Ever Forget?' (1919), *Daily Herald*, 11 November: 1.

Schafer, R. M. (1994 [1977]), *The Soundscape: Our Sonic Environment and the Tuning of the World*, Rochester: Destiny Books.

Scheer, M. (2012a), 'Are Emotions a Kind of Practice (And Is That What Makes Them Have a History)? A Bourdieuian Approach to Understanding Emotions', *History and Theory*, 51 (2): 193–220.

Scheer, M. (2012b), 'Protestantisch fühlen lernen. Überlegungen zur emotionalen Praxis der Innerlichkeit', *Zeitschrift für Erziehungswissenschaft*, 15 (1): 179–193.

Stearns, C. Z. and P. N. Stearns (1986), *Anger: The Struggle for Emotional Control in America's History*, Chicago, IL: Chicago University Press.

Wohlrab-Sahr, M. and M. Burchardt (2012), 'Multiple Secularities: Toward a Cultural Sociology of Secular Modernities', *Comparative Sociology*, 11: 875–909.

Z_R (1924), 'Die Toten-Gedenkfeier', *Vossische Zeitung*, 4 August: 4.

Chapter 11

Amir-Moazami, S. (2016), 'Investigating the Secular Body: The Politics of the Male Circumcision Debate in Germany', *ReOrient*, 1 (2): 147–170.

Amiraux, V. (2016), 'Visibility, Transparency and Gossip: How Did the Religion of Some (Muslims) Become the Public Concern of Others', *Critical Research on Religion*, 4 (1): 37–56.

Asad, T. (2003), *Formations of the Secular: Christianity, Islam, Modernity*, Stanford, CA: Stanford University Press.

Asad, T. (2011), 'Thinking about the Secular Body, Pain, and Liberal Politics', *Cultural Anthropology*, 26 (4): 657–675.

'Assemblée nationale s'attaque aux mariages blancs' (2006), *Le Monde*, 23 March. Available online: http://abonnes.lemonde.fr/societe/article/2006/03/23/l-assemblee-nationale-s-attaque-aux-mariages-blancs_753684_3224.html?xtmc=pascal_clement_et_mariage&xtcr=5 (accessed 23 March 2006).

Belmokhtar, Z. (2006), 'Les annulations de mariage en 2004', *Infostat Justice*, 90. Available online: www.justice.gouv.fr/budget-et-statistiques-10054/infostats-justice-10057/infostat-n-90-10075.html (accessed 6 October 2017).

Cesari, J. (2016), 'Self, Islam and Secular Public Spaces', in N. Göle (ed.), *Islam and Public Controversy in Europe*, 47–55, New York, NY: Routledge.

Clancy-Smith, J. (1998), 'Islam, Gender, and Identities in the Making of French Algeria, 1830–1962', in J. Clancy-Smith and F. Gouda (eds), *Domesticating the Empire: Race, Gender, and Family Life in French and Dutch Colonialism*, 154–174, Charlottesville, VA and London: University of Virginia Press.

Cole, J. (2014), 'Working Mis/Understandings: The Tangled Relationship between Kinship, Franco-Malagasy Bi-National Marriage and the French State', *Cultural Anthropology*, 29 (3): 527–551.

Connolly, W. E. (2011), *A World of Becoming*, Durham, NC: Duke University Press.

Daumas, C. (2007), 'Avec Sarkozy, le Coeur devient une valeur de droite', *Libération*, 24 November. Available online: http://www.liberation.fr/week-end/2007/11/24/avec-sarkozy-le-coeur-devient-une-valeur-de-droite_106998 (accessed 6 October 2017).

Dobie, M. (2001), *Foreign Bodies: Gender, Language, and Culture in French Orientalism*, Stanford, CA: Stanford University Press.

Fadil, N. (2009), 'Managing Affects and Sensibilities: The Case of Not-Handshaking and Not Fasting', *Social Anthropology*, 17 (4): 439–454.

Fassin, É. (2006), 'La démocratie sexuelle et le conflit des civilisations', *Multitudes*, 3: 123–131.

Fassin, É. (2010), 'National Identities and Transnational Intimacies: Sexual Democracy and the Politics of Immigration in Europe', *Public Culture*, 22 (3): 507–529.

Fassin, É. (2014), 'Same-Sex Marriage, Nation, and Race: French Political Logics and Rhetorics', *Contemporary French Civilization*, 39 (3): 281–301.

Fernando, M. L. (2014), 'Intimacy Surveilled: Religion, Sex, and Secular Cunning', *Signs: Journal of Women in Culture and Society*, 39 (3): 685–708.

Foucault, M. (2003), *The Essential Foucault*, eds. N. Rose and P. Rabinow, New York, NY: New Press.

Hall, S. (1996), 'The Question of Cultural Identity', in S. Hall, D. Held, D. Hubert and K. Thompson (eds), *Modernity: An Introduction to Modern Societies*, 595–635, Malden, MA: Blackwell.

Hamel, C., B. L'hommeau, A. Pailhé and E. Santelli (2010), 'La formation du couple entre ici et là-bas', in C. Beauchemin, C. Hamel and P. Simon (eds), *Trajectoires et Origines: Enquête sur la diversité des populations en France*, 85–94, Paris: INED Documents de Travail 168.

Hirschkind, C. (2011), 'Is There a Secular Body?', *Cultural Anthropology*, 26 (4): 633–647.

Hurd, E. S. (2012), 'International Politics after Secularism', *Review of International Studies*, 35 (5): 943–961.

INSEE (Institut national de la statistique et des études économiques) (2011), *Fiche 'Estimation de population par quartier'*. Available online: http://www.insee.fr/fr/ppp/bases-de-donnees/donnees-detaillees/duicq/pdf/em/em_Z_1120040.pdf (accessed 1 October 2016).

INSEE (Institut national de la statistique et des études économiques) (2013), *Commune de Nanterre*. Available online: http://www.insee.fr/fr/themes/comparateur.asp?codgeo=COM-92050 (accessed 1 October 2016).

Jouili, J. (2015), *Pious Practice and Secular Constraint: Women in the Islamic Revival Movement in Europe*, Stanford, CA: Stanford University Press.

Linke, U. (2006), 'Contact Zones: Rethinking the Sensual Life of the State', *Anthropological Theory*, 6: 205–225.

MacMaster, N. (1997), *Colonial Migrants and Racism: Algerians in France 1900–62*, London: Macmillan Press.

Ministère De La Justice (2006), *Projet de loi relatif au contôle de la validité des mariages. Discours de Pascal Clément, ministre de la Justice, garde des Sceaux, 22 mars*. Available online: http://www.presse.justice.gouv.fr/archives-discours-10093/archives-des-discours-de-2006-10094/projet-de-loi-relatif-au-controle-de-la-validite-des-mariages-11232.html (accessed 3 November 2016).

Ministère De La Justice (2010), *Circulaire relative à la lutte contre les mariages simulés, 22 juin*. Available online: http://www.gisti.org/IMG/pdf/circ_civ0910_2010-06-22.pdf (accessed 15 February 2017).

Robledo, M. S. (2011), 'Bleu, blanc, gris … La couleur des mariages', *L'Espace Politique 13*. Available online: http://espacepolitique.revues.org/1869 (accessed 22 January 2016).

Scott, J. C. (1990), *Domination and the Arts of Resistance: Hidden Transcripts*, New Haven, CT: Yale University Press.

Scott, J. W. (2007), *The Politics of the Veil*, Princeton, NJ: Princeton University Press.

Scott, J. W. (2018), *Sex & Secularism*, Princeton, NJ: Princeton University Press.

Segalen, M. (2003), *Éloge du mariage*, Paris: Découvertes Gallimard.

Selby, J. A. (2011), 'Islam in France Reconfigured: Republican Islam in the 2010 Gerin Report', *The Journal of Muslim Minority Affairs*, 31 (3): 383–398.

Selby, J. A. (2012), *Questioning French Secularism: Gender Politics and Islam in a Parisian Suburb. Anthropology of Religion Series*, New York, NY: Palgrave Macmillan.

Selby, J. A. (2014a), 'C'est plus traditionnel ici qu'au bled: Analyse socio-spatiale du traditionalisme religieux dans une banlieue parisienne', *Ethnologie Française*, 44 (3): 515–526.

Selby, J. A. (2014b), 'Islam in France', in J. Cesari (ed.), *Handbook of European Islam*, 23–63, New York, NY: Oxford University Press.

Selby, J. A. (2017), 'Le *bled* en banlieue: Le mariage musulman face à l'État français', *Ethnologie française*, 167 (3): 693–705.

Selby, J. A. and M. L. Fernando (2014), 'Short Skirts and Niqab Bans: On Sexuality and the Secular Body', *The Immanent Frame: Secularism, Religion, and the Public Sphere*. Available online: http://blogs.ssrc.org/tif/2014/09/04/short-skirts-and-niqab-bans-on-sexuality-and-the-secular-body/(accessed 6 October 2017).

Shepard, T. (2012), 'Something Notably Erotic: Politics, "Arab men" and Sexual Revolution in Post-Decolonization France, 1962–1974', *Journal of Modern History*, 84 (1): 80–115.

Stoler, A. L. (2002), *Carnal Knowledge and Imperial Power: Race and the Intimate in Colonial Rule*, Berkeley, CA: University of California Press.

Surkis, J. (2010), 'Hymenal Politics: Marriage, Secularism, and French Sovereignty', *Public Culture*, 22 (3): 531–556.

Warner, M. (2008), 'The Ruse of "Secular Humanism"', *The Immanent Frame: Secularism, Religion, and the Public Sphere*, 22 September. Available online: http://blogs.ssrc.org/tif/2008/09/22/theruse-of-secular-humanism/(accessed 6 October 2017).

Chapter 12

Agrama, H. A. (2012a), *Questioning Secularism*, Chicago, IL: University of Chicago Press.

Agrama, H. A. (2012b), 'Reflections on Secularism, Democracy, and Politics in Egypt', *American Ethnologist*, 39 (1): 26–31.

Agrama, H. A. (2012c), 'Religious Freedom as a Binding Practice of Suspicion', *The Immanent Frame*. Available online: http://blogs.ssrc.org/tif/2012/09/11/religious-freedom-as-a-binding-practice-of-suspicion (accessed 19 May 2015).

Amir-Moazami, S. (2011), 'Pitfalls of Consensus-orientated Dialogue: The German Islam Conference (Deutsche Islam Konferenz)', *Approaching Religion*, 1 (1): 2–15.

Asad, T. (2003), *Formations of the Secular. Christianity, Islam, Modernity*, Stanford, CA: Stanford University Press.

Asad, T. (2006), 'Trying to Understand French Secularism', in H. de Vries and L. E. Sullivan (eds), *Political Theologies: Public Religions in a Post-secular World*, 494–526, New York, NY: Fordham University Press.

Bertelsmann Stiftung (2008), *Religionsmonitor 2008: Muslimische Religiosität in Deutschland*, Gütersloh: Gütersloher Verlagshaus.

Bracke, S. (2011), 'Subjects of Debate: Secular and Sexual Exceptionalism, and Muslim Women in the Netherlands', *Feminist Review*, 98: 28–46.

Brems E., ed. (2014), *The Experiences of Face Veil Wearers and the Law*, Cambridge, UK: Cambridge University Press.

Brettfeld, K. and P. Wetzels (2007), 'Muslime in Deutschland. Integration, Integrationsbarrieren, Religion sowie Einstellungen zu Demokratie, Rechtsstaat und politisch-religiös motivierter Gewalt', report from the German Islam Konferenz, Hamburg University.

CEPOS (2009), 'Indvandrere og Efterkommere Fra Muslimske Lande Er Glade for Danmark' [Immigrants and Descendants from Muslim Countries Are Satisfied with Denmark], report from the think tank CEPOS, Copenhagen.

Cesari, J. (2004), *When Islam and Democracy Meet: Muslims in Europe and in the United States*, Palgrave: Macmillan.

Conseil Sondage Analyses (CSA) (2008), 'Islam et Citoyenneté', survey compiled for Le Monde, August 2008.

Crone, M. (2010), 'Shari'a and Secularism in France', in J. S. Nielsen and L. Christoffersen L (eds), *Shari'a as Discourse. Legal Traditions and the Encounter with Europe*, 141–156, Farnham: Ashgate.

European Agency for Fundamental Rights (FRA) (2008), *EU-MIDIS: European Union Minorities and Discrimination Survey*.

Fales, W. (1943), 'Phenomenology of Questions', *Philosophy and Phenomenological Research*, 4 (1): 60 76.

Fernando, M. L. (2014), *The Republic Unsettled: Muslim French and the Contradictions of Secularism*, Durham, NC: Duke University Press.

Foucault, M. (2007), *Security, Territory, Population. Lectures at the Collège de France 1977–1978*, New York, NY: Palgrave Macmillan.

Fuess, A. (2011), 'Introducing Islamic Theology at German Universities, Aims and Procedures', Lecture given at the Centre for European Islamic Thought, 13 April, University of Copenhagen. Available online: www.islam.ku.dk/lectures/Fuess.pdf (accessed 31 May 2018).

Goldie, P. (2012), *The Mess Inside: Narrative, Emotions, and the Mind*, Oxford: Oxford University Press.

Hacking, I. (1991), *The Taming of Chance*, Cambridge, UK: Cambridge University Press.

Haug, S., S. Müssig and A. Stichs (2009), *Muslim Life in Germany. A Study Conducted on Behalf of the German Conference on Islam*, Nürnberg: Federal Office for Migration and Refugees.

Institute Montagne (2016), 'A French Islam Is Possible', Report Based on Poll from Ifop.

Jacobsen, B. A. (2007), 'Muslimer i Danmark: en kritisk vurdering af antalsopgørelser', in M. Warburg and B. Jacobsen (eds), *Tørre tal om troen: Religionsdemografi i det 21. Århundrede*, 143–165, Højbjerg: Forlaget Univers.

Jacobsen, B. A. (2012), 'Denmark', in J. S. Nielsen, S. Akgönül, A. Alibašić and E. Račius (eds), *Yearbook of Muslims in Europe*, vol. 4, 175–192, Leiden: Brill.

Johansen, B. and R. Spielhaus (2012), 'Counting Deviance: Revisiting a Decade's Production of Quantitative Surveys among Muslims in Western Europe', *Journal of Muslims in Europe*, 1 (1): 81–112.

Koopmans, R. (2014), 'Religious Fundamentalism and Out-Group Hostility among Muslims and Christians in Western Europe', discussion paper, SP VI 2014-101, March.

Korteweg, A. and J. Selby (2012), *Debating Sharia: Islam, Gender Politics, and Family Law Arbitration*, Toronto, ON: University of Toronto Press.

Laclau, E. (1996), *Emancipation(s)*, London: Verso.

Larsson, G. (2012), 'The Fear of Small Numbers: Eurabia Literature and Censuses on Religious Belonging', *Journal of Muslims in Europe*, 2012 (1): 142–165.

Lauritzen, P. (2016), *Spørgsmål, mellem identitet og differens*, Aarhus: Aarhus Universitetsforlag.

Mirza, M., A. Senthilkumaran and Z. Ja'far (2007), *Living Apart Together. British Muslims and the Paradox of Multiculturalism*, London: Policy Exchange.

Nielsen, J. (2010), 'Shari'a between Renewal and Tradition', in J. S. Nielsen and L. Christoffersen(eds), *Shari'a as Discourse. Legal Traditions and the Encounter with Europe*, 1–16, Farnham: Ashgate.

Rose, N. (1993), 'Government, Authority and Expertise in Advanced Liberalism', *Economy and Society*, 22 (3): 283–299.

Rose, N. (1999), *Powers of Freedom*, Cambridge, UK: Cambridge University Press.

Scott, J. W. (2009), *Sexularism. Ursula Hirschmann Annual Lecture on Gender and Europe*, Florence: European University Institute. Available online: http://cadmus.eui.eu/bitstream/handle/1814/11553/RSCAS_DL_2009_01.pdf (accessed 19 May 2015).

Shah, P. (2010), 'A Reflection on the Shari'a Debate in Britain', *Studia z Prawa Wyznaniowego (Studies of Ecclesiastical Law)*, 13: 71–98.

Stern, A. M. (1999), 'Secrets under the Skin. New Historical Perspectives on Decease, Deviance and Citizenship', *Comparative Studies in History and Society*, 41 (3):589–596.

Sunier, T. (2012), 'Domesticating Islam: Exploring Academic Knowledge Production on Islam and Muslims in European Societies', *Ethnic and Racial Studies*, 37 (6): 1138–1155.

Supik, L. (2014), *Statistik und Rassismus. Das Dilemma der Erfassung von Ethnizität*, Frankfurt/M: Campus.

Taylor, C. (2007), *A Secular* Age, Cambridge, MA: Stanford University Press.

Thorne, J. and H. Stuart (2008), *Islam on Campus: A Survey of UK Student Opinions*, Trowbridge: The Centre for Social Cohesion.

TNS Gallup (2006), 'Holdninger Til Integrasjon Og Internasjonale Konflikter Blant Muslimeri Norge Og Den Norske Befolkning Generelt' [Attitudes towards Integration and International Conflicts among Muslims in Norway and the Norwegian Population in General], survey compiled for Norwegian TV 2, Oslo.

Chapter 13

Amiraux, V. (2013), 'The "Illegal Covering" Saga: What's Next? Sociological Perspectives', *Social Identities*, 19 (6): 794–806.

Asad, T. (2003), *Formations of the Secular: Christianity, Islam, Modernity*, Stanford, CA: Stanford University Press.

Astor, A. (2011), *Mobilizing against Mosques: The Origins of Opposition to Islamic Centers of Worship in Spain*, PhD diss, University of Michigan.

Astor, A. (2012), 'Context i conflicte: anàlisi de les fonts d'oposició entorn de les mesquites a Catalunya', *Revista Catalana de Sociologia*, 28: 45–59.

Bader, V. (2010), *Secularism or Democracy?: Associational Governance of Religious Diversity*. Amsterdam: Amsterdam University Press.

Belting, H. (1994), *Likeness and Presence: A History of the Image before the Era of Art*, Chicago, IL: University of Chicago Press.

Brems, E., ed. (2014), *The Experiences of Face Veil Wearers in Europe and the Law*, Cambridge, UK: Cambridge University Press.

Burchardt, M. (2016), 'Recalling Modernity: How Nationalist Memories Shape Religious Diversity in Quebec and Catalonia', *Nations and Nationalism*, 23 (3): 599–619.

Burchardt, M. and S. Höhne (2015), 'The Infrastructures of Diversity: Materiality and Culture in Urban Space, an Introduction', *New Diversities*, 17 (2): 1–13.

Burchardt, M., M. Griera and G. García-Romeral (2015), 'Narrating Liberal Rights and Culture: Muslim Face Veiling, Urban Coexistence and Contention in Spain', *Journal of Ethnic and Migration Studies*, 41 (7): 1068–1087.

Burchardt, M., Z. Yanasmayan and M. Koenig (2018), 'The Judicial Politics of "Burqa Bans" in Belgium and Spain: Socio-legal Field Dynamics and the Standardization of Justificatory Repertoires', *Law and Social Inquiry* online, https://doi.org/10.1111/lsi.12359.

Calhoun, C. (2008), 'Secularism, Citizenship and the Public Sphere', *Hedgehog Review*, 10 (3): 7–21.

Casanova, J. (2009), 'The Secular and Secularisms', *Social Research*, 76 (4): 1049–1066.

Cook, I. R., and M. Whowell (2011), 'Visibility and the Policing of Public Space', *Geography Compass*, 5 (8): 610–622.

Delgado Ruiz, M. (1992), *La ira sagrada: anticlericalismo, iconoclastia y antirritualismo en la España contemporánea*, Barcelona: RBA Libros.

Delgado Ruiz, M. (2006), *El animal público*, Barcelona: Anagrama.

Duyvendak, J. W. (2011), *The Politics of Home: Belonging and Nostalgia in Europe and the United States*, Basingstoke: Palgrave Macmillan.

Elias, N. (1969). *The Civilizing Process, Vol. 1. The History of Manners*. Oxford: Blackwell.

Elias, N. and E. Jephcott (1982 [1969]), *The Civilizing Process*, Oxford: Blackwell.

Fadil, N. (2014), 'Asserting State Sovereignty: The Face Veil Ban in Belgium', in E. Brems (ed.), *The Experiences of Face Veil Wearers in Europe and the Law*, 251–262, Cambridge, UK: Cambridge University Press.

Fernandez González, M. (2014), *Matar al Chino: Entre la revolución urbanística y el asedio urbano en el barrio del Raval de Barcelona*, Barcelona: Virus.

Ferrari, A. and S. Pastorelli (2013), *The Burqa Affair across Europe: Between Public and Private Space*, London: Routledge.

Fournier, P. (2013), 'Headscarf and Burqa Controversies at the Crossroad of Politics, Society and Law', *Social Identities*, 19 (6): 689–703.

Garland, D. (2001), *The Culture of Control*, Oxford: Oxford University Press.

Giffen, J. (2011), 'The Veil of the Ban: A Legal, Social and Political Discourse', *Inter-American & European Human Rights Journal*, 4: 155–173.

Goffman, E. (1971), *Relations in Public: Microstudies of the Social Order*, London: Allen Lane.

Göle, N. (2010), 'Manifestations of the Religious-Secular Divide: Self, State, and the Public Sphere', in L. E. Cady and E. Shakman Hurd (eds), *Comparative Secularisms in a Global Age*, 41–53, New York, NY: Palgrave Macmillan.

Górnicka, B. (2016), *Nakedness, Shame, and Embarrassment*, Heidelberg: Springer.

Griera, M. (2012), 'Public Policies, Interfaith Associations and Religious Minorities: A New Policy Paradigm? Evidence from the Case of Barcelona', *Social Compass*, 59 (4): 570–587.

Grillo, R. and P. Shah (2016), 'The Anti-Burqa Movement in Western Europe', in S. Ferrari and S. Pastorelli (eds), *The Burqa Affair across Europe: Between Public and Private Space*, 197–224, London: Routledge.

Hirschkind, C. (2011), 'Is There a Secular Body?', *Cultural Anthropology*, 26 (4): 633–647.

Hernández-Carr, A. (2011), 'El largo ciclo electoral de Plataforma per Catalunya: del ámbito local a la implantación nacional (2003–2011)', *ICPS Working Papers*, 30.

IDESCAT (2015), Dades de Població. Available online: https://www.idescat.cat/ (accessed 2 February 2018).

Kuru, A. T. (2009), *Secularism and State Policies toward Religion: The United States, France, and Turkey*, Cambridge, UK: Cambridge University Press.

Lévinas, E. (1969), *Totality and Infinity: An Essay on Exteriority*, Pittsburgh, PA: Duquesne University Press.

Mahmood, S. (2009), 'Religious Reason and Secular Affect: An Incommensurable Divide?', *Critical Inquiry*, 35 (4): 836–862.

Mayrl, D. (2016), *Secular Conversions: Political Institutions and Religious Education in the United States and Australia, 1800–2000*, Cambridge, UK: Cambridge University Press.

Mazzarella, W. (2009), 'Affect: What Is It Good For?' in S. Dube (ed.), *Enchantments of Modernity: Empire, Nation, Globalization*, 291–309, New York, NY: Routledge.

Moors, A. (2009), 'The Dutch and the Face Veil: The Politics of Discomfort', *Social Anthropology*, 17 (4): 393–408.

Navaro-Yashin, Y. (2002), *Faces of the State: Secularism and Public Life in Turkey*, Princeton, NJ: Princeton University Press.

Özyürek, E. (2006), *Nostalgia for the Modern: State Secularism and Everyday Politics in Turkey*, Durham, NC: Duke University Press.

Parvez, Z. F. (2011), 'Debating the Burqa in France: The Antipolitics of Islamic Revival', *Qualitative Sociology*, 34 (2): 287–312.

Piatti-Crocker, A. and Tasch, L. (2015), 'Veil Bans in Western Europe: Interpreting Policy Diffusion', *Journal of International Women's Studies*, 16 (2): 15–29.

Pérez-Agote, A. (2010), 'Religious Change in Spain', *Social Compass*, 57 (2): 224–234.
Scheff, T. J. (2000), 'Shame and the Social Bond: A Sociological Theory', *Sociological Theory*, 18 (1): 84–99.
Schutz, A. (1967), *The Phenomenology of the Social World*, Evanston, IL: Northwestern University Press.
Sonesson, G. (2014), 'New Rules for the Spaces of Urbanity', *International Journal for the Semiotics of Law-Revue internationale de Sémiotique juridique*, 27 (1): 7–26.
Spencer, H. (1878), 'Evolution of Ceremonial Government', *The Popular Science Monthly*, 12.
Taylor, C. (2007), *A Secular Age*, Cambridge, MA: Harvard University Press.
Tonkiss, F. (2005), *Space, the City and Social Theory: Social Relations and Urban Forms*, Cambridge: Polity Press.
Warburg, M., B. S. Johansen and K. Østergaard (2013), 'Counting Niqabs and Burqas in Denmark', *Journal of Contemporary Religion*, 28 (1): 33–48.
Wohlrab-Sahr, M. and M. Burchardt (2012), 'Multiple Secularities: Toward a Cultural Sociology of Secular Modernities', *Comparative Sociology*, 11 (6): 875–909.
Yin, R. (1989), *Case Study Research: Design and Methods*, Newbury Park: Sage.

Chapter 14

Bender, C. (2012), 'Practicing Religions', in R. A. Orsi (ed.), *The Cambridge Companion to Religious Studies*, 273–295, Cambridge, UK: Cambridge University Press.
Bennett, J. (2001), *The Enchantment of Modern Life: Attachments, Crossings, and Ethics*, Princeton, NJ: Princeton University Press.
Connolly, W. (1999), *Why I Am Not a Secularist*, Minneapolis, MN: University of Minnesota Press.
Duffy, E. (1992), *The Stripping of the Altars: Traditional Religion in England, 1400–1580*, New Haven, CT: Yale University Press.
Engelke, M. (2013), *God's Agents: Biblical Publicity in Contemporary England*, Berkeley, CA: University of California Press.
Farman, A. (2013), 'Speculative Matter: Secular Bodies, Minds, and Persons', *Cultural Anthropology*, 28 (4): 737–757.
Hirschkind, C. (2011), 'Is There a Secular Body?', *Cultural Anthropology*, 26 (4): 633–647.
Keane, W. (2007), *Christian Moderns: Freedom and Fetish in the Mission Encounter*, Berkeley, CA: University of California Press.
Laqueur, T. (2015), *The Work of the Dead: A Cultural History of Mortal Remains*, Princeton, NJ: Princeton University Press.
Levine, G., ed. (2011), *The Joy of Secularism: 11 Essays for How We Live Now*, Princeton, NJ: Princeton University Press.
Porter, R. (2000), *The Creation of the Modern World: The Untold Story of the British Enlightenment*, New York, NY: Norton.
Robbins, B. (2011), 'Enchantment? No, Thank You!', in G. Levine (ed.), *The Joy of Secularism: 11 Essays for How We Live Now*, 74–94, Princeton, NJ: Princeton University Press.
Schneewind, J. B. (1998), *The Invention of Autonomy: A History of Modern Moral Philosophy*, Cambridge, UK: Cambridge University Press.
Taylor, C. (1989), *Sources of the Self: The Making of Modern Identity*, Cambridge, MA: Harvard University Press.
Taylor, C. (2007), *A Secular Age*, Cambridge, MA: Harvard University Press.

Index

Note: Locators with letter 'n' refer to notes.